low.

PHILOSEMITISM, ANTISEMITISM AND 'THE JEWS'

Philosemitism, Antisemitism and 'the Jews'

Perspectives from the Middle Ages to the Twentieth Century

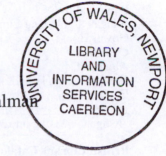

Edited by

Tony Kushner and Nadia Valman

Studies in European Cultural Transition

Volume Twenty-Four

General Editors: Martin Stannard and Greg Walker

ASHGATE

Published by
Ashgate Publishing Limited
Gower House
Croft Road
Aldershot
Hampshire GU11 3HR
England

Ashgate Publishing Company
Suite 420
101 Cherry Street
Burlington, VT 05401-4405
USA

Ashgate website: http//www.ashgate.com

British Library Cataloguing in Publication Data
Philosemitism, antisemitism and 'the Jews' : perspectives
   from the Middle Ages to the twentieth century. - (Studies
   in European cultural transition)
   1. Philosemitism – History 2. Antisemitism – History
   3. Religious tolerance – History
   I. Kushner, Tony (Antony Robin Jeremy) II. Valman, Nadia
   305.8'924'09

Library of Congress Cataloguing-in-Publication Data
Philosemitism, antisemitism and 'the Jews' : perspectives from the Middle Ages
to the twentieth century / edited by Nadia Valman and Tony Kushner.
      p. cm.–(Studies in European cultural transition)
   Includes bibliographical references and index.
   ISBN 0-7546-3678-X
   1. Antisemitism–Europe–History–Congresses. 2. Philosemitism–European–
History–Congresses. 3. Religious tolerance–Europe–History–Congresses. 4.
Christianity and other religions–Judaism–Congresses. 5. Judaism–Relations–
Christianity–Congresses. I. Valman, Nadia. II. Kushner, Tony. III. Series.

   DS146.E85P45 2004
   305.892'404–dc22

                                                          2003028030

ISBN 0 7546 3678 X

Typeset by Bournemouth Colour Press, Parkstone. Printed in Great Britain by
MPG Books, Bodmin, Cornwall.

Contents

Notes on Contributors

David Theo Goldberg is Director of the University of California Humanities Research Institute and Professor of African American Studies and Criminology, Law and Society, and a Fellow in the Critical Theory Institute, University of California, Irvine. He is the author and editor of many books, most notably *The Racial State* (2002), *Relocating Postcolonialism* (2002), *Racial Subjects: Writing on Race in America* (1997), *Multiculturalism: A Critical Reader* (1995) and *Racist Culture: Philosophy and the Politics of Meaning* (1993).

Claire Jowitt teaches Renaissance literature and culture at the University of Wales Aberystwyth. She is author of *Voyage Drama and Gender Politics 1589–1642: Real and Imagined Worlds* (2002) and co-editor of *The Arts of Seventeenth-Century Science: Representations of the Natural World in European and North American Culture* (2002). She is currently editing *Three Renaissance Pirate Plays* for the Revels series and writing a book on representations of piracy and privateering in the Renaissance.

Elliott Horowitz, a native of New York City, is Associate Professor of Jewish History at Bar-Ilan University in Israel. An expanded version of his paper will appear in his forthcoming *Reckless Rites: Purim and the Legacy of Jewish Violence* (Princeton University Press).

Tony Kushner is Professor of Jewish/non-Jewish relations in the Department of History, University of Southampton. He has written widely on British Jewish history, the history of immigration and racism in Britain, the Holocaust and history and memory. He has recently co-authored *The Holocaust* (Manchester University Press) and *We Europeans?*, a study of the social anthropological organisation Mass-Observation, to be published by Ashgate.

Thomas S. Kuttner is on the Faculty of Law at the University of New Brunswick. His teaching and research interests are in public law, including human rights. In addition to his scholarly interests, Professor Kuttner sits as Vice-Chair of the New Brunswick Labour and Employment Board and is active as a labour arbitrator and mediator. He has acted as counsel pro bono in several human rights cases before both the Courts of New Brunswick and the Supreme Court of Canada, and his paper builds upon that experience.

Gavin I. Langmuir received his BA in History from the University of Toronto and his Ph.D. in medieval history from Harvard University, and has taught for most of his career at Stanford University, where he is now Emeritus Professor of History. Initially a scholar of French medieval legal and constitutional history, he has devoted most of his scholarly energy to questions about the nature, formation and causes of intense hostility against Jews in Europe. He distinguishes between antisemitism and other forms of hostility against Jews; by his definition of antisemitism, intense and highly irrational hostility to Jews similar to that of the Nazis first began in northern Europe in the twelfth century.

Mark Levene attempts to combine being Reader in Comparative History at the University of Southampton with environmental and peace work. *The Coming of Genocide*, the first of his three-volume history of genocide in the modern world, is forthcoming.

Irven M. Resnick is Professor of Philosophy of Religion and holds an endowed chair in Judaic Studies at the University of Tennessee (Chattanooga). With Kenneth F. Kitchell, he has translated Albert the Great's *De animalibus* (2 vols; Baltimore 1999) and has in press both an annotated bibliography for *Albert the Great, 1900–2000*, and a translation of Albert's *Quaestiones super de animalibus*.

Ritchie Robertson is a Professor of German at Oxford University and a Fellow of St John's College. His books include *Kafka: Judaism, Politics, and Literature* (1985), *Heine*, in the series Jewish Thinkers (1988), and *The 'Jewish Question' in German Literature, 1749–1939* (1999), and (as editor) *The Cambridge Companion to Thomas Mann* (2002). He has also edited *The German-Jewish Dialogue: an anthology of literary texts, 1749–1993*, World's Classics (1999).

David M. Seymour teaches in the School of Law, Lancaster University. His doctoral thesis and continuing research are in the area of critical theories of antisemitism. He has also published work in film and law studies.

Yvonne Sherwood is senior lecturer in OT/Tanakh and Jewish Studies at the University of Glasgow. Previous publications include *The Prostitute and the Prophet* (1996) and *A Biblical Text and Its Afterlives: The Survival of Jonah in Western Culture* (2000). She is currently working on a monograph on the 'sacrifice' of Abraham's beloved son in Judaism, Christianity and Islam.

Norman Solomon was born in Cardiff, South Wales, and educated at St John's College, Cambridge. He was rabbi to Orthodox congregations in Britain until he became founder–director of the Centre for the Study of Judaism and Jewish/Christian Relations at Selly Oak Colleges, Birmingham. He was Fellow in Modern Jewish Thought at the Oxford Centre for Hebrew and Jewish Studies 1995–2001 and is a member of the Oxford University Teaching and Research Unit in Hebrew and Jewish Studies. He has published several books on Judaism.

Adam Sutcliffe is Associate Professor of European Jewish History at the University of Illinois at Urbana-Champaign. He is the author of *Judaism and Enlightenment* (2003), and is currently working on a study of approaches to nationhood, ethnicity and Jewishness in early nineteenth-century political radicalism.

Nadia Valman is Research Fellow at the AHRB Parkes Centre for the Study of Jewish/non-Jewish relations at the University of Southampton. She has published on nineteenth-century Anglo-Jewish literary history and is working on a study of the representation of the Jewess in Victorian Christian and Jewish literature. She is editor of the journal *Jewish Culture and History*.

General Editors' Preface

The European dimension of research in the humanities has come into sharp focus over recent years, producing scholarship which ranges across disciplines and national boundaries. Until now there has been no major channel for such work. This series aims to provide one, and to unite the fields of cultural studies and traditional scholarship. It will publish the most exciting new writing in areas such as European history and literature, art history, archaeology, language and translation studies, political, cultural and gay studies, music, psychology, sociology and philosophy. The emphasis will be explicitly European and interdisciplinary, concentrating attention on the relativity of cultural perspectives, with a particular interest in issues of cultural transition.

Martin Stannard
Greg Walker
University of Leicester

Preface and Acknowledgements

This volume emerged from a major international conference held at the University of Southampton to mark the centenary of James Parkes' birth. It was attended by scholars from many different countries and backgrounds. The essays included in *Philosemitism, Antisemitism and 'the Jews'* reflect the rich chronological and disciplinary diversity of the conference and highlight the importance of the subject matter of Jewish/non-Jewish relations, the area pioneered by James Parkes. All of the essays included here have been revised and several added to provide balance and coverage. It proved impossible to include all the conference contributions but we would like to take this opportunity of thanking all those who participated in what was an inspiring event. Particular thanks are due to Sarah Pearce and Sian Jones who were my co-organisers and to Chana Kotzin who was the conference administrator. Thanks are also due to Chris Woolgar of the Hartley Institute and the Arts Faculty of the University of Southampton who helped fund the conference, and to Erika Gaffney at Ashgate for her support. Professor Greg Walker has been very patient and encouraging and we are delighted to be included in the series he edits with Martin Stannard, 'Studies in European Cultural Transition'.

Tony Kushner, Southampton

Chapter 1

Introduction: The Wide Field of Relations?

Tony Kushner with Nadia Valman

In August 1956 the 'Parkes Library Limited: A Centre for the Study of Relations between the Jewish and non-Jewish worlds' was formally incorporated. Its main purpose was to provide a Centre 'where non-Jewish sociologists, historians, theologians and other scholars could work in the wide field of relations between Jews and their neighbours, and between Judaism and other religions, and could meet with Jewish scholars engaged on the same work'.

The focus, as outlined in its initial documentation, was on the responsibility of non-Jews to combat antisemitism, a responsibility which its director, James Parkes, believed had still to be taken up, even with awareness of the horrors of the Second World War. Knowledge was needed 'of the many centuries of ignorance, prejudice, and distortion which created modern antisemitic patterns'. Parkes added that the 'destruction of these causes of antisemitism and the creation of normalcy in Jewish/non-Jewish relations' required sustained and concentrated research and hence the creation of and need for the Centre.[1]

James Parkes wrote for fifty years on the 'relations' between the Jewish and non-Jewish worlds. The period from the late 1920s through to the middle 1970s, in which Parkes published, according to his bibliographers, some 329 items, was one of the most traumatic and dynamic in Jewish history. It incorporated mass refugee movements, genocide, the formation of the state of Israel and a fundamental shift in the geographical concentration as well as power structures of world Jewry. Parkes kept pace with the world around him and shaped, with intense skill, some of the early narratives of the history of the Jews and, as a lone pioneer, the history of antisemitism. He was particularly adept in incorporating contemporary history into longer term patterns. He also mastered and often was at the forefront of new approaches to the study of prejudice and the treatment of minorities, Jewish or otherwise. In all his voluminous and varied writings that adjusted to new developments and approaches, however, Parkes' belief in the importance of focusing on the 'relations' between Jews and non-Jews was a constant.

In his study of the origins of antisemitism Parkes was adamant about the central importance of the Christian church: it alone 'turned a normal xenophobia

---

1   'The Parkes Library: A Centre for the Study of Relations between the Jewish and non-Jewish worlds' (leaflet, Parkes Library, 1958?), pp.3–4.

and normal good and bad communal relations between human societies into the unique evil of antisemitism, the most evil, and, as I gradually came to realise, the most crippling sin of historic Christianity'.[2] Few today would accept fully the certainty of Parkes' analysis, although his dogmatic assertion has to be placed in the context of the failure of almost all his Christian contemporaries to accept any such responsibility for the antisemitism of either past or present. Before proceeding further, we need to explore further the nature of Parkes' assumption that there was a 'normal xenophobia' or 'normal good and bad communal relations between human societies'.

Parkes' first book, *The Jew and His Neighbour* (1930) grew out of his involvement in the International Student Service, confronting the intense hostility faced by Jewish students in European universities, which led to violence and exclusion in many different continental countries. The German student movement, for example, was the first major national body to be taken over by the Nazis. By 1931, roughly 60 per cent of German undergraduates were members of the Nazi Student Organization, and more generally support for Nazism in the German universities was 'proportionately twice as great as among the general population'.[3] Indeed, writing about antisemitism in Germany, Austria, Poland, Romania and Hungary, Parkes saw one feature was common to all: 'the predominant role of the student or ex-student class. This has also given European anti-Semitism its other common element – the racial theory'.[4] The problem, as analysed by Parkes, was that many in the universities could not disentangle attitudes towards the individual from those towards a perceived collective entity: to contemporaries, the Jewish student was 'linked indissolubly to his race'. From there, the problems which confronted the Jewish student were 'the same as those confronting other Jews, and the attitude to him on the part of other students [was] but a reflection of the attitude to other Jews on the part of the community'.[5]

In a desperate attempt not to appear partisan by 'exonerating the Jew', Parkes was anxious in this, his first book, to show the two sides to 'the Jewish question'. He was no glib optimist and realised that the prejudices involved were 'the product of centuries'. Nevertheless, he rejected fatalism and believed 'that the roots of the question lie in history and not in the unalterable characteristics of the Jew'. In a post-Holocaust era, Parkes' dismissal of an essentialised, unchanging Jew appears unremarkable. Yet it should be remembered that even those who opposed the Nazis' politicisation of race science during the 1930s accepted the

2   James Parkes, *Voyage of Discoveries* (London: Gollancz, 1969), p.123.

3   Richard Grunberger, *A Social History of the Third Reich* (London: Penguin, 1974), pp.28–30, 388–9.

4   James Parkes, 'Post-War Anti-Semitism in the Light of the Letter of Resignation of Mr James G. McDonald', *The Jewish Academy*, vol.2 no.1 (March 1936), pp.6–7.

5   James Parkes, *The Jew and His Neighbour: A Study of the Causes of Anti-Semitism* (London: Student Christian Movement Press, 1930), p.9.

reality of race and 'race difference'.[6] It has been commented that whilst 'The term "race" was used indiscriminately in the first edition of *The Jew and His Neighbour* to designate Jews as a group', Parkes was careful thereafter not to use the word. Later in 1930 he wrote that 'The falsest of all the slogans is the racial, which bases itself on racial purity and the depravity of racial mixtures. This would be very plausible if either the Jews or their opponents were a "race".'[7]

Parkes related in his memoirs a meeting he organised in Geneva in 1931 in which the German students refused to talk to the Jewish representatives. Jews, apparently, had a 'differentiated plasma' which prevented a symbiosis with the Germans. To the tune of 'My bonnie is over the ocean,' Parkes responded:

> My plasma is over the ocean
> My plasma is awful to see
> My plasma is all of a muddle
> Oh, who'll differentiate me?[8]

Parkes, even in the non-theological realm, was able to deconstruct contemporary discourse on 'the Jew' to a level that made him exceptional, even amongst progressives in the liberal democratic world. Yet, although he was one of the first to see the power and impact of *irrationality* in European history, Parkes retained his faith in human progress and reasonableness – in short, enlightenment ideals. In 1960 Parkes wrote an obituary of his close friend, Charles Singer, who had been Professor of the History of Medicine at the University of London. In summing up Singer's achievements, Parkes could have been writing an account of his own life: 'He was one of that small group of men, Jews, Christians and humanists, who saw from the beginning the menace of racialism and national socialism to all the deepest roots and the highest values which western civilisation had achieved.'[9] Parkes approached the study of the 'Jewish problem' through reason, concluding that, 'given the patience and the goodwill requisite, it is one which can be unravelled by human intelligence and resolved by human action'.[10]

In an article entitled 'Anti-Semitism from Caesar to Luther' (1938), Parkes argued that Jews, like all groups, had been involved in conflict that was not antisemitic. In their long history there had been 'quarrels with their neighbours, in some of which they were wrong, and in some of which it was six of one and

---

6   See, for example, the classic anti-Nazi text *We Europeans: A Survey of 'Racial' Problems* (London: Jonathan Cape, 1935) and Elliot Barkan, *The Retreat of Scientific Racism: Changing Concepts of Race in Britain and the United States Between the World Wars* (Cambridge: Cambridge University Press, 1992), for more general comment.

7   Peter Gilbert, 'The Analysis of Antisemitism in the Theological, Historical and Sociological Criticism of James Parkes' (unpublished PhD, University of Toronto, 2003), p.28.

8   Parkes, *Voyage of Discoveries*, pp.118–9.

9   James Parkes, 'Charles Singer 1876–1960', *Common Ground*, vol.14, no.3 (Autumn 1960), p.3.

10   Parkes, *The Jew and His Neighbour*, p.11.

half a dozen of the other'. It would, he added, for example be 'absurd to call the Philistines or Assyrians "anti-Semites"'. These were *normal* relations within human societies. In contrast 'Anti-Semitism is essentially an *abnormal* hostility.' Again his rationalist critique was employed, Parkes adding that:

> [hostility] to the Jews can only be called anti-Semitic when it is
> abnormal in the sense that there is no adequate explanation for the form
> or the severity of its manifestation in the actual contemporary conduct
> of the Jews against whom it is directed. Its roots will be found at that
> point where something abnormal enters into the ideas of non-Jews
> about their Jewish neighbours.[11]

To Parkes, in contrast to many of his contemporaries in Britain during the 1930s, the tragedy of the situation in Nazi Germany was 'the creation of a Jewish problem where, in fact, none exists'.[12] In eastern Europe, and especially Poland, however, Parkes did feel that there was a 'genuine' Jewish problem. Jews, because of discrimination and exclusion, were concentrated geographically and economically. Here there were 'two sides to the question' and, he wrote in 1930, 'Jewish action is needed as well as non-Jewish to overcome the difficulties involved in their peculiar position'.[13]

There is a parallel between Parkes' belief in 'abnormal' hostility alongside 'normal' relations between Jews and non-Jews and the growth of the term 'race relations' during the twentieth century. The sociologist Michael Banton has identified the first use of 'race relations' in 1911 in a study of Negroes in the American south. Banton argues that before 1914:

> Blacks, whites and yellows were represented as different species within
> the genus *Homo*. So racial relations among humans were to be identified
> by objective phenotypical characters. Nature had made black–white
> relations different from black–black relations [but] after the First World
> War it was argued that the racial classifications of everyday life were
> social constructions based in the popular consciousness. Racial relations
> were therefore to be identified by shared subjective definitions.[14]

By the 1960s, argued Robert Miles, 'race' and 'race relations' were terms treated popularly and by academics as if they were 'real, active subjects ... because people believe that there are "races", then social relations between groups so categorised become described as "race relations"'. The converse was

---

11   James Parkes, 'Anti-Semitism from Caesar to Luther', in *Query Books*, no.2 (London: Query Books, 1938), p.12.

12   James Parkes, 'Post-war anti-Semitism', p.9. See Tony Kushner, *The Holocaust and the Liberal Imagination: A Social and Cultural History* (Oxford: Blackwell, 1994), chapter 1, for an analysis of contemporary reactions in Britain to the persecution of the Jews during the 1930s.

13   Parkes, *The Jew and His Neighbour*, p.145.

14   Michael Banton, 'The race relations problematic', *The British Journal of Sociology*, vol.42 no.1 (March 1991), p.116.

also true, argued Miles: 'any everyday, common description of a situation as one of "race relations" implicitly asserts the existence of "races". This is then objectified as an area of study'.[15] For Miles, coming from a Marxist perspective, the key issues were the reality of racism and the existence, through the development of capitalism, of the need for labour migration. Moreover the failure to provide an academic critique of the 'race relations' paradigm had encouraged the state and political parties to employ it (as with the Race Relations Acts of 1965, 1968 and 1976).[16] There are strengths and weaknesses to Miles' analysis. On the negative side, his argument that immigrant groups need to be treated under the broad category of 'migrant labour' whose arrival has 'prompted a hostile reaction from the indigenous population' oversimplifies and underestimates how all such groups, to a lesser or greater extent, have been subject to a process of racialisation. More positively, Miles provides an analytical critique of academic and governmental approaches to 'race relations' that tends, partly or largely, to blame the minority group for 'poor race relations'. The 'liberal' solution to improve race relations is often for adjustment on both sides alongside immigration control, articulated neatly by Labour Party politician Roy Hattersley in the mid-1960s: 'integration without limitation is impossible; equally ... limitation without integration is indefensible'.[17]

Hattersley's comments are worth exploring further in relation to the approach of James Parkes. The comparison is not aimed at castigating Hattersley but to reveal the differences that emerge between two progressive figures when confronted with cultural difference. In 1964 Hattersley was elected MP for the Birmingham constituency of Sparkbrook as one of a group of aspiring young Labour Party hopefuls. The West Midlands, within which Sparkbrook was part, was the focal point for 'the politics of race' in both the 1959 and 1964 elections. Another Birmingham constituency, Smethwick, had seen a major shift to the Conservatives fighting on the ticket of 'if you want a nigger for your neighbour, vote Labour'.[18] Hattersley achieved a narrow victory but his move from being an opponent of the Conservatives' 1962 Commonwealth Immigrants Act to a supporter of the need for much more stringent controls under the Labour government of Harold Wilson from 1964 was, it must be argued, undoubtedly linked to what he saw as the concerns of his white constituents.

Hattersley's maiden speech in the House of Commons in March 1965 was on New Commonwealth immigration. He stated clearly that with hindsight the

---

15   Robert Miles, *Racism and Migrant Labour* (London: Routledge & Kegan Paul, 1982), pp.32–3.

16   Ibid., introduction and part 1. See also Robert Miles, 'Marxism versus the sociology of "race relations"?', *Ethnic and Racial Studies*, vol.7 no.2 (April 1984), pp.217–37.

17   *Hansard* (HC), vol.721 col.359 (23 November 1965).

18   Paul Foot, *Immigration and Race in British Politics* (Harmondsworth: Penguin, 1965), chapters 1–4, provides the fullest account of Smethwick.

Labour Party had been 'wrong to oppose' the 1962 Act. There was a need to recognise that some controls were necessary and that to have made it into a party political issue in the general election with Labour continuing to object to restriction 'would have done unbelievable harm to the peace and security of this country and put back the cause of *good race relations* [my emphasis] by 50 or 100 years'. Hattersley outlined that his change of heart was largely for social and cultural reasons (with economic factors of less concern): to him the ability of immigrants to assimilate or not was critical in whether they should be accepted. Those from Pakistan, in particular, 'create in our major towns problems a good deal more severe than West Indian immigrants'. Anticipating the right-wing anti-immigrant Conservative, Norman Tebbit, by some quarter of a century, Hattersley called for a 'test which tries to analyse which immigrants ... are most likely to be assimilated into our national life'.[19]

Subsequently Hattersley has distanced himself from some of the Labour government's actions in the 1960s, most explicitly the 1968 Commonwealth Immigrants Act, a blatantly discriminatory measure aimed at excluding East African Asians. In his autobiography, however, Hattersley is circumspect about his maiden speech, only commenting on its success within parliament. He did acknowledge, however, that until he was 'elected for Sparkbrook, I knew nothing of the problems faced by the Black and Asian British. I did not even know – indeed I had hardly met – a member of either community.' Thirty years on, over a third of his constituents were, ironically, of Asian origin and Hattersley's empathy with their day-to-day lives and pressures, including matters of immigration control, had been transformed compared to his early days as an MP.[20]

Placing Roy Hattersley alongside James Parkes, it becomes clear that what was remarkable about the latter, in contrast to the former, was his immediate affinity and understanding of the problems faced by those of whom he knew so little either in terms of history or as people. Rather than turn attention to the minority itself, Parkes looked inwards towards his own culture and religion for the reasons behind the hostility they faced. He set out to read all he could on Jewish history and to meet as many Jews as possible: 'I became familiar with most of the Jewish student centres in Poland, Hungary, Rumania and elsewhere'. In international student conferences he looked for those who could introduce 'Jewish culture, helping to understand Jewry more positively, and to see something of its inner life'.[21] And, whilst Parkes' belief in a genuine 'Jewish problem' has similarities to those of

---

19   *Hansard* (HC) vol.709 cols 379, 381 (23 March 1965). In 1990 Tebbit posed what he called a 'cricket test': which team would those descended from New Commonwealth countries support – England, Pakistan, India or the West Indies?

20   Roy Hattersley, *Who Goes Home? Scenes from a Political Life* (London: Warner Books, 1995), pp.48–9. On his change of heart, see Yasmin Alibhai-Brown, 'Wake up Mr Straw', *The Independent*, 28 October 1999.

21   Parkes, *Voyage of Discoveries*, pp.113–5.

people like Hattersley, who accepted the existence of difficulties in race relations, his solution was somewhat different. In Britain, after the death of Labour leader Hugh Gaitskell in 1963, both major parties accepted that controls were necessary even though the number of black migrants coming into the country was not particularly high, and their needs, particularly those fleeing persecution in East Africa, were often acute. In contrast, during the Second World War, at a time of shortages and strains on the Home Front, James Parkes was willing to support the arrival of as many Jews as was possible into the UK and to denounce the logic of those who argued against it:

> not openly in Parliament, but privately in discussion with deputations or individuals, high officials have betrayed the reason for this attitude. It is not a pleasant one for British honour. It is that these people are not regarded as men or women, not even as children, but as *Jews*. It is said that, if we offered unlimited asylum in our own country or the terrorities we control, it might lead to a dangerous increase of antisemitism. It is even said – as though the idea should terrify instead of rejoicing us – that Hitler might take us at our word, and send us all the Jews still alive in Europe, several million of them.
>
> *There is only one answer for men who still believe there is any nobility in the cause for which we are fighting: WE WILL RECEIVE THEM. AND IF THERE REALLY BE THREE MILLION OF THEM WE WILL THANK GOD THAT WE HAVE BEEN ABLE TO SAVE SO MANY FROM HITLER'S CLUTCHES. AND IF THERE BE A JEWISH PROBLEM TO SOLVE, WE WILL SOLVE IT AS CIVILISED MEN AND NOT AS MURDERERS.*[22]

Parkes believed that past discrimination and hostility had warped Jewish development, leading to certain economic and social concentrations which in specific places had caused a 'Jewish problem'. Three million Jews coming into wartime Britain might do likewise. Most liberals have assumed that influxes of immigrants who are different from the host population have caused a 'race relations' problem. For Parkes and then later proponents of liberal race relations, the existence of antisemitism and racism respectively on the part of the majority is not denied – it would need education and/or legislation to counter it. Yet in both cases the acceptance of the existence of both racism and 'real' problems caused by immigrant or minority groups leads to the analytical confusion outlined by Miles and the tendency in some form or other to blame the victim. Parkes maintained his distinction between the normal 'Jewish problem' and the abnormal 'antisemitism' throughout his writings. As a result, his analysis of the irrational, such as the belief in Jews as ritual murderers or *The Protocols of the Elders of Zion*, was remarkable, paving the way for scholars of the role of collective psychopathology in history such as Norman Cohn.[23]

---

22 James Parkes, 'The Massacre of the Jews. Future Vengeance or Present Help?' (January 1943), Parkes papers, 9/5/1, University of Southampton archive.

23 See 'Proposal for the creation of a centre for research in collective

When it came to analysing the place of Jews as large minorities in countries or as recent immigrants, however, Parkes was more willing to take criticisms levelled at them by contemporaries at face value, leading to accusations from some of his Jewish friends that he was peddling 'sugar-coated antisemitism'.[24] Nevertheless immigration control was not what Parkes had in mind for the solving of the 'Jewish problem': the very fact that he could consider huge transfers of population is evidence enough of his more optimistic outlook. Moreover his 'rational', commonsense approach to contemporary issues, examining behaviour on both 'sides', in no way stopped him appreciating either the validity, integrity and dynamic nature of the world's Jewish communities, or their rich and varied history. Nor did his continued insistence on the difference between a normal 'Jewish question' and an abnormal 'antisemitism' stop his searing examination of the traditions and practices of his own faith, whether it be in founding documents or everyday material culture.

Robert Miles' critique of the race relations paradigm is valuable as it analyses the power bases of society, if admittedly within a somewhat crude Marxist analysis which places almost all the emphasis on the means of production and largely excludes the cultural sphere. In addition, as Michael Banton has argued, Miles and those accepting his position 'tended to neglect interpersonal relations, to aggregate aspects of behaviour that were best examined separately, and to represent racism as something with a life of its own that changed form as circumstances changed'.[25] Parkes in his writings provided what was a dynamic and historically contingent model of antisemitism and thus embraces the more inclusive approach suggested by Banton. James Parkes also stressed the importance of everyday relations between ordinary human actors. Most importantly he realised the critical role played by culture in defining the relations between Jews and non-Jews throughout the ages, especially the power relations between Church and Synagogue from the dawning of the Christian era.

James Parkes was an activist as well as a scholar. Operating largely outside academia, but believing that universities were of central importance, he aimed much of his writing at confronting specific contemporary problems through a critical engagement with the past. He worked on the premise that 'bad history cannot be the foundation of good theology', boldly asking in 1934, as Gavin Langmuir relates in this volume, 'why the attempt to prove the reality of the

---

psychopathology' (Parkes Library, 1965) which was established at the University of Sussex by Norman Cohn with the support of James Parkes and David Astor. See also Norman Cohn, *Warrant for Genocide: The Myth of the Jewish World Conspiracy and the Protocols of the Elders of Zion* (London: Eyre & Spottiswood, 1967).

24   Parkes' notes on his *Enemy of the People: Antisemitism and the Jewish Problem in the Modern World* (1945) in Parkes papers, 7/6/5, University of Southampton archives. See specifically Marie Jahoda, 'Really, Dr Parkes …', *Commentary*, vol.3 (January 1947), pp.97–9.

25   Banton, 'The race relations problematic', p.118.

Divinity of Christ made it necessary to falsify the whole of Jewish history'.[26] Parkes devoted his career, including his publications, to outlining the causes and nature of intolerance. He was equally concerned, however, with creating a theology and sociology of tolerance – how genuine differences could be confronted rather than avoided or removed.

In 1996 the University of Southampton formalised the creation of the Parkes Centre for the Study of Jewish/non-Jewish Relations. It was at this point, the centenary of his birth but fifteen years after his death, that his earlier vision started to be realised. An international conference was organised on the theme 'Tolerance and Intolerance'. Speakers were encouraged to explore from a theoretical perspective the nature and representation of these themes. In particular, research close to the heart of James Parkes were highlighted: Jewish–Christian relations throughout the ages; the role of law and culture in defining the interaction and space between the Jewish and non-Jewish worlds; and the practical implications of academic research in promoting tolerance and fighting intolerance. At the time of writing it is now seven years since the conference. The Parkes Centre has grown and has become the Parkes Institute, aided by support from the government funded Arts and Humanities Research Board in 2000. This growth and success has reflected the academic credibility of the field pioneered by James Parkes, making up to some extent for the marginality and even disdain he faced within the British academic world in his lifetime. Of equal importance, however, is the continuation of the activism that was the essence of Parkes' career: those in the Parkes Institute advise international, national and local governmental and non-governmental bodies and disseminate their research in a variety of media. This volume, based on a careful selection of the conference papers, all of which have been subsequently revised for publication, is part of that process of challenging outreach work.

Gavin Langmuir, one of the great students of the history of antisemitism in the postwar era, developing the foundation created by James Parkes whom he admires deeply, gave the keynote lecture in the 1996 conference. It is appropriate, therefore, that Langmuir's is the first contribution in this volume. Langmuir, like Parkes, poses difficult questions, arguing powerfully that theological beliefs that refuse to acknowledge manifest historical realities are a potent source of intolerance. In contrast, Langmuir suggests that tolerance comes out of an acceptance of historical realities, accepting difference in beliefs, even at the basic and fundamental level of which God it is that is worshipped within monotheistic faiths. Coming from a very different perspective, David Theo Goldberg argues that liberal reliance on tolerance in mediating the recognition of increasing pluralism or diversity in fact masks (intolerant) relations of power

---

26   James Parkes, *The Foundations of Judaism and Christianity* (London: Vallentine Mitchell, 1960), p.x; James Parkes, *The Conflict of the Church and the Synagogue: A Study in the Origins of Anti-Semitism* (London: Soncino Press, 1934), p.96.

since tolerance legitimates dismissal. Difference is 'a problem to be solved rather than a fact to be accepted, let alone people to be respected'. Tolerance, he contends, 'serves to mitigate social power, mapping out a space for individual expression in the face of collective constraint', but ultimately it is an artifice 'powerless to face down power where power seeks more naked expression'. Goldberg contrasts the relatively easy appeal of liberal tolerance compared with the complexities of responsible engagement, of sensitivity and solidarity.

Following on from Goldberg's philosophical analysis, but in the realm of theology, Norman Solomon confronts the difficult but essential issue of how we confront intolerant foundation texts and subsequent legal traditions and practices which are intolerant and discriminatory towards other groups such as women, homosexuals and people of other faiths. Focusing on Jewish holy texts, Solomon concludes that this is possible only through an historical critical approach, enabling a reformulation of the notion of the divine origin of Jewish law as a *metaphor* for the people Israel in covenantal relation with its God. On the other hand, Jewish texts have also, as Yvonne Sherwood discusses, been used within the Christian tradition to produce anti-Judaic readings. Surveying the history of the interpretation of the biblical text of Jonah, Sherwood reveals how scriptural exegesis participated in establishing and perpetuating a dichotomy between the enlightened, universal values of Christianity and the narrow sectarianism of Judaism.

The issues raised by Langmuir, Goldberg, Solomon and Sherwood are ones that very much preoccupied James Parkes. Other essays in this collection would have challenged Parkes himself in their analysis, or opened up areas of study that even he, as an innovative scholar, failed, alongside his contemporaries, to recognise as important. One example of the latter is Mark Levene's analysis of the process of nation building and the problems this has created for ethnic minority groups. Parkes could be typified as a liberal nationalist in the inter-war mode, believing that minority groups could be successfully incorporated within the nation state. Through case studies including post-1918 Poland, the creation of a Jewish state after the Second World War and, most recently, former Yugoslavia, Levene questions the primacy of the nation-state model.

As a historian, James Parkes was best known for his work *The Jew in the Medieval Community* (1938). The contributions of Elliot Horowitz and Irven Resnick consider medieval Christian–Jewish relations from two different perspectives. The Dominican Albert the Great, considered by modern scholarship to have been relatively benign in his attitude to Jews and Judaism, did in fact, argues Resnick, incorporate in his writings thirteenth-century anti-Jewish polemic against the Talmud, and popular perceptions of Jewish moral, intellectual and physiological inferiority. Like other scholastic theologians he emphasized the intentional character of Jewish ignorance of Jesus and, consequently, Jewish guilt for the crucifixion, and thus contributed to the thirteenth-century hardening of anti-Jewish polemic.

In his writings as well as his activism more generally, Parkes believed it was crucial to introduce the voice of the Jews themselves. Rather than viewing Jews as passive victims in medieval Christendom, Elliott Horowitz's essay goes against the grain of Jewish historiography to suggest that accusations against Jews for desecration of the crucifix cannot simply be dismissed as antisemitic inventions, particularly as they are chronicled in Jewish as well as non-Jewish sources. Horowitz reads such accounts from the perspective of Jewish narratives of martyrdom, and argues that acts revealing Jewish attraction to as well as repulsion from the cross suggest the 'tense (and yet sometimes porous) lines of demarcation between the worlds of Judaism and Christianity' in medieval Europe.

Moving to the early modern period and the enlightenment in Britain and the European continent, the essays by Claire Jowitt, Adam Sutcliffe, Ritchie Robertson and David Seymour show the strengths as well as the limitations of thinking about Jews in the history of religious toleration. Jowitt's discussion of the English Quaker writer Margaret Fell, who was writing in the context of the Readmission debate, millenarianism and the messianism of Sabbatai Sevi, shows how Fell moved from conversionist philosemitism towards an increasing intolerance of Judaism, coupled with her appropriation of Judaic motifs as metaphors for the position of Quakers and women. The essays by Sutcliffe and Robertson both demonstrate how Jews marked the outer limit of notions of toleration in the Enlightenment. Sutcliffe stresses the ambiguities and tensions within the early Enlightenment concept of toleration and shows how, as suggested at a more general level by Goldberg, advocating the right of Jews to worship freely did not preclude the simultaneous dismissal of Jewish tradition as fundamentally intolerant. Indeed discourses of toleration can quickly flip from the defence of minority interests in the name of equality through to their denigration as failing to share the necessary values of a tolerant society. Sutcliffe and Robertson both point to a recent manifestation of this tendency with the *Satanic Verses* controversy; it has continued and intensified against Muslims in the post-11 September 2001 world.

German classical drama of the later Enlightenment, Robertson shows, counterposed the corrupting power of ecclesiastical authority against the natural bonds of affection. In these terms, Lessing's *Nathan der Weise* ascribed dogmatic intolerance to the Church and an enlightened humanism to its Jewish hero, Nathan. Yet Lessing's version of religious toleration, which failed to differentiate substantively between religions, was a toleration based on 'indifference': tolerating different beliefs on the assumption that they are not really different, and that one's own ethical values are universal and unchallengeable. Goethe, on the other hand, while advocating 'recognition' rather than 'tolerance', nevertheless shared in the Enlightenment and Romantic critique of Judaism as a legalistic religion without feeling, which once again excluded Jews from the community of the enlightened. David Seymour's discussion of the representation of 'the Jews' in Nietzsche's thought, by contrast, grapples with the contradiction of Nietzsche's philosemitism alongside his characterisation of the Jews in section 7 of the first essay of *On the Genealogy of Morals* as the 'enemies' of the Noble. Nietzsche's irony, Seymour argues, demonstrates and thus illuminates the 'thuggery of thought associated with the man of *ressentiment*', analysing rather than replicating the psyche of the antisemite.

The final two essays in this collection confront post-Holocaust developments. Thomas Kuttner returns to the question of law and how the Canadian legal system has confronted the question of Holocaust denial. The clash between the individual's freedom of expression and respect for communal dignity has been fought out in the Canadian law courts. James Parkes somewhat hesitantly believed that law could have a role in restricting the destructiveness of antisemitism. Kuttner offers an alternative model for challenging antisemitism to criminalizing defamation: the principle that regulates conduct between management and labour in modern collective bargaining legislation, which champions the rights of the collectivity of workers rather than the liberty of the subject. Kuttner also argues that antisemitism must not be universalised but its distinctiveness and imbrication with Christian culture should be recognised by court decisions on Holocaust denial. His analysis of various court cases shows the law's potential, if sophisticatedly handled, to undermine the false invocation of freedom of speech by Holocaust deniers. Such cases are also testimony to the role of activists, Jewish and non-Jewish, in combating prejudice.

The last essay, by Tony Kushner, also has as its focus the Holocaust. In Kuttner's study the Holocaust was used by deniers to denigrate Jews and to promote their own antisemitic world view. The situation in Kushner's case studies is more complex: the use of the Holocaust and representations of the Holocaust to confront contemporary problems including, though not exclusively, that of racism. The essay highlights the dilemmas of instrumentalising the past, even for progressive aims.

The vitality and wide range, both chronologically and thematically, of the essays in this volume, and their multidisciplinary and interdisciplinary approaches, provide, it is hoped, a fitting tribute to James Parkes, described by his colleague and friend Norman Bentwich as 'a Peter Pan among scholars and a Puck in any administration'.[27] The independence of spirit as well as desire to contribute positively is one that lives on in the Institute that seeks to promote the aims of his life work. These essays, spanning the medieval to the modern world, as well as literature, history, politics, religion and theology, law, philosophy and gender studies, cannot provide a complete study of Jewish/non-Jewish relations throughout the ages even when refined through the concepts of tolerance and intolerance. Their very richness, however, reflects not only the importance of

---

27   Norman Bentwich, *Wanderer Between Two Worlds* (London: Kegan, Paul, Trench, Trubner, 1941), p.235.

James Parkes as a pioneer but also how his approach and outlook have inspired (and, it is hoped, will continue to inspire) later generations of scholars and activists.

PART I

Theorising Tolerance and Intolerance

Chapter 2

Intolerance and Tolerance: Only One 'One and Only' God or More

Gavin I. Langmuir

James Parkes was both an historian and a theologian, and the questions posed for this volume in his honour are both historical and religious or ethical. But the premises and methods of historians and theologians differ and can lead to very different, even directly conflicting, results. Whereas belief in a god is a necessary premise for theologians, the only gods that historians can know professionally are constructions of human mental activity. And whereas Christian theologians are monotheists, historians are inevitably polytheists in the strongest sense, for they know that, historically, there have not only been many gods but also several one and only gods. For the historian, the belief that the adherents of the major monotheisms all believe, albeit in differing ways, in the same one and only god conflicts directly with the historical fact that the adherents of Judaism, Christianity and Islam, not to mention other traditions, have believed in different, easily distinguishable, gods.

If there was one Christian scholar prior to 1945 who was acutely aware that theological and historical approaches could be directly opposed, it was James Parkes. In 1934, with great courage, he asked 'why the attempt to prove the reality of the Divinity of Christ made it necessary to falsify the whole of Jewish history'.[1] But he did not discuss the most basic difference between theological and historical interpretations of the relations between Judaism and Christianity, to wit that, although Christians claim to worship the god who made a covenant with the Jews, in historical fact, Christians have not believed in the same god as Jews. Nor, much more recently, did Rosemary Reuther discuss the difference in gods. Although she discussed almost all the distortions involved in the early development of Christian theology about Jews, she had almost nothing to say about the fact that most Christians came to believe that Jesus was divine. She declared that 'the most fundamental affirmation of Christian faith is the belief that Jesus is the Christ. He is that Messiah whom the prophets "foretold" and the Jews "awaited"'.[2] But she said little about the fact that Christians came to believe that Jesus was not simply the Messiah but one of the three persons of their god. Thereby she avoided discussion of the fact that Christians came to worship a different god than did Jews.

---

1   *The Conflict of the Church and the Synagogue* (New York: Atheneum, 1969), pp.96–7.

2   *Faith and Fratricide* (New York: Seabury Press, 1974) p.246.

Recognition of the difference in monotheistic gods has been impeded by the fact that the idea of different one and only gods, if historically obvious, is logically self-contradictory. Moreover, since the adherents of Judaism, Christianity and Islam have been indoctrinated for centuries with the idea there is only one god, they have typically assumed that members of all three monotheistic religions were talking about the same god, even though each side believed that it was talking correctly while the other two were sunk in error. The great theologian Hans Küng has given that belief striking expression: 'It is impossible to understand the Christian God without the Jewish, for the Jewish is in fact the Christian God.'[3] 'Faith in the God of Abraham, Isaac, and Jacob is common to Jews, Christians and Muslims.'[4] Many other writers simply take that position for granted. When Karen Armstrong remarks in her *History of God* that, 'in our own day, many people would say that the God worshipped for centuries by Jews, Christians and Moslems has become as remote as the Sky God', she is simply assuming that Jews, Christians and Moslems have always worshipped the same god.[5]

The assumption that all monotheists believe in the same god has also been protected by the lack of any customary term to direct attention to the historical fact of a plurality of monotheisms with different gods. To remedy that defect I would like to suggest a neologism, 'polymonotheism'. By polymonotheism, I mean the existence or official toleration within a wider society under one government, for example, the England of today, of a plurality of religious societies whose members all believe there is only one god, but whose beliefs about the revelations, nature, actions, commands and required worship of their one god in fact differ so greatly from each other that, despite the belief they have in common that there is only one god and some other similarities, they constitute clearly different monotheistic religions with distinctively different gods. Such polymonotheism is not, of course, a new phenomenon. It has existed in Europe, possibly since the separation of Christianity from Judaism around the year 100 of the Common Era, certainly since Constantine's toleration of both Christianity and Judaism in the Roman Empire.

The idea that the adherents of the three monotheisms all ultimately believe in the same one and only god seems highly attractive for, historically, it has provided a basis for toleration. Thus, whereas Christians have displayed great intolerance toward polytheists, their belief that the Jews had believed and still did believe, however incorrectly or partially, in the god that the Christians worshipped was the basis for the survival of the Jews in Europe. But such

---

3   *Does God Exist?* (New York: Vintage Books, 1981), p.615.
4   Ibid., p.618.
5   Karen Armstrong, *A History of God* (New York: Ballantine Books, 1993), p.4. Or see p.11: 'The ... religion of the One God worshipped by Jews, Christians and Moslems'.

Christian toleration of Jews was highly unstable, for it was based on the empirically false premise that Christians worshipped the same god as Jews. Consequently, whenever Christians suspected the truth – that Jews were not worshipping the same god as Christians – Christian toleration of Jews dropped dramatically.

Historically the adherents of Judaism have never believed in a Trinitarian god who condemned humanity for original sin, one of whose persons was incarnate in Jesus of Nazareth who died and rose again to make eternal salvation possible for human beings. Medieval Jews, for example, referred to Jesus as 'the hanged one' and as a 'putrid corpse'. Conversely Christians, with some very early exceptions, have never believed that their god required them to practise the 613 *mitzvot* prescribed in the first five books of the Bible. Not only, as Parkes emphasized, did the early Christians appropriate and misinterpret Hebrew Scripture, they also appropriated and fundamentally altered the Jewish conception of god in order to construct their own new god, a god which proved to have remarkably broad appeal. What had started as a Jewish interpretation of the Jewish belief in the Messiah became the Christian belief in a new composite divinity that included, indeed centred on, Jesus Christ.

The refusal of Christians to admit that Christians and Jews worshipped different gods was the product of wishfully distorted historical thinking. The first and fundamental denial of historical reality was the refusal of Christians to acknowledge that they were developing a new religion with a new god, a reality obvious to many pagan Romans. As the Emperor Julian 'the Apostate' put it in the middle of the fourth century, 'But you, unfortunately, do not abide by the tradition of the apostles . . . Neither Paul, nor Matthew, nor Luke, nor Mark had the audacity to say that Jesus is God... . John, I say, was the first to have the audacity to make this assertion.'[6]

To avoid the charge that they were creating a new god and to overcome the Jewish denial of Jesus' divinity, Christians claimed that, whereas they believed in the god of the Old Testament, contemporary Jews had been mysteriously blind to the recent great revelation of that god in Christ. And out of that theologically driven distortion of historical reality came a new kind of intolerance, tolerant intolerance. Since Christians believed that they and the Jews worshipped the same one god, they did not feel that Jews were totally wrong or evil. Hence, unlike polytheists, Jews could be tolerated – but not as equals. They were to be tolerated as people who were essentially inferior because they had strayed from, or failed to recognize fully, the one true god.[7] Thus those to whom this new

---

6 *Documents of the Christian Church*, 2nd edn, ed. Henry Bettenson (New York: Oxford University Press, 1963) p.20.

7 Muslims, of course, applied the same sort of thinking to Christians and Jews. See Roger Arnaldez, *À la croisée des trois monothéismes* (Paris: Albin Michel, 1993), p.38; and see also *The Concept of Monotheism in Islam and Christianity*, ed. Hans

moderated intolerance was extended were stamped from the beginning with an enduring badge of inferiority. Even my hero Parkes could not avoid a mild condemnation. Although he recognized that Jews would find belief in 'the Atonement wrought on Calvary' repugnant, he believed that in this they would be in error.[8]

The assertion of inferiority was already present in Paul, the apostle who did the most to separate Christianity from Judaism. The ambiguity and ambivalence of his words have led to considerable disagreement among modern interpreters.[9] But much of his and our confusion was the result of his pride in being a Jew and his effort to maintain his conviction that the god whom he and the Jews had worshipped, and the god in whom he and the followers of Jesus now believed, were one and the same god. It was a difficult position to maintain, for even if Paul thought that Jesus was the Messiah and not God, Torah and Paul's version of the message of Jesus were 'mutually exclusive categories'.[10]

Paul was perfectly aware of how new and crucially different was the image of god and the proper response to god that he was preaching, and he knew equally well that most of his former coreligionists did not agree with his new beliefs.[11] But instead of accepting the fact that most Jews were simply continuing to believe in their god much as they had before, he condemned them cosmically for their blindness to the value of the new conception of god of which he was the major architect. Paraphrasing Isaiah and Deuteronomy, he declared that, to the Jews who did not believe Jesus, 'God gave ... a spirit of stupor, eyes that should not see and ears that should not hear, down to this very day.'[12] And when Paul's belief in the proximity of the second coming of Christ proved false, that postponement made his condemnation much harsher. No longer a matter of one generation, the blindness and hardening of the Jews would be attributed to Jews throughout the centuries and would play a central role in the Christian doctrine about Jews that would prevail for centuries.

On the basis of Paul's ambivalent statements, Christian thinkers from the first

---

Köchler (Vienna: Wilhelm Braumüller, 1982) and Arnaldez, *Three Messengers for One God*, trans. Gerald W. Schlabach (Notre Dame: University of Notre Dame Press, 1994).

8   James Parkes, 'A Theology of the Jewish–Christian Relationship', in *Prelude to Dialogue* (New York: Schocken Books, 1969), p.201.

9   John G. Gager, *The Origins of Anti-Semitism* (New York: Oxford University Press, 1985) provides a good description of the debates and a good example of the agility that can be deployed to protect Paul's reputation.

10   Ibid., pp.201, 247, 263; and see Reuther, *Faith and Fratricide*, pp.96–107.

11   On the theme of the novelty of Christianity, see Wolfram Kinzig, *Novitas Christiana: Die Idee des Fortschritts in der Alten Kirche bis Eusebius* (Göttingen: Vanderhook & Ruprecht, 1994), pp.105–16, 582–6, and *passim*.

12   2 Corinthians 3:14–16. Ibid.: 'But their minds were hardened; for to this day, when they read the old covenant, that same veil remains unlifted, because only through Christ is it taken away.' Or, in Romans 11.8, 25–6: 'A hardening has come upon part of Israel, until the full number of the Gentiles come in, and so all Israel will be saved.'

to the fifth century developed a highly ambivalent doctrine that condemned Jews but justified toleration of them. Of course, the doctrine never acknowledged that Christians and Jews worshipped different gods, but acknowledgment nearly seeped in at times. From an early date, to defend against Jewish disbelief in Jesus, Christians had ransacked Hebrew Scriptures to collect 'Testimonies', passages such as prophecies of the coming of the Messiah, which they interpreted as referring to Jesus. In addition, to justify faith in the multiplicity of the persons of their god, Christians collected passages that could be interpreted to indicate the existence, alongside the god of the Jews, of another divinity, 'the Son' of 'God the Father'. And these efforts to justify the multiplicity *in* their god came very close at times to a recognition of a multiplicity of gods.

The first substantial example of this kind of work dates from around 135. Justin Martyr's lengthy treatise, 'Dialogue with Trypho', is the first extant of a long line of anti-Jewish polemics that defended Christianity and criticized Judaism.[13] Justin justified Christian belief by interpreting many passages of the Old Testament in contorted ways. Although Justin himself did not have a good command of Hebrew,[14] he argued that contemporary Jews gave inaccurate and intentionally distorted translations of the Hebrew Scriptures.[15] And following in the path blazed by Paul and anticipating the similar assertions of Augustine,[16] Justin declared that the Jewish Scriptures were not understood by Jews and did not belong to them but to the Christians.[17]

Justin also wrote two *Apologies* to persuade the emperor Antoninus that Christians should not be persecuted, and here he came very close to recognizing that Jews and Christians worshipped different gods. His major argument for the certitude of Christianity was that the coming of Jesus had been predicted by the Jewish prophets hundreds and thousands of years before Jesus came.[18] But although that argument apparently assumed that the god in whom Justin believed had revealed himself to the Jews, Justin declared that the Jews did not know the true god.

He stated accurately that all the Jews in his day taught that it was the god whom one cannot name who spoke to Moses out of the burning bush. But according to Justin, their teaching only demonstrated that the Jews did not know either the Father or the Son. For, according to the Fourth Gospel,[19] Jesus had said

---

13 'Dialogue with Trypho', in *Writings of Saint Justin Martyr*, vol.6, trans. Thomas B. Falls (New York: The Fathers of the Church, 1948).

14 Saint Justin, *Apologies*, ed. André Wartelle (Paris: Etudes Augustiniennes, 1987), p.16.

15 Ibid., chs 68, 71.

16 Augustine, *The City of God*, 18.43.

17 'Dialogue with Trypho', ch. 29. He also declared that the Christians were the true Israel: ibid. ch. 123.

18 Saint Justin, *Apologies*, ed. Wartelle, 'La Première Apologie', chs 12, 31, pp.113, 136–47.

19 John 8:19, 37–40.

that God the Father could only be known through the Son, and Justin therefore believed that it was Jesus Christ who had spoken from the burning bush.[20] And, at times, Justin's language came even closer to admitting the existence of two different gods. Thus at one point he asserted 'that there exists and is mentioned in Scripture another God and Lord under the Creator of all things'.[21] And, as could be expected, the needs which impelled these defensive distortions also impelled Justin to intolerance. He declared that 'you Jews are a ruthless, stupid, blind, and lame people, children in whom there is no faith',[22] and he asserted that 'circumcision is … essential … only for you Jews, to mark you off for the suffering you now so deservedly endure'.[23]

The only prominent figure in early Christianity who openly proclaimed that Jews and Christians worshipped different gods was Marcion, a contemporary of Justin. Marcion was a Christian dualist. According to him, the god worshipped by the Jews was the inferior god of justice who had created this imperfect world, whereas the newly revealed god worshipped by the Christians, the father of Jesus, was a god of mercy and love.[24] For that belief, as well as his denial that Christ was born of a woman and his belief that the text of the gospels had been corrupted, Marcion was excommunicated in 144,[25] but his teachings attracted a wide following, which provoked Justin to condemn him vigorously:

> Then there is a certain Marcion of Pontus, who even now still teaches his disciples to believe in another and greater god than the Creator. Assisted by demons, he has caused many men of every country to blaspheme and to deny that God is the Creator of the universe, and to proclaim another god to be greater and to have done greater deeds than he.[26]

Marcion's success also impelled others to write arguments against him. Of these, the longest and best known is Tertullian's *Adversus Marcionem*, written around 200.[27] Although Tertullian was mightily concerned to refute the idea that

---

20   Saint Justin, *Apologies*, ed. Wartelle, pp.184–7; see also 'Dialogue with Trypho', chs 55–62.

21   Ibid., ch. 56. For a survey of early Christian expressions of divine multiplicity, see Jaroslav Pelikan, *The Christian Tradition*, vol.1, *The Emergence of the Catholic Tradition (100–600)* (Chicago: University of Chicago Press, 1971), pp.175–200.

22   'Dialogue with Trypho', ch. 27.

23   Ibid., ch.19, p.175.

24   Tertullian, *Adversus Marcionem*, 2 vols, ed. and trans. Ernest Evans (Oxford: Clarendon Press, 1972), I, pp.14–17; Bk I.6: 'For all that, we are aware that Marcion sets up two unequal gods, the one a judge, fierce and warlike, the other mild and peaceable, solely kind and supremely good.'

25   Henry Chadwick, *The Early Church* (Baltimore: Penguin Books, 1969), pp.39–40.

26   'La Première Apologie', ch. 26, in Saint Justin, *Apologies*, ed. Wartelle, pp.132–3; 'The First Apology' in *Writings of Saint Justin Martyr*, trans. Falls, p. 62. See also ch. 58 (Wartelle, pp.178–9; Falls, p.96).

27   See note 24.

Jesus was a novel deity, it is surprising how close one of his rather contorted arguments against Marcion's newly proclaimed superior god was to the charge of novelty that Jews could levy against Jesus' divinity.

> So when I am told of a new god, unknown and unheard of in the old
> world, in old time, under the old God: when I hear that in all those past
> ages he was known to none, was ancient only in men's ignorance of
> him, and that one Jesus Christ, himself new but under ancient names,
> has revealed him, as no one had until now; I am grateful to this
> glorifying of theirs because by its help in particular I shall without
> further ado prove a heresy this profession [Marcionism] of a new
> deity.[28]

The fact that Christians drew on two historically different conceptions of god but proclaimed that theirs was one god and the only god, and their refusal to recognize that they were proclaiming a new god, a god different from the one the Jews had worshipped, created fascinating credal difficulties and heated Trinitarian debates that continued to the end of the Roman period and beyond. All this theological creativity, however, left the relation between the god conceived by the Jews and the god conceived by the Christians peculiarly obscure, as is evident in Augustine's declaration that, 'although God is the God of all nations, even the Gentiles acknowledge him to be in a peculiar sense the God of Israel'.[29] Indeed, to overcome the charge of novelty and to avoid acknowledging that Christians worshipped a different god than the Jews, Christian thinkers developed another duality: they divided the Jews into two opposed groups that mirrored the two different conceptions of god.

The clearest description of the duality was made between 314 and 325 by Eusebius of Caesaria, the very influential historian of the early church. According to Eusebius, God had indeed revealed himself to Jews but only to certain good Jews such as Moses and the prophets, for, from Abraham forward, the vast majority of Jews had strayed from rectitude and resisted God in various ways, as contemporary Jews still did. Eusebius claimed, as Justin had implied and Augustine would later assert, that the good Hebrews in the Bible were the Christians' precursors; that they, not the Jews, had been the true Israel before Christ; and that after Christ, the Christians, not the Jews, continued to be the true Israel.[30]

---

28   *Adversus Marcionem*, I, pp.20–21; Bk I.8.

29   *Contra Faustum* (Corpus scriptorum ecclesiasticorum latinorum, vol.25), 12.24; and see Richard Stothert. trans., *Nicene and Post-Nicene Fathers*, first series., vol.4, pp.155–345.

30   Eusebius, *The History of the Church from Christ to Constantine*, trans. G.A. Williamson (New York: New York University Press, 1966), 1.4; Augustine, *City of God*, 17.7. For a thorough description of these ideas, see Marcel Simon, *Verus Israel: Etude sur les relations entre Chrétiens et Juifs dans l'Empire Romain*, 2nd edn (Paris: E. de Boccard, 1964), pp.104–17.

By the beginning of the fifth century, the development of Christian doctrine about the Jews had found more or less final form with Augustine's formulation, which was somewhat more tolerant than earlier versions;[31] and thereafter the doctrine changed little right down to 1945, except for the thirteenth-century condemnation of the Talmud. But if the theological terms of the doctrine remained remarkably stable, what they meant in practice varied greatly because the doctrine was both highly ambivalent and highly ambiguous. It was highly ambivalent because, although it prescribed that Jews should be tolerated because of their providential role in the history of salvation, it taught hatred or contempt for Jews and attributed a servile status to them because of their denial of Jesus' divinity and responsibility for his death. It was highly ambiguous because it was couched in such general terms that it provided little guidance as to how Jews should be treated in practice, leaving room for a wide range of responses. Consequently, not only did the meaning of the doctrine vary greatly for different people at any one time because of differences in individual personality[32] and local conditions, but over time its meaning varied greatly as historical conditions, Christian mentality and Jewish belief and conduct changed.

Amidst all the historical changes, the religious issue that most directly affected Christian attitudes to Jews was the extent to which Christians felt that contemporary Jews were still, albeit in their peculiarly blinded way, worshipping the god of the Old Covenant. The more Christians thought, according to their Christian understanding of the Old Testament, that Jews were preserving the Hebrew Scriptures and worshipping god as before, the easier it was for Christians to tolerate them despite their refusal to believe in Jesus Christ. But the more Christians felt that what contemporary Jews believed was not based on Scripture and differed from Christian beliefs, the more intolerant Christians became.

By the fifth century, one historical change had greatly increased the distance separating Christianity from Judaism. After the first century, as Judaism became increasingly rabbinic or Talmudic and increasingly inaccessible and unappealing for non-Jews, and as Christianity became overwhelmingly gentile and increasingly philosophical, the difference between Christian and Jewish beliefs in fact increased greatly, but Christians did not realize that, for they were more and more ignorant of what Jews actually believed. Increasingly Christians derived their ideas about Jewish belief and practice, not from any serious experience of what contemporary Jews actually believed and did, but rather from what they garnered from Christian doctrine and their own understanding of their

---

31   See Paula Fredricksen, 'Excaecati Occulta Justitia Dei: Augustine on Jews and Judaism', *Journal of Early Christian Studies*, **3** (1995), 299–324.

32   See my 'The Faith of Christians and Hostility to Jews', in *Christianity and Judaism*, ed. Diana Wood (*Studies in Church History*, vol.29) (Oxford: Blackwell, 1992), pp.77–92.

Old Testament. Moreover the social and political status of the two religions had changed greatly. Whereas Judaism had lost its centre in Jerusalem, Christianity had become the official religion of the Roman Empire, and churchmen were using their political power to depress Jewish legal status.

With the fall of the western Roman Empire came another great historical change that brought a striking reversal, a sharp decline in hostility against Jews.[33] After their conversion to Christianity, most of the Germanic-speaking conquerors of western Europe felt little hostility toward Jews. During the Merovingian and Carolingian periods, for the five centuries from about 500 to 1000, relations between Jews and Christians were, with few, largely episcopal, exceptions, quite friendly both at the elite and the popular level.[34] Although some churchmen enacted anti-Jewish measures in church councils, Jews were generally well treated by the Merovingian and Carolingian kings. Thus, despite the determined efforts of two prominent archbishops of Lyons to get Charlemagne and his son Louis the Pious to lower the legal status of Jews, the emperors refused and continued to treat Jews very favourably.

One reason Germanic Christians were so tolerant toward Jews was that their conception of god closely resembled that of the Jews. Unlike later Christians, they paid little attention to Trinitarian divisions of the divinity and did not focus emotionally on the humanity and suffering of Christ. 'Christ was … made almost the sole representative of the Holy Trinity'[35] and their image of Christ was rather that of the god of the Old Testament than that of Jesus in the New. Like the Jews, they thought of themselves as the people of God, their religiosity was highly ritualistic, and they resonated to the bellicosity of the Old Testament. Since there was little to disturb their belief that they and the Jews worshipped the same god, they felt little strain in tolerating Jews.

Another great reversal began in the eleventh century, a dramatic change in the Christians' conception of their god that brought a deadly increase in hostility. The development of a new interest in the literal meaning of Scripture and in the narrative history in the New Testament focused attention on the humanity and suffering of Jesus and his mother, and the new kind of devotion aroused by these images vastly increased the difference between how Christians thought about

---

33   Bernhard Blumenkranz, *Juifs et chrétiens dans le monde occidental, 430–1096* (Paris: Mouton, 1960).

34   The major exception was the effort of the Visigothic kings between 589 and 711 to impose Christianity forcibly on the Jews in Spain. But that policy seems to have been motivated more by the political desire to unite an ethnically divided kingdom than by purely religious concerns. Indeed it conflicted with the theological doctrine of toleration that Pope Gregory the Great (590–604) was making a matter of ecclesiastical law around 600. In any case, Visigothic Spain was an exception. See Langmuir, *Toward a Definition of Antisemitism* (Berkeley: University of California Press, 1996), pp.78–83.

35   Heinrich Fichtenau, *The Carolingian Empire*, trans. P. Munz (Oxford: Blackwell, 1957), p.49.

their god and what Christians thought Jews believed. The idea that the Jews collectively had killed Christ was now taken very literally, thereby acquiring a powerful new emotional meaning. In 1096, the first of the great massacres of Jews in Europe occurred.

By the middle of the thirteenth century, another change further increased the difference between the Jewish and Christian conceptions of god. After the reception of the Babylonian Talmud in Europe, starting in the tenth century, Europe, particularly northern Europe, gradually became the most important centre of Talmudic studies in the world.[36] Christians, however, knew little or nothing about Talmudic Judaism. A few Christian thinkers did acquire a little distorted knowledge in the twelfth century, but it was not until the middle of the thirteenth century that Christian authorities became fully aware of the fact that what contemporary Jews believed was very different from what Christians had thought they believed.

In 1239, Nichlas Donin, an apostate Jew, drew Pope Gregory IX's attention to the Talmud, charging that it was anti-Christian. The pope ordered that it be thoroughly examined by Christian theologians in Paris. They condemned it in 1242 and had cartloads of Talmuds burned. Yet, while it is true that the Talmud contained a few highly anti-Christian passages, they were remarkably few. The major reason for the condemnation was that the examination had revealed that what contemporary Jews believed was very different from what the Christians who tolerated them had thought they believed. Indeed, as Pope Innocent IV more or less directly implied when he condemned the Talmud again in 1244, it seemed that Jews were no longer worshipping the god of the Old Testament as they had in the time of Jesus:

> They ... throw away and despise the Law of Moses and the prophets, and follow some tradition of their elders.... They rear and nurture their children in traditions of this sort ... but of the laws and doctrines of the prophets they make their sons altogether ignorant. They fear that if the forbidden truth, which is found in the Law and the prophets, be understood – the testimony that the only-begotten Son of God was to come in the flesh – their children would convert to the faith and humbly return to their Redeemer.[37]

Jews were not to be allowed to worship their own god in their own way. If they were to be tolerated, they should believe and worship the way the Christian authorities thought Jews should worship the god of the Old Testament. In fact, of course, the Christian pressure failed, for Jews would not or could not abandon the Talmud, but to Christians, Jews now seemed stranger and more mysterious

---

36   Jacob Katz, *Exclusiveness and Tolerance* (Oxford: Oxford University Press, 1961).

37   Solomon Grayzel, *The Church and the Jews in the Thirteenth Century*, vol.1, 2nd edn (New York: Hermon Press, 1966), pp.250–53.

than ever before. And the change increased the strain on the Christians' belief that the Jews believed, however imperfectly, in the Christians' God the Father. By 1497, Jews had been expelled from almost all of western Europe.

There were many reasons for the various expulsions that treated Jews as little better than polytheists, but one aspect has not been emphasized. Although the expulsions ran counter to the long-established Christian doctrine about Jews, and although the popes would continue to protect the presence of Jews in Rome itself from the Middle Ages to the present, the expulsions from the thirteenth to the fifteenth century occurred without any significant papal protest. As Christians acquired a more realistic recognition of how great the difference was between the Christian and Jewish conceptions of god and how unlikely it was that Jews would convert in any numbers, Christian authorities ceased to be seriously concerned about the religious toleration of Jews.

To sketch the later changes in attitudes through the modern period would exceed the limits of this chapter, but it is worth noting that the Calvinists, who emphasized the Old Testament image of god more than Catholics, thereby diminishing the difference between their and the Jews' conception of god, were also more willing to tolerate Jews than Catholics, and that the rise of Deism, which de-emphasized the importance of the conflicts between the traditional religions with their different gods, encouraged greater toleration of Jews. Today, of course, after the horrors of the Holocaust , the decline of imperialism, the undeniable pluralism of religions and the widespread development of agnosticism and atheism, a great deal of attention is being paid in religious circles in England and elsewhere to religious toleration.[38]

In 1992, a very interesting collection of attitudes toward toleration, *Many Mansions*, appeared in the Canterbury Papers Series. The diverse views expressed provide a convenient summary of recent religious views. The authors of its articles, mostly Christian, divide monotheists into three main camps: exclusivists, inclusivists and pluralists.[39] Needless to say, the members of all three groups profess that there is only one god, but thereafter they diverge sharply. Exclusivists declare that their religion alone has the ultimate and saving religious truth, and they deny any validity to all other religions, even though they might admit that some individuals outside their religion might be saved. Inclusivists are more tolerant, but still brand other monotheists as inferior. Although they believe that the adherents of Judaism, Christianity and Islam

---

38   For example, *Persecution and Toleration*, ed. W.J. Sheils (Studies in Church History, vol.21; Oxford: Blackwell, 1984); *Many Mansions: Interfaith and Religious Intolerance*, ed. Dan Cohn-Sherbok (Canterbury Papers Series) (London: Bellew Publishers, 1992); *Liberalism, Multiculturalism and Toleration*, ed. John Horton (New York: St Martin's Press, 1993).

39   For a good brief discussion of the three categories, see Gavin D'Costa, 'Christianity and Other Religions', in *Many Mansions*, pp. 31–43.

believe in the same one and only god, they nonetheless hold that theirs is the one true, superior religion and that the other monotheistic religions fall short – even though they may be valid so far as they go and may have some valuable elements that the inclusivists' own religion lacks.[40] This was James Parkes' position.[41]

The pluralists would seem the most tolerant, for they stress the validity of all the great religious traditions. But they do so only by rejecting the actual beliefs of those traditions. They assert that 'each of the major faiths represents a culturally conditioned human response to a single divine reality'.[42] But even though they recognize that the adherents of the major faiths would disagree with them, because they have differing conceptions of god and strongly prefer their own forms of monotheism, the pluralists nonetheless disregard those manifest facts in order to proclaim their own belief in a more transcendent god. They reduce what appear to the historian as clearly different monotheisms to being unwitting subsets of their own true monotheism with its patently different, and remarkably abstract, concept of god.

John Hick, for example, has developed a careful, heavily philosophical, highly Kantian, argument for the pluralist position. He believes that the Gods and Absolutes of the different traditions are not purely products of the human imagination but are all manifestations to human awareness of the ultimate reality, 'the Transcendent' that Westerners call God.[43] He asks what can be considered an authentic response to the Transcendent and responds that 'an answer occurs only within the basic circle of faith which affirms that (within the great traditions at least) religious experience is not only a product of the human religious imagination but constitutes at the same time our human response to the universal presence of the Transcendent'.[44] He maintains this position even though he recognizes that his assumption that great traditions are manifestations of awareness of the same single universal ultimate is not compatible with the claims of the different traditions *as they stand*, for each 'holds that its own object of worship or focus of meditation is truly and uniquely ultimate'.[45] The implication is obvious: the different traditions 'as they stand' with their differing, firmly held, conceptions of god are to that extent inferior. Moreover the monotheisms that Hick does not include among the great traditions and considers inauthentic[46] are obviously even more inferior.

---

40 Needless to say, inclusivists may be more or less generous in their recognition of the validity of other religions. Thus Gavin D'Costa takes a very open-minded position: see above, note 39.

41 See above, note 8.

42 Paul Badham, 'The Case for Religious Pluralism', in *Many Mansions*, p.3.

43 John Hick, 'A Religious Understanding of Religion', in *Many Mansions* p.126.

44 Ibid., p.131.

45 Ibid., p.132.

46 For a fuller exposition of Hick's position, see *A John Hick Reader*, ed. Paul

Alan Race has provided a more guarded and more historical argument for the pluralist position.[47] It relies heavily on awareness of the great changes in historical context and in historical and semiotic interpretation that have taken place since the first theological formulations of Christology and the Incarnation were made. Race believes that inter-faith dialogue should be open-minded and need not open with the assumption that Jesus is the 'final' truth of God. For Race, 'the eschatological nature of truth ... [is] reflected pluralistically in the world's different religious visions of the divine life. ... The "particularities" of the world religious traditions are not isolated islands, but territories deeply and necessarily related to one another'.[48]

Thus both Hick and Race recognize but seek to minimize the importance of the differences between the divinities that traditional monotheists have worshipped. But they profess their own different vision of the one God and, highly tolerant though they are, they subordinate the beliefs of the traditional religions to their own vision in a way that most adherents of those religions would not accept. Their monotheism thus continues the habit of most monotheists through the centuries of claiming superiority for their own vision of a single god, of asserting that other monotheisms worship the same god but without the same depth of understanding, and hence are, at least by implication and at least to that extent, inferior.

Ever since the emergence of Christianity, there has been an enduring conflict between the belief that Jews, Christians and Muslims all worship the same god and the historical fact that the ideas about 'God' and the forms of worship of Judaism, Christianity and Islam have differed so widely. And, unfortunately, there is a price to be paid when the protection of theological beliefs necessitates a refusal to recognize historical realities. In this case, as with the distortion of Jewish history that Parkes lamented, the price has been paid by the victims of the religious intolerance that has been such a prominent feature of Judaism, Christianity and Islam through the centuries.

Many theological justifications or rationalizations have been given for that mutual intolerance, and it may be the inescapable result of the logic of monotheistic belief. Some intolerance is inevitable whenever adherents of a monotheism do not recognize that their one and only god is not universal, that their belief in *their* one and only god is a commitment to the requirements of membership, not in humanity, but in their particular human

---

Badham (Houndmills: Macmillan Press, 1990). For a brief critique of his position from an inclusivist position, see Gavin D'Costa, 'Christianity and Other Religions', in *Many Mansions*, pp.35–8. For a fuller exposition of D'Costa's position, see *Theology and Religious Pluralism* (Oxford: Blackwell, 1986). There are, of course, many, many other recent works relevant to religious pluralism and toleration.

47   'Christ and the Scandal of Particularities', in *Many Mansions*, pp.61–72.

48   Ibid., p.72. For a fuller exposition of Race's position, see his *Christians and Religious Particularism* (London; SCM Press, 1983).

community.[49] For, viewed from a purely historical point of view, the fundamental cause of monotheistic intolerance would seem to be the refusal or inability of monotheists – from a variety of motives – to recognize that they have no monopoly of belief in a one and only god. They have been unwilling to accept the historical fact of polymonotheism and to acknowledge that adherents of the other great monotheisms have worshipped and do worship – with equal devotion – a different one and only god, and a god whom they do not think to be but one of several revelations of a more transcendent god.

---

49   I have borrowed that thesis from another pluralist, Paul F. Knitter, *No Other Name?* (Maryknoll, NY: Orbis Books, 1985), pp.184–5.

Chapter 3

The Power of Tolerance

David Theo Goldberg

Introduction

In times like these, it might be insisted, people especially need tolerance towards
each other, towards in particular the political and social and legal positions that
are being circulated in the name of fashioning new sociopolitical orders, whether
in South Africa or Pakistan, Israel and Palestine, Indonesia or Kosovo, the USA
or former USSR.[1] Indeed, it could be said that the Truth and Reconciliation
process that has been so important both to reconstruction in South Africa and to
the representation of its sociopolitical and moral transformation to the world
community has rested precisely on an assumption of the necessities and
possibilities of tolerance. The events both of September 11 and of the dominant
response of powerful states to them, as well as the spiralling violence between
Israelis and Palestinians, have suggested to some an imperative of toleration
above all else. I am afraid what I have to say will burst that bubble, with a view
to replacing it at least tentatively with a set of commitments more compelling.

Tolerance is portrayed usually as powerful in so far as it engenders, in the face
of possibly aggressive and violent responses, a wide variety of viewpoints and
behaviour. Tolerance accordingly is taken to promote – it is even considered the
behavioural analogue of – open-mindedness and patience, ultimately enabling
the emergence of the truth. Tolerance thus articulated is a virtue, a habit of the
heart to be inculcated and cultivated.

Two principal arguments can be identified historically in support of tolerance.
First, a conscience-based account rests on respect for individuals' freedom of
thought, an account that is usually linked more instrumentally to claims about the
emergence of truth and acting on evidence.[2] Second, there is the argument from
civil order. England's Act of Toleration enacted in 1689 under William and Mary
granted freedom of religious worship not because of a commitment to the
inherent value of religious liberty so much as from a concern with maintaining
the peace. John Locke, writing for the political designs of the Earl of Shaftesbury

---

1   This chapter is an adaptation from 'Die Macht der Toleranz', *Das Argument*
(Berlin) Special Issue: Grenzen (Borders), 224 (Spring), 11–27. It is a revised version of
an article on tolerance in the South African context that appeared in Tom Martin (ed.),
Racism and the Challenges of Multiculturalism (College Park: Penn State University
Press, 2002).

2   Here James Mill's 1826 review, published as *The Principles of Toleration*
(New York: Burt Franklin, 1837/1971), is an example.

in 1667, suggested limits to application of the latter principle. Locke restricted toleration from applying to Catholics and atheists, the former because allegiance is paid to external, foreign authority and the latter because obedience to a higher authority is not paid at all and so the grounds of civil authority are supposedly missing in action.[3] Rawls rightly notes that liberalism since has generalized the principle of tolerance to cover other concerns of meaning and value involving deep differences. And Chundran Kukathas has argued in the context of fashioning the normative underpinnings for multicultural states that a tolerance-based liberalism will be more secure than an autonomy-based one, a claim contested by Will Kymlicka.[4] Yet Locke's limitations on tolerance exhibit, at least implicitly, the potential limits of tolerance itself.

It is possible accordingly to reconstruct a genealogy of toleration's conceptual emergence.[5] In the seventeenth and eighteenth centuries tolerance regarding religion in the emergent English liberal tradition developed, if only differentially and partially, as a response to the culture wars at the time, as it did more widely on the stage of the European Enlightenment.[6] Tolerance assumed in the nineteenth century the position of a central utilitarian virtue, the two arguments I have identified with James Mill and John Locke, respectively, combining in the younger Mill's revised utilitarianism. Tolerance supposedly becomes in John Stuart Mill's hands the means to establishing a society more generally happy, productive of the greatest good for the greatest number. 'It is better to be tolerant than not' signifies in this scheme of things that it is more productive of wellbeing (utility) as a rule to tolerate expression, verbal or behavioural, than not. John Stuart Mill makes the most general argument in support of widespread tolerance as a means to enabling and protecting liberty (autonomy) and the production of truth. Here the only legitimate restraint is considered the (potential) production of harm.[7]

---

3   John Locke, *A Letter on Toleration* (Oxford: Clarendon Press, 1968); John Horton and Susan Mendus, 'Introduction', in J. Horton and S. Mendus (eds), *Aspects of Toleration: Philsophical Studies* (London: Methuen, 1985), p.3; Maurice Cranston, 'John Locke and the Case for Toleration', in Susan Mendus and David Edwards (eds), *On Toleration* (Oxford: Clarendon Press, 1987), pp.103 ff.

4   John Rawls, *Political Liberalism* (New York: Columbia University Press, 1993), p.xxviii; Will Kymlicka, *Multicultural Citizenship* (Oxford: Oxford University Press, 1995), p.154.

5   Etymologically, there is little difference between tolerance and toleration, and I will use the terms interchangeably. David Heyd points out that Hebrew derives the words for tolerance and patience from a common etymological root, signifying burden and suffering. The earliest emergence in English of the term 'toleration', in 1517, concerns the endurance of suffering, which only three centuries later is extended to the suffering of others' opinions: David Heyd, 'Introduction', in D. Heyd (ed.), *Toleration: An Elusive Virtue* (Princeton: Princeton University Press, 1996), p.15.

6   Cf. Voltaire's *Traité sur la Tolérance*, 1763 (Paris: Flammarion, 1989).

7   Cf. Mary Warnock, 'The Limits of Toleration', in Mendus and Edwards, *On*

It remains an open question whether as a rule tolerance produces more social utility than any conceivable alternative, as utilitarianism (at least in its rule variety) really demands. In favour of tolerance it might be said that one does not have to wait for the development or acquisition of other virtues and attitudes before tolerance can be expressed,[8] though on reflection (as I suggested at the outset) it does seem tied up with patience and a degree of open-mindedness. Modern liberal moral theory relies heavily on tolerance in mediating the recognition of increasing pluralism or diversity, heterogeneity and multiculturalism.[9] For liberalism socially defined identities such as race and gender are morally irrelevant categories, those on the basis of which moral judgments about persons, pernicious or affirmative, are supposed not to be made. In the face of such reference, psychologically or sociopolitically prompted, liberalism supposedly promotes tolerance of the differences these group categories signify. So tolerance becomes the modern liberal mode – its 'bigness' – in dealing with social identity. Identities are tolerated while being dismissed, or at least non-dominant identities are tolerated by the dominant; begrudging acknowledgment and equanimity are advanced while scowling at the content of the character. Awkwardly, liberalism invokes identities to be tolerated that on principle are supposed to be ignored.

What this all too brief historical reconstruction suggests is that the spreading commitment to liberal tolerance, outwards from religious to broader social applications, developed from the standpoint of domination and power. Ironically some now insist that tolerance may not be all it is cut out to be, that perversely tolerance may be, well, too tolerant, licensing all sorts of excess in the age of multiculturalism and diversity, as though the Other is waiting around to be tolerated.[10] Tolerance, as a concept, a project, a social virtue, a commitment, began to find itself in trouble at exactly the moment the dominance of social regimes identifying themselves as politically liberal came to be openly, provocatively and dismissively challenged. What this suggests also is that tolerance as a project is contingent upon prevailing discursive terms to identify

---

Toleration, pp. 123–5. Instructively, where Mill mentions toleration in *On Liberty*, *Collected Works* XVIII, ed. J.M. Robson (Toronto: University of Toronto Press, 1859/1977) it is generally regarding religion. Regarding religious tolerance he is at odds with Locke. In a footnote, for instance, he chides a British government official for restricting religious tolerance in British India to Christians (ibid., pp.240–41). Mill does use the term to refer more widely to 'tastes and modes of life' once in the closing pages of Chapter Three (pp.272 ff) and again in Chapter Five (pp.292–310).

8   Peter Gardner, 'Tolerance and Education', in John Horton (ed.), *Liberalism, Multiculturalism and Toleration*, (London: Macmillan, 1993), p.100.

9   Rawls, *Political Liberalism*; Kymlicka, *Multicultural Citizenship*, pp.152–78.

10   Cf. S.D. Gaede, *When Tolerance is No Virtue: Political Correctness, Multiculturalism, and the Future of Truth and Justice* (Downer's Grover, IL: InterVarsity Press, 1993).

(to make possible by picking out and legitimating) who as group member permissibly may be tolerated.

Thinking through Tolerance

Now, for tolerance to be invoked, it is generally agreed (though not universally) that it must exhibit the following features: (a) some conduct or expression must be disapproved or disliked; (b) the person disapproving must not act on this disapproval coercively so as to prevent others acting in the disapproved or disliked way; (c) refusing to interfere with the disapproved or disliked expression must turn on more than acquiescence or resignation. In turn, four principled considerations are attendant to this conception of tolerance:

1. *The principle of truth.* Tolerance implicitly makes a claim to truth, to represent, to stand for, to have access to truth, presuming in turn truth's singularity and objectivity.[11] The claim by Europeans to tolerate radical views on immigration they otherwise consider objectionable (whether the insistence upon restricting all immigration or having no restrictions at all) was predicated on the claim of liberals to represent the truth in these matters (moderation and modest quotas in the first instance, the productive power of market economics in the latter).

2. *The condescension effect.* The tolerant implicitly exhibit condescension to the object of tolerance: 'to put up with', to tolerate the tolerated even though they are regarded as repugnant or what they do is disliked or deemed wrong. This is captured by the dismissive ring of the exclamation, 'Well, that's tolerable.' John Stuart Mill's infamous reference to 'nations in their nonage' or perhaps the remark of many middle-class white South Africans in the early 1990s, 'We have to get used to the fact that we are a third world country now' exemplify this feature. Nations in their nonage and their more educated elites – white-like but never quite, as Homi Bhabha puts it – were to be tolerated by the more advanced British who had the right, indeed the calling, to educate Indians and other undeveloped or immature nations (Mill elsewhere mentions West Indians) in the details of government until such time that they are prepared for self-determination. Some white liberals acknowledged begrudgingly in the wake of the Civil Rights Act in the United States or the demise of apartheid in South Africa that increased numbers of black students and faculty as well as black workers should be tolerated in formerly

---

11   Heyd, *Toleration*, pp.4–7. By contrast, Bernard Williams suggests that one source of tolerance among others is a scepticism which those espousing tolerance have about the possibility of truth: Bernard Williams, 'Toleration: An Impossible Virtue?', in Heyd, *Toleration*, pp.20–21. While scepticism certainly theoretically entails tolerance, I am less convinced than Williams that many people as a practical matter are so moved.

overwhelmingly white universities and workplaces. They complained quietly at the same time of the unfairness of affirmative action. Their condescending tolerance was predicated accordingly on longstanding presumptions of racial inferiority and their own superiority, failing to comprehend segregationism and apartheid as a comprehensive and deep-seated affirmative action programme for whites.

3. *The waiting game*. Thus the tolerant tend to be waiting for the tolerated to catch up or on, in knowledge and recognition, in civility and morality, in understanding, patience, in short, in the capacity for self-governance and in action. For example, consider Mill's failed insistence that the English East Indies Company run Indian affairs rather than that India be granted home rule or subjected to British parliamentary rule. And white corporate executives or state administrators assume the initial incompetence of their black counterparts in post-apartheid South Africa that they nevertheless ambivalently tolerate in the name of producing a new society.

4. *Toleration's blindness*. Tolerance tends to be blind because it tends to be superficial: to accept the expression of the tolerated in absence of understanding it; to accept the expression in absence of engaging its content. This is not a necessary condition of tolerance, not part of its definition or conception, but something like an effect that tends from its application. For this reason, too, those who tolerate find themselves less able critically to judge the expression or disposition giving rise to it in a way that is constructive and not just dismissive; in a way, that is, that would enable the criticized to consider the critique seriously. So an English colonialist 'tolerates' the 'native's' expression while silently dismissing it or considering it the expression of an inferior, that is, as *naive*. The tolerated are properly resentful, or dismissive, or angry, rebellious or revolutionary, for in the lack of understanding they (generally) or the expression at issue (in particular) fail to be taken seriously. Susan Mendus is right accordingly in pointing out that religious, ethnocultural or racial intolerance amounts to the rejection of a whole way of life, of who the intolerated essentially are.[12] There is a sense in which one could say this also about the tolerated: In being religiously, ethno-culturally or racially tolerated one is being so in spite of who one at basis takes oneself to be.

David Raphael formalizes this line of argument conceptually in terms of a paradox faced by the notion of tolerance:

> If toleration implies moral disapproval of what you tolerate, and if the criterion of moral approval is conformity to the principle of respect for persons, then toleration presupposes that what you tolerate does not

---

12 Susan Mendus, 'The Tigers of Wrath and the Horses of Instruction', in Horton, *Liberalism*, ed., p.205.

conform to the principle of respect for persons. But on the other hand, so it is suggested, we ought not to tolerate whatever contravenes the principle of respect for persons. So how can there be toleration at all?[13]

If I do not strongly condemn something with which I am prepared nevertheless to live, this is less the case of tolerance than of indifference. And almost all philosophical commentators on tolerance rightly warn against confusing the two.[14] By contrast, if I find something utterly repugnant but I am prepared to live in a society that allows it, I am not so much tolerating it as subsuming it under a competing moral principle that in the hierarchy of values I take to be more important. A person who abhors abortion but is able to live in a society that makes it available is not 'tolerating' abortion so much as determining a woman's choice concerning her own body and self-determination to be more important. So the claim to 'tolerating' abortion or whatever either reduces to mere indifference, which we now know is not tolerance, or is elevated to a more principled though troubled acceptance of the disagreeable practice. Again this is not tolerance but moral conflict. Likewise, the anti-abortionist who fights pro-choice laws regards herself not so much as intolerant as stressing a principle she takes to be more compelling than choice in such matters. And though I may hate country music (or *boeremusiek*) I nevertheless endorse its airtime, not out of tolerance but because I consider freedom of expression more valuable than (imposing) some choice of taste. Thus tolerance is conceptually beside the point. Bernard Williams succinctly characterizes the paradox here by suggesting that for liberalism tolerance is necessary, but impossible.[15]

The Power to Tolerate

If this is so, how is it that tolerance has received so much play as political or social ideal? It being better to tolerate or be tolerated than not, given that at least there is a semblance of coherence to the concept, suggests that the appeal of tolerance is tied up with the appeal of individual liberty. Generally one might say that I would rather my neighbour tolerate my beliefs or actions than not.[16] Nevertheless, when we change neighbour for society – I would rather my society by way of my government tolerate my expression than not (contrary to Heyd I think this eminently possible) – the power behind (or underpinning) tolerance is

---

13   D.D. Raphael, 'The Intolerable', in Susan Mendus (ed.), *Justifying Toleration*, (Cambridge: Cambridge University Press, 1988), p.142.

14   W. Paul Vogt, *Tolerance and Education: Learning to Live with Diversity and Difference* (Thousand Oaks: Sage, 1997), p.30.

15   Bernard Williams, 'Toleration', pp.18–27.

16   Perhaps: I think even this generalization open to exception rather than a truism; I can think of cases (some varieties of paternalism, say) where I would rather not be tolerated so that I know what I'm up against.

laid bare. Most Israelis, for complex reasons, tend to tolerate religious settlements in the West Bank while being increasingly intolerant of Palestinian presence within the boundaries of Israel. It might be said that tolerance serves to mitigate social power, mapping out a space for individual expression in the face of collective constraint. But that the collective constraint is self-consciously placed on hold through tolerance suggests at once the institutional limits of tolerance, that it is an artifice in the end powerless to face down power where power seeks more naked expression. One might even say that tolerance is a form of bad faith, in the final analysis hiding power's expression from (self-)view.

In this sense, tolerance was considered in the nineteenth century to have a civilizing effect, transforming through influence and education the debased character and behaviour of the inferior (the tolerated). Examples abound: the treatment of Jews by middle-class bourgeoisie in Manchester or of the *English* working classes, or Mill's attitude toward the Indian governing classes, or South African liberals towards 'their maids' and 'their boys'. Thus tolerance became a central value, acquiring the status of a virtue, of the English middle-class elites. It lasted as a virtue, to be socialized through English education and practice, so long as the elite remained confident in a relatively stable social order. Consider by contrast the British response to the Indian Rebellion of 1857–8, the apartheid regime's various responses to township rebellion, the Israeli response to *intifida*, or Americans' response to assertive Islamic regimes in the wake of 9/11. Similarly, a white-led anti-racist demonstration in Brussels focusing not insignificantly on voting rights for migrants was widely advertised and received enormous press coverage. A Muslim-organized 'day of reflection' the preceding day in Antwerp, focusing on twenty years of systematic discrimination, passed unnoticed by those outside the Muslim community. As Blommaert and Verschueren comment carefully, 'A show of tolerance on the part of the majority seems to carry more weight than justified expressions of frustration on the part of a minority.'[17] In fact, tolerance is predicated historically on a denial of recognition and respect, public resources and political representation.

Tolerance, well, tolerates. It is a form of 'live and let live'. It does not remove the object population (where the object or target is a group) from the arena of public debate, from remaining a question (as in 'The Negro or Jewish or Woman Question' or now 'The Islamic Question'). It precisely extends and legitimates consideration of the target population as a problem to be solved rather than a fact to be accepted, let alone people to be respected.[18] In fact, tolerance tends

---

17   Jan Blommaert and Jef Verschuren, *Debating Diversity: Analysing the Discourse of Tolerance* (London: Routledge, 1998), p.174. Cf. Avishai Margalit, *The Decent Society* (Cambridge: Harvard University Press, 1996), pp.176–80.

18   Bill Williams, 'The Anti-Semitism of Tolerance: Middle Class Manchester and the Jews 1870-1900', in *City Class and Culture: Studies of Social Policy and Cultural Production in Victorian Manchester*, Alan Kidd and K. W. Roberts, eds. (Manchester: Manchester University Press, 1985), p. 79.

sociologically to be extended more readily to those in some ways like oneself or to those who have little or no power in relation to one: to whites by whites, men by men, or women by men where the women are seen as non-threatening or their desirability in other respects overrides the sense of threat. Nineteenth-century English middle-class elites found it easy to extend tolerance to Jewish middle-class entrepreneurs (in Manchester, for example), or to Indian middle-class or royal civil servants, but not to working-class or poor East European Jewish immigrants or Indian peasants. One might say the same of white liberals in South Africa (in contrast, relatively speaking, to white radicals) tolerating Coloured or African elites while dismissive of the peasant or working classes. Günter Grass recently accused Germans of 'closet racism', of expressing tolerance for Europe's Others while restricting Turkish immigration even as they extend the hand of friendship to Bosnian or Kosovar Albanian (read: European) refugees. Afghans are restricted by contrast largely to the border areas of Pakistan. One could be against anti-semitism or racism while simultaneously against immigration of impoverished Jews from Eastern Europe, Turkish Kurds or Mexican migrant workers in California or Texas. As Bill Williams puts it, a precondition of liberal tolerance in the nineteenth century concerned complementing native (colonial) economic enterprise and extending its scope, rather than competing with it or standing in its way.[19]

Tolerance promotes – indeed, there is a sense in which it is predicated upon the assumption of the possibility of – assimilation of the tolerated who thus have to demonstrate their deserving to be tolerated. The English working classes, or Jewish and Indian and Coloured middle-class elites, are to be tolerated because there is hope for them, in virtue of their ethnoracial, national or class character, to be saved from themselves, so to speak. They are salvageable in character and habit, educable to the virtues of English evenhandedness, reasonableness and the Anglican work ethic.

It follows that tolerance makes actual prejudice and discrimination acceptable (that is, tolerable). 'If we are tolerant, how can we be prejudiced or discriminatory?', it might be asked. Prejudice can go hand in glove with tolerance quite straightforwardly: I am prejudiced but able to tolerate you, the object of my prejudice, in spite of it. 'Look how big I am.' This promotion of prejudice in the name of tolerance is identified formally by Blommaert and Verschueren in the European context in terms of 'the threshold of tolerance'. Tolerance among white Europeans is limited by the maintenance of tradition; permissiveness that threatens or transgresses tradition crosses 'the threshold of tolerance', becoming intolerable. The self-proclaimed virtues of European tolerance and openness, they conclude, are 'cancelled without affecting the basic self-image' of tolerance Europeans pride themselves in promoting. Indeed the

---

19   Bill Williams, 'Anti-Semitism of Tolerance', p.89.

projected elevation of Christianity over Islam in the moralizing calculus of tolerance licenses the former to limit its largesse in the face of the latter's intolerance. It replaces proclaimed civility and openness with severity and oppression as a matter of right in the name of protecting civilisation against invasion by the mere presence of the infidels.[20]

So tolerance offers a politics of disengagement, the view from afar: 'live and let live', 'be and let be', 'minding one's own business' – a politics, in other words, of ignoring and ignorance. The easy possibility of tolerance becomes all too appealing in contrast to the complexities of responsible sensitivity and critical engagement, even as tolerance helps to moderate the more extreme expressions of an exclusionary politics. Better it is for the most part, to be sure, than a politics of interference, self-righteous paternalism and dogmatic dismissal, all in the name of a projected public fabricated for self-fulfilling political purposes. But it closes down the possibility of promoting or nurturing an alternative politics, one of solidarity and engagement, sensitivity and respect, a point to which I return in conclusion.

So, accepting tolerance as the means to civil order or the best a liberal society can hope for in the face of diversity, difference and heterogeneity implies not taking heterogeneity seriously as a good. Indeed it is to assume heterogeneity as an unfortunate fact of life we have to 'tolerate' rather than the central virtue or good of a vital, exciting, stimulating social life or state. Difference tolerated, one might say, is but a step from, or indeed, a step to, difference denied.

The elevation of the category 'hate crimes' in the past twenty years is embraced as evidence of the state's tolerance in the face of multicultural diversity. The 'tolerant' state enables expression of hate crimes it is at once then sufficiently concerned to police, criminalize, and punish. The 'tolerant' state thus balances the freedom to express 'hatefully' with the freedom from the effects of such expression. Thus the state 'tolerates' the expression of the hate the effect of which after the fact it sanctions, thus sanctioning in one sense what it sanctions in another.[21]

Now tolerance is incapable as a conceptual commitment of distinguishing between the freedom to engage in a demeaning expression and the freedom from being so demeaned (between positive and negative freedom, to be crude about it). Tolerating the freedom to demean implies failure to protect freedom from disrespect. Restricting freedom to demean in the name of freedom from disrespect precisely entails a restriction of tolerating the demeaning. Perhaps one

---

20 Blommaert and Verschueren, *Debating Diversity*, pp.77–80. Consider as a prime example Samuel Huntington's awfully popular book in some circles, *The Clash of Civilizations and the Remaking of World Order* (New York: Touchstone Books, 1998).

21 I am grateful to Anjie Rosga for prompting the insight. See also my 'Hate, or Power?' in David Theo Goldberg, *Racial Subjects: Writing on Race in America* (New York: Routledge, 1997).

way a discourse of tolerance might be able to accommodate the distinction is by giving in to it, by admitting that the limits on tolerance lie precisely at the point of empowering the right to be free of demeaning expression. But this is just to admit that the principle of tolerance is subsidiary to principles of solidarity, respect and sensitivity, principles which, I suggest, when properly conceived and considered, vacate the recourse to a principle of tolerance.

So, tolerance acquires its value, its power, by virtue of always being an expression from relative power: personal, social, political or institutional. Glen Newey adds a qualification to the generalization: there are cases where one group may tolerate another because it has calculated that the costs of opposing the other group outweigh the benefits that would follow from such opposition. Here tolerance follows from a certain lack of power, or at least the diseconomies of relative powerlessness, though one may want to name this self-interested instrumentality 'prudent if begrudging acquiescence' rather than 'tolerance'.[22] But this too is problematic. The relative accommodationism of a significant sector of the Coloured middle class under apartheid, begrudging as it was, achieved very limited political and economic benefits at the cost of great psychological stress and withering criticism from anti-apartheid opposition.

Tolerance, I am suggesting then, is a kind of class morality. One way of seeing the dimension of power at work in tolerance is to consider the difference in locutions between 'I am being tolerant' and 'I am being tolerated'. The first is active, the second passive; the first presupposes the power to be other than tolerant, the second suggests that the object of tolerance is fixed, the position of the tolerated *qua* tolerated not quite in the hands of the tolerated to be defined. As Zygmunt Bauman puts it, 'From the point of view of reason-founded human order [of modernity], tolerance is incongruous and immoral.'[23] Tolerance, then, is an all too easy compromise between caring less about the different and a sensitive or committed concern for their equal treatment and respect.

I am suggesting we contrast liberal tolerance with solidarity, respect, mutually engaging comprehension and sensitivity. Tolerance in the sense outlined here is not, as some suggest, a pseudonym for equal respect so much as a poor substitute for it. Respect requires knowledge of and engagement with its object, a concern to comprehend another's standing, even that a person may always be capable of acting in ways other than they have exhibited in the past.[24] Sensitivity presupposes an insightful appreciation of the conditions giving rise to another's situation, of its nuances and implications. The mark of sensitive treatment may be 'measured' (in the sense of assessed; in strict terms it is not measurable at all)

---

22   Glen Newey, 'Fatwa and Fiction: Censorship and Toleration', in Horton, *Liberalism*, p.180.

23   Zygmunt Bauman, *Intimations of Postmodernity* (London: Routledge, 1992), p.xiv.

24   Margalit, *Descent Society*, pp.144–5.

in terms of whether a person reasonably considers him- or herself to have been taken seriously. Being taken seriously has to do, not merely with whether one's views, position(s), and standing have been carefully attended, but whether they have been weighed non-dismissively, inclusively and potentially transformatively in the dialogical relation. Stereotyping especially mitigates, if not obliterates, being considered seriously, if at all, waving magically aside the seriousness of a claim or expression by devaluing (demeaning by denying the complexity of) its proponent. Solidarity involves giving support to another in difficult circumstances, standing shoulder to shoulder, being prepared to be subjected to discomfort in the same way in order to achieve the common purpose of overturning wrongdoing or bringing about a more just state of affairs.

Notice that being treated sensitively or standing in solidarity cannot be invoked formulaically in the way tolerance can: there is no analogue for the object of sensitive treatment to 'the tolerated', indeed virtually no analogue to 'the tolerant' ('the sensitive' or 'those in solidarity' do not trip off the tongue with quite the same alacrity). There is no substantivizing in the grammar of sensitivity as there is with tolerance. Sensitivity and solidarity are predicated on a person strictly adverbially, as a characteristic, even a general condition, of her or his practice. While tolerance may purport to this state, it operates by nature at a moral distance, from a space of disengagement. Tolerance promotes as it presupposes anonymity, begrudgingly giving over if not in to it: the tolerating endure the tolerated action or belief. By contrast, solidarity and sensitivity necessarily require engagement, a resolve to interact with the difference in and of the different, and insight into the conditions prompting and promoting the expression (of difference) in question. This is not tantamount to saying the sensitive necessarily accept the expression; rather it likely transforms the nature and standing of criticism where criticism is deemed necessary. Tolerance, in short, is the disposition of and from distance; solidarity and sensitivity the dispositions of engagement, to change and be changed through interaction.

While it is possible to mobilize sensitivity and solidarity, like tolerance, on consequentialist grounds (stability, security in the first instance, the pleasures and benefits of engagement in the second), their justification rests more squarely on the non-consequentialist commitments of principled respect. I am sensitive to the surroundings and circumstances of a person because and in so far as I respect her; I consider her abstract claim on the conditions that enable a decent life to be morally equal to those of all others. Thus I express solidarity in word and deed with her. The drive for public respect, it could then be said, is at once the pursuit of a politics of recognition,[25] a fair distribution of social resources and political representation in a shared public space. Active anti-apartheid commitments were predicated upon and acted out not the distance of tolerance but commitment to a

---

25   Charles Taylor, *Multiculturalism and the Politics of Recognition* (Princeton: Princeton University Press, 1993).

set of shared principles, and to considered action to institute them in concert with others. A two-state solution to the present Israel–Palestine crisis would seem to be predicated on a similar set of principles.

If I respect someone it makes little sense to say that I tolerate his expression unless that expression flies in the face of his claim on respect (at least in that regard): autonomy is a basic moral principle, and in respecting someone we recognize his or her autonomy. The object of tolerance definitionally is an expression to be considered morally problematic. It is to be tolerated supposedly because we consider autonomy more important than the wrongdoing we consider the expression to represent. But tolerance seems to fall short of respect, its begrudging character hinting at dismissiveness rather than respect. This suggests at least a gap between tolerance and respect, between a judgment of moral dismissal directed at the person's expression and respect for their autonomy so to express themselves. On the other hand, I am sensitive towards someone and their expression not so much in order to show respect, as a means to the end, but more directly as an expression of respect itself, as the way in which respect is manifested. And out of that set of commitments flows the expression of solidarity, of a willingness to act at least broadly in concert to effect common ends.

One principally directs respect to persons as self-directing beings in their own right. Heyd argues that one tolerates a person's or culture's beliefs and expressions in so far as one recognizes the intrinsic humanity, the inherent value, of the persons so believing or expressing.[26] Surely, however, it makes sense to say that one respects a belief or expression for recognition of whatever virtue it may be considered to represent independent of the person expressing it. Indeed a person abhorrent for other reasons may still express a view worthy of respect in spite of her- or himself. And respect here requires sensitivity to the nuance both within expressions (a complex belief) and between one expression and another, as well as comprehension of the complexities of expression. Tolerance all too often substitutes for the absence of a thick description of the background conditions for an expression. Such thick description contextualizes an expression's expressibility and claim to legitimacy, giving to the expression depth, perhaps extending to it even justifiability. It is just such thick contextualizing description that is called for by mutual understanding, sensitivity, respect and solidarity in group formation and dynamics. I do not have the space to pursue an extended contrast of the relative analytic testiness of tolerance with the richness of respect and solidarity in group relations that my account more thickly necessitates. Suffice it here to gesture at the contrasts of a politics of tolerance between (liberal) Jews and Arabs in Israel–Palestine with the possibilities of a politics of respect and solidarity between all inhabitants of the

---

26   Heyd, *Toleration*, p.15.

region in the post-bifurcated and occupied moment.[27] I am pointing to the normative presuppositions underlying the dominant strain of tolerance contrasted with the normative necessitation underlying the possibility of another arrangement of the inhabitants of two states living in respectful relation to each other.

The Anti-politics of Tolerance and a Politics of Respect

In light of this call for a contextualized 'thick' or 'robust' analysis sensitive to the complexities as well as the structurally and culturally located social positionings at work, I want to address the pressing liberal claim that we should tolerate physically non-violent expressions defaming a group or an individual in virtue of group membership. Formulated thus, the question of power is rendered obvious as it is at once made complex, for it raises the question concerning the subjects and objects of tolerance. Who does the tolerating, and who is being tolerated? What social positions enable the relation of tolerance to be enacted? It is not impertinent that Aretha Franklin's hit song should be titled 'R-E-S-P-E-C-T' rather than 'Let's Show Some Tolerance to Each Other'. The imperative to tolerate physically non-violent expressions suggests that it is the social majority, or those in positions of social power, or the state and its representatives (perhaps via legal encoding) that does the tolerating.

Consider the following sorts of claims:

1. 'Jews did not die in the gas chambers'
2. 'Mohammad or Christ were lewd, dishonest, dissembling power seekers'[28]
3. 'Arabs are less intelligent than Jews'
4. 'Hanan Ashrawi is a Palestinian bitch'
5. 'Yassir Arafat is a terrorist'
6. 'Marwan Barghouti is a Hamas leader'
7. 'Yassir Arafat is a murderer'
8. 'Ariel Sharon is a murderer'.

All these statements – and I have heard versions of them all expressed in different contexts in the more or less recent past – seem on the face of it to be making historical or factual claims of some sort. Depending on the context, the point of them all, the point of their assertion (in contrast to their mention), is inevitably to demean. They are designed in their use to demean either the individual as representative of a group – Jews or Muslims, Palestinians or Israelis

---

27 I have elsewhere written in this vein of relations between African Americans and Jewish Americans. See *Racial Subjects*.

28 I adapt these first two examples from Tariq Modood, 'Muslims, Incitement to Hatred and the Law' in Horton, *Liberalism*, p.144.

– or the group *qua* group (and so its members), and in absence at least of any nominal warrantable evidence and, in most of the cases, plenty of counter-evidence. (Perhaps statement 4 alone is a statement for which no amount of evidence conceivably could – or is intended to – apply.) It is as though implicit in the statements, at least on first blush, are prejudgments, a prejudice or bias, concerning the individuals' or groups' alleged power grabbing or inferiority or otherwise supposedly questionable activities. Statements 1, 2, 3 and 4 seem straightforwardly to demean Jews or Muslims, and those with certain sorts of political dispositions, as in the case especially of Hanan Ashrawi. The claim about Mohammad or Christ, like the claims about Barghouti, Arafat and Sharon, may or may not, perlocutionarily, be intended to demean. The context and tone of their expression will reveal whether their assertion is with a view to upset those for whom Mohammad, Arafat and Sharon are important religious or political figures or icons, or whether serious historical scholarship or mere descriptive ascription is at issue. Likewise, it is at least conceivable that there may be empirical issues at stake in the Holocaust denial or Arab intelligence claims. These questions will turn on whether historical claims are being made in the face of overwhelming and incontrovertible or even a preponderance of evidence, whether a 'merely' factual and non-judgmental claim is being made, or whether (as is most likely and presumptively) no more than something demeaning is being imputed in each instance. (The difficult cases will be those fudging the distinction.)

In the case of each of the eight expressions, however, tolerance is either too weak or too strong, and non-trivially. If the expression is demeaning or disrespectful, tolerance is more than those committed to an emancipatory politics can admit (that is 'tolerate'). Respect cannot be mandated. But extreme expressions of intended disrespect can be circumscribed. After all, they circumscribe the conditions of freedom for all thus referenced. Kenan Malik notwithstanding,[29] *The G Factor*, *The Bell Curve*, *The End of Racism* or even *The Clash of Civilizations* and the like are hardly making out new arguments. Nothing requires that their expression be given a forum. I am not suggesting they be censored so much as publicly censured; but surely repeatedly racist expressions, tired for their repetition or designed to infuriate, whether dressed up in academic finery or not, ought to carry no public sponsorship. Note that this line of response walks a careful path between calls for censorship, which I am not endorsing here, and an unqualified emphasis on free expression. It calls for a state considerably more interventionist in its commitments to promoting conditions for public civility and limitations on harmful expression than an absolutist First Amendment insistence makes possible.

By contrast, if the expression has a viable scholarly life with no overtones or

---

29   Kenan Malik, *The Meaning of Race* (New York: New York University Press, 1996).

undertones of disrespect, tolerance is too strong, even misdirected. Perhaps a serious historical case could be made concerning Mohammad's or Christ's dishonesty, and both Sharon's and Arafat's complicity in murder or even their engagement in terrorism, given a reasonably neutral interpretation of the category, if there is one. Indeed such a historical case conceivably could reveal something about human frailty and personal complexity, about political power and its corruption, or might question the respective integrity of each figure in question. Even more emphatically, purportedly empirical claims about historical events or supposedly measurable outcomes call for empirical dis/confirmation. But then it seems all too weak to suggest that such arguments be tolerated rather than seriously considered. To deserve such consideration the arguments need to be made with sensitivity and respect for the nuances of character, historical interpretation, political circumstances and pressures, and religious belief. As they stand, however, all the claims listed above seem to suggest not just disrespect and insensitivity for those who are the individual subjects (or more pointedly objects) of the expression but defamation of the group for whom they are important or appealing religious or social figures. What makes the claims about Sharon and Arafat more complex, nevertheless, is that both persons have been effective in their own ways of prompting or promoting terrible acts of destruction on each other's constituencies behind the cover of charging reckless rhetorical accusations on the part of the other.

Susan Mendus points out that in order to achieve better mutual understanding one needs to license and enable greater (but respectful and sensitive) free speech, not free speech simply as expression but as dialogical intercourse.[30] Free speech on the whole enables rather than restricts mutual understanding. The outcome of this production of sensitive mutual or co-understanding, as Rorty suggests, is the creation of solidarity, through 'increasing our sensitivity to the particular details of the pain and humiliation of other, unfamiliar sorts of people', indeed, of our implication often in their (re-)production.[31] Quite so, but only on the qualification that there is speech that is openly insensitive, obviously dismissive, intended as incivility and the promotion of anti-community (consider the proliferation of insensitivities in and through the anonymous distancing of cyberspace expression). There is speech designed, that is, to undermine solidarity through disrespect, especially in the packed and pressed spaces of urban societies. Nothing in the event of such expression necessitates tolerance, let alone the freedom so to express, though resisting such expression may, indeed must, assume a form sensitive to its circumstance.

There are costs and benefits of the sort of mutual engagement for which I am calling. The costs concern the effort necessary, the emotion spent, the time it

---

30   Susan Mendus, 'Tigers of Wrath', p.205.
31   Richard Rorty, *Contingency, Irony and Solidarity* (Cambridge: Cambridge University Press 1989), p.xiv.

takes to work at the understanding and relation. The benefits have to do with both the exhilaration that follows the effort and the possibility through engagement and understanding to criticize the shortcomings and ineptitudes, the failings and failures of those one has worked to engage, and still be taken seriously for it.

Bhikhu Parekh interrogates this conceptual and social space with considerable subtlety in commenting that 'Space is not often given – it has to be taken. You have to create it, and when a group of people appears to be intolerant, to be demanding that the established norms be opened up a little, it is also to demand to create a space in which a dialogue is possible.'[32] It is to demand that public recognition, fair share of social resources and political representation in a shared public sphere I mentioned earlier. Where space is given rather than taken or established through struggles and confrontations of various sorts it is almost invariably on the terms of those doing the giving. In the case of the tolerant or tolerating, as I have said, it will likely be on the terms of the powerful.

It might be said that tolerance is a moral virtue rather than a political one. Morality in this sense concerns individual decision making and action, practical reason as regards self- and other-regarding action at the individual level, while politics is about collective action. This distinction need not fall back into a normative-denying, positivist sense of the political, a 'realist' conception (as though that is not itself normative, as any conception of the political necessarily is), for what I am suggesting by this is that collective action, politics, invokes, implies or calls upon normative considerations that are often at odds or in tension with the individual(ist) normative considerations that kick in at the level of the moral (whether on deontological, utilitarian, virtue-based or care based conceptions of the moral). Often (though not always) different discursive conceptions order the respective principles that constitute the moral/individualist and political/collectivist domains. The failure of tolerance as an intervention with respect to racist expression, its weakness, in part is that it is an individualist consideration in the face of collectivist expression. Indeed this example reveals that matters are even more fraught than the baldness of the distinction(s) I have drawn suggests. The fact that tolerance is always expressed from a position of relative power implies that tolerance is not merely an individualist moral response to collectivist political expression but its force precisely rests on the implicit and so hidden assumption of political power. Thus having drawn the distinction between the moral and the political there is a sense in which, in the shadow of the complexity of discursive (over-)determination, I am collapsing it in favour of the political. The distinction then is little more than a heuristic to draw attention to the manner in which the domains are differentially discursively ordered. Considerations of power, in short, are always political.

It remains open, at the level of the individual, to offer a counter to the sort of

---

32   Bhikhu Parekh, 'Identities on Parade', *Marxism Today*, June 1989, p.29.

individualist tolerance in relation to others. So others, morally, ought to be considered with sensitivity and respect. And they ought to be so treated with an eye and ear to their similarities and differences, with a view to clearing spaces where people can speak and decide for themselves and be taken seriously in doing so, where people have standing in order to make self-determining claims. But this 'clearing of a space', where relevant and possible without being paternalistic, exactly erodes the space between the moral and the political, between the normativity of doing what is right and the possibilities of power.

I close with two related qualifications of my analysis, and one rejoinder. First, I will not object to folding a politics of recognition, respect, sensitivity and solidarity under a second, progressive, indeed, politicized notion of tolerance, one critical of the first liberal notion in the ways I have suggested, in order to preserve for tolerance a space of (self-)critical engagement. In this sense, I might have followed a venerable philosophical tradition by entitling the paper 'Two Concepts of Tolerance'. Second, and more basically, I have focused my remarks almost exclusively on tolerance, saying little about intolerance. Were I to pursue the analysis by attending primarily to intolerance I should argue similarly that the concept is too broad and analytically weak for the task. As I have argued elsewhere with respect to the concept of 'hate',[33] intolerance takes in too much, eliding the differences between importantly distinguishable wrongs, to which we are simply exhorted 'just [to] say no'. Strategies of response and resistance thus are reduced banally to a superficial singularity, the perpetrators of particular and specific wrongs disappearing in the sea of generality, if not into the welcoming arms of co-conspirators, sympathizers or complicit countries.

Finally one might object that tolerance is not a virtue of first recourse but a back-up, a fail safe of last resort. It kicks in where respect, solidarity, sensitivity and taking others seriously have failed. If there is no recourse to tolerance, all we have left is throwing stones or necklacing, or tanks and bombs, more refugees and mass graves. But in order to have tolerance do the work one has to inculcate it from the start,[34] and the antagonistic critique I have mounted seems to have diminished if not obliterated that possibility. In response it must be said that, far from undermining my critique this point displaces the difficulties faced by tolerance to a different space. If we admit the liberal endgame need for tolerance this admission entails that tolerance must be taught, cultivated, mobilized and encouraged from the outset alongside respect, solidarity, sensitivity and seriousness. But given the relative ease of tolerance and the difficulty of respect and its supplements (in definition, inculcation and practice), it is likely that tolerance will crowd out, by substituting for, the rest. So even if tolerance is necessary as a last instrumental resort, it makes the moral practices of respect and its supplements impossible. So tolerance fails by default.

---

33   David Theo Goldberg, 'Hate, or Power?'
34   This is the gist of Vogt's argument. Vogt, *Tolerance and Education*.

That is the liberal dilemma. It is a dilemma resolved only by rendering primary a political pedagogy of respect, solidarity, sensitivity and taking each other seriously. A full elaboration of the latter would require embedding it in an analytics of democracy and a revised imaginary of national belonging and citizenship. Such an analytics would entail a picture of an incorporative rather than exclusionary social formation, one cognizant of shared resources and common representation, respectful of civility in public and private spheres alike (if that distinction is indeed sustainable) and open to formative virtues of recognising renewable and multiplicitous differences rather than insisting on restrictive and nationalist denials. This is a project the full elaboration of which I must leave to another occasion.

Chapter 4

Reading Intolerant Texts in a Tolerant Society

Norman Solomon

The faithful preach virtue, and appeal to Scripture, mediated by Church or Synagogue, as their authority, the revealed word of God. The appeal is powerful, for the Bible and the traditions rooted in it have provided the language and inspiration for many of the greatest moral achievements of humanity. Yet it is marred, for not infrequently Scripture and other sacred texts appear to make some demand or express some value which we resist, not because it is difficult, but because it is morally repugnant.

One fine summer Sabbath morning I listened to a colleague preaching to his congregation on the theme of tolerance. His sermon was a moving account of how Judaism, in contrast to other religions (by which no doubt he had in mind Christianity and Islam) was a model of tolerance. When had Jews, unlike Christians and Muslims, persecuted people of another faith? When had we aggressively promoted our religion and sought to convert others, as they had constantly done to us? Surely, our holy Torah taught us that the 'righteous of all nations' (meaning of all faiths) had a portion in the World to Come; unlike exclusivist Christianity, it did not deny 'salvation' to those of another faith.

The preacher's words accorded well with a major trend in Jewish apologetic, which can be traced back through such as Leo Baeck, Moses Mendelssohn, Menasseh Ben Israel and Simone Luzzatto,[1] and is not without roots in much earlier Jewish sources. In the days before the Hebron massacre of February 1994,[2] and the Rabin assassination on 4 November 1995, it was perhaps plausible to cite medieval and modern Jewish history as evidence of the pacific nature of

---

A later version of this paper appeared in Hebrew under the title 'B'nei Torah, B'nei Tarbut' in the journal *Tarbut Demokratit*, vol.2 (1999) Bar Ilan University, Israel, pp.113–36.

1   Benjamin Ravid, 'Mystics, Philosophers, and Politicians', in J. Reinharz and D. Swetschinski (eds), *Essays in Jewish Intellectual History in Honor of Alexander Altmann* (Durham NC: Duke University Press, 1982), pp.159–80, drew attention to Menasseh's dependence on Simone Luzzatto.

2   On 19 February, Goldstein, previously known as a gentle and caring doctor, heard *parashat zakhor* read in the Synagogue, including the words, 'blot out all memory of Amalek' (Deut. 25:19). He took this literally and identified the Palestinians with the Amalekites of old. The following Thursday night, Purim, Esther was read, with its narrative of how the Jews executed vengeance on their enemies. On Friday morning Goldstein shot dead several Arabs at prayer in a Mosque in Hebron.

Judaism. Jews did not act violently in the name of their religion, as Christians and Muslims from time to time did; mostly they were passive, even in the face of extreme provocation. True, they had no power, but it seemed safe to suppose that they would not use violence even if they were in the position to do so.

Already in the twelfth century Judah Halevi (c.1080–1140) expressed doubts about this supposition. In Halevi's great philosophical dialogue, the *Kuzari*, the *haver* (rabbi) boasts that the meekness preached but not practised by Christians and Muslims is actually practised by Jews. To this, the as yet non-Jewish Khazar king responds: 'That would be so, if your humility (*tawadu'*) were voluntary, but it is involuntary, and if you had the power, you would kill.'[3] But even if the shaky supposition *were* true, what could one say about the texts? Taking them at their face value, do the main biblical and pre-modern rabbinic texts support the doctrines of tolerance espoused by Menasseh, Mendelssohn and their followers?

The portion of the Torah read on the day I heard the sermon was Deuteronomy 11:26–16:17. It includes the following words:

> And ye shall break down their altars, and dash in pieces their pillars, and burn their Asherim with fire; and ye shall hew down the graven images of their gods; and ye shall destroy their name out of that place. (Deut. 12:3)

So I took my copy of the Torah to the rabbi and asked him how he would harmonise this verse with his contention that Judaism was a tolerant religion.

It says something for the enduring quality of our friendship that we still speak to one another. But I did not receive a satisfactory reply. The present essay addresses the problem of whether and how someone committed to a tolerant, pluralistic view of society can continue to regard as sacred a tradition which contains intolerant, exclusivist texts.

Nature of the Problem

First, two definitions. By 'enlightenment' I mean the whole complex of philosophical and political ideas which took root in Europe in the sixteenth century and of which the most enduring expressions are the scientific revolution from Copernicus onwards, the critical philosophy of Descartes, Spinoza and their successors, and the political ideals of liberty and equality which are enshrined in the American Constitution and in the Universal Declaration of Human Rights adopted by the United Nations in 1948. I do not exclude some recent developments which are referred to as 'post-enlightenment' or 'post-modern',

---

3 Judah Halevi, *The Kuzari*, 2nd ed, trans. Hartwig Hirschfeld, with an Introduction by Harry Slonimsky (New York: Schocken Books, 1964), Book 1, section 114.

since I regard these as critical re-evaluations within the enlightenment tradition; I regret that some authors seem unable to distinguish been 'post-enlightenment' and 'pre-enlightenment' philosophies.

By 'texts' I mean here not just words, but customs, stories, symbols, laws, signs, events, exemplary lives of the saints – all those elements around which a community defines itself, and which make up its distinctive 'language'. Why is there any problem about texts? Why not simply repudiate any traditional texts which we no longer find acceptable? Three factors have to be considered.

1. *Continuity*. Communities, ethnic or religious, seek to preserve their identity. Cultural identity depends on common texts. It is therefore necessary to develop methods of reading which enable the community to continue reading the traditional texts despite the fact that over time people's understanding of the world around them, as well as their grasp of fundamental values, may have changed.
2. *Commitment to equal human rights*. People in the advanced world are committed, by and large, to policies of tolerance, democracy and civil equality which have only been formulated clearly and implemented since the Enlightenment. For example, only in the nineteenth century did slavery become widely regarded as unacceptable and abhorrent; only in the twentieth was the concept of equal rights effectively extended to women, and the process is still far from complete.
3. *The nature of the texts*. Many traditional texts, read in their plain sense, are intolerant, undemocratic, and discriminatory.

The problem arises, then, of whether it is possible to reread biblical and rabbinic texts in terms of the enlightenment political values of democracy and human equality. As the theologian might put it: Can an enlightenment hermeneutic be applied to the Written and Oral Torah? This is not a new problem, nor is it a characteristically Jewish one. Indeed, it is a necessary feature of any society which persists over time, and it affects all cultures and all religions, since their identity arises out of 'texts', as just defined. No text can ever be read exactly the same way twice, for the text is part of a living language, which cannot remain static. Every text constitutive of a society is read in the light of the other texts, and also in the light of the new texts which come into being as the society engages with changing cultures.

Of course, it is possible to *abandon* texts whose content, when they are read in the traditional way, is no longer acceptable. The question then arises, how much can one abandon without loss of identity, or authenticity? If continuity is to be preserved some texts will be retained; how will these be read within the changed inter-textuality brought about by the abandonment of texts with which they were previously associated?

For Judaism, the process of rereading texts in the light of other texts began in

the Bible itself, and is the method by which Talmud, Midrash,[4] religious
philosophy and Kabbala lay claim to authenticity as expositions of Torah.

The Role of Apologetics

Even where Jews do not really share the values of the ambient society they may
find it prudent to interpret their teaching in terms of ambient culture. This may
serve the purpose of defence against possible accusations, or it may be thought
to help in the retention, or reclamation, of acculturated, lapsed Jews within the
faith. Rarely if at all since the fourth century has it served the purpose of mission
amongst non-Jews.

Apologetics has a valid role. However, I am not concerned with it here. What
I want to discover is whether there is some way in which a Jew, or *paribus
passibus* a Christian or Muslim, can in full integrity lay claim to a heritage which
in parts he or she finds morally repugnant.

Tolerance and Tradition

There is a practical aspect to the question, and also a theoretical one. On the
largest scale, the practical aspect is a sociopolitical problem, which for Jews
arises only with regard to the state of Israel. How does the sovereign (the justice
system) handle people of different religions? Is there an established, 'privileged'
religion? If so, are non-conformists (a) merely allowed to live, (b) subjected to
some measure of discrimination, or (c) accorded full and equal civil rights. What
is the nature of the 'secular' state?

On a more limited scale, questions arise at the community or congregational
level. Who is to be included or excluded from (a) membership of the community,
(b) participation in its activities?

Even if the practical issues could be handled in conformity with
enlightenment concepts of human equality, a theoretical problem would remain
to trouble the conscientious believer. This is the theological question of how to
find 'theological space for the other'. The exclusive claim to truth which has
been a normal part of traditional theology does not, in Judaism, necessarily deny
'salvation' to those of other faiths, but it certainly downgrades them and their

---

4   Studies which apply contemporary literary theory to the discussion of
rabbinic reading of Scripture include Daniel Boyarin, *Intertextuality and the Reading of
Midrash* (Bloomington and Indianapolis: Indiana University Press, 1990); Jay Harris,
How Do We Know This? (New York: SUNY Press, 1994); Irving Jacobs, *The Midrashic
Process: tradition and interpretation in rabbinic Judaism* (Cambridge: Cambridge
University Press, 1995); Marc Saperstein, *Decoding the Rabbis: A Thirteenth Century
Commentary on the Aggadah* (Cambridge, MA and London: Harvard University Press,
1980).

beliefs in a condescending fashion which is inconsistent with the more open attitude to truth which finds approval in enlightened society.

Intolerance in the Source Texts

The Bible and rabbinic literature contain resources for tolerance as well as for intolerance. Part of the 'solution' to the problem of handling intolerant texts lies in giving primacy to the tolerant ones. But we must face up to the intolerant ones too. Here are examples of several categories of statement which promote values that 'enlightened' people find unacceptable.

The Torah repeatedly inculcates the virtue of *Qana'ut* (zeal) against idolatry, as in Deut. 12:3, cited above. The positive side of this is the devotion to God, and consequently to justice and compassion, it demands. Compassion, however, is explicitly denied to idolators; of one who leads his fellow-Israelites to idolatry it is said, 'You shall have no pity on him' (Deut. 13:9). It seems that even simple understanding is denied them;[5] their gods are 'but the work of men's hands, mere wood and stone' (2 Kings 19:18 and elsewhere), and there is no hint that anything of value lies behind this form of worship. Whatever my views about the historical circumstances in which Scripture first appeared, it runs counter to my moral convictions that I should be guided by such verses in my relationship with contemporary Hindus or Buddhists, let alone Christians or Muslims.

It is only very recently, on an historical time-scale, that people have begun to think of 'racism' as reprehensible. What we now reject as racist attitudes are normal in Scripture. Genesis 9:25 declares that the 'sons of Ham' (black people) are to be slaves to the 'sons of Shem', and this was frequently cited as a proof-text against the abolition of slavery or in support of the Apartheid system. Canaanites were to be exterminated, and the very name of Amalek blotted out (Deut. 25:19).

Also contrary to enlightenment notions of equality is the privileged status afforded to Cohanim (priests), Levites, Israelites and men. Biblical legislation offers *protection* to foreigners and women, rather than equal status.

The Bible divides people into Israelites (those faithful to God) and 'the nations' (idolators), and takes an overwhelmingly negative view of the latter. The rabbis took a somewhat less malign view of the pagans amongst whom they lived. They were not necessarily idolators in the full biblical sense, but *maase avotehem biydehem*, 'they uphold the deeds of their fathers',[6] that is, they

---

5   Yehezkel Kaufmann, *A History of the Israelite Religion*, 4 vols (Hebrew) (Jerusalem and Tel Aviv: Mosad Bialik 1954–7). The work was translated into English and abridged by M. Greenberg under the title *The Religion of Israel* (Chicago: University of Chicago Press, 1960). Kaufmann demonstrates that the Bible, while polemicising against idolatry, shows no insight into the actual nature of the religions it opposes.

6   Babylonian Talmud (BT) *Hullin*, 13b.

practise through inertia rather than by conviction patterns of idolatrous worship inherited from an earlier, believing generation.

Did God's act in 'electing', that is, choosing Israel from amongst the nations, imply *innate* superiority on their part? According to Deuteronomy, it did not: 'It was not because you were more numerous than any other nation that the Lord cared for you and chose you, for you were the smallest of all nations; it was because the Lord loved you and stood by his oath to your forefathers' (Deut. 7:7,8).

Judah Halevi, building on what the Muslim philosopher al-Kassim claims as the virtue of Shi'ites, states that Jews are the 'choice' of humankind and possess an '*amr al-Allahi*, a 'divine thing', which sets them apart.[7] The Tosafists, in the thirteenth century, suggested that the souls of Jews and non-Jews are kept in separate stores before birth.[8] Kabbalists eventually developed a doctrine of the innate superiority of the Jewish soul. This doctrine occurs in extreme form in the *Tanya* of Shneur Zalman of Liady, the 'bible' of the Lubavitch movement; Shneur Zalman asserts that only Jews have the divine soul which distinguishes human from animal. Whilst this is not standard Jewish doctrine, and is completely contrary to the views of Maimonides and other rationalist philosophers on the soul, its baleful influence on contemporary Orthodoxy cannot be ignored.

The Talmud and Codes incorporate much discriminatory legislation against (a) gentiles, (b) women, (c) 'sinners', defined in terms of *halakha*. Practising male homosexuals would be placed in category (c).

Halakha (Jewish law) as developed in the Talmud assumes a pagan world in which people may be divided exclusively into Israelites, including a subcategory of Jewish heretics, and idolators. For centuries no distinction was made in halakha between idolators on the one hand, and Zoroastrians, Christians and Muslims on the other. Halakha treated all as idolators. In the absence of any other clearly defined category, laws which had once been applied to idolators were presumed to apply to people of any other religion. In Christian countries the wine laws and business partnership laws were relaxed, perhaps for economic reasons, but with the rationale that Christians were not fully idolaters.

Jews in the Middle Ages lived in autonomous communities, and were regarded as a 'people apart'. They adhered to the old rabbinic laws which had been designed specifically to separate Jews from pagans. Jacob Katz documented what he regarded as the relaxation of those laws, particularly in Christian

---

    7   Judah Halevi, *Kuzari* 1:27 and 1:95; the latter passage is a 'Judaization' of al-Kassim. See Shlomo Pines' article, 'Shiite Terms and Conceptions in Judah Halevi', in *Jerusalem Studies in Arabic and Islam II* (Jerusalem: Magnes Press, 1980). The translation of '*amr* in this context is contentious; it may mean something like 'command' or 'classification'. George Lindbeck, at a conference at the Hartman Institute in Jerusalem in 1991, suggested an analogy with a doctrine of 'grace'.
    8   Tosafot on BT, *Avoda Zara*, 5a *s.v. ein ben David ba*.

countries, in the Middle Ages.[9] Indeed, the medieval halakhists were often less stringent in applying the laws of idolatry, wine and interest than the rabbis of the Talmud had been. However Katz's contention that this was a consequence of a more tolerant attitude towards the Christian faith is incorrect; rather, the new theological assessment of Christian teaching was invoked in justification of established customary practice in Western lands.

The old habits die hard, and even those whose theology and personal dealings with Christians betoken a more enlightened attitude persist in treating them halakhically as idolaters. David Hoffman (1843–1921), for instance, who was director of the Berlin Rabbinical Seminary and published articles defending the Talmud and *Shulhan Arukh* against antisemitic detractors, in his responsum on the use of the organ in the Synagogue categorised non-Jews in general as idolaters.[10] Even today many authorities forbid people to enter churches on the grounds that they are places of idolatrous worship.

Strategies

I shall now review some of the strategies employed by rabbis in different ages and localities to reread texts in the light of changing attitudes to other people. The approach will be synchronic rather than diachronic.

Denial of Enlightenment Values

The simplest strategy is to deny the values of pluralism and toleration, and opt for the 'plain sense' of authoritarian, exclusive tradition. Few Jewish thinkers have done this, though several have joined in the current dangerous religious fashion of undermining enlightenment, liberalism and individualism.

Such a position is rarely held consistently, since the people who adopt it belong to minorities which in practice appeal to democratic institutions to protect their own freedom. There is, however, always the ultimate danger that a group of this kind will attain power, as happened in Iran with disastrous consequences for individual freedom.

The strategy should be opposed because (a) it is morally wrong, (b) it constitutes a potential danger to society if adopted by groups who hold the reins of power, and (c) it ignores those elements within the religious tradition which favour the values of democratic government, human equality and individual liberty.

---

9   Jacob Katz, *Exclusiveness and Tolerance* (London: Oxford University Press, 1961).

10   David Hoffman, *Reponsa Melamed l-Ho'il* (Frankfurt-am-Main: Hermon Press), 5686 (1925/6), 5. On page 15 he insists that *avoda zara* ('idolatry') be translated as *Fremder Kultus* rather than *Götzendienst*, thereby including Christianity.

The Prohibition of Idolatry Limited to Israel

This strategy permits 'tolerance' of other religions on the grounds that only Jews, as recipients of God's revelation, are forbidden to worship idols. Its hermeneutic method is to read the Bible's denunciations of idolatry as addressed primarily to Israel; even if Israelites are told to destroy other people's idols it is not because the other people are forbidden to worship them, but because, if they were left around, Israelites might be seduced into their worship.

In this vein Chief Rabbi Hertz, in the mid-1930s, commented sententiously on Deuteronomy 4:19, 'when thou seest the sun and the moon and and the stars, even all the host of heaven … which the Lord thy God hath allotted unto all the peoples under the whole heaven':

> God had *suffered* the heathens to worship the sun, moon, and stars as a
> stepping-stone to a higher stage of religious belief. That worship of the
> heathen nations thus forms part of God's guidance of humanity. But as
> for the Israelites, God had given them first-hand knowledge of Him
> through the medium of Revelation. It is for this reason that idolatry was
> *for them* an unpardonable offence; and everything that might seduce
> them from that Divine Revelation was to be ruthlessly destroyed. Hence
> the amazing tolerance shown by Judaism of all ages towards the
> followers of other cults, *so long as these were not steeped in immorality
> and crime*.[11]

Yehezkel Kaufmann, in his monumental study, likewise contends that according to the Bible only Israel was forbidden to worship idols.[12] Already in the first century both Philo[13] and Josephus[14] argued on a similar basis for tolerance of 'pagan' religions, even though the alleged destruction of temples in Cyrene during the 'Revolt of the Diaspora' under Trajan in 116/7 suggests that some Jews took an opposite view. The rabbis distinguished in this respect between the land of Israel, where no idolatry was to be tolerated, and the lands outside, where gentiles should not be disturbed in their worship.[15] But even if Kaufmann, Philo, Josephus and Hertz were right, this would merely show that God was prepared to 'suffer' idolators for a bit longer, not that his ultimate design was that some people should continue to worship idols.

---

11   J.H. Hertz, *The Pentateuch*, 2nd edn (London: Soncino Press, 1965), pp.759–60 (first published 1936).

12   Kaufmann, *Israelite Religion*.

13   Philo of Alexandria, *De Specialibus Legibus* 1:53 (Vol. VII, p.128 in the Loeb edition). Both he and Josephus have in mind Exodus 22:27(28) and Leviticus 24:15.

14   *Antiquities*, Book IV, 8:10 (4:207). Josephus says that Moses instructed the people: 'Let no one blaspheme those gods which other cities esteem such; nor may one steal what belongs to strange temples; nor take away the gifts that are dedicated to any god' (Whiston's translation). The apologetic intent is clear. See also *Against Apion* 2:144.

15   See for instance BT *Hullin*, 13b and *Jerusalem Talmud* (JT) *Berakhot*, 9:2. Of course, this does not imply that the rabbis did not expect that eventually idolatry would be uprooted from the whole world.

The emphasis on the form rather than the content of 'idolatry' poses a problem today for the Jew, Christian or Muslim who seeks an understanding relationship with Buddhists or Hindus. Is it honest to represent such religions as 'worship of sticks and stones', especially where such a characterisation is categorically rejected by Hindus and Buddhists themselves? We may not feel comfortable with worship directed to or through images, but nor can we any longer feel comfortable with the biblical equation 'idolatry = immorality'. We should also reflect that, from a Buddhist perspective, our own notion of a personal God is a gross form of 'idolatry'.

The boundary before idolatry is always justified by Scripture itself in terms of either (a) a further ethical or moral boundary or (b) a rejection of the literal belief that the image worshipped has power to 'save'. Neither of these arguments supports a condemnation of Hindu or Buddhist religion. Many Hindus and Buddhists are people of high ethical and moral standards, and the simplistic type of belief in idols portrayed in Scripture does not correspond to the reality of Hindu and Buddhist teaching.

The strategy has additional weaknesses. At best, it produces a condescending attitude to people of other religions, as if to say, 'their religions are no good but they cannot be expected to know better, so we shall be kind to them and leave them alone'. It also flatly contradicts the 'Noahide laws', of which more will be said later. Even the most lenient interpretation of these laws does not permit non-Jews to worship idols, though it does permit *shittuf*, that is, to swear by the name of God plus 'something else', as was thought to be the Christian case.[16]

Moreover, although the strategy permits toleration of other religions, it denies that toleration to born Jews who depart from the traditional line.

Radical Reinterpretation

'No Ammonite or Moabite, even down to the tenth generation, shall enter the congregation of the Lord' (Deut. 23:3). Yet, according to the book of Ruth, King David himself was a descendant of Ruth the Moabitess. This apparent inconsistency is discussed in the Talmud as follows:

> Doeg the Edomite said to them, Whilst you are enquiring whether he is worthy to be a king, ask whether or not he is permitted to be a member of the congregation. Why? Because he is descended from Ruth the Moabitess. Abner said to him, We have learned 'Moabite', not 'Moabitess' ... He enquired [in the House of Study]. They said to him, 'Moabite', not 'Moabitess'. Doeg asked all these questions, and they were silent [could not answer]. He wanted to proclaim [that David was disqualified from membership of the congregation]. At once, Amasa arose ... Rava says, he (Amasa) girded his sword like an Arab and said, Whoever does not listen to this halakha (law) will be pierced by the

---

16   See for instance Tosafot on BT, *Bekhorot* 2b *s.v. shema.*

sword. This is the tradition I have received from the court of Samuel of
Rama, 'Ammonite', not 'Ammonitess', 'Moabite', not 'Moabitess'.[17]

What is happening here? This is a radical exercise in intertextuality; one biblical
text is read in the light of another. Since it is inconceivable to the talmudic rabbi
that King David's pedigree should be halakhically unsound, he reads
'Ammonite' and 'Moabite' as gender determined. Rava, well aware that such
grammatical forms are normally inclusive, graphically represents Amasa as
establishing the gender-determined interpretation by force.

This strategy of radical rereading of texts is mandated by the three
assumptions that underlie traditional exegesis, namely that Scripture is
comprehensive, consistent and free from superfluity. It is a difficult strategy to
apply if, as most moderns, one abandons those assumptions. Only if one adopts
an extreme post-modern attitude permitting texts to be read virtually however
one chooses would it be possible to read 'Moabite', not 'Moabitess'. There is
some irony in the convergence of highly contrived rabbinic exegesis with
extreme relativist post-modern freedom of text reading.

Limitation of Sphere of Operation

Judaism in the second century was still a proselytising religion, if not proactive
at least opportunist.[18] In the light of scriptural verses such as 'No Ammonite or
Moabite … shall enter the congregation of the Lord', how could converts from
those nations be accepted? Even on the reading of 'Ammonite', not
'Ammonitess', how could male converts be accepted?

By the time of the Mishna '(do not) enter the congregation of the Lord' was
no longer understood to preclude conversion, but interpreted as a ban on
marriage with a native-born Jewess; proselytes from any nation were to be
welcomed. Matters came to a head in a debate at Yavné, seat of the Jewish court
after the fall of Jerusalem:

> On that day Judah the Ammonite proselyte came and stood before them
> in the House of Study. He said to them, Am I allowed to enter the
> congregation [that is, to marry a Jewess]? Rabbi Joshua said, You are
> permitted. Rabban Gamaliel said to [Joshua], But scripture says, 'No
> Ammonite or Moabite … shall enter the congregation of the Lord; even
> the tenth generation …' Rabbi Joshua replied to him, Are Ammonites
> and Moabites still in their place? Sennacherib, king of Assyria, came up
> and mixed all the nations … They permitted [Judah] to enter the
> congregation.[19]

---

17   BT *Yevamot* 76b–77a.
18   Martin Goodman, *Mission and Conversion: Proselytizing in the Religious
History of the Roman Empire* (Oxford: Clarendon Press, 1994).
19   Mishna, *Yadayim* 4:4. Compare Tosefta, *Yadayim* 2:8.

In the interest of openness to converts, Joshua argued that the circumstances of a biblical law no longer obtained. People are no longer to be identified with biblical nations.

The consequences of this ruling are far-reaching. It runs counter to the midrashic tendency to typology, for instance to identifying Edom with Rome, and to the racism which might be derived from the typology. Certainly it leaves no room for anyone to identify Palestinians with Amalekites.

Yet although Joshua's liberal hermeneutic has removed the practical consequences of an intolerant Biblical law, it has left untouched the theoretical principle that, if Judah really was an Ammonite, his racial inheritance would preclude him from absorption into Jewish life. A satisfactory halakha has been produced, which does not in practice discriminate against individuals on racial grounds, but not a satisfactory theology.

The same strategy has been used in recent times in Israel to justify the non-application of rules about 'idolators' to minorities living within Israel, and to ameliorate the harsh rules of warfare which might arise from the 'straight' application of biblical standards. Indeed, far from encouraging or even condoning biblical levels of violence against the 'enemy', modern rabbinic law has developed the concept of *tohar ha-nesheq*, or 'purity of arms', in accordance with which harm inflicted upon the opposing forces must be minimized, even at some risk to the defending Israelis.[20]

Historical Development: Praeparatio Evangelica

This is hinted at by Sa'adia (882–942)[21] and more fully developed by Judah Halevi (c. 1075–1141) and Moses Maimonides (1135–1204). Islam and Christianity are in error, but can be accommodated as part of the divine design to bring the nations gradually to God. The other monotheistic religions, says Halevi, 'serve to introduce and pave the way for the expected Messiah, who is the fruition, and they will all become his fruit'.[22]

In a paragraph censored from the printed editions of his *Mishné Torah*,

---

20   For English language reviews of contemporary *halakha* on the conduct of warfare, see the volumes of J. David Bleich's *Contemporary Halakhic Problems* (New York: Ktav, Yeshivah University Press). See also 'Combat Morality and the Halacha', by ex-Chief Rabbi Shlomo Goren, in *Crossroads: Halacha and the Modern World* (Jerusalem: ZOMET, 1987/5747), pp.211–32.

21   Sa'adia ben Joseph, *Kitab fi al-Amanat wa-al-Itaqadat* (Arabic) Book II, Chapter 5. Rosenblatt's translation has been republished as Samuel Rosenblatt (trans.), *The Book of Beliefs and Opinions* (New Haven and London: Yale University Press, 1989). Sa'adia is of course highly critical of Christological doctrine, but this does not blind him to the positive aspects of Christianity.

22   Judah Halevi, *The Kuzari*, 2nd edn, tr. Hartwig Hirschfeld, (New York: Schocken Books, 1964).

Maimonides rejects the truth-claims of Christianity and Islam on the basis that they fail to meet the criterion of consistency with the Torah of Moses. Despite this, he assigns both Christianity and Islam a role in the process of world redemption: 'The teachings of him of Nazareth (Jesus) and of the man of Ishmael (Mohammed) who arose after him help to bring all mankind to perfection, so that they may serve God with one consent. For insofar as the whole world is full of talk of the Messiah, of words of Holy Writ and of the Commandments – these words have spread to the ends of the earth, even if many deny their binding character at the present time. When the Messiah comes all will return from their errors.'[23]

Several medieval Jewish thinkers, unlike the rabbis of the Talmud, were familiar with Christian and Muslim texts, and offered comment, whether by way of defence or of instruction. Sometimes this is found in the context of the forced 'disputations' which elicited from Jews much keen apologetic.[24]

The Provençal rabbi Menahem ha-Meiri (d. c.1315) coined the phrase *umot hagedurot bedarkei hadatot* ('nations bound by the ways of religion') to avoid identification of Christians in his own time with pagan idolators, and used this category to justify what was probably already a customary relaxation of certain rabbinic laws.[25] This enabled a positive evaluation, if not of the doctrines, at least of the way of life, of Christians.

The acknowledgment that some truth may be found in other religions is as far as most were prepared to go in the 'age of faith', when religions rested on their absolute truth claims. It is interesting that the concept is common to Judaism, Christianity and Islam. It seems to have arisen first in Christianity, in the attempt to explain its relationship with Judaism. Since Christianity sought to 'prove' itself by claiming to 'fulfil' the Hebrew Scriptures it developed a hermeneutic of those Scriptures as *praeparatio evangelica*, 'preparation for the good news'. That is, the Israelites and the Jews who succeeded them were 'on the way', but had not completed the journey. Mohammed, the 'seal of the prophets', accomplished the same sort of 'completion' for Islam, leaving Judaism and Christianity as steps on the way to full Islam. It is hardly surprising to find that medieval Jewish thinkers adopted the same condescending attitude towards Christianity and Islam.

---

23   Maimonides, *Mishné Torah Melakhim* 11.

24   See H. Maccoby (ed. and trans.), *Judaism On Trial: Jewish–Christian Disputations In The Middle Ages* (London: Associated University Presses, 1982, republished Oxford: Littman Library, 1992); Samuel Krauss, *A Handbook to the History of Christian–Jewish Controversy from the Earliest Times to 1789*, ed. William Horbury, (Tübingen: Mohr, 1996); Daniel Lasker, *Jewish Philosophical Polemics against Christianity in the Middle Ages* (New York: Ktav/Anti-Defamation League of B'nai B'rith, 1977).

25   Meiri's views are expressed in his talmudic commentaries, especially that on *Avoda Zara*. For an English language account and discussion, see Katz, *Exclusiveness and Tolerance*, ch. 10.

Authentic, but Culture-bound, Prophecy

Was it not possible to move beyond 'condescension' to an acknowledgment that authenticity might be found in the 'other'? This further step appears to have been taken by the Yemenite Jewish philosopher Netanel ibn Fayyumi (d. c.1164), who adopted into a Jewish context ideas current amongst the Sufi brethren, the *Ikhwan es-Safa*. Netanel asserts the authenticity of the prophecy of Mohammed, as revealed in the Qur'an, and at least the possibility that there are additional authentic revelations (he does not mention Christianity).

Here are the steps by which Netanel establishes his contention that the prophecy of Mohammed is authentic:

> The first creation of God was the Universal Intellect ... its exuberant
> joy and happiness caused an overflow, and thus there emanated from it
> the Universal Soul. (pp.2, 94)[26]
> Through the necessity of His wisdom ... He mercifully vouchsafed
> unto mortals a revelation from the holy world – the world of the
> Universal Soul – which originated from the overflow of its holy cause,
> the Universal Intellect – which in turn goes back to its originator – may
> He be exalted! This ... expressed itself in an individual man whose
> spirit is free from the impurity of nature and is disciplined in the
> noblest science and the purest works ... [a] prophet. (p.95)
> Know then ... nothing prevents God from sending into His world
> whomsoever He wishes, since the world of holiness sends forth
> emanations unceasingly ... Even before the revelation of the Law he
> sent prophets to the nations ... and again after its revelation nothing
> prevented Him from sending to them whom He wishes so that the
> world might not remain without religion. (pp.103–4)
> .... Mohammed was a prophet to them but not to those who preceded
> (sc. were prior to) them in the knowledge of God.[27] (p.105)
> ... He permitted to every people something He forbade to others.
> (p.107)
> He sends a prophet to every people according to their language.[28]
> (p.109)

Netanel interprets revelation in a 'naturalistic' fashion. It is a universal phenomenon, of which Mohammed is a specific instance. He parallels his philosophical arguments with a skilful use of Jewish midrashic material.

Netanel's position differs radically from the *praeparatio* stance of Maimonides and others. Maimonides, for all his acknowledgment of the purity of Islamic monotheism and the historic function of Islam in preparing for the

---

26   References are to the translation by D. Levine, *The Garden of Wisdom* (New York: Columbia University Press, 1907, reprinted 1966). The best edition of the Judaeo-Arabic text, with a Hebrew translation and notes, is Y. Kafih's second version, *Bustan el-Uqul: Gan ha-Sekhalim* (Jerusalem: Halikhot Am Israel, 5744/1984).

27   Netanel assumes that older equals better.

28   Compare Qur'an Sura 14:4.

Messiah, crudely refers to Mohammed as *ha-meshugga*. Netanel is neither casual nor tongue in cheek in his assessment of Mohammed, but presents the reader with a fully integrated system of thought which allows a measure of religious pluralism. His affirmation of Mohammed's prophetic authenticity is not an *ad hoc* or *ad hominem* argument, but a key statement within an extensively elaborated philosophical system which carries the social implication of respect for the heirs of the prophets, these heirs being the 'imams, administrators, the learned and the wise'.[29]

Netanel, unsurprisingly for a man of his time, maintains the absolute superiority of the revelation through Moses; superior because the Israelites were on a sufficiently high spiritual plane to receive it. What is surprising, and probably unique amongst medieval Jewish philosophers, is his acceptance of plural revelations and of the culture-boundedness of revelation. In this he is far more a philosopher for our time than was the celebrated Maimonides.

Special Concepts: Tiqqun Olam, Darké Shalom, Darké Noam, Qiddush Hashem, Mishum eiva

Rabbinic Judaism fixed its social boundaries most clearly by means of rules, particularly regarding food, idolatry and ritual purity, which were devised by the rabbis and their predecessors with the aim of separating Jews from the heathen environment, as well as from their less devout brethren.[30] This is paralleled by developments within the early Church[31] and other religious societies.

Rabbinic hermeneutic, moreover, restricts the operation of some biblical rules, including 'Love thy neighbour as thyself' (Lev. 19:18), to the faithful among the people of Israel. This restrictive interpretation leaves the rabbis with the problem of how to apply such basic ideas as respect for proprietary rights and regard for human dignity to non-Jews. Their solution, largely ignored by scholars, was masterly. Side by side with the restrictive interpretation of the Bible there emerged a series of broad principles which are used inter alia to govern the relationships of Jews to those outside the bond of faith or peoplehood.[32] These principles include: tiqqun olam ('establishing the world

---

29   Levine, English p.51; Arabic p.31.

30   See Alexander Guttman's discussion of the 'eighteen measures' in his *Rabbinic Judaism in the Making* (Detroit: Wayne State University Press, 1970), pp.102–16.

31   See William Schoedel's essay, 'Theological Norms and Social Perspectives in Ignatius of Antioch', in E.P. Sanders (ed.), *Jewish And Christian Self-Definition*, vol.1 (London: SCM Press, 1980), pp.31f, where Schoedel refers to inter alia the Christian observance of Sunday rather than Saturday as part of the Church's deliberate policy of 'separation' from Jews and Judaism.

32   See Ernst Simon's essay, 'The Neighbour we Shall Love', in M. Fox (ed.), *Modern Jewish Ethics* (Columbus: Ohio State University Press, 1975), pp.29–56 for an

aright'), *darké shalom* ('the ways of peace'), *darké noam* ('the ways of pleasantness'), *qiddush Hashem* ('sanctifying God's name', that is behaving in such a manner as to bring credit to God) and *mishum eiva* ('on account of hatred'). This was invoked to justify departure from the standard law in situations where to follow it might stir up anti-Jewish hatred leading to life danger; it is generally understood as a counsel of prudence rather than as a moral principle governing relations between Jews and non-Jews.

The late Chief Rabbi Unterman of Israel summed up his position in a responsum on *darké shalom* ('the ways of peace'):

> The laws of *darké shalom* flow from the moral fount of the holy Torah whose 'ways are the ways of pleasantness and all her ways are peace' (Proverbs 3:17); they were fixed by our sages of old in their great wisdom and are obligatory upon all of us. They have the power to determine the interpretation of halakha and to permit things which the sages forbade. We find that they even permitted transgression of some Torah prohibitions *mishum eiva* ('on account of hatred'), though with regard to the sabbath they permitted only transgression of rabbinic law ... unless the situation was dangerous [in which case it overrides even Torah law].[33]

Within their operational limits, on Unterman's interpretation, *darké shalom* and the associated concepts are not concessions, but principles for determination and modification of existing laws. That is, halakha itself is in certain circumstances defined by the overriding moral imperative to seek peace.

Selection and rejection of text has been the favoured strategy of Reform Judaism. It raises the problem of continuity. How many 'texts' can be abandoned before it becomes unreasonable to claim that it is still the same religion? Moreover the outright rejection of texts runs up against the fundamental Jewish belief in *Torah min ha-Shamayim*, that the whole Torah was received from God through Moses. Reform theology, however, aided by historical criticism of the Bible, understands revelation as a continuing historical process rather than as the once-for-all appearance of a text out of the sky. This makes it possible to maintain that the more recent 'revelation' of liberal democracy, anti-racism and gender equality enables us to determine which of the earlier texts are of lasting value and which should be abandoned in the light of historical development.

---

attempt to define the application of the 'golden rule' within Judaism. Simon has not clearly grasped the fact that the rabbis used general ethical principles rather than specific scriptural 'rules' to regulate behaviour towards those 'outside the covenant'. *Tiqqun olam* is, strictly speaking, an 'extra-legal' measure introduced within the community to avoid impossible situations arising; cf. BT, *Gittin* 34b, 36a. The *locus classicus* for *darkei shalom* is Mishna, *Gittin* 5:8–9. *Qiddush Hashem* often bears the meaning of 'martyrdom'; for its use in setting standards of moral behaviour in dealings with non-Jews, see BT, *Yevamot* 79a; *Bava Qama* 113a.

33   Issar Yehuda Unterman, 'Darké Shalom v'hagdaratam', in *Qol Torah*, Nisan 5726 (1966), section 4 (Hebrew).

Confidence in this approach has been undermined in the course of the twentieth century as the naïve belief in inevitable human moral progress has been challenged by the barbarities of the age. But surely such challenges should be met by redoubled efforts to implement the newly 'revealed' values, not by retreat into the pre-enlightened past.

Is it possible for the Orthodox to adopt a similar approach? I believe it is, though not without some modification of the traditional doctrine of *Torah min ha-Shamayim*. I reserve further comment for the concluding section.

The final strategy is the one most commonly followed by those Jews who simply follow custom, praying, observing the Sabbath, visiting the sick, helping the needy. Regularity dulls the senses. The rabbi who had not noticed that the passage he read that very morning from Deuteronomy was diametrically opposed to the message of tolerance he preached was neither ignorant nor foolish. He was guided by custom, the custom of regular reading of the Torah, and also the custom of tolerance. Any problems might be safely ignored. One knew that the Torah was perfect, and also that it was good to be tolerant; surely, if there was a contradiction, someone 'in authority', or perhaps one of the old commentators, had sorted it out, so there was no need to worry.

The danger of this naïve faith is that one day somebody – a Barukh Goldstein or a Yigal Amir – will notice what is written and, lacking any positive guidance as to how seriously to take it will act upon its plain sense. Criticism will be muted because the rabbis themselves, or *yeshiva* teachers, have not confronted the morally problematic nature of texts and guided their students on how to handle them.

Conclusions

After the Hebron massacre Dr Jonathan Sacks, Chief Rabbi of the (Orthodox) British United Hebrew Congregations, vigorously denounced the attack as a travesty of Jewish values, and declared: 'Violence is evil. Violence committed in the name of God is doubly evil. Violence against those engaged in worshipping God is unspeakably evil.' He would no doubt have been equally outspoken in his condemnation of the widely reported remark of Rabbi Yaacov Perrin, at Goldstein's funeral on the Sunday after the murders, that 'One million Arabs are not worth a Jewish fingernail'; but evidently Perrin himself, who is not ignorant of Bible and Talmud, did not think the massacre was a travesty of Jewish values.

The problem with Sacks' position is that, much as we may concur with the sentiment, and however many Biblical and talmudic citations we may amass in praise of peace, we are left with numerous texts that *do* summon us to violence in the name of God, and this makes it difficult to argue against Perrin and the like on purely *textual* grounds. Again and again Deuteronomy inveighs against laxity in exterminating the 'seven nations' and Amalek; King Saul was deposed because he disobeyed the divine instruction to destroy (1 Sam. 15); to avoid being caught up in this biblical rhetoric it is necessary either to repudiate it openly or to show why it should not be applied.

Another Orthodox rabbi, David Hartman, in a passionate address to the Jerusalem Fellows' Colloquium on 28 December 1995, reflected upon the assassination of Prime Minister Rabin by Yigal Amir, a young man raised in some of the finest Israeli religious institutions:

> Now, I don't know what the answer is. I don't want neutrality. I don't want halachic relativism because I believe it is extremely important to have anchor points from which you do look at the world, otherwise you are absorbed by the modern world, and you don't know where you are going …
>
> I am not calling for religious neutrality. I am calling for alternative passions. Living in alternative language systems. And alternative stories. Alternative biographies of the self.
>
> As a Jewish philosopher I feel this intuitively, and I know it is correct, with a *posek*,[34] without a Rambam, without anything.
>
> I am straight with you – I have no authoritative position in the tradition to validate this. What validates this is my own sense of human decency. I love Jews, but if they kill goyim it kills me, and it killed me when they said how can a Jew kill another Jew? The issue is not how does a Jew kill.
>
> Are there alternative stories that the Torah suggests? Alternative vocabularies? Alternative frameworks? …
>
> I want to get away from needing validations, or foundational texts, in order to confirm moral intuitions. I believe that moral intuitions grow from some sort of decency …
>
> So people ask me, 'what is the foundation for your morality? What is the source of it?' I have no source, I don't know. It is the accumulated experience of what decent people around the world have come to understand as what civilized behaviour is all about. I have no other source. A *posek*? A *Shakh*?[35] No. I don't have to look at books to find out what a decent person is about …
>
> [Moshe?] Greenberg, in his marvellous thesis on the fear of God in the bible, argues that the concept is one of conscience …
>
> Ramban[36] [commenting on the generation of the Flood, says that their sin was] the loss of *natural* morality …
>
> … the bible has two frames of reference. It has a whole story of judgement … [in the creation story there is no revelatory framework, this only comes at Sinai] … [goes on to argue that Sinai does not displace creation, hence both 'stories' should steer our course – we have the basic human moral intuition from creation, and the halakha from Sinai …]

---

34   One who decides issues of *halakha* (Jewish law).

35   Acronym of Shabbetai ben Meir ha-Cohen, a leading *posek* of the seventeenth century.

36   Moses Nahmanides (1194–1270). The reference is to his comment on Genesis 6:13.

> ... the meaning of being a religious Jew in the modern world is to live
> with the risks of living with numerous vocabularies and multiple frames
> of reference. There is no more security.[37]

Hartman here presents a solution which he has argued at length in numerous books and articles.[38] It may be summed up as a theory of 'two covenants'. One, the creation covenant, was made with all humanity; it depends on some sort of innate, natural law, written in people's hearts. The second, at Sinai, was with Israel only, and is based on a revealed code of law which supplements, rather than displaces, the innate understanding of right and wrong on which the first covenant is based.

This may justify Hartman in living in two worlds at once ('alternative channels of value', he calls it), a world of ethics and a world of halakha, but it leaves the tensions and the risk, and many more problems besides.

First, ethics is a variable quantity. Hartman fails to show why he prefers one ethical system over another. He claims his preferred ethical standards are 'the accumulated experience of what decent people around the world have come to understand as what civilized behaviour is all about'. But this is a circular definition, for how do we decide which people are 'decent'?

Next, where is the boundary at which 'decency' overrides halakha? For instance, does Hartman think that people who seek equal status for women are 'decent', and that this 'decency' should override halakhic considerations? He does move in this direction by admitting women to *shiurim* and to limited Synagogue participation, but why stop at the point at which he does stop? No doubt he would say because the halakha cannot be bent that far. But would counting women as members of a prayer quorum bend the halakha any further than dismissing other intolerant aspects of halakha?

Much has been written on the relationship between ethics and halakha. Gillian Rose, summing up earlier papers by Aharon Lichtenstein[39] and Eugene Borowitz,[40] wrote that Lichtenstein asks whether Judaism recognizes an ethic *independent of halakha*. His question concerns the ethical legitimation of *halakha qua* traditional authority – is it *equitable*? Borowitz, on the other hand, asks what is the authority of the ethical impulse *within halakha*. His question

---

37   These extracts were taken from a poor, 'lightly edited', transcript of the address; minor corrections have been made without consulting the author.

38   See, for example, his *Joy and Responsibility: Israel, Modernity, and the Renewal of Judaism* (Jerusalem: Posner, 1978) and *Conflicting Visions: Spiritual Possibilities of Modern Israel* (New York: Schocken Books, 1990).

39   'Does Jewish Tradition Recognize an Ethic independent of Halakha?', in Marvin Fox (ed.), *Modern Jewish Ethics: Theory and Practice* (Columbus: Ohio State University Press, 1975), pp.102–23.

40   'The Authority of the Ethical Impulse in *Halakha*', reprinted in Eugene B. Borowitz, *Exploring Jewish Ethics: Papers on Covenantal Responsibility* (Detroit: Wayne State University Press, 1990), pp.193–203.

concerns the ethical legitimation of *halakha qua* legal–rational authority – is it *egalitarian*?[41] Hartman clearly recognizes an ethic independent of halakha, and has at the same time, I believe, taken an important step by locating the independent ethic within Torah itself, in the covenant of 'creation'. Although Nahmanides and other medieval authorities also recognised an independent ethic within Torah, they found it within the *halakha*, informing the rest of *halakha* rather than in tension with it;[42] by locating it in a separate covenant, Hartman has made space for the tensions.

Hartman fails to address our main question, which is how to continue reading the texts as sacred literature when we reject them from an ethical perspective. Significantly he does not offer any way to read, for instance, Maimonides' ruling, which he cites with acute discomfort and disapproval, that one should seek any available means, however devious, to encompass the death of traitors and heretics.[43] He rejects as inadequate the statement of the Hazon Ish[44] that such a ruling applies only in times when 'the Shekhina is manifest', not in our day: that is, the 'Limitation of sphere of operation' strategy discussed above. Is his chosen strategy (a) to ignore texts of which he disapproves, or (b) to reject them, to declare them *not Torah*? It looks like the former, but why is he unable or unwilling to adopt the latter?

It seems to me that no satisfactory solution can be reached without reformulation of the doctrine of *Torah min ha-Shamayim* (the divine origin of Torah). Indeed the pretence of Lichtenstein and Borowitz to be arguing about the relationship of ethics and *halakha* is the secondary outcome of a deep disagreement about *Torah min ha-Shamayim*. *Halakha*, for Lichtenstein, is in a rather literal sense the 'voice of God', a transcendent God, who commanded on a specific historical occasion, and commanded specific laws. Borowitz, on the other hand, is a liberal rabbi fully committed to the historical critical approach to holy texts; *Torah min ha-Shamayim* is for him a distant metaphor for a social reality, the people Israel in covenantal relationship with its God, and *halakha* a transient formulation of this relationship.

If we are content to regard *Torah min ha-Shamayim* as a metaphor for the people Israel in covenantal relationship with its God, the path is clear to abandoning, even repudiating, certain texts. We can still say, 'Yes, these difficult

---

41   Gillian Rose, *Judaism and Modernity* (Oxford, UK, and Cambridge, MA: Blackwell, 1993). See my review article, 'Judaism and Modernity: the Whole Agenda', in *Jewish Journal of Sociology*, 36(2) (December 1994), 119–32.

42   The medievals (Jewish, Christian and Muslim) speculated on whether actions are right because God commanded them, or whether God commanded them because they are right. Our discussion proceeds on the latter assumption.

43   Maimonides, *Mishné Torah Rotzeah uSh'mirat Nefesh* 4:10. Compare *Mishné Torah Avoda Zara* 10:1, 2, 6.

44   Acronym of Isaiah Karlitz (1878–1953), one of the most influential *pos'kim* of the century.

texts in Deuteronomy are part of *Torah min ha-Shamayim*, that is, they are part of the document which stands as the historical expression of the myth of Israel's encounter with God, and which cannot be altered, for it (the document) is a fact of history. But this does not bind us to specific provisions which run counter to our moral convictions.' A similar approach might be taken to later sources of Judaism, including the Talmud and Codes. I believe that such a conception arises quite naturally from the rabbinic concepts of Oral Torah and customary law (*Minhag Yisrael*) 'completing' the Written Torah.

Unless such a step is taken, one cannot formally repudiate a Biblical verse or rabbinic formulation of law. Nevertheless all the strategies outlined in this essay remain available to mitigate the impact of morally repugnant elements and to eliminate them from the practical programme of Judaism, even if we continue to live with them as blemishes within its theoretical structure. The very least we can expect from our rabbis and spiritual leaders is that they respond to the heartfelt moral dilemmas of those who turn for guidance to traditional sources, and utilize to the maximum the available strategies for interpretation of 'difficult' texts. Nowhere is this more urgent than in the area of mutual respect and recognition, amongst Jews as well as between Jews and the rest of humankind. *Darké shalom*, the ways of peace, as Unterman wisely observed, 'flow from the moral fount of the holy Torah whose "ways are the ways of pleasantness and all her ways are peace" … they were fixed by our sages of old in their great wisdom and are obligatory upon all of us'.

Ultimately it is not enough to 'read' texts in a far-fetched, if morally acceptable way. This approach lacks intellectual integrity. Somehow one must find the courage to say No!

Chapter 5

The Limits of Tolerance: Nation-State Building and What it Means for Minority Groups

Mark Levene

Arriving at Ruskin College, Oxford in September 1971, Atallah Mansour is invited to stand up and introduce himself. He does so: 'Atallah Mansour from Jerusalem, Christian, Catholic, Greek Catholic, Israeli, Arab' – everyone bursts into laughter.[1] The passage opens his delightful yet painful autobiography, *Waiting for the Dawn*, whose first chapter I use as a key text for a course on the British mandate in Palestine. My students, unlike those at Ruskin, generally do not fall around laughing but they are, more often than not, perplexed. An Israeli and Arab and apparently proud of it too? And all those other identities? Surely it is all too complicated, even schizophrenic? Yet in the complication, even possibly contradiction, might one not read one, possibly even two, more positive messages about the modern world? Here we have a man who has been moulded by the rich ethnic and cultural diversity of his homeland, Palestine. To have an identity on one level does not prevent him having others too. One might go further and suggest that there is also some grain of a Western, enlightenment idea here; that our citizenship does not preclude, or override, or undermine either the individual or collective attributes of our social and cultural existence; that we have, in short, the possibility or, perhaps more accurately, the potentiality, to be whatever we want to be.

If we turn to international protocol this good idea seems also to be on offer as best practice. Many historians would locate its origins in the articles of the Treaty of Westphalia, in 1648, which confirms the right to religious difference within the state. But further expressions and amplifications are to be found in, for instance, the Treaty of Berlin of 1878, the Minorities Treaties associated with the Versailles Peace of 1919, the United Nations (UN) Charter of 1948 and, very noticeably, in the 1975 Helsinki Accords.[2] Cumulatively they seem to offer a

---

1   Atallah Mansour, *Waiting for the Dawn* (London: Secker & Warburg, 1975), p.1.

2   See Lucien Wolf, *Notes on the Diplomatic History of the Jewish Question* (London: Jewish Historical Society of England, 1919) for pre-1919 international treaties referring to religious tolerance. For the text of the Helsinki Accords see Gale Stokes (ed.), *From Stalinism to Pluralism: A Documentary History of Eastern Europe since 1945* (Oxford: Oxford University Press, 1991), pp.160–62.

mandate for citizens of states to be free and unhindered in their linguistic, ethnic and religious orientation. Walk on the streets of London, Paris or New York and best practice seems to be directly observable: people speaking different tongues, often wearing a variety of defining religious garb, apparently tolerating each other's right to be. As the global economy, on one level, makes us more and more the same, multilayered identities of the Atallah Mansour type, closely linked to an aware cosmopolitanism, seem to offer the basis for a personal equilibrium in what could be, after all, the best of all possible worlds.

But surely I am confusing my terms? Or, perhaps, the confusion is a function, or dysfunction, of the world we live in. We consume within a global economy, we may have a McDonalds round the corner, whether our home is Sydney, Singapore or Seville, but we live in and are primarily defined by our status as nationals of states, more specifically nation-states who themselves operate in an international system of nation-states: another clear product both of the enlightenment and of the impact of the West. And while nation-states, most of which have emerged since the First or Second World Wars, are required by the international conventions of an essentially Western-designed and Western-led system to repeat the formulae of racial, religious and ethnic tolerance, this essay begins with the premise that limits on that tolerance are implicit within the design itself. Nation-states do not exist to promote diversity; on the contrary, their role is to streamline, make homogeneous, organise people to be uniform in some sense, in order that their societies may compete, survive and develop within the system. Or as Michael Ignatieff, an avowed cosmopolitan himself, has aptly put it in his book, *Blood and Belonging*, 'Globalism in a post-imperial age only permits a post-nationalist consciousness for those cosmopolitans who are lucky enough to live in the wealthy west. It has brought chaos and violence for the many small peoples too weak to establish defensible states of their own.'[3] Tolerance, in other words, is, in the late 1990s, not a function of who you are but where you live. Yet its Western liberal version is also, via a Western-dominated political economy, at least in some sense, directly responsible for its breakdown.

Having thus posed a disparity, if not a contradiction between, on the one hand, a societal ideal of tolerance and, on the other, pragmatic, political efforts to forge nation-states, our focus here recalls two attempts to reconcile them. Both attempts were imbued with the ideal of tolerance, as understood in the best Western enlightenment tradition. Yet both had to grapple with fraught political situations where the imminent creation of nation-states was bound to infringe upon the wellbeing, not to say safety, of peoples who could, or would not, be easily absorbed into them. Both cases, moreover, would have been of particular interest, if not very close to the heart of James Parkes, not least because Jewish–Gentile relations were involved. Parkes, indeed, had much to say on the

---

3   Michael Ignatieff, *Blood and Belonging: Journeys into the New Nationalism* (London: Vintage, 1994), p.9.

first of the cases in his *Emergence of the Jewish Problem*.[4] I propose to reserve judgment, however, on the degree to which he would have been sympathetic to proposals emanating from the second.

As for the cases themselves, they relate to the international imprimatur for the creation of two modern polities, firstly that of Poland, by the Western Allies at the Paris Peace Conference in 1919, out of lands partitioned over a century earlier by three imperial powers, secondly that of Israel, in 1948, the endorsing body being, on this occasion, the UN, in its capacity as supervisor of the British imperial mandate for Palestine which was being terminated in favour of the partition of the mandated territory into two independent states.

In each instance, Jews were directly affected. In the former, this was as one of several ethnic and linguistic groups who, being considered distinct from the Polish 'majority', were to be recognised and given status as 'minorities'; in the latter, as the group entitled to exercise sovereign powers, even though its 'majority' position was, in population terms, only by the smallest margin over its Arab 'minority'.[5] It is, moreover, pertinent to this discussion to recall the close parallels in the creation of the two states. These might be outlined as follows.

1. Born-again nations. Poland had not existed as a sovereign state since 1795, a Jewish state had not existed for more than 1700 years prior to that. Yet both new entities made their claim to sovereignty over particular territories by claiming historic rights, which in turn were based on allegedly continuous national relationships to them. This was more remarkable in the case of Israel, given the extreme remoteness of the historical relationship in question, the diaspora existence of the vast majority of Jews since then and the fact that most Jews in Palestine, in 1948, were first or second generation incomers. Poles, at first sight, were in a much stronger position on this score. But they also made claims that were highly contentious, though backed by a strong diaspora, and with a keen sense that exile and resurrection were intrinsic to their understanding of their own identity.[6] In both instances, the idea of the nation strongly preceded the state and was, in a critical way, responsible for its emergence.

---

4   James Parkes, *Emergence of the Jewish Problem 1878–1939* (London: Oxford University Press, 1946).

5   On the basis of the 1921 census the Polish national composition by percentage was 69.2 per cent Poles, 14.3 per cent Ukrainians, 7.8 per cent Jews, 3.9 per cent Germans and Byelorussians, 0.9 per cent (mostly Lithuanian) others. See Joseph Marcus, *Social and Political History of the Jews in Poland 1919–1939* (Berlin: Moulin, 1983), pp.16–17. In the UN proposed Jewish state in Palestine, 520 000 Jews faced 350 00 Arabs. Including Jerusalem, the total population, noted Ben-Gurion, would be about one million, on a 60:40 ratio in favour of the Jews. See Benny Morris, *The Birth of the Palestinian Refugee Problem 1947–1949* (Cambridge: Cambridge University Press, 1989), p.28.

6   See Neal Ascherson, *The Struggles for Poland* (London: Joseph, 1987), p.7.

2. Sacred and profane. The notion of a unique, even messianic, mission, leading to the redemption of all nations[7] was germane not only to the Jewish but also to the Polish claim to statehood. This particular combination of historical memory with religious metaphor did not, however, preclude the framing of their demands in terms of a Western practice which identified the rule of law and the equality of all state citizens regardless of religion, race or creed before that law, as the sine qua non for their legitimation.

3. Historic multculturalism. Though Poles and Jewish Zionists proposed to create nation-states, the ethnic composition of the territories thus earmarked were of considerable diversity. Some previous imperial regimes had sought to accommodate these realities through the provision of generous schemes of religious toleration and group self-regulation, amounting to self-government. Under the Polish–Lithuanian commonwealth, for instance, this system reached its apotheosis in the sixteenth and seventeenth centuries, when state Catholicism nevertheless allowed for a variety of autonomous non-Catholic communities, including a trans-state network of Jewish *kehillot*, the Va'ad Arba Arazot (Council of the Four Lands).[8] Likewise, up to 1917, under the state Islam of Ottoman rule, non-Muslim national–religious groupings, including Jews, in Palestine were entitled to similar provisions under the still extant, if decaying, millet system.[9]

4. Outside help. In spite of the rather dubious narratives associated with, for instance, Pilsudski and Begin, to the effect that national liberation had been self-induced, neither the Polish nor the Jewish state was capable of coming into existence of its own volition. Each was dependent on the political support of the leading Western powers in the international community, both the Poles and Zionists receiving statements of legitimation from this source in 1917, the Poles particularly, though not exclusively, via President Wilson's fourteen points, the Zionists in the form of the somewhat problematic British Balfour Declaration. These endorsements helped pave the way to statehood, in the Polish case at the end of the First World War, in the Jewish case, thirty years and a further world war, involving specific Jewish catastrophe, later.

5. Territorial expansion and psychosis. In spite of international determination of their state boundaries, both Poland and Israel dramatically expanded their territorial dimensions under cover of national wars of independence. Paradoxically, both continued to suffer from collective psychoses of vulnerability, to the point where the aggressive intentions of neighbouring

---

7   Ibid., pp.6–7, 9–10.

8   Ibid., pp.20, 40. See also Norman Davies, *Heart of Europe: A Short History of Poland* (Oxford: Oxford University Press, 1986).

9   See Kemal H. Karpat, 'Millets and Nationality: The Roots of the Incongruity of Nation and State in the Post-Ottoman State', in Benjamin Braude and Bernard Lewis (eds), *Christians and Jews in the Ottoman Empire: The Functioning of a Plural Society*, vol.1 (New York and London: Holmes & Meier, 1982), pp.140–60.

states were perceived to threaten their own imminent liquidation. These fears were framed with reference to the demise of their original, 'authentic' and historic states. Nevertheless the fears also had some considerable justification. In 1939, Poland, in the wake of a disastrous war, was repartitioned and ceased, for nearly six years, to exist, while Israelis' fear that they would be literally driven into the sea and off the map were only eased after the *annus mirabilis* victory of 1967.

6. Demographic politics. The initial territorial expansion of Israel in 1948, like that of Poland in 1919–20, underscored the question of the relationship between ethnic grouping and loyal citizenship. Or, put more starkly, how did either nation-state propose to remain viable with so many potential fifth-columnists within its midsts; how would Poles deal with the yeshiva students of Pinsk when these were considered to be agents of Bolshevism; how would a nascent Israel behave towards the population of Ramle or Lydda when these were supposedly part of a sea of encroaching Arabism?[10]

If, then, there are acute parallels in the Polish and Jewish experience of nation-state creation, there are connecting threads which go beyond these, suggesting a closer, even incestuous, interconnection between the two. The historic Polish lands had been the demographic power house of European Jewry since the eighteenth century, though it was almost a century after Polish partition that a Jewish national consciousness began to emerge there. Initially diverse in its tendencies, its Zionist strand increasingly came to reject the possibility, or even desirability, of Western-led models for Jewish emancipation and assimilation in favour of the creation of its own national community in Palestine. A Zionist maximalism, founded in historic Poland yet rejecting, on national grounds, the possibility of a Jewish place within it, was mirrored in the parallel emergence of a Polish national movement which, in its maximalist form, also had no cultural, social or economic place for Jews.[11] Thus, for some Polish patriots as for some Jewish patriots, the idea of their would-be nation-states was premised not on toleration, or even majority–minority coexistence, but on the elimination of 'the other'. Polish and Jewish nationalism, in these maximalist versions, agreed that Jews should go to Palestine. By the same token, presumably anybody

---

10   For 1919–20 Polish accusations and actions against Polish Jews, see Norman Davies, *White Eagle, Red Star: The Polish–Soviet War 1919–1920* (London: Macdonald & Co., 1972), pp.162–3. For parallel 1948 Israeli leadership views towards Arabs, see notably those of Shertok, in Morris, *Palestinian Refugee Problem*, pp.140–46.

11   For Polish ultra-nationalist rejection of Jews, see Alexander Groth, 'Dmowski, Pilsudski and the ethnic conflict in pre-1939 Poland', *Canadian Slavic Studies*, vol.3 (1969), pp.69–91; also A.M. Fountain II, *Roman Dmowski: Party, Tactics, Ideology 1895–1907* (Boulder, CO: East European Monographs, 1980). For conditions leading to the development of Zionism in nation-state Poland, see Ezra Mendelsohn, *Zionism in Poland: The Formative Years, 1915–1926* (New Haven and London: Yale University Press, 1981), especially pp.12–18.

in Palestine who was not Jewish would similarly be required to vacate possession and go somewhere else. One ultimate, all-important irony here: neither Polish nor Jewish nationalists were able to translate these desired goals into practice by themselves. Push could only come to shove through an outside agency which, as it turned out, was the deadly enemy of all Jews and all Poles: Nazi Germany. Its direct physical elimination of Jews, primarily on Polish soil, catalysed international demands for a statist solution to the Jewish question, at the end of the war, which paved the way for the creation of Israel. Similarly, not least through the physical liquidation of nine-tenths of Polish Jewry, alongside a numerically but not proportionally equivalent number of non-Jewish Poles, it provided some of the conditions whereby the postwar reincarnation of Poland was, for the first time, a more or less ethnically homogeneous nation-state.

If, unlike the Nazis, neither Polish nor Jewish nationalists, in power, could be charged with desiring or enacting genocide, the very notion that they might have considered the forcible removal of Jewish and/or other populations from Poland, or Arab ones from Palestine, in the interests of their own national self-determination, raises a rather large question mark regarding their avowed adherence to Western ideals of tolerance.

It was with this danger in mind that Lucien Wolf, the first of my protagonists, rebuked his friend and sometimes sparring partner, Israel Zangwill, who was an early proponent of Arab population 'transfer' (a veiled euphemism for expulsion) thus: '1. Principle: if the Zionists establish themselves in Palestine, it must be on the basis of justice and fair play. 2. Expediency: if we evict Arabs, anti-semites in Europe will evict Jews.'[12] Wolf was writing just before the Paris Peace Conference, where his remit, as political secretary to the Joint Foreign Committee of British Jews (JFC), was to safeguard and protect the interests of Jewish and, for that matter, other minorities in Poland and the other 'new' states of Eastern Europe which were to be recognised by the Western Allies. Pragmatically Wolf recognised that any Zionist intolerance towards Arabs in Palestine would have knock-on effects for the great majority of Jews who remained 'at home'. But by trying to ensure that they would be legally secured 'firmly and explicitly in the nationality of the lands of their birth',[13] Wolf laid himself open to the severest Zionist censure. For them, as well as for succeeding Zionist historiography, Wolf was simply proving himself to be a classic 'assimilationist' and, thereby, an enemy of the Jewish 'nation'. In one respect, of course, this was true. A disciple of Western liberalism, a believer in the Westphalia model, a proponent of the idea that religious difference need not impede one's patriotism as a Briton, a Frenchmen or, indeed, a Pole, Wolf's

---

12   See Mark Levene, *War, Jews and the New Europe: The Diplomacy of Lucien Wolf 1914–1919* (Oxford: Oxford University Press, 1992) p.120.

13   YIVO archive, New York, Mowschowitch collection, 1603–4, Lucien to George Wolf, 9 April 1920.

intrinsic vision was of a world of nation-states in which civic status, not ethnic background, determined one's nationality.

Wolf's colour-blind premise, was not, however, naturally founded on some conceptual notion associated with the idea of multilayered identities. His odyssey in that direction only came through years of persistent struggle against the 'national postulate',[14] a Zionist version of the more general Central and East European tendency to view the nation in ethnic terms. This being so entirely at odds with the Jewish ideology of emancipation, Wolf was at pains to offer a counter-formula, but not in some hackneyed form whereby he would simply be repeating emancipation doctrine. The quest, however, was made urgent, in the context of the First World War, when it became apparent that Zionists might actually win Britain and other Western states to their cause. Through David Moschowitch, his adviser on Eastern European affairs, Wolf was thus fortunate to learn about the Renner principle.

Karl Renner was a leading Austro-Marxist theoretician who, in 1902, had proposed a remedy for the intensifying nationality conflicts in the sprawling, multi-ethnic dual monarchy. Renner's solution lay in the separation of 'nationality' from 'citizenship', an idea that was not itself new but rather expounded in a novel way. In the classic nation-state either one's nationality was synonymous with citizenship because the state was ethnically homogeneous, or the dominant group's nationality was synonymous with citizenship and other groups had either to integrate themselves accordingly or recognise their eternal subordination to the dominant group. There were one or two variations on this theme. The peoples of Britain, for example, found themselves remoulded, in the eighteenth century, into a new hybrid nationality, the British. This formula, however, was intended to fuse the concepts of citizenship and nationality, not to detach them.[15]

In addressing the competing claims of an Austria–Hungary in which at least fourteen significant nationalities resided, Renner offered some lateral thinking. Why not make citizenship, on the one hand, the common privilege of everybody residing in the boundaries of the state and nationality, on the other, a matter of one's personal identification and affiliation? Go on from this to recognise each of these nationalities as a distinct corporation under public law and provide them with national secretariats who would be responsible for all matters pertaining to each group's national life, specifically those relating to language and education. Most importantly, and this was where Renner's formula was radically new, divorce the idea of nationality from any assumption regarding its territorial space. Renner's two-tier system, in other words, would operate equally across

---

14   Levene, War, *Jews*, pp.110–19.

15   Linda Colley, *Britons: Forging the Nation, 1707–1837* (New Haven, CT: Yale University Press, 1992). See also Robin Cohen, *Frontiers of Identity: The British and the Others* (London and New York: Longman, 1994), pp.5–13.

the breadth of the state. There would be an apparatus of state, which would be answerable to the whole enfranchised populace through state elections and there would be national bodies, answerable to everybody in each national community, through their own elections.

Renner's scheme was, of course, a federal idea but with an intriguing slant. It was specifically designed to avoid one nationality being more important in the state than any other, or with rights to state resources disproportionate to the others. This principle of proportionality represented the only impediment, for instance, to a national secretariat setting up one of its schools in an area where its communal numbers were small. The limiting factor in such a case would not be national resources but total state ones. The concept of nationality as territorially non-specific remained sacrosanct. Interestingly, too, Renner did not propose a single offical language for his reformed 'Danubian Federation'.[16]

In writing in depth about Renner's scheme in an important article in the *Edinburgh Review* in 1917,[17] Wolf not only signalled his interest in an idea which is now almost forgotten in the history of nationalism but also thereby endorsed Renner's view on the non-applicability of the Western national model to eastern Europe. This was a major departure for the Anglo-Jewish diplomat who had previously held to the notion that Jews could only genuinely achieve tolerance through their adoption of the 'nationality' of the state. In recognising that in eastern Europe the Western model could only be a recipe for intolerance, Wolf thus affirmed that the only way forward, in these countries, was to make a virtue out of multinationality. Succeeding interviews and discussions with Polish diplomats, throughout 1917 and 1918, could only confirm Wolf in this conviction.

A sovereign Polish state, whatever its final shape, would be a state which, like Austria–Hungary, would be a composite of many ethnic groups (albeit with Polish speakers as something in the region of a two-thirds majority), but unlike the latter would be specifically a nation-state. Polish diplomats insisted, over and over again, to Wolf that this would not detrimentally affect minorities, Jews included, because they would be guaranteed in their rights through the application of the Western liberal principle of full equality before the law. The problem was: what did this mean in practice? Would the minorities be able freely to speak and practise their own languages and culture? Would they be able to be schooled in their mother tongue? Would their distinct non-Polish nationality be

---

16 Karl Renner, *Der kampf der osterreichischen Nationen um den Staat* (Leipzig and Vienna: F Deuticke, 1902). For more on the Austro-Marxist model, see Uri Ra'anan, Maria Mesner, Keith Ames and Kate Martin (eds), *State and Nation in Multi-Ethnic Societies: The Breakup of Multinational States* (Manchester: Manchester University Press, 1991), notably Theodor Hanf, 'Reducing conflict through cultural autonomy: Karl Renner's contribution', pp.33–52.

17 Lucien Wolf, 'The Jewish National Movement', *Edinburgh Review* (April 1917), 303–18.

recognised as such? Would specific Jewish concerns such as the right to trade on Sundays in a largely Catholic country be guaranteed? Indeed, would they, as ethnic non-Poles, be entitled to the citizenship and equality before the law which the diplomats promised, or would they rather be allocated to a nether region outside of Polish citizenship and thereby beyond what the genocide scholar, Helen Fein, has referred to as 'the universe of obligation'?[18]

Though Renner, in his original scheme, had not been thinking specifically of the Jews, Wolf could see that the singularity of the Jewish demographic position in Poland, dispersed throughout the country but with strong, often majority, urban concentrations, made the application of his ideas both relevant and urgent. The problem was that not only none of the Poles but hardly any of the policy makers were among the Western Allies prepared to see it that way. As the official British publication on the Paris Peace Conference stated:

> the recognition of national rights of the Jews of Poland would have
> been completely inconsistent with the territorial sovereignty of the
> state, which is the basis of our whole political system. The view taken
> by the British delegation throughout and supported by the
> Plenipotentaries was that if there was to be a Jewish nationality it could
> only be by giving the Jews a local habitat and enabling them to found
> in Palestine a Jewish state. Any Jew who was, however, a national of
> the Jewish state would ipso facto cease to be a Polish citizen.[19]

As the possibility of some sort of multinational federal framework, on the Renner model, faded and then disintegrated, paradoxically, with the defeat of Germany and the collapse of the old empires at the end of 1918, it was replaced by a Wilsonian interpretation of national self-determination, which, in effect, meant the nation-state. And as this was being given a mandate by the Western Allies, it thus also represented a green light for the strongest national elements in the East, to carve out for themselves the largest available space from the imperial vacuum, at the expense of the weaker ones.

There was little that Wolf could do about any of this. All he could do was point out to the peace conference decision makers what the consequences might be. Ultra-Zionist assertions that they wanted recognition of a Jewish nationality, as leverage towards the creation of an immediate sovereign Jewish state in Palestine, were playing straight into the hands of ultranationalist Poles who used

---

18   Helen Fein, 'Scenarios of Genocide: Models of Genocide and Critical Responses', in Israel W. Charny (ed.), *Toward the Understanding and Prevention of Genocide: Proceedings of the International Conference on the Holocaust and Genocide* (Boulder and London: Westview Press, 1984), pp.3–31.

19   H.W.V. Temperley, *A History of the Paris Peace Conference*, vol.V (London: H Fowde and Hodder & Stoughton, 1921), p.137, from the chapter 'Treaties for the Protection of Minorities'. For more on British views, see Alan Sharp, 'Britain and the Protection of Minorities at the Paris Peace Conference, 1919', in A.C. Hepburn (ed.), *Minorities in History* (London: E. Arnold, 1978), pp.171–88.

the assertions to argue that Jews, therefore, did not need, let alone have the right to, Polish citizenship. The Popular National Union, associated with Roman Dmowski's National Democrats, made no bones about its rejection of the idea of a multinational federation, or its desire to Polonise both economy and society by removing up to three million of its Jewish inhabitants.[20] Some of the Zionists, in turn, seemed to agree that such a divorce was the only solution,[21] and the precedent, once created, could be used not only against other ethnic groups in Poland but elsewhere too. The mass misery all this would have caused would have been obvious. However, Wolf's only real chance of success with the hardened statesmen of Versailles was to emphasise how the ensuing destabilization would threaten the wider peace. Bereft of Renner's federal raft, he, Louis Marshall, Judge Julian Mack and Cyrus Adler, the most influential American Jewish spokesmen in Paris, put forward compromise proposals which, while confirming Polish sovereignty on the Western model, also sought to offer something more than that Jews should 'not be penalised qua Jews in the eyes of the law and for purposes of citizenship'.[22]

That Western diplomats listened to Wolf is evident from the key articles of the Minorities Treaties with which he collaborated in drafting. Every new state, beginning with Poland, was required to sign such a treaty, each of which provided international guarantees not only for the full rights of citizenship for minority groups within the state but also for the protection of their cultural autonomy. Particular emphasis in this regard was given to language rights, requiring state signatories not only to allow schools to operate in the mother-language of the minority group but also to provide public funding for them.[23] This might be held to be a significant, perhaps even paradigmatic breakthrough. For the first time, the modern nation state was, via international protocol, being hedged in with caveats regarding group rights in the public domain. If the treaties did not acknowledge minority national rights as such, the fact that minority ethnic and linguistic autonomy was being recognised represented a considerable departure from a previous international wisdom which had conferred minority religious freedom but in all other respects treated people of different ethnic backgrounds as if they were the same. The Minorities Treaties, by contrast, seemed to acknowledge difference. There was just a murmur of multiculturalism here, a hint that, in place of social engineering, forced assimilation, pogrom and expulsion, there could be room for different groups, living side by side within a state framework, being equally entitled to rights of common citizenship, yet with access to state resources

---

20   Antony Polonsky, *Politics in Independent Poland 1921–1939* (Oxford: Clarendon Press, 1972), p.58.

21   See Levene, *War, Jews*, pp.223–24.

22   Public Record Office. FO 371/ 3419/199696, Sir Eyre Crowe minute, 11 December 1918.

23   For the full text of the Polish Minorities Treaty see Parkes, *Emergence*, pp.119–23, and Levene, *War, Jews*, pp.312–15.

for the purposes of their autonomous cultural and social life. For Polish and other Jews, moreover, the treaties meant very specifically a recognition of their right to live in situ, as Jews, and have their identity and security guaranteed as such.

But how much was this really a victory for Wolf, or for a more open-ended, flexible view of the nation-state? The treaty articles had actually given away very little, even, one might say particularly, with regard to that all-important barometer, language instruction in schools.[24] In spirit, they could at best be described as a rather grudging recognition that the only way domestic peace in Poland, and in the other new states, could be ensured was by provisions which would prevent the dominant group totally subordinating the rest or, as in the case of the Polish Germans, giving cause for a minority to kick up a fuss with a neighbouring state where they were a majority. At worst, however, the treaties might be viewed as a sort of empty paper tokenism (discernible in the fact that there was no serious workable machinery for their enforcement) thus potentially making the position of Jews and other minorities more, not less, precarious.[25]

All this could be taken as evidence that the intolerance implicit in the nation-state principle had not really been dented. Poland had been created in the interests of Poles, not Jews, or Germans, or Ukrainians. Certainly, Poland had been used as a test-case by the drafters of the Minorities Treaties and, as expected, the Poles had responded bitterly by denouncing the peacemakers' demands as both an infringement upon, and depreciation of, their sovereignty. If there were those, among Poland's new intelligentsia, mostly on the political left, who were sympathetic to the minorities, it was nearly always on the understanding that they would use their new-found citizenship in order to lose their 'other' identity in favour of Polonisation. For those on the Dmowskite right, when it came to the Jews, not even this option was available. Their socioeconomic position was seen as an obstacle to Polish state building, as was their supposed political orientation, the right consistently blanket-charging them with allegiance, if not responsibility, for Russian bolshevism, which thus branded them as a collective security risk inimicable to the interests of the Polish state. If Celia Heller is off-track when she proposes that Polish anti-semitism provided the seed bed which enabled the Nazis to undertake the destruction of European Jewry specifically in Poland, nevertheless it is true to say that no Polish politician was reconciled to the idea of sharing Poland with Jews, or any other minority group.[26]

---

24 Levene, *War, Jews*, p.299. Mother-tongue instruction was to be allowed in primary schools only.

25 For analyses, see C.A. Macartney, *National States and National Minorities* (London: Royal Institute of International Affairs, 1934), Jacob Robinson, *Were the Minorities Treaties a Failure?* (New York: Institute of Jewish Affairs of the American Jewish Congress and the World Jewish Congress, 1943) Oscar Janowsky, *The Jews and Minority Rights 1898–1919* (New York: Columbia University Press, 1933).

26 Celia Heller, *On the Edge of Destruction: The Jews of Poland between Two World Wars* (New York: Columbia University Press, 1977).

The Minorities Treaties were thus, from the Polish standpoint, in large part a dead letter almost before the sealing wax had dried. Certainly the imperatives of state and nation building made it so, long before the official Polish government repudiation in 1934. By then, conditions of acute economic crisis were additionally poisoning any hope for a modus vivendi between Jews and Poles. Proposals for the transfer of the bulk of Jews to Palestine had been the monopoly of an ultra-Polish and ultra-Zionist rhetoric. Now they entered into mainstream discourse and planning, to the degree that the Polish colonels' regime, in the spring and summer of 1939, began secretly training and arming members of the ultra-Zionist Betar and Irgun movements, with a view to facilitating a mass Polish–Jewish invasion of British Palestine.[27]

While the colonels' actions may seem a bizarre and hare-brained attempt to put their fantasy wish fulfilment into practice, though where one would place this on the spectrum of political madness in the run-up to September 1939 is a matter for speculation, one might conversely argue that what they were doing was simply a logical extension of Poland's nation-building agenda – all the more so when one puts Poland's actions alongside those of other emerging nation-states in a First World War and after time-frame. The leaderships of such polities, on occasions, showed a determined propensity not simply to contemplate but to act out their visions of a homogeneous nation cleansed of ethnically extraneous elements. One, the Ittihad, the radical nationalist regime which governed the Ottoman empire in its very final years, went so far as to attempt the physical annihilation of its Armenian population. Under the cover of war, in 1915 and 1916, as many as one million of them were done to death, and only those who were able to flee, or who lived either in the major cities or at the empire's non-Anatolian margins, escaped being caught up in this first total genocide of the twentieth century.[28] The Jewish author Franz Werfel later wrote a novel, *The Forty Days of Musa Dagh*, about these events, with the primary aim of warning the world that the same fate could also befall the Jews.[29] Similarly, in 1933, the still very much minority Jewish community in Palestine, the *yishuv*, was alarmed by reports of events in newly independent Iraq, where the regime and its generals

---

27   See Laurence Weinbaum, *A Marriage of Convenience: The New Zionist Organisation and the Polish Government 1936–1939* (Boulder: CO: East European Monographs, 1993), pp.143–60.

28   There is now an extensive literature on the Armenian genocide for which see Richard G. Hovannisian, *The Armenian Holocaust: A Bibliography relating to the Deportations, Massacres and Dispersion of the Armenian People 1915–1923* (Cambridge, MA: American Heritage Press, 1980) and more recently, Hamo Vassilian (ed.), *The Armenian Genocide: A Comprehensive Bibliography and Library Resource Guide* (Glendale CA: American Reference Books, 1992). Successive Turkish governments, as well as a number of otherwise reputable Western specialists, have continued to deny the charge of genocide.

29   Vahakn N. Dadrian, *The History of the Armenian Genocide: Ethnic Conflict from the Balkans to Anatolia to the Caucasus* (Oxford: Berghahn Books, 1996), p.xv.

had attempted to liquidate their problem Assyrian population. Only the intervention of the former British mandatory power put a stop to the killing, in this, now largely forgotten, 'Assyrian Affair'.[30]

If direct massacre presented one way of removing unwanted minorities from new nation-states, the scale of the undertaking, not to say the potential international opprobrium it might attract, turned some regimes to consider replacing or, possibly supplementing, the procedure with other methods. The idea of an 'exchange' of populations had the advantage of sounding not only less brutal but even ethically virtuous. The fact that in 1922 and 1923 such an 'exchange' had been enacted under League of Nations supervision with regard to several million Greeks in Anatolia, for a lesser number of ethnic Turks in the Greek islands, seemed to prove the point. When other states, or would-be states, considered and cited it both as a precedent and as an example of legitimate practice, they thus generally preferred to overlook what had precipitated it in the first place, namely a vicious Turco-Greek war resulting in massacres and 'ethnic cleansing' on both sides.[31] Falling into this category of overlookers were the very same leaders of the *yishuv*, who were simultaneously evincing so much post-Assyrian Affair anxiety about their own victim status.

However, as Nur Masalha's devastating book on the subject makes clear, Zionist political thought by the 1930s was directed, not towards the possibility of a Jewish removal from Palestine, but to the removal of their vastly more numerous Arab neighbours.[32] This, on one level, sounds strange and contradictory, not least because the official *yishuv* position, stated quite clearly by David Ben-Gurion as far back as 1918, was that there was room enough in Palestine for everybody, both Jew and Arab.[33] Nor did a succession of top-level Zionist secret committees to consider 'exchange', or 'transfer' as it was otherwise called, seem to recognise some of the ironies they were churning up in the process. Thus one highly considered destination for the Arab 'exchangees' was the Jazirah, the desert triangle straddling Iraq and Syria where, in 1915–16, so many of the Armenian deportees from Anatolia had ended their miserable

---

30   R.S. Stafford, *The Tragedy of the Assyrians* (London: G. Allen & Unwin 1935), pp.20–40 and more recently, David Omissi, 'Britain, the Assyrians and the Iraqi Levies 1919–1932', *Journal of Imperial and Commonwealth History*, 17 (1989), 301–22. For Jewish concern, see Neil Caplan, *Futile Diplomacy*, vol ii, *Arab-Zionist Negotiations and the End of the Mandate* (London: Frank Cass, 1986), p.103.

31   Arnold Toynbee, *The Western Question in Greece and Turkey* (New York: Howard Fertig, 1970 [1922]) notably chapter 7, 'The War of Extermination'.

32   Nur Masalha, *Expulsion of the Palestinians: The concept of 'transfer' in Zionist political thought 1882–1948* (Washington, DC: Institute for Palestine Studies, 1992). See also Morris, *Palestinian Refugee Problem*, pp.23–8.

33   David Ben-Gurion, *My Talks with Arab Leaders* (Jerusalem and New York: Keter, 1972), pp.7–8. More generally see Neil Caplan, *Palestine Jewry and the Arab Question, 1917–1925* (London: Frank Cass, 1978) and Yosef Gorny, *Zionism and the Arabs, A Study of Ideology, 1882–1948* (Oxford: Clarendon Press, 1987).

existences.[34] Moreover, the idea, returned to time and time again between 1939 and 1941, that this might become some designated reserve for Palestinian resettlement coincided with Nazi plans to turn a large tract of eastern Poland around Lublin into a reservation for Jews, pending 'a final solution'.[35]

The Zionist leadership, of course, would have protested vigorously against any suggestion that their transfer proposals were comparable with the Nazi quest for *lebensraum*. Moreover there was no way, in the 1930s or early 1940s, that the *yishuv* could have relocated Arabs to the Jazirah, or elsewhere, without the support of the British and other Arab states, as well as the international community. But the conviction of a prime mover like Ben-Gurion that moral and practical support for the scheme might well be forthcoming from these quarters is, perhaps, what makes it all the more disturbing. In October 1941, Ben-Gurion wrote:

> in the present war the idea of transferring a population is gaining more sympathy as a practical and the most secure means of solving the dangerous and painful problem of national minorities. The war has already brought the resettlement of many peoples in eastern and southern Europe, and in the plans for post-war settlements the idea of a large-scale population transfer in central, eastern and southern Europe increasingly occupies a respectable place.[36]

Ben-Gurion was right. The British Peel commission recommendations for the partition of Palestine in 1937 had assumed exactly what Ben-Gurion was stating: that Arabs in the Jewish state would have to be moved elsewhere.[37] A month prior to Ben-Gurion's confidential memorandum, Benes, the avowedly liberal Czech prime minister, in exile in London, had publicly stated that transfers could 'be made amicably under decent human conditions'.[38] As Ben-Gurion and the Jewish Agency, and for that matter the Peel commissioners, had done among themselves so here Benes misappropriated and distorted the truth about the Greek–Turkish exchange in order to give a moral sanction to what in effect would be a population expulsion, of the Sudeten and other Germans, in Czechoslovakia at the end of the war. However, while both he and Ben-Gurion, in the autumn of 1941, were wrestling with the problem of how to remove their problem populations, in the Russian borderlands, Hitler's Einsatzgruppen were busy showing how you could short-cut the problem altogether by simply killing them

---

34   Masalha, *Expulsion*, pp.137–40.

35   See Christopher Browning, 'Nazi Resettlement Policy and the Search for a Solution to the Jewish Question, 1939–1941' in *The Path to Genocide: Essays on Launching the Final Solution* (Cambridge: Cambridge University Press, 1992) pp.3–27.

36   Quoted in Masalha, *Expulsion*, p.128.

37   Cmd 5479: Palestine Royal Commission Report (London: HMSO, 1937), pp.389–92.

38   Oscar I. Janowsky, *Nationalities and National Minorities* (New York: Macmillan, 1945), p.136.

in situ. Nor were the Nazis alone in adopting this more radical approach. Axis allies, such as Romania and Hungary, were also willing to follow suit with their own deportations and mass killings of Jews and gypsies, while Stalin's NKVD, in 1943 and 1944, attempted a Soviet version of the deportation/extermination mix, with regard to a number of minorities, including Volga Germans, Tatars and several Caucasian Moslems, all of whom were collectively slated as 'enemies' of state and people.[39]

If it was, then, the totalitarian states who, in the context of the Second World War, dealt with their troublesome minorities in the most deadly genocidal fashion, Western sanction for the avowedly non-genocidal concept of 'transfer' still offered, in its immediate aftermath and to those who wanted to be seen to be liberal, an alternative route to national 'homogenisation'. For states in Eastern Europe who wanted to go down this route, an explicit green light came from Churchill, no less:

> Expulsion is the method, which as far as we have been able to see, will
> be the most satisfactory and lasting ... I am not alarmed by the
> disentanglement of populations, nor even by these large transferences,
> which are more possible in modern conditions than they ever were
> before.[40]

Between 1945 and 1947, some ten to twelve million people, mostly German people, were evicted on this say-so, with horrendous suffering and huge death tolls en route.[41] And if the liberal West could contemplate with equanimity the ethnic homogenisation of Poland and Czechoslovakia in this way, why not Palestine too?

It is Masahla's contention that in the Zionist camp this desired goal was not confined to the more obviously ultra-rightist groupings associated with Zionist revisionism but rather was central to the mainstream *yishuv* agenda. If he is correct, aligned to my suggestion that the broader international community was increasingly ready to turn a blind eye to, countenance, or even endorse the active implementation of ethnic cleansing programmes by other new, duly constituted and recognised nation-states, then the proposals of the second of our protagonists must seem all the more remarkable.

The group Ihud (Unity) was founded in Palestine in 1942. Its leading lights and guiding spirits were two internationally renowned figures, Martin Buber and

---

39   See Robert Conquest, *The Nation Killers: The Soviet Deportation of Nationalities* (New York: Macmillan, 1970) and Aleksandr Nekrich, *The Punished Peoples: The Deportation and Tragic Fate of Soviet Minorities at the End of the Second World War* (New York: W.W. Norton, 1978).

40   Churchill speech to House of Commons, 15 December 1944, quoted in Neal Ascherson, 'The tragically easy path to "ethnic cleansing"', *The Independent on Sunday*, 9 August 1992.

41   See Alfred-Manuel de Zayas, *The German Expellees*, English edn, (Basingstoke: Macmillan, 1993).

Judah Magnes, and it was they who presented the Ihud case to an international body, the Anglo-American Committee of Inquiry, when they considered the future of Palestine in 1946. Buber and Magnes were both committed Zionists but theirs was a distinctly minority tradition in Zionist thought. Buber, a Viennese-born theologian and philosopher, combined a mystical, even visionary love of Judaism – (and *Eretz Israel*) with an acute desire for dialogue with the universal in all mankind. Magnes, the president of the Hebrew University of Jerusalem, where Buber, from 1938, was a professor, was a self-confessed dissenter from conventional wisdoms. In his native America in the First World War, he had raised hackles in establishment quarters by denouncing militarism in favour of what became a lifelong commitment to pacifism; even before that he had rejected political state-oriented Herzlian Zionism in favour of the cultural version associated with the writings of Ahad Ha'am.[42]

Ihud's origins, thus, lay firmly in the idea of a Zionist modus vivendi with native Palestinian Arab society, as pursued in the 1920s and early 1930s by the pacifist-leaning Brit Shalom ('Covenant of Peace'), of which Buber and, indirectly, Magnes were also leading players. Of course, as has often been pointed out, Brit Shalom, and its immediate successor Kedma Mizraha ('Forward to the East') were extremely marginal to the Zionism of this period. They were neither movements, nor parties, so much as a small circle of like-minded liberal Jewish academics and intellectuals, which was also, incidentally, notable for the absence of like-minded Palestinians.[43] Nevertheless what they lacked in numbers, Jewish or Palestinian, they made up for with proposals for the future of Palestine which, because they were intrinsically different from those of mainstream Zionism, amounted to an alternative political programme.

Thus, while the mainstream from 1942 onwards had been explicit in its demands for a Jewish state in Palestine, either in all or in part, Ihud, arguing on a basic Brit Shalom premise, rejected the notion completely. Like Renner earlier, this did not entail the renunciation of the idea of 'nation'; on the contrary, it celebrated it. But, as Ihud declared in its 1946 submission to the Committee of Inquiry, Jewish national goals 'must of necessity be carried out without encroaching upon the vital rights of any other community'.[44] What was actually meant by this was that, if the foundation of a Jewish polity in Palestine involved partition and population transfer, this would, in its eyes, be morally and

---

42   For more on Buber's thought and life see Martin Buber, *On Zion: The History of an Idea* (New York: Schocken Books, 1973), Paul A. Schilpp and Maurice Friedmawn (eds), *The Philosophy of Martin Buber* (La Salle, Il.: Open Court, 1967). For Magnes, see A.A. Goren, (ed.), *Dissenter in Zion: From the Writings of Judah L. Magnes* (Cambridge, MA and London: Harvard University Press, 1982).

43   On Brit Shalom, Paul R. Mendes-Flohr (ed.), *A Land of Two Peoples: Martin Buber on Jews and Arabs* (New York, 1983), pp.9–10, 72–75.

44   *Arab-Jewish Unity: Testimony before the Anglo-American Commission for the Ihud (Union) by Judah Magnes and Martin Buber* (London, 1947), p.47.

politically unacceptable. Even with the urgency for the immediate immigration of the remnant of Holocaust survivors, Buber and Magnes, therefore, were rejecting the standard nationalist assumption of *sacro egoismo*, namely 'that the egotistic pursuit of the interest of one's own group, even if it involves the disregard and abuse of another group, is "sacred" and hence morally self-sufficient'.[45] Or, put another way, if tolerance of the 'other' is genuinely to mean anything, this can only be achieved politically through accommodation, compromise and cooperation. In the context of Palestine, this could only mean relinquishing the idea of one's own national state and instead learning to share both it and its land with the other people who inhabited it. In short, Ihud advocated binationalism: one Palestine, one state, two nations – Arab and Jewish – preferably in turn integrated into a broader, federal system of Middle Eastern states.

Retrospectively one can see that Ihud's proposed mechanism for arriving at this formula was deeply flawed. In an attempt to avoid the problems of a majority/minority imbalance it advocated controlled Jewish immigration over a protracted period of time in order to create a demographic equilibrium between the two communities. If this amounted to a rather clumsy and unsatisfactory technical fix it was, nevertheless, an acknowledgment of the primary difference between nation-states and binational or multinational ones. In the former, the issue of minority community access to national resources either does not arise or is entirely at the discretion of the state. By contrast, in consociational experiments such as Canada, former Yugoslavia and Belgium, the equitable sharing of resources among national communities has been of the essence, while failure to deliver on this score has also, in the recent case of Yugoslavia, obversely been a key factor in its downfall.

All this is reminiscent of the problems of national intolerance Renner had been trying to circumvent in Central Europe. Ihud did not advocate his scheme per se but, in insisting on a non-territorial, decentralist solution, with the Swiss cantonal system as its model for emulation, the Ihud plan clearly had many aspects in common with Renner. And, like Renner's champion, Wolf, Ihud would have preferred not to have been speaking about minorities or minority rights at all, noting that the distinction between majority and minority was what had failed at the Paris Peace Conference.[46] Both Renner's scheme and Ihud's scheme were thus implicitly geared towards a concept of state in which resources were intended to be equitably shared between different ethnic communities. Which is why perhaps, in the last analysis, and putting aside the straightforward hatred which many Arabs and Jews were feeling for each other in 1946, mainstream Zionism so unequivocally rejected the Ihud plan.

It is not, and has never been, enough for the modern state simply to be. Its

---

45   Quoted from Mendes-Flohr, *A Land of Two Peoples*, p.16.
46   *Arab-Jewish Unity*, p.28.

survival is dependent on the success of its developmental agenda, which entails not only what it can seek to deliver to those who are defined within its 'universe of obligation' but also how it can successfully define its place within a politically and economically competitive system of nation-states. To achieve this elusive goal requires both the sense that the state is genuinely sovereign and, hence, more problematically but crucially, its ability to harness and indeed maximise whatever natural resources or assets, including people, are available within its territorial space. By proposing both decentralisation and joint action between the two communities, Ihud was accused by the Zionists of holding their would-be developmental agenda as a hostage to fortune. 'The problem is how to make of independence an instrument of development not a stranglehold on development,' argued Moshe Shertok, the avowedly doveish political secretary of the Jewish Agency.[47] The Ihud plan, in his view, would give to the 'static' element, that is the Arabs, a veto over the 'dynamic' one, the Jews, implying that this would cramp its style and slow the pace of what would of necessity (given the Zionist agenda for a mass absorption of Jewish immigrants) have to be a fast-speed developmental programme. James Parkes, interestingly, in also rejecting binationalism at this time, seems to have shared these sentiments: 'The Arabs have shown complete unwillingess to accept the pace or further growth of the Jewish community' which, he noted, was 'a vigorous body … which has performed miracles in the restoration of fertility and activity to the country'.[48]

But if Arabs and Jews could not share Palestine any more than Jews and Poles in Poland, did this, then, amount to a zero-sum game? Parkes, albeit guardedly, implied as much when he ventured that 'Arabs who might find it intolerable to live under Jewish rule' might move to surrounding underpopulated Arab countries.[49] Parkes did not go on to propose exactly how this would happen, except to cite, as others had done previously, the highly misleading precedent of the Greek–Turkish exchange, as if to suggest that, under the aegis of the League's successor authority, the UN, any such relocation could be both humane and acceptable.

In practice, what followed with regard to Palestine was neither. The UN was, nevertheless, deeply implicated. In proposing the partition of Palestine in 1947, it allotted some 350 000 Palestinian Arabs to the would-be state of Israel. The majority of these people, as well as more significant numbers in border territories seized by Israel under cover of its war of independence in 1948, were then expelled, not primarily, it should be added, by 'aberrant' elements, such as Irgun

---

47   Moshe Shertok, 'Statement to UNSCOP', July 1947, quoted from extract 'Bi-nationalism is unworkable', in Paul R. Mendes-Flohr and Jehuda Reinharz (ed.), *The Jew in the Modern World* (New York and Oxford: Oxford University Press, 1980), pp.475–76.

48   James Parkes, *An Enemy of the People: Antisemitism* (London: Penguin, 1945) p.136.

49   Ibid.

and Lehi, on the extreme right of the Zionist spectrum, but by the newly-created Israeli defence forces acting on directives issued by prime minister Ben-Gurion and his senior advisers. Some three quarters of a million Palestinians in all were ethnically cleansed in this way.[50]

It is only against the actual 1948 and after record of Israel, as of that of post-1919 Poland, that a fair evaluation of the Ihud plan, and that of Wolf's compromise of Renner, can be set. Both attempted to put into practice a moral politics, both sought to initiate dialogues with the 'other' side, founded on compromise and mutual recognition in place of national chauvinism and conflict. Each also represented, in its own way, an attempt at lateral thinking, diluting the idea of national sovereignty at a time when it was was becoming an unquestionable, and hence non-negotiable, wisdom. In so doing, their alternative state models offered otherwise unconsidered possibilities for coexistence, especially of value to ethnically mixed societies. But in a world where the attempt to translate the idea of national self-determination into nation-states was increasingly de rigueur, the problem of ethnic diversity in the state was hardly a marginal or isolated one.

Perhaps it is no accident, therefore, that attempts to find a genuine and humane solution came so often from Jewish sources. Of all peoples, Jews historically knew what it meant to be not simply a persecuted minority but a dispersed one at that. Their specific predicament was now, however, fast becoming a universal one. In 1945, Oscar Janowsky, who had devoted his scholarly life to the issue, warned that, unless we 'find the way not only to tolerate national–cultural differences but also to unite majorities and minorities organically in the structure of the state', the alternative would be violence and extermination.[51] At the same time, another Jewish intellectual, the jurist Raphael Lemkin, was almost single-handedly lobbying the UN to introduce a convention on genocide, which in the light of wartime events in Europe, he demanded, needed international action in order to safeguard minorities for the future.[52] The paradox was that the convention duly became part of international law in 1948, at the very juncture when the UN charter was reaffirming the nation-state's right to non-interference from outside powers, as if this principle was sacrosanct. If

---

50 Historiographical equivocation, obviating Israeli government responsibility for the post-April 1948 expulsions, must be put to rest with the archival findings of Benny Morris's *The Birth of the Palestinian Refugee Problem* even though he, himself, found no written evidence of an actual 'expulsion policy'. Similarly, Masalha, *Expulsion*, who also covers these events through the archives concerning the then current transfer committee, notes on p.194 that Ben-Gurion, in his war diaries, freely referred to it as the Committee for Removal and Expulsion. It was the censors, after the events who renamed it the Committee for Evacuation and Repatriation.

51 Janowsky, *Nationalities*, p.5.

52 Raphael Lemkin, *Axis Rule in Occupied Europe* (Washington, DC: Carnegie Endowment for International Peace, 1944).

genocide scholars, among others, today look to the UN, its genocide convention and international law as the best way to safeguard minorities and protect them from violence and collective abuse from the state, one needs to weigh against this the words of Leo Kuper, the authoritative and sober doyen of the subject: 'the United Nations, for all practical purposes' defends the right of 'the sovereign territorial state … as an integral part of its sovereignty … to commit genocide'.[53] Michael Ignatieff, after visiting Halabja, the Kurdish town which was the site of an infamous Iraqi chemical attack in 1988, reached his own conclusion: 'you realise one thing very clearly: autonomy will never do … for a people who have known genocide, there is only one thing that will do: a nation-state of their own'.[54]

These sobering thoughts might incline one to be less kindly disposed to the proposals of either Wolf or Ihud, to see them as at best naïve, at worst the sort of meddling which actually makes the situation of minority groups more, not less, vulnerable. Certainly, Wolf in the First World War and its aftermath, and the Buber–Magnes group in the period leading up to Israeli independence, were often vilified as well as marginalised by mainstream Zionism not only for daring publicly to challenge its claim to primacy within Jewish politics but also for undermining the logic, and indeed morality, of its nation-statist case. Israeli leaders today would not be diffident in reminding us that Jewish victimhood and suffering are the strongest single reason why there has to be a Jewish state. Polish leaders would similarly intone their own tragic narrative as just cause for the existence of Poland. Yet these 'two saddest nations on earth'[55] would also insist that they have been scrupulous in their treatment of minority groups, that in Poland today, German, Jewish and Byelorussian minorities have equality before the law; that in Israel, Arabs have not only full rights of citizenship but, as Muslims and Christians, an autonomy based on the traditional millet system. Even Begin, the ultra-rightist disciple of Zionist revisionism, claimed in his period post-1977 as prime minister, a scrupulous regard on this account, pointing out that the national minority rights which were part of the Zionist platform for Poland and elsewhere in the diaspora were always intended to be honoured with regard to Israel's non-Jewish inhabitants, and that this extended to the occupied West Bank and Gaza, should these territories have been formally annexed by Israel.[56] After all, independent post-1919 Poland, like post-1948 Israel, can justly claim to have been neither notably nasty nor totalitarian polities. All they asked for was to be normal, like other 'nations'.

---

53   Leo Kuper, *Genocide: Its Political Use in the 20th Century* (New Haven, 1981), p.161.

54   Ignatieff, *Blood*, p.151.

55   The verdict of a poem by Antoni Slominski restated in Eva Hoffman, 'On the two saddest Nations on Earth', *2B* vol.iv (1996), pp.166–73.

56   See Colin Shindler, *Israel, Likud and the Zionist Dream: Power Politics and Ideology from Begin to Netanyahu* (London: I.B. Tauris, 1995) p.89.

Yet it also has to be recognised that their achievement of 'normality' was founded on the fact that the majority of those who did not fit into their conceptions of peoplehood were ultimately removed or expunged from their state territories. In the case of Poland, outside forces were clearly critical: the German genocide of the Jews, and then the Allies' rubber-stamping of the expulsion of millions of Germans as part of the 1945 Yalta deal by which the country's eastern and western borders were recast. In the case of Israel it was, in first president Weizmann's words, the 'miraculous clearing of the land: the miraculous simplification of Israel's task',[57] as if what had happened to the Arabs in 1948 was the result of some deus ex machina power. Yet can one imagine what Poland and Israel would be like if these events had not taken place and if the majority of these diverse peoples had not been so ejected or eliminated? In Israel, today, Arabs are only tolerated because they are now an absolute minority. Largely isolated, vulnerable, the butt of a constant hostility, as attested to, for instance, in a 1958 letter from Atallah Mansour to Martin Buber,[58] Israeli Arabs remain, in practice, second class citizens with no stake in the Jewish state, and with few friends in it bar those like Buber, who, until his death in 1965, remained constant to his tolerant, multicultural vision. In Poland, there is a difference. There is a nostalgia for the country's lost Jewish community, so much so that it is now apparently even chic to claim Jewish descent. But would this still be the case if, as in the 1920s and 1930s, 10 per cent of the country's overall population, or 30 or 40 per cent of its major towns' population, were actually composed of Jews? Of course, Poland today does treat the remnants of its Jewry with considerable care. But one might cynically argue that this is because good diplomatic and commercial relations with the West demand it. Instead of the Jews, it is Poland's gypsies who are abused, attacked and forced to flee.[59] If this does not add up to Poland or Israel being comparable in their treatment of minorities with, say, modern Serbia or Turkey, if their present-day homogeneity has been good luck rather than premeditated and malicious design and if, indeed, they can be exempted from a good two score of post-1945 genocides perpetrated by states mostly against minority peoples,[60] neither, nevertheless, can claim to be the product of a moral politics.

But perhaps this is where Wolf and Ihud were at their most naïve. Both

---

57   Quoted in Masalha, *Expulsion*, p.175.

58   Mendes-Flohr, *A Land of Two Peoples*, pp.281–2.

59   For the gypsies' current situation in Poland, see Margaret Brearley, 'The Roma/Gypsies of Europe: a persecuted people', Jewish Policy Research (JPR) Policy Paper no.3 (1996), p.27. Antisemitism also continues to flourish on the ultra-right of the Polish political and societal spectrum. See JPR's *Antisemitism: World Report, 1996* (London and New York: JPR, 1996), pp.189–97.

60   See the research findings of Barbara Harff and Ted Robert Gurr, 'Toward Empirical Theory of Genocides and Politicides: Identification and Measurement of Cases since 1945', *International Studies Quarterly* (1988), pp.359–71.

believed that the antidote to nation-state *realpolitik* was an operation of humanistic principles wielded by a superior authority: an international community which would act for justice, fair play and tolerance. Both Wolf's proposals and Ihud's did, indeed, receive sympathetic hearings before such higher authorities, but with no serious long-term outcome. Consider, instead, the more recent parallel, Bosnia, and the degree to which the international community via the Owen–Vance plan, or even the later Dayton accord, actively promoted or endorsed the destruction of a multi-ethnic society, the degree to which it helped facilitate the creation of a greater Serbia, or an enlarged Croatia – the degree to which it was at the very least, an accessory, after the fact, to both ethnic cleansing and sub-genocide.[61]

In other words, before we can even consider a contemporary international politics of tolerance we have to recognise the international system's irredeemably schizophrenic nature. Intellectually its leadership claims the moral high ground: liberal, tolerant, concerned for minorities, ready to listen at every opportunity to the latter-day likes of a Wolf or a Magnes. The actual reality of this Western-dominated world order, its political economy, and hence its power relations, is, by contrast, little short of social darwinian. The only way to survive in it is either to start out strong or to become so. And whether this is by a top-down, command economy like centralisation, involving the absolute control and consolidation of one's territorial resources and assets, or by the more fashionable embrace of the global market, one thing does not seem in doubt: one's population will be required to adapt themselves accordingly. And where parts of it cannot adapt, cannot be socially engineered, cannot or will not conform to some preconceived national 'type', they simply become a surplus to requirement or, more dangerously still, an obstacle to the nation-state building agenda. This is the logic of the nation-state, a logic which actually does not need toleration because having nicely tidied up or airbrushed out the elements that do not or will not fit, there is nothing sufficiently different to tolerate. When Janowsky, thinking of eastern Europe, wrote in 1945 that 'the tolerant nation-state is not enough' he was of course more than right.[62] The tolerant nation-state is a contradiction in terms. The very idea of minorities in such a state ought to fill us with alarm. The moral as well as political strength of Renner, Wolf, Buber or Magnes is that they offer us quite different directions, away from the language of national agendas, dominations and endgoals towards one of orientations, communities, regions, decentralised federations – and, by inference, one might venture, away from global economies to a sustainability of human scale. Ihud's programme talked of a politics of 'together with', 'alongside' not 'against'. Is this part of the healing, the *tikkun*, I wonder, which

61   See, for instance, Noel Malcolm, *Bosnia: A Short History* (London and Basingstoke: Macmillan, 1994), pp.241–51.

62   Janowsky, *Nationalities*, p.134.

the planet's peoples in the twenty-first century so desperately need, if they are to have a chance of collectively surviving it?

Acknowledgment

This paper was first published in *Patterns of Prejudice*, vol.34 no.2 (2000), http://www.tandf.co.uk/journals/titles/0031322X.html.

PART II

Philosemitism, Antisemitism and Intolerance

Chapter 6

Jonah the Jew: The Evolution of a Biblical Character

Yvonne Sherwood

Extracting a sense of a character from a biblical text is by no means a simple process.[1] Biblical narratives are notoriously gap-filled and enigmatic and, unlike characters in nineteenth-century realist fiction, the characters are not so much described as inferred through a process of reader response. This chapter explores how the figure of Jonah has been read through Christian eyes in a way that validates the Christian 'universalistic' gospel and denigrates the anachronistic 'nationalist' Jew. Pictures of a dour, snarling Jonah, watching bitterly as the gentiles are forgiven, still cast their shadow over twentieth-century Christian readings, ironically exposing the unwitting sectarianism of a tradition that has prided itself on its universalism.

Making Characters

The literary theorist Roland Barthes claims that readers form an impression of a character in a novel by unconsciously picking up elements of characterisation, which he terms *semes*. These 'semes' can be hints of traits from the character's actions, evocation of the character's internal thoughts, as well as the most obvious clues, the adjectives attached to the character by the narrator. Reading *Middlemarch*, for example, we mix the author's observations about Dorothea (that she is 'open, ardent and not in the least self-admiring') with her admiration for Casaubon and evidence from her own thoughts, which are rather too heavily weighed down with altruism and extracts from Pascal's *Pensées*.[2] These semes mix to create the illusion of a person, the flavour of a personality, which Barthes compares to the odour of a dish or the bouquet of a wine.[3]

As has often been observed, reading a biblical text is quite a different matter to reading nineteenth century realist novels because, as Eric Auerbach famously

---

1   The original paper was first written and presented in 1996. Since then, I have had time to develop some of the ideas here into a book-length study: Yvonne Sherwood, *A Biblical Text and Its Afterlives: The Survival of Jonah in Western Culture* (Cambridge: Cambridge University Press, 2000).

2   G. Eliot, *Middlemarch* (Penguin: Harmondsworth, 1985), p.32.

3   R. Barthes, *S/Z*, trans. R. Miller (Oxford: Basil Blackwell, 1990), p.67.

commented, everything is 'fraught with background'.[4] The biblical authors only attach adjectives to characters on a need-to-know basis. Thus we are told that Bathsheba is beautiful and that Esau is 'an hairy man' and Jacob 'a smooth man' (as the Authorised Version gloriously puts it) because these adjectives are essential to the working of the plot. Very rarely do we get intimations of the character's psychology by a brief glimpse into his/her mind, as when Hezekiah, having been told that his sons will be carried away to Babylon thinks '[at least] there will be peace and security in my days' (Isa. 39.8; 2 Kings 20.19). Characters in the biblical world, like people in our own world, do not come conveniently wearing labels that sum up their characters in a few pithy adjectives, but are revealed only by their words, actions and interactions with other characters, all of which are open to multiple interpretations.

If you want to get a sense of the difference between biblical narrative and the modern novel, compare the biblical intimations about David, in many ways the Hebrew Bible's most developed and rounded character, with Joseph Heller's *God Knows*,[5] which transforms the biblical David into the male lead in a modern novel. The biblical text sketches in David's actions, but leaves us guessing about his motives;[6] *God Knows* begins inside David's head, as he watches Abishag, describes her at sensuous length, and ruminates on the disillusionment of old age. Bathsheba, in Heller's novel, is not simply beautiful but is swamped in adjectives: 'large and wide-hipped', 'tall, brazen, selfish and formidable',[7] and we are even told how she dyes her hair with a mixture of saffron and loofstrife. The relationship with the reader is far more intimate and more confessional than the biblical text: it is as if David, as a man very much of our times, has a painful desire to bare his soul to the reader–analyst and to tell us everything, indeed to tell us too much, so that the picture becomes saturated and overblown with detail.

Such a picture could not be more removed from the biblical narratives, as they tell their story starkly, mysteriously, as if words were on ration. These texts, by their very omissions, make us aware of the work we have to do as readers, the inferences that we have to make, the gaps we have to fill, if we are to give even the vaguest outline to the biblical characters. The sheer sparsity of the biblical

---

4   E. Auerbach, 'Odysseus' Scar', in D. Lodge (ed.), *Twentieth Century Literary Criticism: A Reader* (London: Longman, 1972), pp.316–32.

5   J. Heller, *God Knows* (London: Black Swan, 1995).

6   Thus Shimon Bar-Efrat muses, 'Why did [David] bring Michal back to him after she had become the wife of Paltiel the son of Lish/ Was it because of love, because he had wed her at the price of a hundred foreskins of the Philistines, or perhaps because she was the daughter of the former king (2 Sam. 3.14–16)?' For an entire list of whys and speculations about David's motives, see S. Bar-Efrat, *Narrative Art in the Bible* (Sheffield; Almond Press, 1989), p.78. For a discussion of characterisation in the Hebrew Bible, see also Adele Berlin, *Poetics and Interpretation of Biblical Narrative* (Sheffield: Almond Press, 1983), pp.23–42.

7   Heller, *God Knows*, p. 8.

narratives makes them an excellent prooftext for the theories of the 'reader-response' critics such as Stanley Fish who argue that readers are active, rather than passive, in the act of reading and that readers in a very real sense *make* characters and texts.[8] According to Fish, readers construct the characters and themes of narratives according to the ideology of the interpretative communities to which they belong.

This chapter is about the evolution of a particular biblical character, Jonah, and one of the strongest of interpretative communities, the Christian church. It is a study of Jonah and Fish, not in the old-fashioned sense of speculations over whether Jonah's scaly friend was shark or whale, myth or reality,[9] but a study that looks at the way the evolution of Jonah the Jew seems to confirm some of Stanley Fish's claims about what readers do with texts. In this study I shall be looking at the way in which the history of Jonah's development confirms Fish's two main theses: that readings are not governed by the text and are potentially arbitrary, and that readings are controlled by the needs and preconceptions of interpretative communities. I shall also be looking at the durability and strength of this Christian reading of Jonah which is now taken as self-evident, natural and somehow *in* the text.

Making Jonah: Jonah–Christ and Jonah–Jew

Jonah begins his 'life' more as a symbol than a character, as an Old Testament type of Christ. The tradition of strong and audacious Christian reading is inaugurated by the Jesus figure himself,[10] when he interprets himself, cryptically, as representing the so-called 'sign of Jonah'. The statement is open to multiple interpretations. Luke sees the point of the analogy being Christ's and Jonah's mission and imagines this present generation being condemned by the Ninevites for failing to repent at the preaching of one greater than Jonah (Lk. 11:29–32).

---

8   S. Fish, *Is There a Text in This Class? The Authority of Interpretative Communities* (Cambridge, MA: Harvard University Press, 1980).

9   During the nineteenth century, under the joint pressure of scientific advance and conventions of realism in fiction, commentators felt obliged to explain that there was nothing 'fishy' about the book of Jonah, and that a man-swallowing fish and a fish-surviving man could exist. Explanations ranged from fisherman's yarns of sharks and sea calves found with entire oxen or men inside them, to the more prosaic thesis that Jonah was rescued by a ship called *The Big Fish*, and accommodated for three nights in an inn called *At the Sign of the Whale*. For a fascinating tour of the various proposals, see E.D. Pusey, *The Minor Prophets with a Commentary, Explanatory and Practical* (London: Walter Smith and Innes, 1891), pp.257–9.

10   As the Douai Old Testament puts it in a marginal note: 'who could have thought that Jonas had been a figure of our saviour's death and resurrection unless [Jesus] himself had so expounded it', cit. R.H. Bowers, *The Legend of Jonah* (The Hague: Martinus Nijhoff, 1971), p. 39.

Matthew takes the analogy further and, fiddling the maths a bit, compares Jonah's three days in his fishy Sheol to Jesus' three days in the tomb (Matt. 12.38–40).

The Church Fathers, as disciples of Christ, follow the precedent set down in the gospels, copying not only the Jesus–Jonah equation, but the interpretative freedom with which it is developed.[11] In early Christian readings, only two points are fixed: the fact that Jonah is *somehow* a sign for Jesus, and the fact that the Old Testament is properly interpreted by being subsumed in a Christian master narrative,[12] and around these two strands the Church Fathers weave elaborate, chaotic and infinitely creative typologies. Jonah's flight is the incarnation; the storm is the suffering of humanity *or* Christ's passion; the sailors are Pilate or the Roman authorities; and the fish is variously the devil, time, death or hell. Most commonly, Jonah descending into the fish is a symbol of Christ's harrowing of hell, Jonah's vomiting forth is a sign of the resurrection, and Jonah preaching to the Ninevites is a sign of Christ's ministry to the 'gentiles' or, as St Bede majestically put it, 'the Church ornate with the glory of all virtue'.[13]

The tradition of reading the book of Jonah as a symbolic microcosm of the Christian gospel upgrades the peculiar narrative into a triumphant tale of heroism and sacrifice, and the figure of Jonah, not surprisingly, comes off well from the Christ–Jonah equation. It is this interpretation (represented in Figure 6.1) that is enshrined in the stained glass in our churches and cathedrals, where Jonah is depicted as a noble, dignified character, triumphantly stepping free from the fish's maw with the dignity of a Christ figure and the heroism of a St George. Crucially, though the Fathers relish the way in which the repentance of the Ninevites, the uncircumcised, humiliates the circumcised,[14] Jonah, at this stage in his development, is not a Jew. On the contrary, he is one of 'us', rather than one of 'them', the proto-Christ figure who acts as a prologue to the master-narrative and conveniently anticipates the transition from the Old to the New Testament.

Within this strong collective reading, however, a single dissident voice makes itself heard. Augustine, unlike his contemporaries, sees Jonah as an

---

11   'For freedom Christ has set us free,' claims the writer to the Galatians (Gal. 5:1) and, in his interpretation of Jonah, Christ releases his followers into interpretative freedom. (This claim comes, incidentally, after a very creative reading of the Abraham narrative.) If one sense of being Christian is to read texts like Christ, then this adds a whole new dimension to the motif of shaking off the yoke of the law.

12   For a discussion of Christianity as the ultimate master-narrative, see F. Jameson, *The Political Unconscious: Narrative as a Socially Symbolic Act* (London: Methuen, 1981), especially pp.22ff.

13   St Bede, cit. Bowers, *The Legend*, p.40.

14   St Jerome, 'The foreskin believes; but circumcision remains faithless' (*creditit praeputium et circumcisio permanet infidelis*), cit. P. Antin (ed.), *St Jerome's In Ionam* (Sources Chrétiennes 43) (Paris: Les Editions du Cerf, 1956), p.95.

6.1 Jesus-Jonah striding confidently from the fish's maw/the tomb. *Jonah en de walvis*, by Dirk Crabeth 1564 in St Janskerk, Gouda. Copyright Stitching Fonds Goudse Glazen.

embodiment of 'carnal Judaism'[15] infuriated at the idea that God is extending his project of salvation to the gentile nations. Until the Reformation this reading lies dormant, as a muted counter-voice, but in the interpretation of Luther it grows and swells. Luther's reading is a new departure because it no longer interprets Jonah purely as a type, a symbol or cardboard cut-out pointing to Christ, but as a creature with a psychology, a motivation, a character (almost). Criticising the Fathers for their 'silly deference'[16] to the prophet and their inability to see his faults, Luther goes on to remedy the omission with zeal. He describes how Jonah refused to go and preach because he still retained an outmoded 'Jewish, carnal idea of God' as the 'exclusive' property of Israel,[17] and how he thought, like the psalmist, typically 'Jewish' thoughts such as 'Pour out your anger on the nations who do not know you and the kingdoms who do not call on your name' (Ps. 79:6).[18] Luther's reading is a turning point because instead of seeing Jonah as a representative of carnal Judaism, as Augustine does, he starts to look at Jonah's character and to ask what is going on in his mind. We even begin to glimpse elements of an external appearance, albeit rather caricatured, as Luther suggests how Jonah's green eyes flash with jealousy over the forgiveness of the Ninevites.[19]

In Luther's reading, the Christ–Jonah equation is loosened, and saint- or Christ-like qualities are stripped from Jonah and transferred entirely to the gentile Ninevites. Instead of being a suprahuman Christ-like figure, Jonah, eyes flashing green with jealousy, begins to appear as a subhuman monstrous, 'odd' figure,[20] while the Ninevites and sailors, the Gentile representatives in the text, 'shine forth' in contrast as 'saints' and 'pure angels of God'.[21] For Luther, Jonah becomes 'the first to make Judaism contemptible and superfluous',[22] for by preaching to the Gentiles he participates in the invalidation and anachronisation of his own tradition.[23] Once the theme of the text – the supersession of Judaism by Christianity – is established, Luther finds it everywhere: in a vague line from Jonah's psalm, which Luther interprets as being a criticism of those who 'rely on law' and 'snub the gospel of grace',[24] and even in the parable of the plant and the

---

15   Augustine, *Epistulae* 102: 6, 35, cit. Y. Duval *Le livre de Jonas dans la littérature chrétienne grecque et latine*, vol.2 (Paris: Etudes Augustiniennes, 1973), p.515.

16   Luther, 'Lectures on Jonah', in H.C. Oswald (ed.), *Minor Prophets II: Jonah, Habakkuk* (*Luther's Works*, 19) (Saint Louis: Concordia, 1974), p.45.

17   Luther, *Jonah*, p.50.

18   Ibid., p.93.

19   Ibid., p.93.

20   Ibid., p.91.

21   Ibid., p.85.

22   Ibid., p.94.

23   This theme of Jonah working against his own interests comes into its own in twentieth-century satirical readings (see p.108).

24   Luther, *Jonah*, p.81.

worm, which Luther reads as a symbol of the 'wild fruitless plant' of Judaism being destroyed by the poor crucified worm, Christ.[25]

If the contours of Jonah the Jew are sketched by Augustine and Luther, Jonah the Jew as a character comes into his own in the Enlightenment, with the birth of critical biblical studies. Enlightenment thinkers and the first biblical critics imagined themselves shaking themselves free of the 'tutelage' of the past and stepping boldly out into a new objectivity,[26] but in fact the *philosophes* carried over the image of the Jew from Christian mythology and reinscribed and secularised Christian anti-semitism.[27] Similarly, critical biblical scholars, who saw themselves as escaping from the naïveté of the pre-critical era, reinscribed an Augustinian and Lutheran reading of the text. The language may be more sophisticated and Luther's embarrassingly overcreative interpretations of the plant and worm may have been dropped, but once the surface rhetoric is scratched away and you look at the deep mythology, a clear line of continuity can be traced between Augustine's description of Jonah as an embodiment of 'carnal Judaism', Luther's idea that Jonah had a 'Jewish, carnal idea of God',[28] and modern sketches of Jonah as a representative of '*die fleishlichen Juden*' (the 'carnal' or 'fleshy' Jew).[29]

In the Enlightenment the character of Jonah is not only fleshed out, but is defined by his unspiritual fleshiness. The flicker of characteristics that we have noticed in Luther – the green-eyed envy, the hatred of other nations – swells and grows until Jonah becomes a fully rounded, recognisable character, the image of a stigmatised European shtetl Jew. It is probably no accident that, at the time of the rise of the novel, Jonah evolves into a character, and it is certainly no accident that he is shaped by images of Jews as a racial subclass. If you look up Voltaire's entry for '*juifs*' in the *Dictionnaire Philosophique* you find that they are 'an ignorant and barbarous people, who have long united the most sordid avarice with the most detestable superstition and the most invincible hatred for every people by whom they are tolerated and enriched':[30] if you look up Jonah in a

---

25   Ibid., p.103 (cf. Matt. 21.19).

26   'Enlightenment is man's release from his self-incurred tutelage. Tutelage is man's inability to make use of his understanding without direction from another ... *Sapere aude*! [Dare to know]': I. Kant, *What is Enlightenment?*, ed. and trans. L.W. Beck (Chicago: 1955), p.286.

27   Thus the historian Arthur Herzberg writes 'the vital link, the man who skipped over the Christian centuries and provided a new, international, secular, anti-Jewish rhetoric in the name of European culture rather than religion was Voltaire' (A. Herzberg, *The French Enlightenment and the Jews*, New York: Columbia University Press, 1968, p.313). For a brief discussion of modern secular anti-semitism see also R.S. Wistrich, *Antisemitism: The Longest Hatred* (London: Methuen, 1991), pp.43–53.

28   Luther, *Jonah*, p.50.

29   Compare C.F. Keil (1833), cit. P. Friedrichsen, *Kritische Ubersicht der Verschiedenen Ansicheten von dem Buche Jonas* (Leipzig: 1841), p.172.

30   Voltaire, 'Juifs', *Dictionnaire Philosophique*, XLI, cit. R.S. Wistrich, *Antisemitism*, p.45.

Bible dictionary, you find that he has become a magnet for the same litany of adjectives, becoming, among other things, proud, vicious, envious and superstitious.

In the beginning of professional Biblical Studies was the context; biblical scholarship was not born into a vacuum. It is revealing to see just how far the book of Jonah became a mirror for this context, reflecting back to the readers their own situation. The Fathers never pretended that they were doing anything but a Christian reading of the now Old Testament, but the Enlightenment critics thought that they were looking for the real historical meaning of the text. They claimed that what they had found was a book written by a singularly enlightened Jew, designed to attack the sectarian views of a narrow nationalist group, whose views are represented in the books of Ezra and Nehemiah. Once you scratch the surface of this historical reading, however, you find that it is a mystification, a biblicised, pseudo-historicised version of contemporary political conflict. The central question of the book, which Bleek helpfully defines as 'whether it is *right* for the Jews to entertain such a hostile mindset towards all other nations',[31] locates the so-called Jewish question at the heart of the biblical text. The singularly enlightened author, is of course an image of the reader: he is a proto-philosophe, a liberal academic, a biblical Nathan the Wise and even, as Tom Paine suggests, taking the reasoning to an extreme, a *gentile*.[32] Seeing the *author* in their image gives these readers *authority* and at the same time validates the Christian position as ordained by God even during the period of the Old Testament. As the Fathers had once, less sophisticatedly, read Jonah as a sign of Christ, so the text was now read as a manifesto for universalism, a version of the New Testament question, 'Is God the God of the Jews only, or of the Gentiles also?'(Rom. 3.29) to which the only *reasonable* answer was, of course 'Yes, of the gentiles also.' The book thus became a kind of biblical *Merchant of Venice*, with Jonah, as a kind of Shylock figure, glowering over Nineveh, crying out for his pound of flesh, and the Christians arguing, sweetly and reasonably, for the mercy that droppeth as the gentle dew of heaven. Thus polemicised, and

---

31   F. Bleek, *Einleitung in das Alt Testament*, p.574, cit. E. Bickerman, 'Les deux erreurs du prophète Jonas', *Revue d'histoire et de philosophie religieuse*, 45 (1965), 232–64; my italics). For other studies of anti-Judaism in Jonah studies, see Bickerman (above) and F.W. Golka, 'Jonaexegese und Antijudaismus', *Kirche und Israel*, 1 (1986), 51–61.

32   Paine reasons 'as the book of Jonah, so far from treating of the affairs of the Jews, says nothing upon [the book's authorship], but treats altogether of the Gentiles, it is more probable that it is a book of the Gentiles than of the Jews; and that it has been written as a fable, to expose the nonsense and satirise the vicious and malignant character of a Bible prophet, or a predicting priest (T. Paine, *The Theological Works of Thomas Paine*, Boston: The Advocates of Common Sense, 1834, p.119). The author is still, as Jonathan Magonet points out, habitually seen as a liberal-minded, proto-Christian: see J. Magonet, 'Jonah', in D.N. Freedman (ed.), *The Anchor Bible Dictionary* (New York and London: Doubleday, 1992), pp.936–42.

polarised, the text became a tract for the times, a call to Jews to abandon superstition and exclusivity and come to claim their 'admission ticket to western culture'.[33] As a representative of the undesirable qualities of Judaism and a retrograde nationalist Old Testament, Jonah is given an ultimatum by God: to modernise, progress, or be thrown 'overboard'.

Neither eighteenth-century readers, nor readers who followed them in the tradition which they had defined, suspected that they were doing anything other than locating the text's real meaning. Reading in 1782, one of the earliest figureheads of professional biblical studies, J.D. Michaelis, was gratified by how easily the book yielded its message, observing that 'the meaning of the fable hits you right between the eyes'.[34] A nineteenth century writer, Friedrichsen, marvels at the way Michaelis and Eichhorn, though working independently, produced an almost identical reading, thus proving the inherent rightness of their interpretation.[35] Writing in the twentieth century, E.M. Good notes the 'remarkable unanimity … among biblical scholars (a notoriously quarrelsome lot) which might seem suspicious were it not so welcome'.[36] Convinced by the air of unanimity, an intimidating cacophony of big names, with whom it was becoming hard to disagree, Friedrichsen argues that the book is about God softening Jonah's 'hard (Jewish) heart',[37] while Good, almost two hundred years later than Michaelis, reads the book as a protest against 'xenophobia'.[38] Reading the yellowing pages of Friedrichsen in the British Library, I was struck by how contemporary the readings he was cataloguing sounded, clearly demonstrating how the earliest critics set the 'limits of the thinkable',[39] and how quickly their situated reading became canonised in the tradition.

What hit Michaelis right between the eyes, however, was not so much the secret of the words on the page, but the prevalent symbols and ideologies of his own culture. Regrettably biblical critics have not yet appreciated the fact that all readers, even our 'big names' and founding fathers, are 'cultural artefacts',[40] a product of prejudices of the *Aufklärung* as well as its advances. As we have universalised their reading, regarding it as timeless, transcendent and true, so we

---

33   Heinrich Heine, cit. E. Manuel, *The Broken Staff: Judaism Through Christian Eyes* (Cambridge, MA: Harvard University Press, 1992), p.294.

34   J.D. Michaelis, *Deutsche Übersetzung des Alten Testaments mit Anmerkungen für Ungelehrte* (Göttingen, 1782), p.106.

35   Friedrichsen, *Kritische Übersicht*, p.113.

36   E.M. Good, 'Jonah: The Absurdity of God', in *Irony in the Old Testament* (London: SPCK, 1965), pp.39–55.

37   Friedrichsen, *Kritische Übersicht*, p.116.

38   Good, 'Jonah: The Absurdity of God', p.54.

39   A. Sinfield, *Faultlines: Cultural Materialism and the Politics of Dissident Reading* (Oxford: Clarendon Press, 1992), p.172.

40   C. Geertz, *The Interpretation of Cultures* (New York: Basic Books, 1973), p.51.

have been duped by their use of the word 'universalism'. For on closer examination it becomes clear that the description of the book as an argument against sectarianism is itself based on sectarian premises. As Tamar Garb observes:

> The secularising and universalising dream of emancipation whilst purporting to be inclusive and democratising, resembled the proselytising ethos of the Christian missionaries in a fundamental way. It was premised on an eradication of difference that was by no means reciprocal. There was no negotiation of a new shared culture for Christians and Jews, involving a give and take, a symbiosis or universal respect. Rather Jews were expected to discard their cultural specificity for a more 'rational', modern', 'universal' identity and thereby enter into the 'common culture of man'.[41]

While the values of the Christian communities were valorised and made to stand for rational, universal values, the practices of Jews were devalued, parochialised and stigmatised. As Michaelis's phrase 'hitting between the eyes' unwittingly suggests, every culture has its range of vision and its blind spots, and ironically a critique of the Jews on the basis of their narrow sectarianism, is itself based on a very narrow and implicitly *Christian* understanding of what 'universalism' might mean.[42]

The picture of Jonah that emerges from the Enlightenment and that is represented in Figure 6.2 could not be further removed from the dignified Christ-like figure sanctified in stained glass. As the Christ-like Jonah is usually identified with a particular moment in the narrative – his triumphant exit from the fish tomb – so this new Jonah has a typical posture and a typical narrative moment: his anger over God's forgiveness of the Ninevites. Jonah is depicted as a repellent figure, squirming, unable to get comfortable with God's new policy of mercy, or as a vengeful character, stamping and shaking his fists. Perhaps because characters are more durable than ideas, this vengeful Jonah is now indelibly stamped on the critical imagination: we feel as if we know him, and this is not surprising, for he has not changed significantly over the last two hundred years. If the biblical text lacks adjectives and direct authorial statement, the critical tradition has stepped in and taken the author's place. If the biblical text leaves us wondering what qualities we would fix to Jonah, the critical tradition has rushed to the rescue, George Eliot-fashion, to dissipate all confusion and to

---

41   T. Garb, 'Modernity, Identity, Textuality', in L. Nochlin and T. Garb (eds), *The Jew in the Text: Modernity and the Construction of Identity* (London: Thames and Hudson, 1995), pp.20–30.

42   I myself find 'universalism' a far too roomy term to be useful: it tends to obscure cnflict by conveniently accommodating sentiments from missionary zeal to moral relativism. For an excellent critique of the way 'universalism' is used in Biblical Studies, see H.M. Orlinsky, 'Nationalism–Universalism and Internationalism in Ancient Israel', in *Essays in Biblical Culture and Bible Translation* (New York: KTAV, 1974), pp.78–116.

6.2 Repellent Jonah, furious at God's new (characteristically 'Christian') policies of universalism and mercy. Carol Christian, *Jonah* (Macmillan Bible Stories; London: Macmillan, 1996), p.37. © Illustrations Macmillan Education Ltd, 1996, reproduced by permission of Macmillan, Oxford.

pass a moral judgment. The range of adjectives that are now considered as typical of the prophet has swelled to 'mulish',[43] 'blind',[44] 'petty',[45] 'ludicrous',[46] 'good-for-nothing',[47] 'disobedient and hypocritical',[48] and even, in adjectives reminiscent of the blood libel, 'bloodthirsty', 'poisonous' and 'monstrous'.[49] And his internal world has been delineated with increasing precision: Paul Trudinger fills out the contents of Jonah's thought-bubble, as if he were a cartoon character, thus: 'It's just like God to forgive these wretched Ninevites, these outsiders. Now we will have to welcome them as fellow-members in the community of faith!'[50]

Throughout the twentieth century, Jonah as book and character remains mirror-like and conveniently reflective: as a 1920 political pamphlet on 'Biblical antisemitism' described how Jonah was a '*Judenspiegel*', a mirror for the Jewish character and Jewish guilt,[51] so Otto Kaiser, writing in 1975, sees Jonah as '*ein Bild des Judentums*', a picture of Jews, who would like God to 'annihilate their enemies with fire and sulphur'.[52] In 1912, Julius Bewer, in the still well-used ICC commentary, described how the purpose of the narrative is to teach 'the narrow, blind, prejudiced, fanatic Jews, of which Jonah is but the type',[53] that 'the love of

---

43   H.W. Wolff, *Obadiah and Jonah*, trans. M. Kohl (Minneapolis: Augsburg, 1986), p.176.

44   G. von Rad, *Old Testament Theology II; The Theology of Israel's Prophetic Traditions*, trans. D.M.G. Stalker (London: Oliver and Boyd, 1965), p.291.

45   J. Holbert, '"Deliverance Belongs to YHWH!", Satire in the Book of Jonah', *Journal for the Study of the Old Testament*, 21 (1981), p.74.

46   M. Burrows, 'The Literary Character of the Book of Jonah', in H.T. Frank and W.L. Reed (eds.), *Translating and Understanding the Old Testament: Essays in Honour of H.G. May* (Nashville: Abingdon Press, 1970), pp.82–105 (86).

47   Wolff, *Obadiah and Jonah*, p.109.

48   J.C. Holbert, 'Deliverance Belongs to YHWH!', 59–81.

49   Von Rad calls Jonah a 'religionspsychologisches Monstrum' (G. von Rad, *Der Prophet Jona*, Nuremberg: Laetare, 1950, p.11), while Leslie Allen asks 'What religious monster is this?' (L.C. Allen, *The Books of Joel, Obadiah, Jonah and Micah*, London: Hodder and Stoughton, 1976, p.229). The re-emergence of semes such as bloodthirstiness and poison reveals the deep divisions between progress and regress, myth and empiricism in the advance of modernism. For a discussion of the Enlightenment double-think, see T. Adorno and M. Horkheimer, *Dialectic of Enlightenment* (London: Verso, 1989), p.175.

50   P. Trudinger, 'Jonah: A Post-Exilic Verbal cartoon?', *The Downside Review* (April 1989), pp.142–3.

51   K. Gerecke, *Biblischer antisemitismus: Der Juden weltgeschichtlicher Charakter, Schuld und Ende in des Propheten Jonah Judenspiegel* (1909) cit. E. Bickerman, 'Les deux erreurs du prophète Jonas', p.248.

52   O. Kaiser, 'Wirklichkeit, Möglichkeit und Vorurteil. Ein Beitrag zum Verständnis des Buches Jona', *Evangelische Theologie*, 33 (1973), 91–103. (*Vorurteil* – prejudice – is an interesting title for this article, that rebounds on the writer somewhat).

53   J.A. Bewer, 'Critical and Exegetical Commentary on Jonah', in G. Mitchell Hinckley, John Merlin Powis Smith, Julius Brewer, *Critical and Exegetical Commentary on Haggai, Zechariah, Malachi and Jonah* (Edinburgh: T. and T. Clark, 1912), pp.3–65.

God is wider than the measures of man's mind/ And the heart of the Eternal is most wonderfully kind',[54] that is, to soften those hard Jewish hearts with the soothing words of Christian hymns, while Leslie Allen, writing in 1976, used Romans 3.29 as an intertext and concluded that the lesson of the text was clearly that 'Israel has no monopoly of God's loving care'.[55]

Apart from a slight modification of tone, there is little difference between pre- and post-war readings, and despite talk of Christian theology (in the abstract) being traumatised by the Shoah, there is little sense that Jonah criticism is yet feeling the reverberations. The book is still almost universally seen as a prologue to the New Testament, a trailer for the main film: thus Wilhelm Rudolph argues that the Old Testament book encapsulates the very 'quintessence of the gospel',[56] and Allen observes, without reflection or irony: 'As so often the effect of this OT book is to lay a foundation on which the NT can build.'[57] A Lutheran hierarchy between an exhausted anachronistic Judaism and a new vibrant Christianity is still in operation in the writing of prominent biblical critics. Edwin Good shows how the myopic Jonah exposes 'the untenability of the understanding of the ways of God that was then prevalent in Israel',[58] while Hans Walter Wolff observes how, by questioning God's choice of a particular people, the text 'calls into question Israel's beliefs and her ministry in the world'.[59]

As long as you look no further than the field of 'critical' biblical studies, this impression of Jonah seems unanimously supported by a whole panoply of major scholars and hence, to all practical purposes, 'true'. You only begin to feel dissonance if, for example, after a day reading about how Jonah embodied the legalistic, narrow mentality that Jesus came to rectify, you happen to look up at a stained glass window in which Jonah appears as Christ's image, rather than Christ's antithesis. Under such circumstances, you might experience the giddiness of historical relativism and interpretative vertigo, and begin to wonder how the same character can be both Christ, and if not exactly the anti-Christ, certainly the embodiment of the kind of sentiment that popular speech would label 'un-Christian'. If you are more suspicious than Edwin Good about the testimony of consensus, you might begin to suspect that the two readings have been considered persuasive not because of the way they use the details of the text (for they use them oppositely) but because they support contemporary understandings of a Christian master-narrative. In the early reading, Jonah himself is a type of Christ and prefigures a literally interpreted gospel: in the

---

54   Bewer, 'Jonah', p.64.
55   L.C. Allen, *The Books of Joel, Obadiah, Jonah and Micah*, p.194.
56   W. Rudoph, *Joel, Amos, Obadja, Jona* (Gütersloh: Gerd Mohn, 1971), p.371.
57   Allen, *The Books of Joel, Obadiah, Jonah and Micah*, p.194.
58   E.M. Good, 'Jonah: The Absurdity of God', p.54.
59   H.W. Wolff, *Obadiah and Jonah*, p.176.

post-Enlightenment readings the sentiments of the *book* of Jonah anticipate the sentiments of Christ, interpreted in a more reasonable, ecumenical, universalist fashion. Whatever chain of thoughts the contrast sets in motion, you have to admit there is something fishy here that (with apologies for the pun) seems to validate Fish's thesis that the limits on a reading are imposed, not so much by what is in the text, but by the question of how well it validates and conforms to the beliefs of the interpretative community. Perhaps the objective mandarin stance of scholarship masks a desire to be pleased, rather than convinced by a reading; perhaps readings hit us right between the eyes because we know, in advance, what a text must say.

Two Recent Twentieth-century Mutations: 'Jonah the Clown' and 'Jonah the Zionist'

Though twentieth-century critics continue to read the figure of Jonah along Enlightenment lines, they adjust his outline to suit contemporary tastes. In a recent comic twist, readers have started to read the book as a satire, using laughter to reinforce the humiliation and denigration of the prophet. The starting point of this reading was already implicit in Luther when he observed how Jonah the Jew participated in the invalidation of his own tradition, for the premise of this rather unfunny 'comic' reading is that Jonah, the fervent nationalist, converts the sailors and Ninevites despite and against himself and so hurts himself, inadvertently, like a slapstick clown. 'How the narrator laughs,' writes Wolff, 'at the Hebrew who takes great pains to flee from his God, and in the process and quite against his will, brings non-Israelites to believe in this God.'[60] Instead of merely depicting Jonah as a malevolent character and encouraging us to criticise him, the enlightened author is now seen as setting Jonah up as a figure of fun and getting us to expel him by the force of collective laughter. Everything Jonah does suddenly becomes funny: his flight is funny because no-one can escape from God, his psalm in the fish's belly is funny because it is so hypocritical, and his resentment of the Ninevites is funny, for he is a 'dismally mulish' 'pupil', a stubborn child.[61] Critics no longer read Jonah's exit from the fish as a dignified symbol of the resurrection, but exult in the explicitness of the text, which describes (using the verb קיא) how Jonah was, literally, 'vomited out'. In one of the best critical one-liners in biblical scholarship, James Holbert observes that the fish is 'literally *sick* of this man and his false piety' and 'it is no wonder that immediately after Jonah shouts "Deliverance belongs to Yhwh!", the big fish throws up'.[62]

---

60   Ibid., p.109.
61   Ibid, pp.176, 183.
62   J. Holbert, '"Deliverance belongs to YHWH!"', p.74.

In this now very popular image of Jonah emerging from the fish on a tide of fish vomit (represented in Figure 6.3), Christian readings have gone full circle. The image of Jonah being expelled from the fish is the exact opposite of his Christ-like triumphant exit, and the fish's disgust and the author's laughter at Jonah acts as a cue to the reader to treat this distinctly unsavoury character with the contempt he deserves. As laughing at someone implies a superior vantage point, laughter between the proto-Gentile author and a Gentile audience at the expense of Jonah the Jew repeats the impression, albeit more subtly and pleasurably, that Gentiles know rather more about God and humanity than Jews. Jonah's comic ineptitude as he trips over the truth of Romans 3.29 reinforces Gentile superiority: as Linda Nochlin observes, in a different context, 'Once more irony puts Jewish figures in their place.'[63]

A second, more disturbing, twentieth-century mutation of Jonah takes his place beside Jonah the clown, namely Jonah the Zionist, or Jonah the Israeli. In eighteenth and nineteenth-century readings Jonah is not usually Israeli but Jewish (an epithet reserved for anti-heroes, rather than figures such as Moses and Abraham), and very rarely in Jonah criticism do you find the more neutral term

6.3 Eminently 'vomitable', satirical Jonah. Kathy Singleton and Arthur Baker, *Jonah and the Big Fish* (Bury St Edmunds; Kevin Mayhew Ltd, 1993), pp.16–17 © 1996 Kevin Mayhew Ltd, Buxhall, Stowmarket, Suffolk, IP14 3BW. Used by permission from *Jonah and the Big Fish*, Licence No 307042.

---

63 L. Nochlin, 'Starting with Self: Jewish Identity and its Representation', in L. Nochlin and T. Garb (eds), *The Jew in the Text*, pp.7–19.

Israelite, or Israel (a term with which the church, as new Israel, subconsciously identifies *itself*). After 1948, however, the term 'Israel' curiously starts to creep back into the critical tradition. An article in the *Interpreter's Bible* of 1956 calls Jonah a 'first class national expansionist ("Israel first") who hates all foreigners',[64] while a popular commentary written in the 1980s boldly claims that 'From the book of Jonah itself it is evident that Jonah was an ardent nationalist, pro-Israel and anti-foreign – at least anti-Assyrian'.[65] Rather than reflecting an increasing respect for the historicity of the text and a desire to make at least some kind of distinction between the historical Israelites and Judeans and contemporary Jews, the re-emergence of the term 'Israelite', or more revealingly *Israeli*, merely reflects changes in contemporary Jewish stereotypes.

Once an emblem of the anti-assimilationist ghetto Jew, Jonah now mutates into the hard-hearted expansionist Zionist, and nowhere is this change in Jonah's identity more clearly marked than in Rosemary Radford Reuther and H.J. Reuther's denunciation of Zionist ideology under the title, *The Wrath of Jonah*.[66] The Reuthers' book presents its argument in iconic form on the very first pages, where a map entitled 'Territories captured by Israel in 1948 and 1949' is placed opposite God's question to Jonah, 'Should I not pity Nineveh, that great city, in which there are more than a hundred and twenty thousand persons' (presumably they drop the phrase 'and much cattle' because it would inject too much levity). As the Reuthers explain, they use the title 'The Wrath of Jonah' because Jonah is an 'angry chauvinist prophet' who wants God to be a 'punitive and partisan God', and who must learn that God wants him to 'live in the peace that springs from repentance and obedience … rather than in violence and the desire for the annihilation of others'.[67]

In a none-too-subtle allegory, Jonah becomes a symbol for the aggressive Zionists who, like the prophet, need to learn some lessons about peace and tolerance, while the Ninevites are transformed from exemplary and angelic Gentiles into equally exemplary Palestinians. The Reuthers proclaim that their book is written 'out of concern for both wounded peoples',[68] but whereas the Palestinians are 'wounded in body but not in spirit', having 'sustained over many years of suffering an enormous sense of moral unity in the rightness of the cause', the Israelis are depicted as 'militarily strong but wounded in soul'.[69] The symmetry of language (both peoples are wounded) cannot mask the dissymmetry of the analysis as Jonah becomes, once again, a symbol for Judaism gone wrong,

---

64   J.S. Meek and W. Pierson Merrill, 'Jonah', in *The Interpreter's Bible*, vol.6 (New York: Abingdon, 1956), pp.875–94.

65   D. Stuart, *Hosea-Jonah* (Waco: Word Books, 1987), p.431.

66   R. Radford Reuther and H.J. Reuther, *The Wrath of Jonah* (New York: Harper and Row, 1989).

67   Ibid., p.xvii.

68   Ibid., p.xv.

69   Ibid.

an early manifestation of the sick aggressive Zionist soul, which for the Reuthers belies the true Jewish spirit of the diaspora (in their analysis, the true Jew is a diaspora Jew).

By pushing the reading to extremes and overlaying it on a fraught and complex contemporary political situation, the Reuthers' interpretation of Jonah (which has just, I believe, gone into a second reprint) exposes the serious limits of a Christian pseudo-universalistic understanding of Jonah the character and Jonah the book. Their stereotypical reading of Jonah the Jew, which, as David Biale comments, is merely another version of the Jews – that 'stiff-necked people',[70] at least does us the service of exposing the huge distance between the monochrome stereotype and the Jewish people who are (and this seems so obvious that it hardly needs saying, and yet so repeatedly needs saying) 'neither purely a religion nor purely a nation, neither strictly universalists nor solely exclusive nationalists'.[71] Read this way, the book of Jonah tells us nothing: the character is thin and static (nothing like as complex as Dorothea Brooke); the lesson, which has a jargonistic, sing-song quality to it, is merely that we should prefer love over hate, and be open-hearted towards others and, irony of ironies, it proclaims this childish lesson in studies that 'practise moral parochialism under the mask of promoting universal ethics'.[72] The redundancy of this very simple jangling lesson is embarrassingly exposed as soon as we apply it to any form of actual human life, let alone a situation as nuanced and complex as Middle Eastern politics.

If Jonah Really Were a Jew ...

Throughout the history of modern biblical studies, the image of Jonah glowering over Nineveh (and his twentieth-century equivalents) has cast a huge shadow over our understanding of this little book. But in fact the narrative is far more open than our readings have allowed, even at the level of the word: for example, the phrase commonly translated 'and Jonah was very angry', the textual cell from which the body of the glowering Jonah develops, can also be translated 'and Jonah was saddened' or 'and Jonah was terribly upset'.[73] If a single word or phrase can accommodate different interpretations, how many different possibilities can be accommodated by this lightly sketched and provocative

---

70   D. Biale, 'The Philo-Semitic Face of Christian Anti-Semitism', *Tikkun*, 4.3 (1989), pp.99–102. Biale offers a sustained critique of *The Wrath of Jonah*, that accuses the Reuthers of 'stealing a Jewish book and telling us how to read it' and 'turning the Hebrew Bible into a stick with which to beat the Jews' (p.101).

71   Biale, 'The Philo-Semitic Face', p.101.

72   Z. Bauman, *Postmodern Ethics* (Oxford: Basil Blackwell, 1993), p.14.

73   See J.M. Sasson, *Jonah: A New Translation with Introduction, Commentary and Interpretation* (The Anchor Bible) (New York: Doubleday, 1990), pp.273–5.

narrative? In this final section I want to look at some refreshing alternatives to the image of Jonah the Eminently Vomitable Nationalist and to pursue some Jewish cues for reconceiving Jonah as both character and text.

From the very first, Jewish interpretation has been aware that biblical interpretation is a political activity, and that how you read is determined not so much by constraints in the text as by pressures in your cultural environment. If you compare equivalent passages in *Bavli* and *Yerushalmi*, you find that, while *Bavli* extols the repentance of the Ninevites (who were so determined to do right that even if they had stolen a single beam and built it into a palace, they would raze the entire building to give it back),[74] *Yerushalmi* cynically suggests that the Ninevites practised a 'repentance of deception'. While the Babylonian *ta'anim* were writing in a relatively uncluttered interpretative space, the Palestinian writers had to define themselves against strong readings like St Bede's, in which the Ninevites were already firmly linked with the Church. Thus the Palestinian interpreters strategically and deliberately inverted the image of the exemplary Ninevites and did not reuse it until after the Arab conquest in the seventh century CE.

As *Yerushalmi* cunningly replied to Christian sectarian readings, so we can perhaps use Jewish readings to reply to, and subvert, the critical mainstream. For, whereas mainstream interpretation works by applying loaded abstracts and seeing Jonah's nationalist vindictive viewpoint as absolutely wrong and God's benign universalist policy as absolutely right, the Rabbis tend to see the relation of Jonah to his God as more two-sided, nuanced and problematic. Operating on the principle that, as Elie Wiesel puts it, 'The Jew ... may oppose God as long as it is in defence of God's creation',[75] the *Mekilta* starts from the premise that Jonah is not wrong to want to protect his own people. For according to the *Mekilta* the ideal prophet (and perhaps the ideal reader) must see a situation not only from God's point of view, or only from the nation's point of view, but from both perspectives simultaneously.[76] The readers of the *Mekilta*, reading from both sides at once, empathise with Jonah as he is placed in an impossible dilemma, and imagine him worrying (justifiably) that, as a result of his actions and the repentance of the Ninevites, Israel might be condemned. According to the *Mekilta*, Jonah did not resist a simple mission of mercy but, faced with an impossible dilemma, made his voyage to drown himself in the sea. Because he preferred suicide to cooperating in Israel's potential destruction, Jonah is ranked alongside David and Moses, heroes willing to give their lives for their nation (Exod. 32.32; 2 Sam. 24.17). Whereas modern readings lampoon him, the *Mekilta* takes him seriously: whereas the mainstream labels him as anti-prophet, the *Mekilta* lists him in the *Who's Who* of Jewish tradition.

---

74   *Ta'anit*, 16a.

75   E. Wiesel, *A Jew Today* (New York: Vintage, 1978), p.135.

76   Lauterbach (ed. and trans.), *Mekilta de Rabbi Ishmael* (Philadelphia: Jewish Publication Society of America, 1933), Tractate *Pisha*, pp.7–9.

Jonah becomes a poignant nuanced and complex book when you look at it from God and Jonah's point of view, for, as Emmanuel Levinas comments, 'as soon as two are involved, everything is in danger'.[77] But the book becomes more complex, and more potentially disturbing still, when you follow Abravanel and read the Ninevites not as a cipher for 'the gentiles' but 'the Assyrians'. Nineveh is not a neutral place, like Meggido, but the capital of Assyria, the nation responsible for the exile, and disappearance of the northern kingdom of Israel. Suddenly it becomes possible to take Jonah's perspective very seriously indeed, and to imagine him not merely sulking and stamping his feet over the kindness of God, but rather suffering depression at the prospect of exile which he (as a prophet) now knows will come upon his people.[78]

These Jewish readings, and many others that could easily become another paper, or a book, in their own right, are simply more *interesting* than the Sunday School lesson that has dominated critical scholarship, and seem better suited to a world where ethics is increasingly seen as an area for debate (rather than a boxing ring for antitheses) and where sectarian hierarchies like 'universalistic Christian versus sectarian Jew' are (I like to think) coming apart at the seams. These more complex versions of the character of Jonah are better suited to post-Victorian tastes in fiction, where we are less well-disposed to the realist novel and its convention of pinning down characters by adjectives, like butterflies with pins.[79] There is space for at least another reading, one that exploits the 'backwaters and underbellies' of the book's interpretative heritage to challenge some of the assumptions of the 'mainstream'. But, interpretative communities being what they are, it is by no means a foregone conclusion that these repressed strands of interpretation will have the power to counter this biblical Shylock, Jonah the Jew: at the time of writing he has long passed his use-by date and yet still remains relatively durable.

---

77 E. Levinas, *Nine Talmudic Readings*, trans. A. Aronowicz (Bloomington: Indiana University Press, 1990), p.16.

78 For a much fuller discussion of Jewish interpretation of Jonah, see Sherwood, *A Biblical Text and Its Afterlives*, pp.97–137.

79 See S. Rimon-Kenan, *Narrative Fiction: Contemporary Poetics* (London: Routledge, 1994), pp.60–61.

Chapter 7

The Jews and the Cross in the Middle Ages: Towards a Reappraisal

Elliott Horowitz

On their raiment, wrought with gold,
See the sign we hateful hold.

These lines were written, not by a European Jew of the Middle Ages, but rather, by a nineteenth-century English scholar and divine (Edward Plumptre) who, in a remarkable feat of empathy, spoke through the former's voice, describing the experience of Jewish martyrdom during the Crusades.[1] They may serve, therefore, as a useful opening to an essay written in memory of another Oxford-educated English divine of rare empathetic gifts, James William Parkes. When speaking in his own voice of the cross of Christ, in one of his numerous essays, Plumptre had asserted that a 'a man may put forth his own hand and eat of the fruit thereof, and live for ever'.[2] Yet he was also able to understand that many a medieval Jew regarded the sign of the cross with unmitigated hatred.

As we shall see below, this is not something that many Jewish historians have openly acknowledged. Rather exceptional in this regard has been Jacob Katz, who, as rector of the Hebrew University in Jerusalem, conferred upon Parkes an honorary fellowship in 1970.[3] A decade earlier Katz had written with admirable frankness in his now classic study *Exclusiveness and Tolerance* of the repulsion with which the visible signs of Christianity were regarded by medieval European Jews. 'Even had their religion not emphatically prohibited visible representation of the Godhead,' he wrote, 'such representations would still have repelled the Jews, who had not shared the intellectual and emotional experiences which made these representations meaningful to Christian worshippers. Throughout the literature of the time we find the rejection of Christianity expressed in the form of the repudiation of one of its visible symbols, more particularly that of the crucified Christ'.[4]

---

1   E.H. Plumptre (1821–91) in Joseph Friedlander (compiler) and G.A. Kohut (ed.), *The Standard Book of Jewish Verse* (New York, 1917), pp.217–18. On Plumptre, who began his career as chaplain at King's College, London, and rose eventually to be dean of Wells, see the entry in *Encyclopaedia Britannica* (*EB*), 11th ed, 21, 856.

2   'The Tree of Life', in E.H. Plumptre, *Biblical Studies* (London and New York, n.d), p.64. The essay was written before 1869.

3   See the photograph of Parkes and Katz accompanying the entry on the former in *Encyclopaedia Judaica* (*EJ*), 13, 121.

4   J. Katz, *Exclusiveness and Tolerance: Jewish–Gentile Relations in Medieval and Modern Times* (Oxford: Oxford University Press, 1961), pp.22–3.

This chapter will attempt to go beyond Katz's pioneering remarks both by examining the specific forms, especially non-verbal, which such repudiation took, and also by looking into the (paradoxically) related issue of the cross's attraction to medieval Jews, by whom it could be regarded, I shall argue, not only as an idolatrous object, but also as one of illicit desire. These two dimensions could dovetail in such brazen actions as urinating or rudely exposing oneself in the presence of the cross, actions which, not surprisingly, were often followed by martyrdom. But in a society that regarded martyrdom as its highest ideal, such actions were not rare. A more common (and less gender-specific) form of repudiating the cross and all it stood for was the act of spitting.

We may cite an example from R. Ephraim of Bonn's account of an incident that occurred on the outskirts of Mainz during the Second Crusade. Three Jews of Bacharach and their families had fled to the Stahlbeck fortress which, on the eve of Shavuot, they were obliged to leave. 'The errant ones [Crusaders] rose up against them and pursued them, demanding that they defile themselves [become baptized]. But they refused, for they deeply loved their Creator, even unto death. Mr. Kalonymos spat conspicuously upon an image of the Crucified One, and they slew him on the spot.'[5] Was this daring act on the part of Mr Kalonymos wholly spontaneous, or had he perhaps thought to himself over the years, while passing crosses and other Christian images in the streets and thoroughfares, 'May it be God's will that I shall be privileged to spit before the Gentiles upon one of these abominations ere I die?' Or was he prompted, perhaps, by the heightened religious tension which must have pervaded the community of Mainz (in which he and the other two martyrs were buried) during the days between the third of Sivan, which marked the anniversary of the slaughter of Mainz Jewry during the first crusade half a century earlier,[6] and the sixth of that month, which marked the giving of the Law to Moses at Sinai? Rather than attempting to choose one of these three possibilities over the others, I would prefer to point to the complex web of memory confronting a twelfth-century Rhenish Jew as he confronts the cross on the eve of Shavuot and contemplates martyrdom.

Before returning to this complex web of memory I would like to place side by side with the story of Mr Kalonymos another which also took place on the eve of Shavuot, not in Germany, but in England, approximately a century later. 'In England there was a learned, wealthy, and diligent student of the Talmud, the late R. Yom Tov, who hanged himself on the eve of Shavuot. His father, Rabbi Moses the Pious, did not leave his room, nor did he shed a tear, but studied in his library

---

5   A.M. Haberman (ed.), *Sefer Gezerot Ashkenaz ve-Zarfat* (Jerusalem: Tarshish, 1945), p.118; S. Eidelberg (trans. and ed.), *The Jews and the Crusaders: The Hebrew Chronicles of the First and Second Crusades* (Madison: University of Wisconsin Press, 1977), p.125. Here and elsewhere I generally follow Eidelberg's translation, with minor changes.

6   Haberman, *Saefer Gezerot*, p.30; Eidelberg, *Jews and Crusades*, p.29.

as if no evil had befallen him, asserting that his son had caused his own death.' The anonymous author of the account reports that 'on that night he [the deceased] appeared to me in a dream, and he looked well, better than he had in life. And he also appeared to others that night, reporting that he had seen a great light'. Later in his account the chronicler provides some background information concerning the late R. Yom Tov: 'And he was somewhat afflicted by a demon [*vegam mikzat shed haya bo*] … and he would say (it is not clear whether the following words were said in life or after death) that the demon would place before him the sign of the cross and press him to commit idolatry.' The anonymous author concluded with the following advice: 'It is better for man to perform penance in this world through self-affliction and flagellation',[7] – apparently intending thereby to transform R. Yom Tov's death from one of depressive suicide to one of heroic martyrdom.

This short but striking passage was redeemed from obscurity by the late Hayyim Hillel Ben-Sasson in one of his last articles, bearing the somewhat provocative title (for a Jerusalem Jewish historian): 'Assimilation *in* Jewish History'. Ben-Sasson saw in the above quoted passage testimony that according to a contemporary of R. Yom Tov's 'the cross had penetrated, ineluctably, the mental world of a learned and God-fearing medieval English Jew'.[8] One could of course argue with the assertion that the cross's penetration was ineluctable, but Ben-Sasson's words remind us that the cross could arouse not only passionate revulsion among Jews but also passionate attraction, and just as the former response could lead Mr Kalonymos to his tragic death, so could the latter response lead R. Yom Tov to a similar end – and both on the eve of Shavuot.

The stories when taken together allow us to grasp the complicated nature of the medieval Jew's attitude toward the cross, a matter which comes across also from the rich lexicon devised by medieval Jews so as to avoid calling it by its true name. Within this lexicon I would like to focus on the twin (masculine and feminine) words *ti'uv* and *to'evah*, both meaning 'abomination'. Thus the above-mentioned Ephraim of Bonn, when describing acts of martyrdom in Würzberg during the Second Crusade, mentions the case of a young maiden 'who was brought into their place of idolatry in order to be defiled [baptized], but she sanctified the name of God and spat upon the abomination [*ti'uv*]. They then struck her with stone and fist'.[9] Similarly, when R. Elazar Rokeah came to describe the background to the suffering of the Jews of Mainz during the Third Crusade he mentions hearing before Hannukah (of 1187) that the Muslims had

---

7   E. Kupfer, 'A Contribution to the Chronicles of the Family of R. Moses ben R. Yom-Tov "the Noble" of London', *Tarbiz*, 40 (1971), 384–7, (Hebrew).

8   H.H. Ben-Sasson, 'Assimilation in Jewish History', *Molad*, 7 (1976), 305 (Hebrew), idem, *Continuity and Variety*, ed. J. Hacker (Tel Aviv: Am 'Oved, 1984), pp.61–2 (Hebrew).

9   Haberman, p.119; Eidelberg, *Jews and Crusaders*, p.127.

taken Acre and the areas outside of Jerusalem 'and that they had captured the abomination [*to'evah*] upon which Jesus had been crucified … and had taken the abomination with them to the land of Ishmael'. The same author utilized similar language to describe the arrival of the returning Crusaders at the gates of his own city: 'And the uncircumcised had marked themselves with the signs of their abomination (*ba-ti'uv shelahem*) by the hundreds and thousands.'[10]

One could add dozens if not hundreds of examples, but I would like to pause for a moment to examine the particular resonances of the word 'abomination' when used by medieval Jews in reference to the Christian cross. On the one hand it alluded to such biblical verses as Deut. 7:26, 'And you shall not bring an abomination into your house, and become accursed like it', where the reference is to artifacts of idolatry, but also, on the other hand it alluded to verses where the context is one of prohibited intimacy. These include Lev. 18:22: 'You shall not lie with a male as with a woman; it is an abomination' and Ezekiel 22:11: 'One commits abomination with his neighbour's wife.' The abominated cross was regarded by medieval Jews as an idolatrous object, but also, I would argue, as a potential object of illicit desire. Recognizing that Jewish violence against the cross could stem, not only from undiluted hostility, but also from anxiety engendered by an object of illicit desire, we are in a better position to take Christian reports of Jewish cross desecration seriously rather than dismissing them as anti-semitic inventions. There is also no paucity of references to such conduct in Jewish sources (some of which have already been mentioned), but these have all too often either been quietly passed over by Jewish historians or tendentiously misrepresented.

As an example of the first, let me cite the 1941 anthology of Jewish heroism and martyrdom, *Sefer ha-Gevura*, edited by Israel Halpern (the first book published by the Histadrut's 'Am 'Oved press founded by Berl Katznelson). In the section dealing with Jewish heroism during the Second Crusade, Halpern included from R. Ephraim of Bonn's chronicle the story of Samuel b. Isaac of Worms who, when attacked on the road to Mainz, managed to wound 'three of the enemy' before he was killed, and that of Ms. Gutalda of Aschaffenburg, who refused baptism 'and drowned herself in the river'.[11] He chose, however, to pass over the story of Kalonymos of Bacharach who 'spat conspicuously upon an image of the Crucified One' before being put to death, which appears in R. Ephraim's chronicle between the two aforementioned tales of heroism. Halpern also left out the above-mentioned story of the young woman from Würzberg who 'sanctified the name of God and spat upon the abomination' when she was brought into Church to be baptized.[12] Were the former two deeds more heroic or

10   Haberman, pp.162–3.

11   I. Halpern (ed.), *Sefer ha-Gevura* (Tel-Aviv: Am Oved, 1941), p.64.

12   Both these cases have recently been mentioned by C. Cluse, 'Stories of Breaking and Taking the Cross: A Possible Context for the Oxford Incident of 1268',

more worthy of emulation (by 1941 standards) than the latter two? Or did Halpern perhaps doubt that these Jewish martyrs actually spat upon the cross before meeting their deaths? It may be noted in passing that spitting has historically been associated not only with the expression of contempt but also with neutralizing the powers of evil spirits,[13] and Jewish spitting in the presence of the cross, a practice which lasted for centuries, may well have contained both of these elements.

As an instance of (what appears to me) misrepresentation we may note Abraham Grossman's recent discussion of a responsum sent by R. Joseph Tov-Elem of Limoges, early in the eleventh century, to the community of Sens. The neighbouring community of Troyes had imposed upon the Jews of Sens a tax for the redemption of captives, 'but when the missive arrived in Sens,' wrote R. Joseph, 'the Jews there declared themselves free of any obligation, giving as grounds the great troubles which surrounded them ... The messenger from Troyes found them greatly troubled by the calamity which had befallen them as a result of the shattering of an "abomination" (to'eva) in their locality'.[14] R. Joseph would appear to be passing on matter-of-factly the information that the Jews of Sens had smashed a crucifix (perhaps on Purim) and were now paying the price.[15] Grossman, however, without explanation and in contrast to previous scholars who have discussed the responsum, speaks rather of an 'accusation against the Jews of Sens',[16] suggesting that, in his view, they probably were not guilty of smashing the item referred to disdainfully by R. Joseph as an 'abomination'. In this connection it may be apt to redeem from obscurity the bold observation about medieval Jews made (in a footnote) by Solomon Grayzel in 1933: 'It is clear ... [that they] were indiscreet, but one must remember that they

Revue d'Histoire Ecclesiastique, 90 (1995), 438–9. I thank Yisrael Yuval for bringing this important article to my attention.

13   See W. Crooke, 'Saliva', in James Hastings (ed.), *Encyclopaedia of Religion and Ethics*, XI (Edinburgh: T & T Clark, 1920), 100–104; J. Trachtenberg, *Jewish Magic and Superstition: A Study in Folk Religion* (New York: Behrman, 1939), pp.107, 120–21, 159, 162, and the sources cited there, to which may be added *Sefer Hasidim* (ed. R. Margoliot) (Jerusalem: Mosad ha-Rav Kook, 1957), no. 235 (p.209). I thank John Gager for suggesting that I pursue this line of inquiry.

14   I. Agus, 'Democracy in the Communities of the Early Middle Ages', *Jewish Quarterly Review*, 43 (1952), 166–7, idem (ed.), *Responsa of Tosephists* (New York: Talpioth, 1954), no. 1; idem, *Urban Civilization in Pre-Crusade Europe*, I (New York, 1965), p.176.

15   On Purim violence against the cross since the early fifth century, see E. Horowitz, 'The Rite to Be Reckless: On the Perpetration and Interpretation of Purim Violence', *Poetics Today*, 15 (1994), 9–54.

16   A. Grossman, *The Early Sages of France: Their Lives, Leadership and Works* (Jerusalem: Magnes, 1995) p.20 (Hebrew). In addition to Agus (note 14) contrast Haym Soloveitchik, *The Use of Responsa as Historical Source: A Methodological Introduction* (Jerusalem: Zalman Shazar Centre, 1990), ch.8 (Hebrew).

had not yet learned the self-effacement which the subsequent centuries were to teach them.'[17]

Jewish indiscretion had for centuries expressed itself in both words and deeds, as in the practice, mentioned in the Theodosian law of 408, of burning a crucified figure on the holiday of Purim. Centuries later, Jewish converts to Christianity in the Byzantine Empire were required not only generally to renounce 'every Hebrew law, custom, and ceremony', but specifically to 'curse those who keep the festival of the so-called Mordecai ... nailing Haman to wood, and then mixing him with the emblem of the cross and burning them together'. Such a pre-baptismal oath, dating from some time between the eighth and early eleventh centuries, has come down to us from the Byzantine East.[18]

In this connection we may also note the letter sent by Doge Pietro II Candiano of Venice to the German Emperor Henry I and to Archbishop Hildebert of Mainz, apparently after the Erfurt conference of 932, informing them of reports he had received concerning a Jew who had recently been in Jerusalem and was now in their vicinity in the guise of anti-Christ, uttering curses against 'our Lord the Messiah' and the Holy Sepulchre. In truth, continued the Doge, there had indeed been a religious disputation in Jerusalem between Jews and Christians, but (as the Patriarch of Jerusalem had informed the Byzantine Emperor Romanus), it had concluded with a great miracle at the Church of the Sepulchre, after which many Jews of Jerusalem converted to Christianity. The Doge concluded his letter to the Emperor and Archbishop with a particular request: that this story be told to the Jews under their jurisdiction and that they be forced to accept Christianity. Should any Jew fail to do so, 'let it be commanded throughout their kingdom that his polluted hands shall not be permitted to touch the sign of the cross on any item of metal or cloth, or any other merchandise'.[19]

Although many (though not all) scholars have doubted the report concerning the disputation in Jerusalem and its alleged consequences, none has (to my knowledge) challenged the authenticity of the Doge's letter. Yet the full import of its attempt to distance Jews from the sign of the cross has not been appreciated. Salo Baron confidently asserted, some forty years ago, that it was economically motivated: 'Though couched in terms of extreme Christian sensitivity,' he wrote,

---

17   S. Grayzel, *The Church and the Jews in the Thirteenth Century*, rev. edn, (New York: Hermon Press, 1966), p.29, n.42.

18   See Horowitz, 'Rite to Be Reckless', pp.25–9.

19   For the Latin text with German translation, see Julius Aronius, *Regesten zur Geschichte der Juden im fränkischen und deutschen Reiche* (Berlin, 1902), pp.53–4. For a discussion of the letter and its background, see Zvi Baras, 'Jewish–Christian Religious Disputation in Jerusalem (932)', *Cathedra*, 63 (1992), 31–51 (Hebrew).

'the doge's recommendation could not conceal his intention to place insuperable obstacles in the way of Jewish traders handling merchandise, which *often* bore the sign of the cross in its commercial markings.'[20] Similarly Cecil Roth, writing (evidently under Baron's influence) a decade later, claimed that 'the economic jealousy behind this ostensibly pious ejaculation is obvious'.[21] Neither Baron nor Roth, however, provided any evidence that tenth-century commercial markings frequently included the sign of the cross, nor did either explain why it was 'obvious' that the doge's pious language derived, not from concern that crosses on commercial merchandise might be desecrated by Jews, but from the desire to avoid Jewish competition in trade. It is perhaps worth noting the opinion of *Sefer Hasidim*, the bible of Ashkenazic pietism (many of whose traditions derived from early medieval Italy), that, if a Jew acquired 'a dish, or cup, or any utensil upon which which the sign of the cross (*sheti va-'erev*) had been placed, he should not use it until [the cross is] removed'.[22]

Baron's reluctance to entertain the possibility that the doge was actually worried about Jews desecrating the sign of the cross would seem to go hand in hand with his scepticism concerning the report by the Christian chronicler Yahya ibn Sa'id (Eutychius) that in 937 (five years after the Doge's letter) Jews had participated, together with Muslims, in the burning of St. Mary's Church in Ascalon [Ashkelon].[23] The same chronicler reports that some thirty years later the Jews of Jerusalem participated in the anti-Christian riots which broke out between Ascension Day and Pentecost, during which three of the city's churches were badly damaged and the Patriarch John VII was cruelly murdered. According to ibn Sa'id's testimony, which Goitein has taken considerably more seriously than did Baron, 'the Jews exceeded the Muslims in acts of destruction and ruin'.[24] If these reports of Jewish violence against churches in tenth-century Palestine do indeed reflect wider eastern Mediterranean realities (and there is reason to believe that they do), the Venetian Doge's concerns about Jews desecrating objects carrying the sign of the cross may well have been quite genuine.

---

20 S.W. Baron, *A Social and Religious History of the Jews* (hereafter *SRH*) vol.IV (Philadelphia: Jewish Publication Society, 1957), p.25.

21 Cecil Roth, 'Italy', in idem (ed.), *The World History of the Jewish People: The Dark Ages* (Tel-Aviv: Masada, 1966), p.116. The economic explanation of the Doge's motives is also favoured by Baras, 'Jewish–Christian Disputation', p.50, without mention of its having been advanced previously.

22 *Das Buch der Frommen*, 2nd edn, ed. J. Wistinetzki (Frankfurt: M. A. Wahrmann, 1924), p.176.

23 According to Baron 'this tale is too strictly in line with the Church's traditional accusations of Jewish involvement in anti-Christian persecutions to merit full credence'. See idem, *SRH*, III, p.137. On Eutychius and Jewish anti-Christian violence, see also below, note 31.

24 See S.D. Goitein, 'Jerusalem in the Arab Period (638–1099)', in *Yerushalayim*, I (1953), p.94; idem, *Palestinian Jewry in Early Islamic and Crusader Times*, ed. J. Hacker (Jerusalem: Yad Ben Zvi, 1980), p.17 (Hebrew).

After the year 1000 reports of such activity appear on the European continent itself, beginning, in fact, in the very capital of western Christendom, during the spiritually tense years between the millennium after Christ's birth and the millennium after his death. This was also a period during which the image of the crucifix became much more prominent and widespread in Western Christian piety on both popular and elite levels,[25] a development which was undoubtedly noted by European Jews. Early in the eleventh century, during the papacy of Benedict VIII (1012–24), a number of Roman Jews were executed on what Cecil Roth has called the 'improbable charge of mocking a crucifix'.[26] According to the contemporary chronicler Ademar of Chabannes (d.1034) this occurred after an earthquake accompanied by a severe storm erupted on Good Friday, prompting a Roman Jew to inform the papal palace that some of his coreligionists had mocked a crucifix in their synagogue. After those found guilty were beheaded the earthquake ceased.[27] Ademar claims that these events took place 'circa 1020', although a later chronicle (by Baronius, d.1607) gives the date as 1017.[28] Baronius also adds the important information that the storm lasted through Vespers on the following Saturday. A century ago Vogelstein and Rieger, in their monumental history of the Jews of Rome, suggested 1021 as the most likely date, based on external testimony that an earthquake had occurred in that year. They implicitly accepted the testimony of Baronius, however, that the earthquake lasted through the Saturday before Easter, although they expressed serious doubt (echoed by Roth half a century later) that the Jews of Rome might have actually

---

25   E. Delaruelle, 'La crucifix dans la piété populaire et dans l'art, du VIe au XIe siècle', in idem, *La piété populaire au moyen âge* (Turino: Bottega Dierasmo, 1975), pp.27–42; R. Landes, *Relics, Apocalypse, and the Deceits of History: Ademar of Chabannes, 989–1034* (Cambridge, MA: Harvard University Press, 1995), pp.301–2.

26   C. Roth, *The History of the Jews in Italy* (Philadelphia: Jewish Publication Society, 1946), p.72.

27   For Ademar's account of the events in Rome, see *Monumenta Germaniae Historica: Scriptores*, vol.IV (Hannover, 1841), p.139, and the summary in H. Schreckenberg, *Die christlichen Adversus-Judaeos-Texte und ihr literarisches und historisches Umfeld* (1.–11. Jh.), rev. edn (Frankfurt: Peter Lang, 1990), pp.541–2. Kenneth Stow has strangely attributed to Ademar the report that 'Pope Benedict VIII burned twenty Roman Jews at the stake for desecrating a holy image and causing an outbreak of plague.' See idem, *Alienated Minority: The Jews of Medieval Latin Europe* (Cambridge, MA: Harvard University Press, 1992), p.95. Yet the chronicle clearly refers to an earthquake ('terrae motu') and to the Jews as having been beheaded ('decollatis'), with no number given. On Ademar's chronicle, see now Landes, *Relics*, who has little, however, to say about the Rome incident. It is also curiously omitted (as is the aforementioned letter of the Venetian Doge) in J. Shatzmiller, 'Desecrating the Cross: A Rare Medieval Accusation', *Studies in the History of the Jewish People and the Land of Israel*, 5 (1980), 159–73 (Hebrew).

28   See Ceasar Baronius, *Annales Ecclesiastici*, vol.16, ed. A. Theiner (Bari, 1849), p.42.

engaged in such 'absurd conduct' as mocking a crucifix, endangering thereby the entire community.[29]

Yet conduct which appeared absurd to German Jews late in the nineteenth century might well have appeared less so to Roman Jews of the early eleventh. Vogelstein and Rieger, who suggested 1021 as the most likely date for the Roman incident, apparently failed to note that in that year Easter and (the first day of) Passover fell on the very same day (2 April) and that Good Friday was therefore both the day of the burning of *hametz* and the eve of 'the Great Sabbath'. If the Jews of Rome had indeed mocked the crucifix on that Friday (upon which Christians prayed for their conversion), it may well have been by burning a crucified figure together with the remnants of their leavened bread. And if one of them had indeed informed the papal authorities of the sacrilege, it may well have been after hearing, on 'the Great Sabbath' (and Easter eve) the prophetic reading from *Malachi* which spoke of 'the coming of the awesome, fearful, day of the Lord' (3:23) – words eminently capable of arousing apocalyptic feelings (especially in times of millennial excitement) and also, perhaps, feelings of guilt and contrition, when accompanied by heavy gusts and an earthquake's aftershocks.

In both the other years mentioned as possible dates for the Roman incident, 1017 and 1020, Good Friday fell on the eve of the intermediate Sabbath of Passover, the Sabbath upon which Ezekiel's vision of the dry bones returning to life (ch.37) was read in the synagogue, a custom explained in a contemporary responsum as being rooted in the belief that the resurrection of the dead would take place in the month of Nisan (during which Passover fell).[30] Reminding Jews in this way of the difference between their Resurrection narrative and that of the Christians undoubtedly added to the already tense and emotionally charged atmosphere prevailing for centuries during the days from Holy Thursday through Easter, when 'the lines of demarcation between Christian and Jew were most clearly drawn'.[31] Why, then, should it appear unlikely that Jews residing in

---

29   H. Vogelstein and P. Rieger, *Geschichte der Juden in Rom*, vol.I (Berlin: Mayer und Müller, 1896), pp.212–13. Roth (note 26), who gives the date of the incident as '1020 or 1021', had clearly seen their discussion.

30   See the responsum attributed to R. Hai Gaon (d.1038) in B.M. Lewin (ed.), *Otzar ha-Geonim: Megillah* (Jerusalem: Hebrew University Press, 1932), pp.63–4, and the sources cited there.

31   See Baron, *SRH*, III, pp.50–51, and more recently B. Brennan, 'The Conversion of the Jews of Clermont in AD 576', *Journal of Theological Studies*, 36 (1985), 327, from whom the quotation is drawn. For the claim (by the chronicler Eutychius) that as part of their revolt against Byzantine rule the Jews of early seventh-century Tyre had hoped to murder all the city's Christians on Easter night see D. M. Olster, *The Politics of Usurpation in the Seventh Century: Rhetoric and Revolution in Byzantium* (Amsterdam: Adolf Hakkert, 1993), p.103. On the critical dialogue between Passover and Easter since the early centuries CE see Yisrael Yuval, 'The Haggadah of Passover and Easter', *Tarbiz*, 65 (1995), 5–25 (Hebrew).

Christendom's Western capital during the period between the millennium of Christ's birth and the millennium of his crucifixion might have mocked a crucifix on the very anniversary of the latter?

Some four decades later a similar accusation was made against the Jews of Aterno, near Pescara.[32] This accusation occurred during the lifetime of R. Joseph Tov-Elem, who, as noted above, mentioned rather matter-of-factly the 'smashing of an abomination' by the Jews of Sens. It is noteworthy, then, that shortly after the turn of the millennium and well before 1096 Jewish violence against the crucifix, as a response, I would argue, to the new prominence of the latter, begins to appear in Western Europe. If the experience of the first Crusade did not initiate such violence, it seems to have raised it to new heights.

R. Solomon b. Samson, the primary Jewish chronicler of the first crusade, reports that, on the first day of Passover, 1096, Crusaders from France led by Peter the Hermit arrived in Trier and soon after began to desecrate the community's Torah scrolls. The Jews 'undertook penitence and charity, and fasted six weeks from day to day [during the daytime hours], from Passover to Shavuot'.[33] Acts of martyrdom, some quite dramatic, began only after the Christian Pentecost, when the local bishop (before whom a large cross was customarily carried in procession that day) began to demonstrate a less protective attitude toward the town's Jews.

Tensions between Christians and Jews in Trier (which in the tenth century had acquired the status of a 'second Rome') had emerged as early as 1066. In that year, according to the *Gesta Trevorum*, Archbishop Eberhard threatened the town's Jews with expulsion if they would not convert by the Saturday before Easter. The Jews, it was claimed, burned a wax figure of the bishop which they had arranged (through bribery) to have baptized, and thus caused his death on that very Saturday.[34] It is difficult, of course, to accept every detail of this report, the earliest record of a Jewish presence in Trier, at face value,[35] but it is

---

32   Peter Browe, 'Die Hostienschändungen der Juden im Mittelalter', *Romische Quartalschrift für christliche Altertumskunde und Kirchengeschichte*, 36 (1926), 170; Roth, *Italy*, p.72.

33   Haberman, 52–3; Eidelberg, *Jews and Crusades*, pp.62–3, Robert Chazen, *European Jewry and the First Crusade* (Berkeley: University of California Press, 1987), pp.287–8.

34   On Trier as a 'secunda Roma', and on the processional consequences therof, see H. Fichtenau, *Living in the Tenth Century: Mentalities and Social Orders*, trans. P. Geary (Chicago: University of Chicago Press, 1991), pp.9, 11, 13, 49, 54–5. On the alleged events of 1066 see, among others, Aronius, no. 160 (p.76).

35   See the important comments of Moritz Güdemann, *Geschichte des Erziehungswesen und der Culture der abendländischen Juden*, I (Vienna: Alfred Hölder, 1888), p.224.

noteworthy that, in 1066 too, Easter eve coincided with the intermediate Sabbath of Passover. It would appear, therefore, that the *Gesta*'s story of the pressure exerted by the bishop upon the Jews to convert and their revenge upon the former by means of the baptized wax image reflect the tensions created during the early years of Jewish settlement in Trier by the significant overlap between the opposing holidays of Passover and Easter. Similar tensions, fanned by outside forces, smouldered three decades later during the overlap between the Jewish seven week cycle bridging Passover and Shavuot and the Christian seven week cycle between Easter and Pentecost.

The most dramatic incident in Trier narrated by R. Solomon b. Samson is the martyrdom of Asher b. Joseph the *Gabbai*, who was put to death first before the gate of the bishop's palace 'so as to instill fear and terror in the rest'. On the way to his death, Asher invited other members of the community to join him in welcoming the Divine Presence; an invitation to which only the youth Meir b. Samuel responded affirmatively. 'When they emerged from the gate of the palace, the crucified one was brought before them so that they would bow before him. *They cast a branch at the abomination*, and the two pious men were slain in sanctification of the [Divine] Name.'[36]

How did the two pious Jews of Trier provoke their slayers? The Hebrew phrase '*hitilu zemora*' was translated rather literally by Shlomo Eidelberg as 'they cast a branch', but I would prefer the no less literal 'they *thrust a rod*'. The phrase, as scholars have noted, clearly alludes to a cryptic verse in Ezekiel (8: 17): 'Then he said to me, "Have you seen this, O son of man? Is it too slight a thing for the house of Judah to commit the *abomination* which they commit here, that they fill the land with violence ... Lo, they put the *branch* to their nose."' Thus in the Revised Standard Version, closely following the Authorized Version. In the new JPS translation the last words are rendered: '*thrust* the branch to their nostrils'. My preference for the verb 'thrust' comes not from tribal loyalty to the JPS translation, but because it fits better the phallic connotations of 'rod' (like 'Rute' in German), well illustrated in one of Ezra Pound's *Cantos*: 'his rod hath made god in my belly'.[37]

I am not suggesting (as did Graetz) that *zemora* necessarily means 'phallus' in the above-mentioned verse from Ezekiel,[38] but rather, that its most likely use among medieval Ashkenazic authors would have been in the phallic sense. This

---

36   Haberman, p.55; Eidelberg, *Jews and Crusaders*, p.65; Chazan, p.291. I have adopted elements of both translations.

37   See R.W. Burchfield, *A Supplement to the Oxford English Dictionary* (Oxford: Oxford University Press, 1982), vol.III, 1320; Eric Partridge, *A Dictionary of Slang and Unconventional Language*, 8th edn (London: Routledge, 1984), p.983.

38   H. Graetz, 'Die euphemistische Bedeutung des Wortes [zemora] im hebräischen,' *Mon. für Geschichte und Wissenschaft des Judentums*, 25 (1876), 507–8. See also A. Kohut, *Aruch Completum*, vol.III (Vienna, 1926), pp.300–301.

usage was prominent in midrashic literature,[39] especially in the legends concerning Amalek's attack upon the Israelites shortly after their exodus from Egypt, in some versions of which the circumcised phalluses of the latter were cut off and insolently thrown heavenward by the Amalekites.[40] These legends, in turn, became the basis for some of the liturgical poems composed by R. Elazar Kallir, in early medieval Palestine, for recitation on *Shabbat Zakhor*, the Sabbath before Purim devoted to the memory of Amalek and his descendants. In these poems Kallir uses the term *zemora* when referring to the circumcised phalluses victimised by the Amalekites, a matter not always understood by his modern translators.[41] Among medieval Ashkenazic Jews, however, Kallir's poems were not only widely recited, but also carefully studied and extensively commented upon, achieving a canonical status akin to that of rabbinic literature.[42] In the commentary composed by R. Eliezer b. Nathan (R. Solomon b. Samson's younger contemporary and fellow chronicler of the First Crusade) two possible explanations were offered for this usage.[43] There can be little doubt, therefore, that R. Solomon was familiar with the liturgical poems of Kallir in which *zemora* was used as a term for the circumcised phallus, and that its usage in his chronicle conformed to that of the revered poet.

When we are informed, then, that two Jews in Trier 'thrust a rod' upon the crucifix when it was offered to them, what R. Solomon seems to be saying is that they urinated upon it. These Jews are not the only martyrs of 1096 to whom R. Solomon attributes such brazen conduct. Earlier in his chronicle he recounts the death (some months later) of Natronai b. Isaac, one of the martyrs of Xanten: 'Some priests of his acquaintance had come to him throughout the previous day attempting to persuade him to defile himself in their evil waters, for he was a handsome man, pleasant to sight. He threw a branch in their mouths (*zarak zemora be-fihem*) and said: "God forbid that I should deny God-on-High ..." He slaughtered his brother and then himself.'[44]

What sort of branch (or rod) did Natronai throw in the mouths of the priests

---

39 In addition to Kohut (previous note) see J. Levy, *Wörterbuch über die Talmudim und Mirashim*, vol.I (Berlin and Vienna, 1924), p.544.

40 See, for example, *Pesikta de Rav Kahana*, 2nd edn ed. B. Mandelbaum, (New York: Jewish Theological Seminary, 1987), p.49 (and note 4 there); and the translation by W.G. Braude and I. J. Kapstein (Philadelphia: Jewish Publication Society, 1975), pp.52–3.

41 See, for example, that by (Rabbi Dr) Joseph Marcus, *Yozerot for Shabbat Shekalim, Zakhor* (New York: Pardes, 1965), p.9.

42 See the important comments of Grossman, *Early Sages of France*, pp.331, 534, and the literature cited there.

43 (1) The root *zmr*, used as a verb in the sense of pruning (Leviticus 25), suggests circumcision. (2) the shape of the phallus is similar to that of a branch (or rod). R. Eliezer's commentary is quoted by Solomon Buber in the notes to his edition of *Tanhuma* (Vilna, 1885) II, p.42.

44 Haberman, p.49; Eidelberg, *Jews and Crusaders*, pp.57–8.

before his martyrdom? Shlomo Eidelberg, in his aforementioned annotated translation, states that 'the reference is to an act of disdain toward the offered baptismal rites', but refrains from suggesting precisely what sort of act. Robert Chazan says even less.[45] In contrast to those prudent historians who have not been willing to go out on a limb, I would suggest that Natronai is described by our chronicler as having disdainfully linked his (exposed) phallus with the baptismal waters, either by actually urinating or by merely indicating his readiness to do so. When Solomon says that Natronai 'threw a rod' in the mouths of the priests, he may have meant to say that he used his 'rod' to shut their mouths – in a manner evidently not unlike the late American president Lyndon Johnson, who when repeatedly asked in a private conversation with reporters why the United States was still in Vietnam, 'unzipped his fly, drew out his substantial organ, and declared "this is why!"'[46]

R. Solomon, it is clear, described two separate acts of First Crusade martyrdom (one in Xanten and the other in Trier) as having involved the provocative use of the Jewish phallus to express disdain for Christianity's hallowed symbols. That the male organ in particular was chosen for this purpose (whether by the martyrs themselves or by their later chronicler) is not especially surprising, for in medieval Europe it symbolized, in its circumcised form, the quintessential difference between Christian and Jew. During the First Crusade and its aftermath the internal sign which the Jew bore on his lower body seems to have been consciously pitted against the external sign (of the cross) which the crusader wore on his upper body, to which the Hebrew chroniclers referred by the same word (*ot*) used in the Bible (Gen. 9: 12, 17) for the sign of circumcision.[47] Whether or not R. Solomon's descriptions of these brazen acts which preceded martyrdom are accurate in all their details, what is hardly less important is that he recorded narrative traditions which were circulating in his day,[48] and which he regarded as worthy of transmission to future generations.

From the Continent let us return to England, and to a remarkable story narrated by Matthew Paris in his *Historia Anglorum*. I refer to the 1222 incident later given the rather picturesque title 'The Deacon and the Jewess' by F.W. Maitland

---

45   Eidelberg, *Jews and Crusaders*, p.155; Chazan, *European Jewry*, p.283.

46   R. Dallek, *Flawed Giant: Lyndon Johnson and His Times, 1961–1973* (New York: Oxford University Press, 1998), p.491. Dallek's source was Arthur Goldberg.

47   See Haberman, pp.24, 72; Eidelberg, *Jews and Crusaders*, pp.21, 79.

48   For recent debate on the issues of 'facticity' and 'narrative', see the recent study by Jeremy Cohen (favouring post-1096 narrativity over 1096 facticity), 'The "Persecutions of 1096" – From Martyrdom to Martyrology: The Sociocultural Context of the Hebrew Crusade Chronicles', *Zion* 59 (1994), 169–208 (with ample bibliography) (Hebrew).

in his eponymous article 'delightful in form as well as original in substance,' first published in 1886.[49] Matthew Paris, who died in 1259, claims to have heard this version from an eye-witness, Master John of Basingstoke. According to Matthew (in Maitland's translation):

> An English deacon loved a Jewess with unlawful love, and ardently desired her embraces. 'I will do what you ask' said she 'if you will turn apostate, be circumcised, and hold fast the Jewish faith'. When he had done what she bade him he gained her unlawful love. But this could not long be concealed and was reported to [Archbishop] Stephen [Langton] of Canterbury. Before him the deacon was accused ... he was convicted and then confessed all these matters, and that he had taken part in a sacrifice which the Jews made of a crucified boy. And when it was seen that the deacon was circumcised, and that no argument would bring him to his senses, he solemnly apostasised before the archbishop and the assembled prelates in this manner: – a cross with the Crucified was brought before him and he defiled the cross ['et minxit super crucem'] saying 'I renounce the new-fangled law and the comments of Jesus the false prophet' and he reviled and slandered Mary ... and made against her a charge not to be repeated' ... Thereupon the archbishop, weeping bitterly at hearing such blasphemies, deprived him of his orders.[50]

In this particular version of the story, the ex-deacon was grabbed, as he left the church, by a certain Fawkes of Bréauté, and shortly thereafter decapitated. So scrupulous a historian as Maitland could hardly accept every detail of this story as accurate. 'Eye-witness and archdeacon though Master John of Basingstoke may have been,' he wrote, 'we cannot believe all that he had said.' Among other problems in the account, Maitland saw it as unlikely that 'the assembled prelates gave the apostate an opportunity of manifesting his change of faith in a fashion at once very solemn and very gross'.[51] One suspects, however, that, had Maitland been familiar with the Hebrew sources from Germany and France discussed above, he would have been less sceptical about the possibility that the deacon had learned how to die defiantly, the Jewish way, having perhaps even heard stories of the brave martyrs in Xanten and Trier.

Maitland found the former deacon's action so gross that he could not even bring himself to translate it precisely, rendering it euphemistically as 'defiled the cross' and discreetly inserting in a footnote the Latin original: 'et minxit super

49   The article was originally published in the *Law Quarterly Review*, II (1886), 153–165, and reprinted in Maitland's *Roman Canon Law in the Church of England* (London, 1898) and then in *The Collected Papers of Frederic William Maitland*, ed. H.A.L. Fisher (Cambridge: Cambridge University Press, 1911), pp.385–406. See also *Transactions of the Jewish Historical Society of England*, 6 (1908–12), 260–76, where it was again republished with an important introduction by Israel Abrahams (ibid., pp.254–9), whose admiring description I have quoted.

50   Maitland, 'The Deacon and the Jewess; or, Apostasy at Common Law', in *The Collected Papers*, I, 399.

51   Ibid., p.400.

crucem'. Curiously, whereas Matthew Paris and his informant had no problem reporting that the circumcised deacon had urinated on a crucifix, the latter's indecorous charge concerning Mary was not deemed worthy of repeating, even euphemistically. Maitland, by contrast, writing during the reign of Queen Victoria, was more squeamish about the deacon's 'very gross' act than about his blasphemous words.

Nonetheless he was willing to provide considerably more information about that act than was, in our own century, the Anglo-Jewish historian Cecil Roth. In his *History of the Jews in England* (published during the Holocaust), Roth briefly narrated the story of the thirteenth-century deacon 'who had been induced through the study of Hebrew to adopt Judaism and had married a Jewess', mentioning the former's blasphemy but not his defilement of a crucifix. A decade later, in his 1951 monograph on *The Jews of Medieval Oxford*, Roth was a bit more generous with details concerning the former deacon's last moments: 'When a crucifix was brought before him,' wrote Roth, 'he defiled it with the words "I renounce the new-fangled law and the comments of Jesus the false prophet", adding also blasphemies against the Virgin Mary.'[52] Roth did not bother to specify the nature of the defilement, even in his lengthy footnote on the incident. Yet it is hardly clear that the charges against Jesus and Mary, quite reliably, in Roth's view, attributed to the ex-deacon, possess greater facticity than Matthew's report that he also urinated on a crucifix. Historians may sometimes think themselves scrupulous when they are simply being squeamish.[53]

Returning then to our less squeamish medieval chroniclers, we have Solomon bar Samson in twelfth-century Germany speaking of two Jews in Trier urinating on a cross offered to them at the moment of martyrdom, and Matthew Paris

---

52   C. Roth, *A History of the Jews in England* (Oxford: Clarendon Press, 1941) p.41; idem, T*he Jews of Medieval Oxford* (Oxford: Clarendon Press, 1951), p.20. On Roth, see, most recently, F. Krome, 'Jewish History for Our Own Needs', *Modern Judaism*, 21 (2001), 216–37.

53   Note, for example, the various treatments by Jewish (or philo-Semitic) historians of the expulsion of the Jews from Antioch in the late sixth century after one of their coreligionists was accused of urinating on an image of the Virgin Mary. See J. Parkes, *The Conflict of the Church and the Synagogue* (London: Soncino Press, 1934), p.293, who wrote that the Jews of Antioch had insulted an image of the Virgin 'in repulsive fashion'; shortly afterward Joshua Starr, 'Byzantine Jewry on the Eve of the Arab Conquest (565–638)', *Journal of the Palestine Oriental Society*, 15 (1935), 283, who described the act as 'a sacrilege perpetrated by an individual Jew', and Baron, over two decades later, who wrote that the community was punished 'for the transgression of a single coreligionist' (*SRH*, III, p.19). Baron, despite his critique of lachrymosity in Jewish historiography, gave no hint as to the nature of the transgression which caused the entire community of Antioch to be punished. M. Avi-Yonah, in his *The Jews under Roman and Byzantine Rule* (Jerusalem: Magnes, 1984), originally published (in Hebrew) in 1946, omitted the events of 592–3 in Antioch entirely. Contrast with all the above D.M. Olster, *Roman Defeat ... and the Literary Construction of the Jew* (Philadelphia: University of Pennsylvania Press, 1994), p.4.

reporting a case of similar behaviour in thirteenth-century England. Both chroniclers are writing at a distance of two or three decades from their subjects, and both explicitly state that they have their information at second hand. Their accounts may be seen as corroborating each other, if perhaps less on a factual level than on a mental one. To both Jews and Christians of their time (unlike historians of recent generations) it was not difficult to imagine a Jew, whether naturally born or converted, urinating on a cross if given the opportunity. Unlike ritual murder or host desecration, this form of imagined conduct, it may be added, was not limited to Christian sources.

The tragic story of the former deacon who denied the cross may be linked, somewhat paradoxically, with that of his aforementioned countryman and contemporary, Yom Tov b. Moses, who met his death on account of his attraction to the very same sign. Both point to the centrality of the cross as symbolizing the tense (and yet sometimes porous) lines of demarcation between the worlds of Judaism and Christianity. And both may be linked with a third, well documented, story from thirteenth-century England: the snatching and trampling of a processional cross by a Jew of Oxford as an ecclesiastical procession passed through the centre of the town's 'Jewry' on Ascension Day, 1268.

'A certain Jew of the most consummate impudence,' as Tovey later wrote, 'violently snatched it from the bearer, and trod it under his feet, in token of his contempt for Christ.'[54] News of this event came to King Henry III, who intervened personally in the matter, demanding that the Jews of Oxford be thrown into jail until they had made reparation, and that they not be permitted to administer their property until they had given adequate security for the replacement they would provide. This, it was determined, would consist of a stately marble crucifix picked out in gold, with a figure of the crucified Jesus on one side and the Virgin on the other, which was to be erected at the place where the crime had been committed. At the top of the cross was to be an inscription containing the cause of its erection. Likewise they were to present a portable crucifix of silver, of the size that was usually carried before archbishops, to be given to the Chancellor and the scholars of the university for use on such occasions when they went in procession.[55]

---

54   D' Blossiers Tovey, *Anglia Judaica: or the History and Antiquities of the Jews in England* (London, 1738), p.168. See also Roth, *Medieval Oxford*, pp.151–3; Trachtenberg, *The Devil*, p.118.

55   Tovey, *Anglia Judaica*, p.168; Roth, *Medieval Oxford*, p.152. For the Latin original of the King's letter, see *Close Rolls of the Reign of Henry III ... A. D. 1268–1272* (London: His Majesty's Stationery Office, 1938), pp.14–15. I thank Mary Minty for acquiring for me a photocopy. The loose translation I have offered draws on both Tovey and Roth.

The 1268 cross snatching by an Oxford Jew, which Tovey, an eighteenth-century fellow of Merton College, called a 'most astonishing crime', was discussed with evident discomfort by a later Jewish resident of Oxford, Cecil Roth, who in his aforementioned monograph attempted to put an acceptable 'spin' on the incident:'It may be that some Jew was pushed accidentally against the Cross or else dragged towards it by the mob, and made the bearer stumble, or possibly a demented iconoclast may have taken it into his head to make this foolish gesture.' But Roth was not the only Jewish historian to seek an explanation in the realm of psychopathology. As late as 1980 Joseph Shatzmiller suggested that the Oxford Jew had attacked the cross 'in a moment of temporary madness'. More recently Christopher Cluse, while describing Roth's attempt at explanation as 'fully valid', especially since it was offered 'so soon after the Holocaust' (in 1951), has advanced the 'daring' (in his view) hypothesis that an Oxford Jew did intentionally snatch and smash a processional cross on Ascension Day, 1268. He has also gone beyond the event to examine its 'narrative', which, he suggests, emerged 'in an atmosphere dominated by the preaching of the crusade and [Lord] Edward's preparations for taking the Cross on St. John's Day (24 June), 1268', an atmosphere of religious tension in which the story 'made sense' to both 'Jews and Christians alike'. In addition to pointing to previous accusations of cross desecration which bear some degree of verisimilitude, Cluse has made the important observation that, in the year 1268, Ascension day fell on the third of Sivan, the first of the three 'days of limitation' before Shavuot, and the anniversary (as noted above) of the massacre of Mainz Jewry in 1096.[56]

It would be of course 'very speculative', as Cluse himself has admitted, 'to think that the Oxford Jew who broke a processional cross on Ascension day 1268' was influenced by the memory of that distant event. But one should note nonetheless the heightened tensions which must have frequently prevailed between Christians and Jews in the years after 1096 when the commemorations of three momentous events overlapped or occurred in close proximity: the ascent of Moses 'up to God' (Ex: 19:3) in order to receive the Torah; the ascent of Jesus 'into heaven' (Acts 1:9–10) after his resurrection; and the ascent 'to God, all together' of the martyrs of Mainz.[57] And just as the overlap between Passover and Holy Week could give rise to religious tensions between Jews and Christians resulting in crime (on the part of the former) and punishment (on the part of the

---

56   Roth, *Medieval Oxford*, p.152; Christopher Cluse, 'Stories of Breaking and Taking the Cross: A Possible Context for the Oxford Incident of 1268', *Revue d'Histoire Ecclésiastique*, 90 (1995), pp.369–442, p.161; Joseph Shatzmiller, 'Desecrating the Cross: A Rare Medieval Accusation', *Melakanim be-Toledot 'am Yisrael Ve-eretz Israel*, 5 (1980) pp.403–5, 428, 430–31.

57   See Solomon bar Samson in Haberman, pp.29–30; Eidelberg, *Jews and Crusaders*, p.29.

latter, as in Clermont and Rome) so too could the clash between the dates commemorating the ascent of Moses on Mount Sinai (for forty days) and the ascension of Jesus on the Mount of Olives (after forty days) create a similarly explosive environment.[58] This, of course, would only be magnified for those who recalled the martyrs of Mainz in 1096.

As Shatzmiller aptly noted, the anonymous assailant of the processional cross in Oxford was a contemporary of the unfortunate Yom Tov who took his life on the eve of Shavuot after 'a demon showed him an image of the cross and pressed him to worship it'. To these two 'mad Englishmen' of the thirteenth century I have added a third, the deacon who 'loved a Jewess with unlawful love' and embraced her religion with such ardour that he was willing (according to Matthew Paris) to urinate (with his newly circumcised phallus) upon the crucifix he once revered above all else. In doing so he followed, whether knowingly or not, the tradition of rude and reckless denial of Christianity associated in European Jewish memory with the martyrs of the Crusades. It was a tradition, however, for which Israel Halpern found no place in his 1941 anthology of Jewish valour, just as Cecil Roth, in his history of English Jewry published in the very same year, found no place for the former deacon's defilement of a cross. In this essay I have attempted to return these 'demented iconoclasts' to the realm of Jewish historical memory, and to explain how their actions could have made sense to them and to their Christian contemporaries. As Emily Dickinson wrote: 'Much Madness is divinest Sense/ to a discerning Eye.'

---

58   On the link between the biblical accounts of the ascension of Moses and the ascension of Jesus see Georg Kretschmar, 'Himmelfahrt und Pfingsten', *Zeitschrift für Kirchengeschichte*, 66 (1954–5), 217–18. I thank Daniel Schwartz for securing for me a photocopy of Kretschmar's article.

Chapter 8

Albert the Great on the Talmud and the Jews

Irven M. Resnick[1]

Despite a traditional anti-Judaism in patristic and medieval Christian theological literature,[2] tolerance for Jews and religious difference coexisted in Christian culture into the twelfth century. This may seem something of a paradox given that more polemical treatises written *contra Judaeos* were penned in the twelfth century than in all of the earlier Christian centuries combined.[3] Yet many of these, perhaps the majority, display an irenic spirit at variance with the image conjured up by the term 'polemic'. By the middle of the twelfth century, however, several Christian polemical treatises had assumed a more vicious tone, for example Peter Alphonsi's *Dialogues of a Christian and a Jew*,[4] which displays the religious zeal of a Jewish convert to Christianity, Guibert of Nogent's *Treatise on the Incarnation against the Jews*,[5] and Peter the Venerable's

1   I would like to thank the Oxford Centre for Hebrew and Jewish Studies for a research fellowship in 1995 that enabled me to begin the original paper. I would also like to thank Dr Daniel Frank (formerly of the Oxford Centre for Hebrew and Jewish Studies) and Professor Menachem Kellner of the University of Haifa for their helpful responses to particular inquiries. Although presented under the present title at 'Tolerance and Intolerance: An International Conference to mark the Centenary of James Parkes' Birth', it was published, subsequently, under the title 'Talmud, *Talmudisti*, and Albert the Great' in *Viator*, 33(2002), 1–18 and is reprinted here, with only minor additions, with the permission of the editor.

2   See Gerhart B. Ladner, 'Aspects of Patristic Anti-Judaism', *Viator*, 2 (1971), 355–63.

3   For a survey of Christian polemical literature, see Peter Browe, 'Die Judenmission im Mittelalter und die Päpste', *Miscellanea Historiae Pontificiae*, 6 (Rome, 1973), 99–121.

4   *Dialogi ex Judeo Christiani, Patrologia cursus completes, series Latina* (*PL*), ed. J.P. Higne (Paris: 1844–5) 157, 535-672. For a good discussion of Peter Alphonsi's *Dialogi*, and his role in Jewish–Christian polemics, see Jeremy Cohen, *Living Letters of the Law: Ideas of the Jew in Medieval Christianity* (Berkeley, Los Angeles and London: University of California Press, 1999), pp.201–18; and his 'The Mentality of the Medieval Jewish Apostate: Peter Alfonsi, Hermann of Cologne, and Pablo Christiani', in Todd M. Endelman (ed.), *Jewish Apostasy in the Modern World* (New York: Holmes & Meier, 1987), pp.20–47. My annotated translation of *Dialogi* is forthcoming from the Catholic University of America Press, The Fathers of the Church, Mediaeval Continuation.

5   PL 156, 489–528. For a discussion of Guibert's anti-Judaism, see A.B. Sapir Abulafia, 'Christian Imagery of Jews in the Twelfth Century: A look at Odo of Cambrai

Against the Inveterate Stubbornness of the Jews.[6]

Several different explanations have been offered for this shift. However one of the more compelling is Jeremy Cohen's contention that it is rooted in a growing conviction among Christians that living Jewish communities had substituted the Talmud for the Old Testament, thereby abandoning the single most positive function St Augustine thought Jews performed, namely, to preserve and carry with them the text and the Law of the Old Testament.[7] In part because the Talmud was thought to be filled with attacks upon Christian doctrine and theological absurdities, Peter the Venerable (ca.1092–1156), the first Christian polemicist to refer directly to the Jews' dependence on the Talmud,[8] despaired even of the Jews' capacity for reason. He concluded that no hope remained that Jews might be persuaded to see the truth of Christianity any more than the brute

---

and Guibert of Nogent', *Theoretische Geschiedenis* (Historiography and Theory), 16.4 (1989), 383–91; and Jeremy Cohen, *Living Letters of the Law*, pp. 192–201.

6   See Peter the Venerable, *Adversus Judeorum inveteratam duritiem*, ed. Yvonne Friedman, CC CM, vol. 58 (Turnhout: Brepols, 1985). This text can be dated to the fourth decade of the twelfth century.

7   See, for example, Augustine's *Sermo* 200.2, 'quid aliud hic significavit divina providentia, nisi apud Judaeos solas divinas Litteras remansuras, quibus Gentes instruerentur, illi excaecarentur; quas portarent non ad adjutorium salutatis suae, sed ad testimonium salutatis nostrae? ... si forte Pagani, quos lucrari volumus, dixerint non eas tanto ante praedictas, sed post rerum eventum, ut haec quae facta sunt propheta putarentur, a nobis esse confictas; Judaeorum codices recitamus, ut tollatur dubitatio Paganorum' (How else has divine providence indicated [in Matt. 2: 5–7] that they are blinded unless by the fact that only the divine texts, by which the Nations will be instructed, will survive among the Jews, but not as an aid to their salvation but as a testimony to ours? ... [so that] if perhaps the pagans, whom we want to win over, should say that these [testimonies] were not so much prophesied as they were fabricated by us after the event, so that the things that occurred might be thought to have been prophesied, we read from the Jews' codices, so that the Pagans' doubts may be lifted') (PL 38, 1030). Cf. also *De fide rerum quae non videntur*, c. 6.9, PL 40, 179: 'Ergo occisi non sunt, sed dispersi: ut quamvis in fide, unde salvi fierent, non haberent; tamen unde nos adjuraremur, memoria retinerent, in Libris suffragatores, in cordibus nostri hostes, in codibus testes' ('Therefore they have not been slain but dispersed, seeing that although they do not embrace the faith in which they may be saved nevertheless – our enemies in their hearts, our witnesses in their codices, our supporters in their books – they preserve the memory whereby we are adjured') (*De civitate Dei*, *XI–XXII*, 18.46, CCSL 48/2 (Turnholt: Brepols, 1955); and *Ennarrationes in Psalmos*, LI-C, CCSL 39 (Turnholt: Brepols, 1956), pp.744–5. For Jeremy Cohen's treatment, see both his *The Friars and the Jews* (Ithaca: Cornell University Press, 1982) and *Living Letters of the Law*. See also the classic study of Bernhard Blumenkranz, 'Augustin et les Juifs – Augustin et le Judaïsme', *Recherches Augustiniennes*, 1(1958), 225–41.

8   See Friedman's remarks in *Adversus Judeorum inveteratam duritiem*, p.xv. For some discussion, too, of the increasingly frequent attacks on the Talmud in anti-Jewish polemics, see also Kurt Schubert, "Das christlich–jüdische Religionsgespräch im 12. und 13. Jahrhundert', in Alfred Ebenbauer and Klaus Zatloukal (eds), *Die Juden in ihrer mittelalterlichen Umwelt* (Cologne: Böhlau, 1991), pp.223–50.

beast could be persuaded.[9] With Peter, Gavin Langmuir remarks, not only had the fear of the Jew become irrational but even the Jew himself.[10]

Although fourteenth-century Christian polemicists would investigate the Talmud both in search of concealed evidence to confirm Christian doctrine and to refute rabbinic claims,[11] in the first half of the thirteenth century it was especially the alleged blasphemies it contained against Christianity that elicited a dramatic Christian response in Paris resulting in (as some scholars interpret the evidence) its condemnation for heresy.[12] Following several decrees issued by Pope Gregory IX in June 1239 to ecclesiastics and rulers,[13] King Louis IX confiscated rabbinic texts and called Jewish scholars to Paris to defend the Talmud against such charges, initiating a series of public disputations which drew attention to the claim that it was the Talmud that was responsible for the Jews' departure from the Mosaic religion.[14] By 1242, the Talmud had fallen victim to politics and polemics, and perhaps as many as twenty-four cartloads of the Talmud were burned in Paris.[15]

---

9   For the significance of this shift in tone and its implications for Jewish–Christian relations, see also Anna Sapir Abulafia, 'Twelfth-Century Christian Expectations of Jewish Conversion: A Case Study of Peter of Blois', *Aschkenas*, 8.1 (1998), 45–70. For Sapir Abulafia, the perceived irrationality of Jews presented Christian polemicists with a paradox: a growing awareness of the impossible futility of persuading Jews by reason of the superiority of Christian claims, and the compelling need to make just such attempts in order to provide Christians with appropriate defences for their faith.

10   See Gavin Langmuir, *Toward a Definition of Antisemitism* (Berkeley, Los Angeles and Oxford: University of California Press, 1990), p. 207.

11   For a Jewish response to this new Christian tactic, see David Berger's 'Christians, Gentiles, and the Talmud: A Fourteenth-Century Jewish Response to the Attack on Rabbinic Judaism', in Bernard Lewis and Friedrich Niewöhner (eds), *Religionsgespräche im Mittelalter*, vol.4 (Wiesbaden: Otto Harrasowitz, 1992), pp.115–32.

12   See Jeremy Cohen, *Living Letters of the Law*, pp.317–34, for a vigorous defence of the claim that the attack on the Talmud stemmed from the view that it constituted heresy. For evidence of a growing tendency from the middle of the twelfth century to conflate Judaism and heresy, see Raoul Manselli, 'La polémique contre les Juifs dans la polémique antihérétique', in *Cahiers de Fanjeaux*, vol.12, *Juifs et judaïsme de Languedoc* (Toulouse: Édouard Privat, 1977), pp.251–67.

13   See Shlomo Simonsohn, *The Apostolic See and the Jews*, vol.1, *Documents: 492–1404* (Toronto: Pontifical Institute of Mediaeval Studies, 1988), pp.171–4, nos. 162–5.

14   See Benjamin Z. Kedar, 'Canon Law and the Burning of the Talmud', *Bulletin of Medieval Canon Law*, 9 (1979), 78–83, and Robert Chazan, 'The Condemnation of the Talmud Reconsidered (1239–1248)', *Proceedings of the American Academy for Jewish Research*, 45(1988), 11–30.

15   For the history of the burning of the Talmud, and its basis, see Joel E. Rembaum, 'The Talmud and the Popes: Reflections on the Talmud Trials of the 1240s', *Viator*, 13 (1982), 203–23; and Judah M. Rosenthal, 'The Talmud on Trial. The Disputation at Paris in the Year 1240', *Jewish Quarterly Review*, n.s. 47(1956), 58–76,

Ecclesiastical attempts to confiscate or eliminate the Talmud continued in Europe,[16] but it was in France that the impact on the intellectual life of the once-flourishing Jewish community may have been most devastating. Repeatedly, Jewish scholars appealed to the papacy and declared that without the Talmud, Jews could not properly understand or fulfil the precepts of the Bible. They rallied to the defence of the Talmud and related literature in the late 1240s, and found some support from Pope Innocent IV.[17] Such support was, however, inadequate to restrain the zeal of the papal legate in Paris, Odo of Tusculum (Odo of Châteauroux), who continued to press efforts to locate and destroy these Jewish books.[18] In 1247, he formed a commission of inquiry in which numerous scholars and theologians of the University of Paris participated. The outcome of the commission is revealed in Odo's proclamation of 15 May 1248 in Paris, which rails against the Talmud for its innumerable errors, abuses, blasphemies and nefarious attacks on Christianity. Such books clearly should not be tolerated any longer in Christendom.[19] Within a generation, these attacks on the Talmud had aroused increasing antipathy and intolerance of the Jews themselves.[20]

145–69. To my knowledge, Christian awareness of a resurgence in Jewish messianism in France did not figure in the attack on the Talmud. The fifth Jewish millennium began in the Christian year 1240 and this combined with news of the Mongol invasions to create a messianic atmosphere. In France, Ezra of Moncontour prophesied that Elijah would come in 1226, the messiah in 1233 and redemption in 1240. See Elisheva Carlebach, 'Between History and Hope: Jewish Messianism in Ashkenaz and Sepharad', 3rd Annual Lecture of the Victor J. Selmanowitz Chair of Jewish History (17 May 1998), (New York: Graduate School of Jewish Studies, Touro College, 1998).

16   Papal documents from the 1250s and 1260s, from Alexander IV and Clement IV, and 1320, from John XXII, renewed calls to confiscate the Talmud and other Jewish commentaries. See Shlomo Simonsohn, *The Apostolic See and the Jews*, vol.1, *Documents: 492–1404*, pp. 215–16, 233–6, 321–2, nos 211,.228–9; 309. Similar orders for its destruction were issued in 1415 and 1553. See Kenneth Stow, 'The Burning of the Talmud in 1553, in Light of Sixteenth-Century Catholic Attitudes toward the Talmud', in Jeremy Cohen (ed.), *Essential Papers on Judaism and Christianity in Conflict: From Late Antiquity to the Reformation* (New York: New York University Press, 1991), pp.401–28.

17   Cf. *Chartularium universitatis Parisiensis*, ed. Heinrich Denifle, 4 vols (Paris: Delalain, 1889–97), 1, 202, no. 173; see also Simonsohn, *The Apostolic See and the Jews*, vol.1: *Documents: 492–1404*, pp.196–7, no. 187.

18   Odo (d.1273), former chancellor of the university of Paris, had been named cardinal bishop of Frascati by Innnocent IV in 1244. In October 1245 he returned to France to preach the sixth crusade.

19   'quia eos [books of the Talmud] invenimus errores innumerabiles, abusiones, blasfemias et nepharia continere … quod predicti libri secundum Deum sine fidei christiane injuria tolerari non possunt' (*Chartularium universitatis Parisiensis*, 1, 209, no. 178.

20   See the appendices in Joseph Schatzmiller's *La deuxième controverse de Paris. Un chapitre dans la polémique entre chrétiens et juifs au Moyen Age* (Paris and Louvain: Editions E. Peeters, 1994), which contain accounts of a public disputation, or disputations, held in Paris ca. 1270. In Appendix III, Schatzmiller provides a French translation of a Hebrew record of an encounter between Abraham ben Samuel of Rouen

Among the forty scholars and ecclesiastics (members of Odo's commission of inquiry) who affixed their signatures to this document appears the name of the great Dominican scholar Albert the Great (*Albertus Theotonicus*; d.1280).[21] Indeed this seems to be the first document in which Albert's name appears. Only a little more than a month after signing this decree, Albert left Paris for Cologne to assume responsibility for the Dominican *studium generale* there.

Although Albert composed no systematic polemic against Judaism, scattered throughout his writings one finds a few references to the Talmud, to the writings of medieval Jewish scholars, and to Jews or Judaism itself. Yet no study has attempted to examine Albert's understanding of Judaism and the Talmud. Nevertheless, despite Albert's prominence in the new mendicant movement, which Jeremy Cohen has argued raised anti-Jewish polemics to a harsher, more aggressive level, Cohen absolves Albert with the assurance that Albert's attitude toward Jews and Judaism was relatively benign and traditional (that is, Augustinian).[22] Here, I intend to examine this claim, to explore in Albert's writings his views of Jews and Judaism, and to discuss his relationship to the increasingly aggressive missionary effort directed toward the Jews by Albert's fellow Dominicans.

Albert the Great in Paris and the Talmud's Condemnation

Weisheipl remarked, quite correctly, that 'The first forty years of Albert's life are relatively obscure.'[23] We are not certain in what year Albert entered the Dominican order, although it is likely that he was received into the order between 1223 and 1230. From 1230 to 1243, a chronology of Albert's life is hardly more straightforward, and especially vexing is a controversy over the date of his arrival in Paris. Weisheipl suggested that Albert went to Paris in either 1243 or 1244.[24] More recently, Simon Tugwell has argued that Albert arrived in Paris as

---

and his Christian opponent, whom Schatzmiller identifies as Pablo Christiani. The Christian in the debate insists that, precisely because the Talmud offers evidence for Christian messianic claims, the Jews' rejection of Jesus is all the more incomprehensible. As they slew him, they deserve to be slain and a curse on all those who tolerate them (p.76, fol.109a).

21   Contemporary or near contemporary documents variously identify Albert as Albert the German (*Albertus Teutonicus*), Albert of Cologne, or simply as Albert the Great (*Albertus Magnus*). For these different appellations, see Adolf Layer, 'Namen und Ehrennamen Alberts des Grossen', *Jahrbuch des historischen Vereins Dillingen an der Donau*, 81(1979), 41–3.

22   'The Jews as Killers of Christ from Augustine to the Friars', *Traditio*, 39 (1983), p.18.

23   James A. Weisheipl, 'Albertus Magnus', in *Dictionary of the Middle Ages* (New York: Scribner, 1982), I, p.127.

24   One notes that Weisheipl also seems uncomfortable with 1243/44 for

early as 1240. If Tugwell is correct, Albert would have been in Paris for the outbreak of the first attack upon the Talmud. This attack accompanied the famous Parisian public inquisition of 1240, involving R. Yehiel of Paris, three other rabbis, and numerous Christian adversaries, including the Jewish convert to Christianity, Nicholas Donin of La Rochelle, and William of Auvergne, Bishop of Paris.[25]

This attack on the Talmud had been sparked by Nicholas Donin, who had complained to Pope Gregory IX as early as 1236 of Jewish insults to Christianity in the Talmud and other Jewish books. In 1239, Gregory wrote to William of Auvergne in Paris instructing him to collect these books during Lent the following year, 1240.[26] The Talmud was legally charged and tried by the Inquisition. A clerical court condemned it and ordered it burned at the stake. Twenty to twenty-four wagon loads (10 000–12 000 volumes) were burned in Paris in 1242. In 1244, Pope Innocent IV repeated a request to King Louis IX to burn copies of the Talmud.[27] As a participant in this process, Nicholas Donin compiled a treatise of over 100 folios in which he included the noxious passages of the Talmud (entitled the *Extractiones de Talmut*) as well as another work listing similarly offensive passages from the Jewish liturgy (entitled *Articuli litterarum pape*).

Albert's arrival in Paris. In an earlier study he suggests 1241 as the year in which Albert was sent to Paris to prepare to become a master in theology See his 'Albert the Great', in the *New Catholic Encyclopedia* (1967) 1, p.254.

25   An account of this disputation was completed some twenty years later by R. Yehiel's pupil, Joseph ben Nathan Official, in the *Sefer Yosef ha-Mekane*. Hyam Maccoby provides a paraphrase of both this (Hebrew) account and a Latin text in his *Judaism on Trial: Jewish-Christian Disputations in the Middle Ages* (Rutherford, NJ: Fairleigh Dickinson University Press, 1982), pp.153–67. For a discussion of the *Sefer Yosef ha-Mekane* and its position among Jewish–Christian polemics,see Hanne Trautner-Kromann, *Shield and Sword: Jewish Polemics Against Christianity and the Christians in France and Spain from 1100–1500* (Tübingen: J.C.B. Mohr, 1993), pp.91ff. For the particular talmudic passages at issue, see especially Judah M. Rosenthal, 'The Talmud on Trial. The Disputation at Paris in the Year 1240'.

26   See Simonsohn, *The Apostolic See and the Jews*, vol.1, *Documents: 492–1404*, pp.171–2, 174, nos 162–3, 165. William of Auvergne's role in the attack on the Talmud has been evaluated by Lesley Smith in 'William of Auvergne and the Jews', Diana Wood (ed.), in *Christianity and Judaism*, Studies in Church History, 29 (Oxford: Blackwells, 1992), pp.107–17. Smith sees William as sympathetic to the Jews and suggests that although he was dragged into this conflict, his influence stalled its progress from 1240 to 1242.

27   See Simonsohn, *The Apostolic See and the Jews*, vol.1, *Documents: 492–1404*, p.180, no. 171. Note too that the Parisian *Summa Theologiae* attributed to Alexander of Hales, and completed in the 1230s or early 1240s, also recommends burning for these Jewish books which blaspheme against Christianity. See *Alexandri de Hales, Summa Theologica*, 4 vols (Quaracchi: Collegium S. Bonventurae, 1948), S.T. Inq. III, tr. VIII, sect. I, q.1., tit. II, M.1, c.1.

Talmud, Talmudists and Jewish 'Philosophers'

Regardless of the date of his first appearance in Paris, Albert's activities there and his involvement in the Commission of Inquiry of 1247 would have made him aware of some of the controversial claims located in the talmudic literature condemned by Odo of Tusculum in 1248. Albert's knowledge of the Talmud must, of course, be strictly derivative. He did not have the linguistic skills required for access to the texts themselves: Albert knew no Hebrew or Aramaic (nor for that matter Arabic, and very little Greek). Perhaps he had already become acquainted with Nicholas Donin himself – both Donin's and Albert's signatures appear on the document condemning the Talmud – and learned something of the Talmud's contents from him,[28] or perhaps from Odo of Tusculum who also was involved in the original investigation of the Talmud in 1240, or perhaps from the synopses of Talmudic errors composed by the convert Thibaut de Sezanne (to which Nicholas Donin provided the appendix) for Odo of Tusculum.[29]

In the end, it may be impossible to identify the source of Albert's information on the Talmud. Nevertheless, while talmudic literature does not figure prominently in Albert's own writings, he does make mention of it. One example is found in his commentary on the Lombard's *Sentences*, on which Albert had laboured since his arrival in Paris and which he completed for publication by 1249.[30] There Albert criticized as a talmudic 'heresy' the claim that Job denied the doctrine of resurrection. Albert attributes this heresy found among the Jews to a Rabbi Nasse who, he claims, 'composed [*composuit*] the Talmud'.[31] Albert presumably has in mind R. Judah ha-Nasi, credited with the codification ca. 200CE of the Oral Law or Mishnah, one component of the Talmud. In another text, Albert attributes to several Jewish sages, including one Rab Vasse (perhaps

---

28   Cf. *Scriptores ordinis Praedicatorum*, ed. J. Quétif (Paris: 1719–21), 1, p.166.

29   His *Excerpta Talmudica* or *Extractiones de Talmud* which, Rosenthal remarks, was edited between 1249–55. See 'The Talmud on Trial. The Disputation at Paris in the Year 1240', pp.74–5.

30   Internal evidence makes clear that Albert was still working on this as late as 1246. See *Commentarii in IV Sententiarum*, Opp. 27, ed A. Borgnet, vol.30 (Paris: L. Vivès, 1894), p.139. For a chronology of his works, cf. James A. Weisheipl, 'Albertus Magnus', in *Dictionary of the Middle Ages*, I, pp.129–30.

31   'Scias autem, quod in ista auctoritate Job duae haereses sunt radicatae circa resurrectionem, quarum una est Judaeorum, scilicet Rabbi Nasse, qui composuit Talmuth, qui dicit Job resurrectionem non credidisse et negasse' (*Commentarii in IV Sententiarum (dist. 23–50)*, dist. 43, A, art. 1, ed A. Borgnet, vol.30 (Paris: L. Vivès, 1894), p.301. The name Rabbi Nasse does not appear in the papal documents concerned with the confiscation of the Talmud and assembled by Simonsohn or, explicitly, in the accounts of the Parisian disputations of 1240 or 1270, rendering all the more interesting its appearance in Albert's work.

a scribal error for Rabbi Nasse, identified above) the claim that God gave to the Jews a 'double law' (*duplicem legem*): the first written on stone and the second in the hearts of the wise.[32] This 'double law', an expression that recalls Jerome's reference to the *deuterosis* or oral law of the Jews,[33] Albert criticizes for its 'carnal' and imperfectly spiritual understanding of basic commandments. The suggestion that R. Nasse 'composed the Talmuth', morever, indicates Albert's ignorance of its origins and development.

It is not immediately clear from Albert's criticism of talmudic heresy in his commentary on the *Sentences* whether he regards as heretical the view that *Job* denied the resurrection, or whether he supposed that rabbinic *Jews* denied the doctrine of the resurrection, based on mistaken talmudic interpretations of Job and other books in the Bible. The notion that rabbinic Judaism understood Job to have denied the resurrection is mistaken. Although Job 14:12 might be read this way (If a man dies can he live again? He shall never be roused from his sleep) other passages from the same book (for example, Job 28:13; 33:30) were typically invoked to support a doctrine of the resurrection, considered an essential rabbinic belief.[34] Indeed the resurrection of the dead appears as one of Maimonides's thirteen essential principles or fundamentals of Judaism. In another work, however, it becomes clearer that Albert's criticism supposes a 'carnal' interpretation of the resurrection, and that this is, in fact, a talmudic 'heresy'. In his commentary on the *Ecclesiastical Hierarchy* of Pseudo-Dionysius the Areopagite, Albert again criticizes the Talmud for its doctrine of the resurrection.[35] He notes that Dionysius introduces four false opinions regarding the resurrection, and one that is true. Of the false opinions, the first is attributed to Empedocles, viz. that after death the soul withdraws into non-being;

---

32   'Dicebant enim Rab Vasse et Rab Iosua et Rab Iohanna et alii scribae, quod deus dedit duplicem legem, unam scriptam in lapidibus et aliam scriptam in cordibus sapientium' (*Super Matthaeum, capitula 1–14*, 5.43, Cologne ed. vol.21(1)) (Münster, 1987), p.160, 20f.

33   *Commenataria in Abacuc*, 1.2.9 (PL 25: 1297D).

34   Note too that Christian exegetes frequently interpreted Job 14:12 in a manner that would avoid impugning either the book's authority or the doctrine of the resurrection, insisting on treating the statement as a conditional: that is, that the dead will not be raised until, as Job says in the preceding passage, the heavens are opened. See Gregory the Great, *Moralia*, 12.7–8 (PL 75: 991B-992D); Odo of Cluny, *Moralia in Job*, 12.11–12 (PL 133: 236A–B); Garnerius of St. Victor, *Gregorianum*, 7.4 (PL 193: 294D). Moreover, although Peter Alphonsi attacks his interlocutor, Moses, for inconsistencies in his belief regarding the resurrection and for the notion that those resurrected will be returned to live on earth, he does not doubt that rabbinic Jews embrace a belief in the life to come. See his *Dialogi*, 3 (PL 157: 588D–589A). The source of Albert's information, then, remains unclear.

35   Albert began lecturing on the Ps. Dionysian corpus in Paris after 1245, when he assumed his chair as regent master, and wrote his commentary on the *Ecclesiastical Hierarchy* in Cologne in 1249. See *Super Dionysium de ecclesiastica hierarchia*, ed. Maria Burger, Cologne edn 36(2) (Monasterii Westfalorum: Aschendorff, 1999), p.i.

the second, to Plato, viz. that souls are not corrupted at the death of the body but return to the stars; the third, to Origen, viz. that, although the soul is reunited to the body after death, it is not rejoined to the same body it had, but to a body of subtle ether; the fourth error admits that the soul is reunited to the same body it had, but insists that it will continue to need food and will enjoy corporeal pleasures. This last formulation, notes Albert, is the error of Papias,[36] the Apollinarists,[37] Mohammed and also the Jews,[38] who say in the Talmud that following the resurrection the just will eat geese and Leviathan. The correct view of the resurrection, he insists, proclaims that the saints will be like the angels; in the life to come they will achieve with the angels rest in God, and their delights will not be of the body.[39] Their food will be spiritual and not corporeal.[40]

Here Albert recognizes that the Talmud acknowledges the resurrection of the body but he criticizes its doctrine as insufficiently spiritual. In doing so, he seems to have incorporated polemical attacks articulated at the Paris disputation of 1240. In the Talmud, Rabba b. bar Hanna does describe the very fat geese which will be Israel's portion in the world to come.[41] This passage was certainly known to Nicholas Donin since, in the Hebrew account of the Paris disputation of 1240, Donin refers to it, albeit in another context.[42] Similarly, in the Latin record of the disputation, R. Yehiel responds directly to Donin's complaints of talmudic 'absurdities' with a defence of the claim that at a messianic banquet Israel will

36   Papias (ca. 60–130) was Bishop of Hierapolis.

37   Apollinarius (ca. 310–ca. 390) was the Bishop of Laodicea, whose christological error was condemned at the second ecumenical council, at Constantinople.

38   'Quarta opinio ... dicebat, quod resurget anima cum corpore eodem, sed illud corpus utetur cibis sicut nunc et aliis delectationibus corporalibus, et in hoc esse beatitudinem. Et hoc dicit Papias Hierapolites, quem secuti sunt etiam in hoc Appollinaristae, et hoc etiam dicit Machumet in lege sua, et similiter Iudaei in Talmuth quod comedent anseres in alia vita et leviathan' ('The fourth opinion ... stated, that the soul will rise up with the same body, but that body will be accustomed to food just as it is now as well as other bodily delights, and that beatitude consists in this. And Papias of Hierapolis said this, as did the Apollinarists who followed him on this matter, and Mohammed also said this in his Law, as did the Jews in the Talmud [who say] that they will eat geese and Leviathan in another life) (*Super Dionysium de ecclesiastica hierarchia*, c.7, pp.148, 38–46.

39   'Quartam reprobat per hoc quod sanctis est repromissa vita similis angelis ... unde iniustum esset eis materialem vitam dicere futuram' (ibid., p.148, 55–8). Cf. Thomas Aquinas, *Summa contra gentiles*, 4.83, where Thomas criticizes the view that food or sex shall have any place among the saints in the life to come.

40   *Super Dionysium de ecclesiastica hierarchia*, c.1, p.16, 42–53. For Albert's treatment of food (corporeal and spiritual) the reader may wish to consult Philip Lyndon Reynolds, *Food and the Body: Some Peculiar Questions in High Medieval Theology* (Leiden and Boston: E.J. Brill, 1999), pp.215–310.

41   See Babylonian Talmud (B.T.), *Baba Bathra*, 73b.

42   See Maccoby, *Judaism on Trial: Jewish–Christian Disputations in the Middle Ages*, p.158.

eat Leviathan. Yehiel insists that 'there are several scriptural evidences for this'.[43] Leviathan, a dragon-like creature mentioned in the Bible that shares the characteristics of a serpent and a sea monster (Cf. Isa. 27:1; Job 3:8 and 40:25; and Ps. 104: 26), in Jewish art generally is depicted as a large fish engaged in an eschatological battle with Behemoth.[44] According to the Babylonian Talmud, having created Leviathan both male and female, God castrated the male and killed the female. The female was preserved in salt to be put before the righteous in an eschatalogical banquet.[45] The notion that then the righteous will eat Leviathan is explicit in Eleazar of Worms' (ca. 1165–1230) comments on its creation (Gen. 1:21). Speaking of Leviathan, he remarks: 'And in the future to come God will command Michael and Gabriel to hunt him, and he will stand on his tail before them, and his head will reach the Throne of Glory. They will flee from him immediately, until he is destined to fall at the hands of Jonah ... And who will eat him? People of truth who are involved with the Torah of truth.'[46] It is also found in Jewish *exempla* literature.[47] By contrast, Christian exegetes generally treated Leviathan allegorically, as a figure for Satan or the devil, who is struck down by Christ's divine power.[48] For the latter, then, Talmudic legends of Leviathan were a clear reflection of the 'carnality' of Jewish biblical interpretation and, in this instance at least, Albert's inclination to assign these 'errors' to the Talmud has some basis.

While here Albert identifies the Talmud as a source of doctrinal error, he nevertheless sometimes speaks approvingly of the teachings of talmudic sages, as well as of the work of more contemporary Jewish scholars, such as the eighth-century astrologer Messahala, Isaac ben Solomon Israeli (a Jewish physician–philosopher influenced by Neo-Platonism, who died ca. 955) and Maimonides – despite the fact that some Dominicans in France had publicly burned many of Maimonides' writings in 1232.[49] Yet, apart from occasionally

---

43   Ibid., p.162. See also Rosenthal, 'The Talmud on Trial. The Disputation at Paris in the Year 1240', p.165, where the belief that the just will feast on Leviathan appears among 35 charges or articles against the Talmud.

44   For a discussion of these motifs, see Marc Michael Epstein, *If Lions Could Carve Stones...': Medieval Jewry and the Allegorization of the Animal Kingdom. A Textual and Iconographic Study* (Ann Arbor, MI: UMI, 1992), p.286.

45   B.T., *Baba Bathra*, 74b.

46   *Perush HaRokeach Al'HaTorah*, Genesis 1:21 ed. Hayyim Konyevsky (Bnei Brak: Y. Klugman, 1978), p.62, quoted by Epstein, *Medieval Jewry*, p.274.

47   See the story of Emperor Antoninus the Pious, who inquired of R. Judah the Holy if he would allow him to feast on Leviathan in the world to come with the Jews (*Ma'aseh Book*) vol.1, trans. Moses Gaster (Philadelphia: Jewish Publication Society, 1934), p.145.

48   See Peter Damian, *Sermo*, 17bis (*De Sancto Vitale Martyre*), PL 144: 593D; *Sermo*, 46 (*Homilia in nativitate beatissimae virginis Mariae*), PL 144: 751B–C.

49   See Daniel J. Silver, *Maimonidean Criticism and the Maimonidean Controversy, 1180–1240* (Leiden: E.J. Brill, 1965), pp.148ff.

approving remarks, Albert also criticizes Talmudists (*Talmudisti*) and other Jewish thinkers for errors in biblical exegesis rooted in philosophical or scientific speculation.[50] Indeed, it is especially for their erroneous arguments in the realm of philosophical theology that Albert condemns certain Jewish exegetes. Albert criticizes both Arab and Jewish 'moderns', but especially Maimonides, for identifying the celestial intelligences of Aristotelian cosmology with the angels.[51] Similarly, in his commentary on the *Sentences* (I, dist. 37, L, art. 24: 'Whether Angels move in time?') Albert criticizes Jewish 'philosophers' explicating the Old Testament, like R. Moses (Maimonides), R. Elieser and R. Joanna, who have said that angels move, and that all the (celestial) virtues obey them with respect to their will. But this, proclaims Albert, is contrary to Scripture and is heretical.[52] Similarly Albert criticizes a position he wrongly attributes to Maimonides, that individual humans are the only particulars God and the angels know.[53]

---

50   Cf. *De animalibus*, 7.21 and 26.32(40), ed. Hermann Stadler, *Beiträge zur Geschichte der Philosophie des Mittelalters*, 15 and 16 (Münster: Aschendorff, 1916–1920). For a translation, see *Albertus Magnus On Animals. A Medieval Summa Zoologica*, trans. Kenneth F. Kitchell Jr. and Irven M. Resnick, 2 vols (Baltimore, MD: Johns Hopkins University Press, 1999), I, p.594; p.1762.

51   'novi quidam, et tantum quidam Arabes et quidam Judaei, Arabes sicut Avicenna et Algazel, Judaei autem sicut Isaac et Moyses Aegyptius, quem Rabbi Moysen, hoc est magistrum Moysen, vocant' (*Problemata determinata*, q. 2, in *Opera omnia Alberti Magni*, hereafter, cited as Cologne ed., ed. J. Weisheipl, vol.17(1) (Münster im Westf.: Aschendorff, 1975). Cf. *De causis et processu universitatis a prima causa*, 1.4.8, ed. Winfried Fauser, Cologne ed., vol.17(2) (Münster im Westf.: Aschendorff, 1993). This is a position Albert gradually came to reject. Cf. James A. Weisheipl, *Nature and Motion in the Middle Ages* (Washington, DC: Catholic University of America Press, 1985), pp.160–61. For Albert's treatment of Maimonides generally, see Manuel Joel, *Verhältniss Alberts des Grossen zu Moses Maîmonides. Ein Beitrag zum Geschichte der mittelalterlichen Philosophie* (Breslau: H. Skutsch, 1863).

52   'Philosophi enim quidam explicantes Vetus Testamentum de missionibus Angelorum, sicut Rabbi Moyses, et Rabbi Elieser, et Rabbi Joanna, dixerunt Angelos moveri, sed obedire eis omnes virtutes quoad nutum … et hoc (quia sacrae Scripturae contrarium est) haeresis est' *Commentarii in I Sententiarum (dist. 26–48)*, dist. 37, L, art. 24, ed A. Borgnet, vol.26 (Paris: L. Vivès, 1893), pp.265–6. Albert is evidently criticizing here the view that God created *ex nihilo* only the first universal form and universal matter, from which all subsequent things are made by the intelligences or 'angels', working according to divine command. For Albert's critique of such views, see James A. Weisheipl, 'Albertus Magnus and Universal Hylomorphism: A Note on Thirteenth-Century Augustinianism', in Francis J. Kovach and Robert W Shahan (eds), *Albert the Great. Commemorative Essays* (Norman, OK: University of Oklahoma Press, 1980), pp.239–60. For Maimonides's views on angels and their relationship to the Aristotelian separate intellects or intelligences, see *Guide of the Perplexed*, 2.6.16bf., trans. Shlomo Pines (Chicago: University of Chicago Press, 1969), pp.262–3.

53   *Super Dionysium, De caelesti hierarchia*, ed. Paul Simon and Wilhelm Kübel, Cologne ed., vol.36(1) (Monasterii Westfalorum: Aschendorff, 1993), pp.108, 70f. The argument over the extent of God's knowledge of particulars is evident in Averroes's *Decisive Treatise Determining the Nature of the Connection Between Religion and*

Albert's criticism, however, need not imply that these errors are specific to Jewish thinkers or to Judaism. Often he relies on Maimonides as a commentator on Aristotle,[54] and in no way is he singled out as a source of error. Albert frequently identifies by name Avicenna and Al-Ghazali, as well as other Arab commentators, as guilty of error. For Albert, however, *Jewish* thinkers err, not only in their understanding of Aristotle or the natural world, but also in their efforts to support their doctrines with evidence from the Bible. Consequently the 'errors' of Maimonides or other Jewish thinkers represent for Albert a more direct challenge to Christian truth, and elicit a harsher response than do errors found among Aristotle's Arab commentators. A greater familiarity among Scholastics with the works of Jewish scholarship, as Jeremy Cohen has reminded us, did not ensure greater tolerance for Jews or Judaism.[55]

The Jewish Character

Albert sometimes appeals to Jewish scholars for support and does not hesitate to praise their philosophical accomplishments when he finds himself in agreement with them.[56] Nevertheless he does not fail to introduce certain attacks on flaws in the Jewish character that are grounded in religious ethics, customs or in the Jews' physical constitution. He compares Jews, heretics and pagans to unclean dogs, because of both their insidious customs and their lack of faith. This lack of faith is a manifestation of the special perfidy of the Jews,[57] whom Albert identifies as worse than the demons because Jews not only deny divinity to Jesus, but actually perceive his power as demonic (cf. Matt. 9:34).[58] Commenting on Lk. 21:21 and

---

Philosophy, where Averroes rebuts Al-Ghazali's complaint that, according to the Peripatetics, God knows no particulars. See the selection appearing in Arthur Hyman and James J. Walsh (eds), *Philosophy in the Middle Ages* (Indianapolis: Hackett Publishing Company, 1977), p.295. With respect to Maimonides' views on divine knowledge of particulars, Albert is simply mistaken. For Maimonides' discussion of divine knowledge, see *Guide of the Perplexed*, 3.16–24 and especially 3.19.39b–3.21.44b, pp. 477–85.

54   See, for example, his use of Maimonides' summary of arguments for the eternity of the world at *Physica* 8.1.11, Cologne ed., vol.4(2) (Monasterii Westfalorum: Aschendorff, 1993), pp.570–72.

55   See the arguments in Cohen's 'Scholarship and Intolerance in the Medieval Academy: The Study and Evaluation of Judaism in European Christendom', *Essential Papers on Judaism and Christianity in Conflict: From Late Antiquity to the Reformation*, ed. Jeremy Cohen (New York: New York University Press, 1991), pp.310–41.

56   Describing Issac Israeli, for example, as 'in philosophia magnus'. Cf. *Metaphysica, libros 6-13*, 2.2.10, Cologne ed., vol.16(2) (Monasterii Westfalorum: Aschendorff, 1964), pp.495, 70–73.

57   *Super Matthaeum*, Cologne ed., vol.21(1) (Monasterii Westfalorum: Aschendorff, 1987), p. 247, 12 and p. 276, 81.

58   *In Evangelium Lucae*, 8.28, ed. A. Borgnet vol.22 (Paris: L. Vivès, 1894), p.561.

24, Albert condemns Jews for avarice, repeating a story he attributes to Hegesippus:[59] During the fall of Jerusalem (70 CE) Roman soldiers, when they heard that the Jews had swallowed all the gold which they had hidden earlier, attacked all the city's inhabitants with the sword: men, women and children. The Romans sliced open their bellies looking for the gold, and thus was Job's prophecy fulfilled: 'The riches he devoured, he vomited forth, and God drew them out of his stomach' (Job 20:15).[60] Avaricious, perfidious, worse than the demons – these are the characteristics Albert attributes to Jews.

Just as Jewish avarice is illustrated by the story above (and had become part of popular culture, in so far as Jews and usury were closely identified), so too Albert repeated the popular tale of the Magus and the Jew to illustrate Jewish misanthropy. This story, which Albert claims Pseudo-(Ps.) Aristotle handed down to Alexander the Great in his *De regimine dominorum*, describes an encounter between a Jew and a Gentile traveller in the desert. The Jew was on foot, while the Gentile rode a mule. As they travelled, they discussed their laws and customs. The Gentile said it belonged to his law to hold faith with all and to show compassion to all. The Jew said that it belonged to his law to hold faith with and to show compassion only to one who belonged to the same people (*contribulus*). Finally, when the Jew was exhausted by the journey, the Gentile placed him on his own mount, with a little food and drink. The Jew immediately spurred the mount, and abandoned his benefactor in the desert. But a vengeful God sent a wild beast after the Jew, who was thrown from the mount, which the Gentile was able to recover. When the Gentile demanded of the Jew, why did you return evil for good? the Jew replied that the Law commanded him to do ill to foreigners, even if they had done him some kindness.[61]

---

59   A second-century Church historian. Only fragments of his work now survive, and almost all of these are included in Eusebius' fourth-century *Ecclesiasticae Historiae*. It is possible that his entire work may have survived in European libraries as late as the 16th–17th centuries.

Perhaps Josephus provided a basis for the story which follows, explaining that some wealthier Jews during the siege of Jerusalem defected to the Romans, but 'to frustrate the bandits they swallowed their gold pieces, and deserting to the Romans had only to empty their bowels to have ample provisions for their needs' (Josephus, *The Jewish War*, 5.421, trans. G.A. Williamson (New York: Penguin Books, 1981), p. 312. Perhaps Roman soliders assumed that Jews who had remained in the city had also hidden their wealth in the same manner. Much later, Fulcher of Chartres recorded an observation that during the first crusade Christian crusaders ripped open the bellies of the Saracens in search of gold besants, and then burned the bodies, searching through the ashes for more gold. See *The First Crusade: The Chronicle of Fulcher of Chartres and Other Source Materials*, ed. Edward Peters (Philadelphia: University of Pennsylvania Press, 1971), p.77.

60   *In Evangelium Lucae*, 21.21, ed. A. Borgnet, vol.23 (Paris: L. Vivès, 1895).

61   *In Evangelium Lucae*, 10.32, pars 2, ed. A. Borgnet, vol.23 (Paris: L. Vivès, 1895). For a similar account, see Roger Bacon, *Secretum secretorum*, ed. Robert Steele, *Opera hactenus inedita Rogeri Baconi*, fasc. 5 (Oxford: Clarendon Press, 1920), pp.146, 110b.

For Albert, this 'Jewish' behaviour directly contradicts the New Testament commandment to love one's neighbour and even one's enemies. Commenting on Matt. 5:43 ('You have heard that it is said: Love your neighbour, etc.'), which he describes as the end and form of all the commandments (*finis et forma omnium mandatorum*), Albert notes that the Jews argue that this does not require love for one who is *not* one's neighbour. The source of their conclusion, he avers, is that 'double law' or oral tradition Jews claim was handed down to Jewish scholars and which is recorded in talmudic literature.[62] And it is from the latter that the Jews deduce that it is unnecessary to love one who is not one's neighbour, and employ a very narrow concept of 'neighbour', which is carnal rather than spiritual.[63]

Just as Jews are distinguished from Christians by their avarice and misanthropy, Albert alleges that they display as well distinctive biological or physiological characteristics. Because their diet or nourishment is especially thick and salty, their blood is thick and earthy. Moreover, thin blood is generally preferable and is more suitable for intellectual operations. Thus, he remarks in *De animalibus*, 'Thick blood feeds the body more and has less sensation, for which reason the things fed off it also have less sensitivity. Thin blood is more suitable for intellect, and the same is so for cold blood.'[64] Although Albert does not apply this observation to Jewish physiology, his readers would likely make the association of thick blood and Jewish 'carnality' and intellectual deficiency, which Albert laments has rendered the people Israel even without a capacity for wisdom.[65] This intellectual deficiency is matched by physical defects. For example, Albert adds that haemorrhoids, caused by a superfluity of thick blood,

---

62   *Super Matthaeum, capitula 1–14*, 5.43, Cologne ed., vol.21(1) (Münster: Aschendorff, 1987), p. 160, 20f. This claim was among those presented earlier by Nicholas Donin. Cf. Rosenthal, 'The Talmud on Trial. The Disputation at Paris in the Year 1240', p.146.

63   Jewish authorities did debate the extension of the concept of 'neighbour' according to the commandment to love one's neighbour as oneself (cf. Lev. 19:18). Did it apply only to other members of the community of Israel, or to all humanity, and, if to Israel alone, to all or only part? Maimonides argues that the commandment applies only to members of the community of Israel and, among these, only to those who accept the obligatory thirteen principles of faith. Those who reject them are outside of Israel and therefore beyond the application of this commandment as well. For a discussion, cf. Marvin Fox, *Interpreting Maimonides* (Chicago and London: University of Chicago Press, 1990), pp.214–18. For a definition of 'Israel' in Maimonides' work, cf. also Menachem Kellner, *Maimonides on Judaism and the Jewish People* (Albany: SUNY Press, 1991), pp.61–64.

64   *De animalibus*, 12.29.

65   See Albert's *In Osee prophetam enarratio*, 9,7 (in *Super prophetas minores*, ed. A. Borgnet, vol.19, p.77), where Albert describes foolish (*stultus*) Israel and explains, 'Stultus dicitur a stoliditate, qui non sapiens tantum non est, sed etiam capax sapientiae non est' ('A fool is so called from stupidity, and is not only not wise but has not even a capacity for wisdom.')

are especially common among Jews (and, elsewhere, in particular among Jewish men):

> Haemorrhoids are caused by a superfluity of gross blood, because when such blood is abundant in the body it descends below, namely to the womb, where there are a number of veins, and then often one or two of these veins burst and the blood sometimes flows on account of this opening of their veins. This occurs according to nature especially among people who thrive on gross and salty nourishment, *like the Jews.*[66]

Moreover, the perceived frequency of bleeding haemorrhoids among Jews represents for Albert, as well as for other Christian authors, a divine punishment and visible fulfilment of Ps. 77:66: 'He struck them in the posterior and gave them perpetual opprobrium.'[67]

In the next generation medieval physicians repeated Albert's observation that haemorrhoids constitute a 'Jewish affliction' and related this defect to alleged Jewish crimes. Although most scholars no longer accept the *De secretis mulierum* as a genuine work by Albert, nevertheless it is likely a product of Albert's circle from around 1300 and it also propounds the notion that bleeding haemorrhoids are 'found in Jews more than in others, for their natures are more melancholic, although it is said that they have this flow because of a miracle of God, and there is no doubt that this is true'.[68] Bernard de Gordon (b. ca. 1258), the author of a well-known practical treatise on medicine, also commented on the prevalence of bleeding haemorrhoids among Jews. This he attributed to three causes: first, Jewish idleness; second, Jewish fears and anxiety, which increased the melancholic blood; and, third, divine punishment, as recorded in Ps.77: 66. Bernard may have also believed that Jews regularly perform ritual murder because they must continually seek Christian blood in order to replace the blood lost from these haemorrhoids[69] (a belief that appears among other thirteenth-century authors as well).[70] Both he and Albert made contributions to the bizarre

---

66   'Haemorroidae causantur ex superfluitate sanguinis grossi, quia quando talis sanguis abundat in corporem descendit inferius, ubi est pluralitas venarum, scilicet in matrice, et tunc frequenter rumpitur una vena vel duae, et tunc fluit sanguis propter apertionem earum venarum aliquando. Unde illud maxime accidit viventibus ex nutrimento grosso et salso, sicut Iudeis, per naturam' (Albertus Magnus, *Quaestiones de animalibus*, 9, q.7, Cologne ed., vol.12 (Monasterii Westfalorum: Aschendorff, 1955), p.206.

67   See Albertus Magnus, *Commentarii in secundam parten psalmorum (LI-C)*, ed. A. Borgnet, vol.16 (Paris: L. Vivès, 1882), p.343.

68   *Women's Secrets: A Translation of Pseudo-Albertus Magnus's De Secretis Mulierum with Commentaries*, trans. Helen Rodnite Lemay (Albany: SUNY Press, 1992), p.74.

69   See Luke E. Demaitre, *Doctor Bernard de Gordon: Professor and Practitioner*, Studies and Texts 51(Toronto: Pontifical Institute of Mediaeval Studies, 1980), p.9. Bernard's comments appear in *Lilium medicine*, 5.21, fol.77r.

70   For a brief discussion of the connection between a Jewish requirement for

medieval Christian fantasy that feminized Jewish men and depicted them as suffering from regular bleeding around the anus, cursed like Eve with a form of male menstruation.[71]

Jewish Guilt in the Death of Jesus

It was a commonplace of Christian theology that the Jews, and not the Romans, were collectively responsible for the crucifixion. Yet until the twelfth century Jewish guilt was mitigated by the belief that at least the Jewish masses had been ignorant of Jesus' true nature. The Jews had sought his death for what they perceived to be the crimes of blasphemy and other violations of the Law. Although they may have acted out of malice, they also acted out of ignorance. Augustine even suggests that, in so far as they perceived Jesus to have violated the Law, they acted rationally in seeking his death. They rightly understood his claim to be the Son of God, equal to the Father (and in this respect revealed more understanding, says Augustine, than the Arians), but perceived it as false and blasphemous.[72]

Jack Watt has shown that, among Parisian theologians at the end of the twelfth century, Peter Lombard and Peter Cantor re-examined Augustine's doctrine, modifying protestations of the Jews' ignorance and harshly accentuating Jewish guilt.[73] Similarly, Jeremy Cohen has argued that in the thirteenth century a shift occurs in the treatment of Jewish guilt, especially among mendicant theologians like Hugh of St Cher, St Bonaventure and, at the end of the thirteenth and beginning of the fourteenth century, Duns Scotus and Nicholas of Lyre. These masters attribute greater intentionality to Jewish actions and suggest that at least some Jews, the leaders, or *maiores*, at the time *knew* that Jesus was the promised messiah and perhaps the Son of God as well. Although the masses or *minores* may not have had the same degree of knowledge as their leaders, nevertheless increasingly Christian theologians, such as Alexander of Hales, emphasized that they *should have known* Jesus' true identity from the miracles he performed, but chose instead to accept the judgment of their leaders.[74] Therefore, even the

---

Christian blood and haemorrhoids, cf. Joshua Trachtenberg, *The Devil and the Jews: The Medieval Conception of the Jews and its Relation to Modern Antisemitism* (New Haven: Yale University Press, 1943), pp.50, 148.

71   For a discussion and bibliography see my 'Medieval Roots of the Myth of Jewish Male Menses', *Harvard Theological Review*, 93(3) (2000), 241–63.

72   Cf. *Tractatus in Joannis Evangelium*, 17.16 and 18.2, CC SL 36 (Turnholt: Brepols, 1954), pp.178, 180.

73   Jack Watt, 'Parisian Theologians and the Jews: Peter Lombard and Peter Cantor', in Peter Biller and Barrie Dobson (eds), *The Medieval Church: Universities, Heresy, and the Religious Life: Essays in Honor of Gordon Leff* (Woodbridge, Suffolk and Rochester, NY: The Ecclesiastical History Society, 1999), pp.55–76.

74   Alexander of Hales, *Glossa in Quattuor libros sententiarum Petri Lombardi,*

minores are not without guilt for his death. Their crime stems from a failure to know what they could have (and should have) known. Knowledge emphasizes both Jewish guilt and irrationality: to kill the Son of God knowingly is a crime against reason itself.

Inflammatory proclamations of Jewish guilt stemming from the crucifixion were features central to the Jewish–Christian public disputations of the thirteenth century, and Christian polemicists repeatedly insisted that contemporary Jews endure exile and collective punishment because they killed Jesus on the Cross. Jewish respondents replied that if, as Christians believe, the crucifixion occurred according to the divine plan and will of God, and since Jesus himself prayed that those responsible should be forgiven (cf. Lk. 23:33), Jews inherit neither guilt nor punishment for the death of Jesus. Their exile is rather owing to their failure to fulfil perfectly the precepts of Torah.[75]

Guilt and responsibility for the death of Jesus, then, was a much contested issue in the debates, and received accordingly more attention from Scholastic theologians. Moreover, the belief of some mendicant theologians that Jews knowingly killed the messiah enabled them not only to justify increasingly numerous and violent attacks upon Jewish communities, but also to support a polemical strategy that sought to find in the Talmud concealed testimony in support of Christian claims. Since at least Jewish leaders were thought fully to have known that Jesus was both messiah and Son of God, the Talmud should contain the evidence. And, if the true identity of Jesus could be demonstrated from the Talmud itself, then the rejection of Christian claims by contemporary Jews can only be understood as wilful ignorance, and a form of heresy justly punishable by the Inquisition.

Albert the Great was certainly one of the most eminent Dominican theologians about the middle of the thirteenth century, serving as regent master in Paris until 1248.[76] At the time of his arrival in Paris the Dominicans possessed

---

4, dist. 18, 5b, ed. Collegii S. Bonaventurae (Quaracchi, Florence: College of St. Bonaventure, 1957), vol.4, pp.384–5. In his *responsum*, Alexander blames the Jews (even the *minores*) for the crucifixion, because even though they witnessed abundant signs of his divinity, they accepted instead the judgment of others (the *maiores*): 'Iudaei autem plus peccaverunt, quia opera viderunt, quae plus erant quam aliqua testimonia; nec contra hoc testes essent recipiendi, quia maius est testimonium de caelo quam de terra.' Jack Watt suggests that this view of the guilt of the *minores* hardened still more in the *Summa Theologiae* attributed to Alexander of Hales. See Watt. "Parisian Theologians and the Jews: Peter Lombard and Peter Cantor', pp. 64–6.

75   This defence had appeared already in the second half of the twelfth century. See *The Book of the Covenant of Joseph Kimhi*, trans. Frank Talmage (Toronto: Pontifical Institute of Mediaeval Studies, 1972), pp.75–7; also see Joseph Schatzmiller, *La deuxième controverse de Paris. Un chapitre dans la polémique entre chrétiens et juifs au Moyen Age* (Paris, Louvain: Editions E. Peeters, 1994), pp.24, 76–7.

76   The date of Albert's inception is impossible to determine precisely. Henry of Herford indicates that he left Paris for Cologne after serving for three years as master. If

only two chairs in theology at the university, held by Godfrey of Bléneau and Guerric of St-Quentin. Not long after his arrival, Albert became the first German Dominican to hold one of these chairs (probably filling the vacancy caused by the death of Guerric of St-Quentin in 1244 or 1245) and he was regent master in Paris until 1248. It was in Paris, toward the end of 1245, that Albert acquired his most famous pupil, Thomas Aquinas. But it was also in Paris that Albert likely had another student, more important for the history of Christian–Jewish polemics: Raymond Martini, the author of the monumental *Pugio Fidei* (*Dagger of Faith*),[77] upon which Albert may have exerted both a literary and an intellectual influence.[78] Shlomo Simonsohn remarks that, as part of his polemical strategy, 'Martini injected the element of intentional error on the part of the Jews; that the misinterpretation of Scripture and all that followed from it – oral law and its evolution, the rejection of Jesus and the refusal to accept Christianity – were done with malice.'[79]

Regarding Jewish guilt and the crucifixion, Thomas Aquinas reflects this same hardening of attitude. He clearly distinguishes between the leaders of the Jews (*maiores*) and the crowd (*minores*). The former knew that Jesus was the messiah, but not that he was divine. Still they witnessed the manifest signs of his divinity, but rejected these from hatred and envy. Their 'ignorance', then, is hardly a mitigating factor: it is intentional (*ignorantia affectata*). Indeed it makes their crime worse: they remain ignorant because they did not wish to know the truth, and therefore Aquinas maintains that the *maiores* crucified Jesus not only as man but even as God. The 'crowd', however, is guilty of the same *type* of sin as the Jewish leaders, but in their case their guilt is somewhat mitigated (but not eliminated) by the extent of their ignorance. Nevertheless their guilt remains

---

he left in 1248, then one may assume that he incepted in 1245. For his inception speech, see Nancy Katherine Spatz, 'Principia: A Study and Edition of Inception Speeches Delivered before the Faculty of Theology at the University of Paris, ca. 1180–1286', (PhD dissertation, Cornell University, 1992), ch. 4.

77   Raymond Martini, *Pugio Fidei* (Leipzig, 1687; reprint Farnsborough: Gregg Press, 1967). This text was likely written ca. 1280. On the importance of this work, Robert Chazan remarks 'No other work can match the *Pugio Fidei* for its dedicated effort to probe the Jewish psyche, for its massive collection of Jewish sources, for its careful and sophisticated argumentation on the broadest possible range of theological issues' (*Daggers of Faith. Thirteenth-Century Missionizing and Jewish Response*, Berkeley, Los Angeles and London: University of California Press, 1989, p. 115).

78   'Los contactos conceptuales y textuales entre fray Ramón Martí y san Alberto Magno pueden ser suficientes para justificar, por una parte, la affirmación de que el 'opus' albertino es una de las fuentes literarias de la producción apologético-teológica del dominico catalán, y, por otra, la conveniencia de seguir el 'rastro' albertino de las ideas filosóficas del discípulo (Pedro Ribes y Montané, 'San Alberto Magno, Maestro y fuente del apologeta medieval Ramon Marti', *Doctor Communis*, 33.2 (1980), 192.

79   Shlomo Simonsohn, *The Apostolic See and the Jews*, 8 vols (Toronto: Pontifical Institute of Mediaeval Studies, 1991), vol.8, p.314.

more weighty than that of Pilate or the Roman soldiers because the Jews (all of them) *should have known* Jesus as messiah and Son of God, since unlike the Romans they had been given the witness of the prophets.[80]

What position did Albert adopt on this question of Jewish guilt for the crucifixion? In his commentary on Matt. 21:38, Albert directly raises the question of the extent of Jewish knowledge of Jesus' identity at the time of the crucifixion. Although some scriptural evidence indicates that Jews did know his true identity,[81] Albert introduces other evidence to support a tradition of Jewish ignorance, in particular I Cor. 2:8 ('if they had known him, they never would have crucified the Lord of Glory') and Acts 3:17 ('I know that you have acted from ignorance, as have your leaders'). Moreover, Albert adds, Anselm objected that, if the Jews had knowingly killed the Son of God, their sin would be irredeemable, since it is infinitely worse to sin against God than against humanity. But it is clear that their sin is redeemable since, by the end time, a faithful remnant at least will proclaim their faith in Christ. Therefore they must have acted from ignorance.[82]

The discussion seems to require some definition of knowledge and ignorance. Albert explains that one can be said to know something in two ways: first, in its principles or premises (*principia*) and second, in the conclusions drawn from these. Certainly the Jews had the intellectual *principia* necessary to know that Jesus is the Son of God. From these they would have known him as such if their own faithlessness and carnality had not covered their eyes (cf. Jn 15:24). Jesus' works, which he performed in their midst, were sufficient to reveal him to them, just as someone who points to the sun with his finger provides some knowledge of the sun. If this fails, it is not the fault of the finger, but of the eye looking at it. This, for Albert, is the sense of two passages in the Gospel of John that he conflates (Jn 15:22, 24): 'If I had not done works among them which no one else had done, they would not have sin; now, however, they have no excuse for their sin.' Albert believes that, in terms of having the necessary intellectual equipment and the proper indications, the Jews had the capacity to know; but from the blindness caused by their faithlessness, they are said to be ignorant.[83]

In ordinary circumstances, ignorance may mitigate guilt. But Albert suggests that Jewish ignorance entails culpability. Commenting on Jn 8:19, Albert

---

80   *Summa theologiae* 3.47.5–6, in *Opera omnia*, vol.11 (Rome: 1903), pp.460–61. For a synthetic approach to Thomas's view of Jewish guilt for the crucifixion, see John Y.B. Hood, *Aquinas and the Jews* (Philadelphia: University of Pennsylvania Press, 1995), pp.64–76.

81   Albert lists, among others, Mich. 7:10, Job 16:10, and Jn. 1:14.

82   Cf. *Cur Deus Homo*, 2.15, *Opera omnia*, ed. Francis Salesius Schmitt (5 vols) (Edinburgh: Thomas Nelson and Sons, 1946–51), vol.2, p.115.

83   *Super Matthaeum*, 21.38, Cologne ed., vol.21.2 (Monasterii Westfalorum: Aschendorff, 1987), pp.525–6. According to Weisheipl, the definitive version of this commentary appeared after 1270.

maintains that Jewish ignorance does not stem from a defect in the intellect but rather from a malicious or perfidious will.[84] Albert pursues this theme further in his commentary on Jn 5:40 ('And you do not wish to come to me in order to have eternal life').[85] Here, Albert explains, it is evident that the unbelieving Jews are not to be excused.[86] It is not ignorance, but wilful malice that prevents their conversion. Although Acts 3:17 seems to contradict this view, since it stresses Jewish ignorance, nevertheless on account of the testimonies of Scripture the Jews had a strong 'suspicion' regarding Jesus' identity and their ignorance could have been easily overcome.[87]

Similarly, commenting on Lk. 23:33 ('Father, forgive them, for they know not what they do, etc.'), Albert remarks that Jesus prays here only for those who acted out of ignorance.[88] But who are they? Albert remains perhaps intentionally unclear, insisting that 'Some were *unwilling* to know him on account of the envy they bore him and these cannot be called ignorant, nor can they be excused ... [thus] he may not be said to pray on behalf of those men who knowingly crucified the Son of God.'[89] But that some were *unwilling* to know Jesus as Son of God does not necessarily imply that the rest were *unable* to have such knowledge or that their ignorance is excusable. This broad sense of Jewish culpability also informs Albert's response to the self-justification that, under the Law, Jesus had to be judged guilty of blasphemy and other transgressions, and therefore had to be punished (cf. Jn 19:7). This explanation emphasizes Jewish obedience to the Law, rather than malice, as a rational basis for Jesus' death. But Albert insists that certainly the Jews were not motivated by obedience to the Law, but by envy, evil intent and a bad conscience.[90]

---

84   'Ad hoc dicendum, quod in veritate ductu rationis per opera Filii, et per Scripturas poterant cognoscere Filium, quia Filius Dei est, et sic novissent et Patrem. Sed per aversionem invidiae et perversae voluntatis, ad hanc collationem non pervenerunt', *In Evangelium Joanni*, 8.19, ed. A. Borgnet, vol.24 (Paris: L. Vivès, 1899), p.341. Cf. also Jn. 8.54–5 (pp.367–8) for similar views. Albert's commentary on John, though written ca. 1256, was revised between 1270 and 1275.

85   Albert completed this work ca. 1256, but revised it between 1270–1275.

86   'Hic ostendit ... Judaeos incredulos inexcusabiles esse', *In Evangelium Joanni*, 5.40, p.229.

87   'quamvis veram de ipso scientiam non habuerunt, tamen propter testimonia quae inducta sunt, vehementem de ipso habebant suspicionem, et de facili vincibilem ignorantiam' (ibid., p.229).

88   Albert completed this commentary in 1261–62 and revised it between 1270 and 1275.

89   'Quidam enim ex invidia quam ad eum habebant, scire eum nolebant: et illi non dicuntur ignorantes, nec excusantur ... propter homines scienter Filium Dei crucifigantes non dicatur orare', *Ennarationes in secundam partem evang. Lucae (10–24)*, 23.33, ed. A. Borgnet, vol.23 (Paris: L. Vivès, 1895), p.726. This text was completed ca. 1261–2 and revised between 1270 and 1275.

90   *Commentarii in III Sententiarum*, dist. 20, art. 13, ed A. Borgnet, vol.28 (Paris: L. Vivès, 1894), pp.371–2.

Reason, he explains, which ought to rule the soul, judges or perceives that something ought to be done, and its law is known as 'conscience'. Conscience is defined as 'a judgement (that is knowledge or determination) of reason, which binds either to do or not do something'.[91] But reason can err, Albert adds, and likewise conscience. For example, one may know a universal principle through reason, but err when dealing with the concrete particular. Thus I may know in the abstract that every mule is a sterile animal, but, when, through the senses, I observe that a particular mule's belly is swollen, I may judge in error that it is pregnant. At the level of the universal, reason knows rightly what to do or not do, but at the level of the particular it can err in judgment, owing to its reliance on the senses. Similarly the Law says: every blasphemer must be punished and killed, and reason says this correctly, in harmony with the divine Law. Now whoever makes himself out to be the Son of God is a blasphemer. This too is true and correct. But when later reason says, *this* man, namely Jesus, falsely makes himself out to be the Son of God and therefore must be punished, this is an error grounded in a sensitive appetite or desire (*sensualitas*). But as here reason errs, conscience too is in error. While the Jews seem to have been constrained by conscience to kill Christ as a blasphemer, nevertheless, their conscience was in error and they – not all, perhaps, but most? – remain guilty.[92]

Moreover it does not seem that the Jews' reason was misled unwillingly by sensitive appetite. Elsewhere Albert reiterates his claim that they *could* have known Jesus' identity, had they wanted to. Therefore there would seem to be an element of intentional error, malice and deliberate (or even deliberative) unbelief at work. As a result, the appeal to the Law's stricture regarding blasphemy provides no justification, because it is evident that Jesus is the Son of God from his acts and from the witness of the Scriptures.[93] Thus, although the Pharisees accused Jesus of blasphemy and for violating the Sabbath, and used this to justify their persecution of him, the true causes behind their enmity were envy, superstition, vainglory and their reprobate sense.[94] It is this same reprobate sense which, Albert insists, remains at the bottom of Jewish guilt in his own time. It is

---

91   'conscientia est iudicium sive scientia sive dictamen rationis artans ad faciendum vel non faciendum', *Quaestiones*, q. de conscientia, art. 3, Cologne ed., vol.25(2) (Münster: Aschendorff, 1993), pp.24, 45–7.

92   'Lex dicit: omnis blasphemus est puniendum vel occidendum, hoc bene dicit ratio recta, quae concordat legi dei; sed quicumque se facit filium dei et non est, blasphemus est; adhuc verum dicit et recte iudicat. Sed cum postea dicitur: Iste homo, demonstrato Christo, se facit filium dei, et non est, ergo est puniendus: hic est error, quia cum videt hunc hominem Christum mortalem et passibilem, iudicat ratio, quod non est deus, et ita iudicat hunc esse puniendum, et sic [est] ratio tracta per sensualitatem male iudicat, et sic sententia rationis sive conscientia est erronea. Et ita Iudaei artari videbantur per talem conscientiam ad hoc quod Christus erat occidendus ut blasphemus. Tamen eorum conscientia erat erronea et deponenda' (Ibid., pp.25, 2–16).

93   *In Evangelium Joanni*, 19.7, p.649.

94   *Super Matthaeum*, 12.14, p.375, 50f.

not only that Jews in each generation bear collectively the guilt for the crucifixion – as all, according to a doctrine of original sin, bear the guilt of Adam's sin – but they *remain unwilling* to find in the salvific blood of Jesus that which will remove their guilt.[95] Jews in his own day, therefore, are at least as guilty as those of the first century because they recapitulate the intentional unbelief and hatred for Christ found among their forebears.

Conclusion

Although Albert was indebted to Jewish scholars and philosophers, his attitude towards Jews and Judaism was neither entirely Augustinian nor relatively benign, as Jeremy Cohen has suggested.[96] Indeed Albert seems not to have distinguished as clearly as Thomas between the guilt of the *maiores* and the *minores*. Moreover Albert, like other Scholastic theologians, emphasises the intentional character of Jewish ignorance and, consequently, Jewish guilt for the crucifixion. Although some Jews were, and remain, ignorant of Jesus' true identity, their ignorance is itself the product of a malicious will and therefore culpable. For the same reason, it seems, Albert condemns the Talmud and its authors for blasphemy and heresy, while Albert's scientific endeavours led him to propose the existence of distinctive Jewish physiological characteristics which helped to explain the Jews' *sensualitas*, carnality and intellectual torpor.

I am unaware of any documentary evidence showing that Albert had any encounters with living Jewish communities although, during his brief residence in Regensburg (1260–61) as Bishop, it is possible that he had some dealings with its very old and substantial Jewish population which had enjoyed imperial privileges since the latter part of the eleventh century.[97] Albert may also have encountered Jewish communities as he satisfied his papal commission to preach

---

95   See Albert's remarks on Matt. 27: 25 ('His blood is upon us and upon our children'), *Super Matthaeum*, 27.25, p. 642, 13f.

96   'The Jews as Killers of Christ from Augustine to the Friars', p.18. Note, too, that Cohen's conclusion may rest in part on a mistranslation of Albert's commentary to Matt. 21.38, cited above. Cohen understands 'in principiis' and 'in conclusione' to be temporal references, referring to the beginning or end of Jesus' lifetime. There is no justification for this reading. Here, and in other works, Albert commonly distinguishes the principles of knowledge from the conclusions derived from such principles. See, for example, *De animalibus*, 11.18.

97   For a history of the Jewish community in Regensburg, see Raphael Straus, *Regensburg and Augsburg*, trans. Felix N. Gerson (Philadelphia: Jewish Publication Society of America, 1939), pp.87–170. At least until the late 1260s, the Bishop of Regensburg maintained some control over Regensburg's Jews and, particularly, over the taxes received from them. It may be instructive, however, that Straus's history omits any mention of Albert's episcopacy in Regensburg.

the Crusade in German lands (1263–4),[98] although once again I am not aware of any documentary evidence of interreligious encounter. In 1274, his signature does authenticate a papal document from Pope Gregory X that threatens Christians in Germany who molest the Jews with ecclesiastical punishment.[99] Apart from his role in the Parisian commission of inquiry of 1248, however, Albert was not directly involved in polemics against Judaism. Nevertheless his condemnation of the Talmud and certain of its doctrines, his attacks on the *talmudisti* and his emphasis on Jewish guilt and intentionality in the death of Jesus may well have provided material for other mendicant apologists and encouraged a shift in the Christian ideology of Judaism.[100]

---

98   For a few passing references to Albert's contribution, see Christoph Maier, *Preaching the Crusades: Mendicant Friars and the Cross in the Thirteenth Century* (Cambridge and New York: Cambridge University Press, 1994).

99   Shlomo Simonsohn, *The Apostolic See and the Jews*, vol.1: *Documents: 492–1404*, pp.245–6, no. 237; vol.7: *History*, p.56 (Toronto: Pontifical Institute of Medieval Studies, 1988).

100   See Pedro Ribes y Montané, 'San Alberto Magno, maestro y fuente del apologeta medieval Ramón Marti', *Anthologica Annua*, 24–5 for 1977–8 (1980): 593–617; Rpt. *Doctor Communis*, 33.2 (1980),169–93.

Chapter 9

'Inward' and 'Outward' Jews: Margaret Fell, Circumcision and Women's Preaching

Claire Jowitt

There is neither Jew nor Greek, there is neither bond nor free, there is neither male nor female ... for ye are all one in Christ Jesus.

This quotation from Paul (Galatians 3:28) appears egalitarian since, as Daniel Boyarin has argued, it represents 'an ideal of a human essence, beyond difference and hierarchy' where fleshly or bodily particularities are subordinated to a universalist notion of the spirit.[1] Paul's words were appropriated and included by Margaret Fell in her 1668 text *A Call Unto the Seed of Israel* as, ostensibly, a way of expressing her commitment to racial, religious, class and gender equality.[2] However, neither Paul's text, which bluntly admonished the 'Foolish Galatians' (Galatians 3:1) for adulterating the gospel of Christian freedom with elements of Jewish legalism, nor Fell's use of this excerpt were so egalitarian as the out-of-context quotation would imply. In fact, Paul's text was a blistering attack on his Galatian converts who, after being visited by Judaisers, were once more observing the Jewish calendar and food laws and, most importantly of all, had again started to practise circumcision. The result was that Paul's Christian converts reverted to demonstrating outward and visible signs of their Jewish religion on their bodies.[3] In other words, the Galatians had failed to understand the spiritual and salvational equality that

---

1   Daniel Boyarin, *A Radical Jew; Paul and the Politics of Identity* (Berkeley: University of California Press, 1994), p.7.

2   Margaret Fell, *A Call unto the Seed of Israel, that they may come out of Egypt's darkness* (London: Robert Wilson, 1668) Ii3r. Any discussion of 'race' as distinct in this period is, of course, complex since issues of race and religion frequently intersect and overlap. In this essay I use the term to mark cultural differences between groups of people, rather than as a fully formed or discrete system of categorization. For a fuller discussion of these issues, see Margaret T. Hogden, *Early Anthropology in the Sixteenth and Seventeenth Centuries* (Philadelphia: University of Pennsylvania Press, 1971); Bryan Cheyette, *Constructions of 'the Jew' in English Literature and Society: Racial Representations 1875–1945* (Cambridge: Cambridge University Press, 1993) pp.1–12; Margo Hendricks and Patricia Parker (eds), *Women, 'Race' and Writing in the Early Modern Period* (London: Routledge, 1994).

3   For further details see J.D. Douglas and N. Hillyer (eds), *New Bible Dictionary*, 2nd edn, (Leicester: Inter-Varsity Press, 1982), pp.400–401.

Paul's teachings offered and remained wedded to bodily and fleshly particularities.

In 1668, Margaret Fell's attitudes to Renaissance Jews appear to correspond to Paul's castigation of the doubly apostate Galatian people. In her earlier texts addressed to the Jews, *For Menasseth ben Israel. The Call of the Jewes out of Babylon*, and *A loving salutation to the seed of Abraham among the jewes*, published in 1656 and 1657, respectively, her arguments had been explicitly apocalyptic and universalist as she confidently awaited the imminent conversion of Jewish peoples to Christianity, specifically Quakerism.[4] In these 1650s texts, similar to the practice of her Quaker brethren, most prominently her later husband George Fox, Fell had used the Pauline metaphor of 'inward' and 'outward' Jews to argue for the future spiritual equality of all Quakers – whether they had converted from Judaism, Catholicism or other reformed Protestant denominations – before God.

By 1668, when Fell appropriated Paul's letter to the Galatians, she had been incarcerated for over four years in Lancaster Castle for non-conformity.[5] She was also disappointed that the expected apocalypse had failed to materialise, and pessimistic that the Jews would ever convert to either Quakerism or any other Christian persuasion. Consequently Fell's later texts, similar to Paul's Epistle to the Galatians, are much sterner towards the Jews, reflecting her increasing disenchantment with the English political and religious situation and her growing realisation that the apocalypse was not imminent. This chapter examines the attitudes Fell demonstrates towards Jews in her first batch of pamphlets in 1656 and 1657 and compares them to her later pamphlets. It suggests that developments within the Quaker movement itself, the different religious and political climate of the latter period, as well as Jews' messianic claims concerning Sabbatai Sevi, were responsible for the changes between her mid-1650s work and the pamphlets published in the 1660s. Since Fell no longer expected the Jews to convert because they had not responded to her earlier universalist, salvational message, her attitudes to them became considerably more brutal. Renaissance Jews remained attached, like Paul's Galatian converts, to fleshly particularity. Indeed, I will suggest that, in her later 1660s work, Fell's central concern was no longer with Jewish conversion to Quakerism. Rather it was women's marginal status within Quakerism which was now (still using the

---

4   Margaret Fell, *For Menasseth ben Israel. The Call of the Jewes out of Babylon* (London: Giles Calvert, 1656); Margaret Fell, *A loving salutation to the seed of Abraham among the jewes: where ever they are scattered up and down on the face of the earth* (London: Thomas Simmons, 1657). The Thomason collection gives the date of *For Menasseth ben Israel* as 20 February 1656 and for *A loving salutation* as 31 October 1657.

5   For biographical information about Margaret Fell, see Bonnelyn Young Kunze, *Margaret Fell and the Rise of Quakerism* (Basingstoke and London: Macmillan Press, 1994); see also Isabel Ross, *Margaret Fell: Mother of Quakerism* (London: Longmans, Green & Co, 1949), pp.191–204.

same metaphors of 'inward' and 'outward' Jewishness with which she had proselytised Renaissance Jews in the 1650s), being questioned by Fell's work. Hence I will argue that Fell's later work addresses, similar to Renaissance Jews, Paul's Galatian converts, and those Quakers and other Christians that argued for the silence of women in Church, issues of fleshly particularity – specifically the difference between men and women – in an attempt to persuade the Quaker movement to maintain in practice the universalist, salvational equality of all before God. Consequently, Paul's egalitarian words were appropriated by Fell in 1668 as a way of expressing her ideal of salvational equality but, at the same time, they were used to criticise both Renaissance Jews who had failed to understand their message and those Friends who argued for the inequality of women within the Quaker movement.

I: Fell's Early Pamphlets and the Readmission Debate

Fell's first pamphlets to the Jews were written in the immediate aftermath of the Whitehall Conference about Jewish readmission, which had been called by Oliver Cromwell in December 1655. It is unlikely, but not impossible, that Margaret Fell had met any Jews when she wrote her first pamphlets in 1656 and 1657. Though Anglo-Jewish historians have established that there were small communities of Sephardi Jews, either disguised as New Christians from Spain and Portugal or living as 'aliens' in London and other cities at this time, since Fell lived at Swarthmoor in Northumberland and did not visit the capital until June 1660, it is doubtful whether she had any first-hand contact with these groups.[6] Consequently her knowledge of the Jewish religion was derived from contemporary myths about Jews, her reading of the Bible, the arrival of broadsheets conveying news from London, the circulation of information between Quakers by letter and the publication and distribution of pamphlet literature concerning important spiritual issues.[7]

In the 1650s Jewish readmission to England was a particularly significant religious issue. During the previous hundred years there had been a growing conviction that the Jews would be converted to Christianity, specifically

---

6   For details of Fell's visits to London, see Kunze, *Margaret Fell and the Rise of Quakerism*, pp.131–42; for a recent discussion concerning the number of Jews in England in the seventeenth century, see David Katz, *The Jews in the History of England 1485–1850* (Oxford: Clarendon, 1994), pp.107–44; see also James Shapiro, *Shakespeare and the Jews* (New York: Columbia University Press, 1996), pp.43–88.

7   For further information concerning the importance of letters in the maintenance of a sense of religious community, and the exchange of information between Quakers, see N.H. Keeble, *The Literary Culture of Nonconformity in Later Seventeenth-Century England* (Leicester: Leicester University Press, 1987), pp.78–81; see also Maureen Bell, 'Mary Westwood: Quaker Publisher', *Publishing History*, 23 (1988), 5–66.

Protestantism, as a prelude to the Second Coming and the millennium ushering in Christ's thousand-year earthly reign.[8] However, according to the book of Isaiah, such events would only occur when the 'dispersed of Judah' were gathered together 'from the Four Corners of the earth' (Isaiah 11:12). Jews were already in two corners, Russia and Palestine. The third corner had recently been identified as South America, since it was believed that the Ten Lost Tribes had been discovered there.[9] The fourth was thought to be England since, as David Katz points out, in Hebrew literature England was called 'the end of the earth'.[10] As a result, theologians argued that the millennium would not occur until Edward I's 1290 royal order banishing Jews from England was revoked. Bernard Capp's study of the English clergy in the first half of the seventeenth century argues that 70 per cent of the ministers who published books in the period believed in the imminent second coming of the messiah and, crucially, they also believed that Christians were compelled to use all available means to bring about the return of Jesus.[11] Furthermore there were many who argued that, it order to convert the Jews, it was first necessary to bring some of them to England, since the chief reason why the Jews persisted in their religion was that they had never seen the pure Protestant faith in its English interpretation.[12] The favoured dates for these prophetic events were, according to exegesis from Daniel and Revelation, the years 1650–56 or, alternatively, 1666.

The renewed interest in Jewish readmission to England culminated in Dutch rabbi Menasseh ben Israel's meeting with Oliver Cromwell in September 1655 and, in the following month, the formal submission of a petition for the readmission of Jews into England to be considered by the Council of State.[13] At the time of the conference itself and in its immediate aftermath many writers published texts on this subject. From the end of 1655 well into 1656 and beyond, a pamphlet

---

8   See Christopher Hill, 'Till the Conversion of the Jews', in Richard H. Popkin (ed.), *Millenarianism and Messianism in English Literature and Thought 1650–1982* (Leiden: Brill, 1988), pp.12–36.

9   See Claire Jowitt, 'Radical Identities? Native Americans, Jews and the English Commonwealth', *The Seventeenth Century*, 10, (1995), 101–119.

10   See David S. Katz, 'The Phenomenon of Philo-Semitism', *Studies in Church History*, xxix (1992), 327–361.

11   B.S. Capp, *The Fifth-Monarchy Men: A Study in Seventeenth-Century English Millenarianism* (London: Faber & Faber, 1972).

12   See David Katz, *The Jews in the History of England*, pp.112–13.

13   This document made seven requests: it asked that the Jews be readmitted as ordinary citizens, that they be allowed to have a public synagogue and cemetery and that their religion be tolerated. It also requested that Jewish people be allowed to trade freely in all varieties of merchandise, and that they be allowed to try their cases by Mosaic Law. The entire apparatus of readmission, Menasseh ben Israel maintained, could be supervised by a person of quality who would receive the passports of immigrant Jews and swear them to fidelity to England. Finally, it requested that any anti-semitic legislation be annulled in order to give the embryonic Jewish community a measure of security. See Katz, *The Jews in the History of England*, pp.121–32.

and counter-pamphlet debate was conducted which discussed the merits of Jewish readmission. For example, arguing against readmission, the Presbyterian polemicist William Prynne published, in two parts, *A Short Demurrer to the Jewes*, which described, in horrific terms, ritual murders perpetrated by Jews against Christians.[14] At the end of his text, Prynne summarised a 'few general heads concerning the Jews, to which they are reducible'. He then catalogued an enormous list of crimes supposedly committed by Jews against Christians, including 'circumcising and crucifying Christian children, breaking the crucifix in Oxford, and trampling it under foot in the midst of the Universities solemne Procession ... extorsions, clipping and falsifying moneys, Charters, usuries, frauds, rapes, murders, forgeries'.[15] Another anonymous pamphlet, *The Case of the Jewes stated* (1656), after asserting that the Jews use 'filthy blasphemous words' in connection with their bodily functions, coyly continues that 'their chamber morals are so lascivious written upon their walls, as it is unfit for chaste ears'.[16]

By contrast, several writers, including Joseph Copley in *The Case of the Jew is Altered* (1656) and Thomas Collier in *A Brief Answer* (1656), attempted to refute such ethnocentric descriptions. Indeed Collier dedicated his tract to Cromwell and the Council of State in an effort to counterbalance the objections to Jewish readmission outlined by Prynne. Though Copley and Collier were in favour of readmission, they were not wholly positive in their descriptions of Jewish peoples and culture. Collier, for example, acknowledges some of Prynne's criticisms of the Jews to be valid: Jews did kill Christ, they also practised usury and attempted to convert Christians. However his strategy for Jewish readmission is one of containment: Jews' behaviour, he argues, could be controlled by the introduction of various rules and regulations. Indeed he concludes his pamphlet with a direct address to the Protector, 'Who knowes? ... but God may make you ... an instrument in his hand to help them into their own Country, for thither they shall return by whom or by what means, time will manifest.'[17] Though Collier's descriptions of Jews represent them as a threat to the English nation, he concludes that new legislation would be able to protect the native Christian population. The fear that the readmission of Jews engendered in the English population is well expressed by an incident involving Cromwell's advisor and Secretary of State, John Thurloe. Ralph Josselin, a minister, experienced a troubling dream he had in January 1655 where 'Thurloe was turned Jew'.[18] Whatever the reasons behind Thurloe's Jewishness – Josselin

---

14   William Prynne, *A Short Demurrer to the Jewes*, 2nd edn (London: Edward Thomas, 1656).

15   William Prynne, *A Short Demurrer*, R3r.

16   For further details, see David Katz, 'English Redemption and Jewish Readmission in 1656', *Journal of Jewish Studies*, 34 (1983), 73–91.

17   Thomas Collier, *A Brief Answer* (London, 1656). Quoted by David Katz, 'English Redemption and Jewish Readmission', pp.78–9.

18   For further details, see Shapiro, *Shakespeare and the Jews*, pp.55–6.

seems uncertain whether the report was a 'mistake' or a politic assumption on Thurloe's part 'to ingratiate with the Jews' – the conversion of a person so near the centre of government points to profound anxieties about the religious and social stability of Cromwell's regime.

Not only had Cromwell's readmission scheme to contend with this increasingly vitriolic pamphlet debate but it was also hampered by the lack of support it received from philosemitic Conference members. For example Henry Jessey, who had previously written in favour of Jewish readmission and was nicknamed 'Jessey the Jew', turned against the proposal when it was put into concrete form.[19] Jessey suggested a compromise by which the Jews might be admitted to England's declining ports and towns on the condition that they paid higher customs duties. This was, however, considerably different from either Cromwell's recommendation or Menasseh ben Israel's proposals.[20] Even John Dury, a committed and well-informed philosemite, did not support readmission. Importuned for his opinion on the issue by Thurloe, and by his friend Samuel Hartlib, Dury advised caution, stating that England should 'go warily, and by degrees'. Dury argued that the Jews 'have ways beyond all other men, to undermine a state, and to insinuate into those that are in offices, and prejudicate the trade of others; and therefore, if they be not wisely restrained, they will, in short time, be oppressive'.[21]

The reverberations from Prynne's hostile pamphlets, the loss of Dury's support and the confining schemes of Collier and Jessey all hindered the endorsement of Cromwell's readmission policy. Indeed, when Cromwell concluded the final meeting of the Whitehall Conference on 18 December 1655, he was compelled to make clear that his only interest in Jewish readmission was to fulfil scriptural prophesy as 'he had no ingagement to the Jews but what the Scriptures held forth'.[22] Though it is evident that Cromwell had hoped the conference would reach a firm decision he was forced to conclude that the issue 'was left more doubtful to him and the Council than before'. All he could hope was that through 'their prayers ... the Lord would direct them so as might be for his Glory, and the Good of the Nation'.[23] However pragmatic he appeared in

---

19   For more information see David Katz, 'Menasseh ben Israel's Christian Connection: Henry Jessey and the Jews', in Yosef Kaplan, Henry Méchoulan ad Richard H. Popkin (eds), *Menasseh ben Israel and his World* (Leiden: E.J. Brill, 1989), pp.117–38.

20   For further details, see William Cortez Abbot, *The Writings and Speeches of Oliver Cromwell*, 4 vols (Cambridge, MA: Harvard University Press, 1947), vol.IV, p.53.

21   John Dury, *A Case of Conscience, Whether it be Lawful to Admit Jews into a Christian Common-wealth?* (London, 1656), reprinted in W. Oldys (ed.) *The Harleian Miscellany* (London, 1808–13), VII, 251–6.

22   Nathaniel Crouch, 'The Proceedings of the Jews in England in the Year 1655', in Robert Burton, *Judaeorum Memorabilia, or Memorable Remarks Upon the Ancient and Modern State of Judea and the Jewish Nation* (Bristol: W. Matthews, 1796), p.210.

23   Nathaniel Crouch, *The Proceedings of the Jews*, p.210. For another account,

public, the Protector had suffered a political defeat. John Thurloe described how in the following week the Protector was 'put to exercise every day' with 'peevishness and wrath'.[24] As late as 1661 the issue of Jewish readmission still possessed political currency for marshalling arguments against the now dead Protector. For example, in the Royalist writer Abraham Cowley's satiric text, *A Discourse Concerning the Government of Oliver Cromwell* (1661), Cromwell was represented as prepared 'to sell St. Pauls to them [the Jews] as a Synagogue, if their purses and devotions could have reacht to the purchase ... he did it only for love of their Mammon; and would have sold afterwards for as much more St. Peters (even at his own Westminster) to the Turks for a Mosquito'.[25]

So why did the Whitehall Conference fail to follow the wishes of the Protector? The merchants who took part in the conference, including Alderman Dethick (Lord Mayor of London) and Alderman Pack (late Lord Mayor), were concerned that readmission would 'enrich foreigners and impoverish the natives of the land'.[26] Believing that the Protectorate no longer valued their opinions or supported their interests in the same way that the Commonwealth had done in the early 1650s, these merchants were concerned to protect their trade networks from Dutch–Jewish rivals.[27] The lawyers and clergy on the conference panel, though they agreed that there was no legal obstacle, appeared anxious about the subversive possibilities of the return of a Jewish community to Britain. What this group seemed to fear was the fact that 'people at this time were so soon drawn aside to new opinions'.[28] In a thinly veiled reference to the Quakers, followers of the 'light within', Lord Lawrence and Major General Lambert described how 'persons were now carried away with the notion of farther light, and of new discoveries of Christ, and the gospel'.[29] Indeed Mr Newcomen, one of the clergymen appointed to the Whitehall Conference, argued against readmission since he believed that it would agitate an increasingly credulous populace: 'And some other opinions had been lately broached, which sober Christians judge to be impious and monstrous, yet have found too many followers and receivers of them.'[30] Read against such aspersions against the 'impious and monstrous'

---

see Henry Jessey, *A Narrative of the late Proceeds at White-Hall* (London, 1656), p. 9. For an assessment of the Whitehall Conference, see Katz, *The Jews in the History of England*, pp.121–32. See also William Cortez Abbot, *The Writings and Speeches of Oliver Cromwell*, vol.IV, 18–19, 34–6, 45, 51–3.

24   See ibid., 53.

25   Abraham Cowley, *Essays, Plays and Sundry Verses*, ed. A.R. Waller (Cambridge: Cambridge University Press, 1906), pp.368–9.

26   Nathaniel Crouch, *The Proceedings of the Jews*, p.210.

27   For details concerning the economic arguments concerning readmission see Edgar Samuel, 'The readmission of the Jews to England in 1656, in the context of English economic policy', *Jewish Historical Studies*, 31 (1988–90), 153–69.

28   Nathaniel Crouch, *The Proceedings of the Jews*, 204.

29   Ibid.

30   Ibid.

Quaker faith which had 'too many followers', it is not surprising that Fell felt licensed to correct the view that Friends would be so fickle as to be converted to Judaism. Furthermore Cromwell's half-hearted remarks as he closed the Whitehall Conference that through 'prayers ... the Lord would direct them so as might be for his Glory, and the Good of the Nation' also functioned as an invitation of sorts for Fell to offer her own rather more urgent prayer for Jewish conversion to her own denomination.

One of Fell's key metaphors in her proselytising of the Jews in all her pamphlets was the idea of a difference between a 'Jew outward' and a 'Jew inward'. Fell shared an emphasis with George Fox on this Pauline image (Romans II: 28–9), which they both used to distinguish between true and superficial faith. Indeed the first oration by Fox that Fell heard was when he interrupted the minister at St. Mary's Church, Ulverston near Swarthmoor in 1652 and asked to be allowed to speak. He then exhorted each member of the congregation to become a 'Jew inward'. Fell later described this incident: 'His first words were: 'He is not a Jew that is one outward; neither is that circumcision which is outward: but he is a Jew that is one inward; and that is circumcision which is of the heart.'[31]

Fox's motif greatly affected Fell: she describes how she 'stood up in my pew and wondered at his doctrine ... then he went on to rebuke those that understood the Scriptures only of themselves, without the illumination of the Spirit of Christ ... This opened me so, that it cut me to the heart; and I saw clearly that we were all wrong. So I sat down in my pew again, and cried bitterly'.[32] Fox's motif became a fundamental vehicle for the expression of Fell's theological ideas. The label 'outward Jew' applied, in Fell's texts, just as much to non-Quaker Christians as to Jews. It was a term that referred to all those who failed to value the Spirit and concentrated instead on outward, ritualised and 'fleshly' religious practices. What this terminology reveals is that Quakers were 'inward Jews': an identification that is both positive and negative in terms of contemporary seventeenth-century representations of Jewishness. Fell identified 'inward Jews' with the Biblical Hebrew nation. According to Fell, Quakers were the spiritual heirs of the Hebrews since, similar to the sufferings of the Jews under Babylonian captivity, in 1650s England, Friends were a righteous minority persecuted by the vagaries and corruption of the reformed Protestant Church.

Thus far, then, in Fell's work Judaism was represented positively. However, contemporary Jews were 'outward Jews' since they had, according to Fell, succumbed to idolatrous practices and rejected God's 'statutes, and his Covenant'.[33] As such they were 'outward Jews' until, as she argued in her 1657 pamphlet *A Loving Salutation*, the 'seed of Abraham ... scattered up and down

---

31   Quoted by Isobel Ross, *Margaret Fell: Mother of Quakerism*, p.11.
32   See Isobel Ross, *Margaret Fell: Mother of Quakerism*, p.11.
33   Margaret Fell, *For Menasseth ben Israel*, p.2.

upon the face of the earth' were converted to the 'light' of Quakerism which would be 'an everlasting Covenant'.[34] Fell's rhetoric here performs a sleight of hand. By identifying the Quakers with Biblical Jews it allows her to urge contemporary Jews to convert to Quakerism/Biblical Judaism since it is represented not as a different religion but simply as a more pure and spiritual form of Judaism. As she argues in *For Menasseth ben Israel*, 'the out-casts of Israel' who are now 'gather[ed] together ... in this our day in this Nation' will be able to see the error of their ways through the contrast with 'living and faithful God' of the Quaker religion: 'Therefore you who from the Lord is turned and gone astray, see from whence ye are fallen, from the living and true God, are yee driven and separated.'[35]

In her 1656 and 1657 texts, Fell appeared confident that Jewish conversion to Quakerism was imminent and, as she reveals in *For Menasseth ben Israel*, she expected England, which she calls 'a Land of gathering', to be the site of this harbinger of the apocalypse.[36] In February 1656, according to Thomason the date of publication of this pamphlet, it seems that Fell believed that the Whitehall Conference would be successful in allowing Jews back into England to be proselytised. Indeed the tone throughout this pamphlet is one of breathless anticipation as Fell 'calls' to Jewish peoples represented by the figurehead of Menasseh ben Israel 'who are come into this English Nation with all the rest of thy brethren'.[37] Fell appropriates and transposes the chosenness of the biblical Hebrew nation onto the Quakers and uses this to construct a connection with seventeenth-century Jews. She argues that a divinely calculated future time is visible in the present: 'the day of the Lords power is come'.[38] Consequently the Jews' imminently expected conversion invites Quakers to treat them proleptically in terms of their impending position as saved. Through such beliefs in these early pamphlets Fell questions racial categories as she argues for a brand of millenarian egalitarianism and spiritual universalism. As recent feminist historical studies have shown (most prominently by Bonnelyn Young Kunze and Judith Kegan Gardiner) in Fell's 1656 and 1657 texts, both Christians and Jews are addressed in terms of the biblical past they have already experienced and, significantly, in terms of the equality before Christ which they will soon share.[39] Fell appears confident that the Jews will indeed leave their 'outward sacrifice' and become 'inwardly' Jews since she talks in definite terms of '*when* you [the

---

34 Margaret Fell, *A Loving Salutation*, p.3.
35 Margaret Fell, *For Menasseth ben Israel*, p.3.
36 Ibid.
37 Ibid.
38 Ibid., p. 21.
39 For further details see Bonnelyn Younge Kunze, *Margaret Fell and the Rise of Quakerism*, pp.211–28; see also Judith Kegan Gardiner, 'Margaret Fell Fox and Feminist Literary History: A "Mother in Israel" Calls to the Jews', *Prose Studies*, 17 (1994), 42–56.

Jews] come to know this condition'(my emphasis), rather than phrasing Jewish conversion to Quakerism as a mere possibility.[40]

Thus, in 1656 and 1657, Margaret Fell represented the Jews comparatively positively. In *For Menasseth ben Israel*, for example, she only uses Old Testament references and images, rather than concentrating upon New Testament descriptions of Christ as the Son of God.[41] Indeed, compared to George Fox's 1656 admonitory text, *A Visitation to the Jews*, Fell's tone in these pamphlets is diplomatic.[42] Fox opened his text with a blunt attack on the Jews as Christ-killers.

> From them that are the seed of Abraham, to all the scattered Jews
> according to the flesh, who have the law of God, the form of it, but
> being found out of the life of it, have not possessed that which Moses
> saw, who received the law from God, which law you have the form of,
> and your fathers in ages past had, who put Christ to death, and slew
> him that is the end of law, God's righteousness, Christ Jesus, and the
> end of God's righteous law, to keep out of all unrighteousness.[43]

Here, it seems, God's law and righteousness are equatable with 'Christ Jesus'; therefore the act of Christ killing by the Jews meant, for Fox, their forfeiture of true righteousness and law so that Jews were merely left with 'the form of it'. Fox described the way in which biblical Jews 'killed him [Christ], they cast him out, and delivered him up to the Gentiles to be mocked, scourged, and crucified'.[44] Indeed, with a certain degree of satisfaction, Fox mocked the situation of contemporary Jews: 'Now consider, what hath become of you since, of you husbandmen? Have you not been laid waste?'[45] However Fox was keen to point out that this lack of Jewish righteousness was not irredeemable. Once the Jews acknowledge Jesus Christ as the son of God they will, according to Fox, be saved: 'receive the covenant of light, and the power of God Christ Jesus, that you may come to life, regeneration, and conversion.'[46] It is important to recognise that, as David Lowenstein has argued, other pamphlets written by Fox at this time were filled with 'violent scriptural language and vivid apocalyptic images' in order to conduct an 'impassioned warfare ... against false churches, worldly rulers, and the social order'.[47] For example, in *To All that would Know the Way to the Kingdom* (1654), a text which urges readers 'to turn your minds within',

---

40   Margaret Fell, *For Menasseth ben Israel*, p.20.
41   For further details, see Kunze, *Margaret Fell and the Rise of Quakerism*, p.217.
42   George Fox, *The Works of George Fox*, 8 vols (New York: AMS Press, 1975), vol.IV, pp.53–75.
43   Fox, *A Visitation to the Jews*, *Works*, IV, 53.
44   Ibid., 54.
45   Ibid.
46   Ibid., 74.
47   David Lowenstein, 'The War of the Lamb: George Fox and the Apocalyptic Discourse of Revolutionary Quakerism', *Prose Studies*, 17 (1994), 25–41.

dwell in the light and wait upon the Lord, Fox accentuates the power of the 'word of the Lord [which] is a fire, burns up all the corruptions, burns up all that is hewn down … that nothing can stand it'.[48] In this text Fox argues that the coming of Christ and his kingdom will be accompanied by apocalyptic forces which will disrupt all contemporary religious, social and political institutions. Using intensely graphic and physical language, he describes the terror of the apocalyptic judgment as mountains 'melt', 'rocks cleave' and 'the sword of the Almighty … hew[s] down Baal's priests, corrupt Judges, corrupt Justices'.[49] In comparison to the violent millenarian language demonstrated by concurrent texts, Fox's pamphlets to the Jews are noticeably mild and, like Fell, Fox believed Renaissance Jews could lose their 'outward' Jewishness in order to become spiritually equal Quakers, or 'inward' Jews. In both Fox and Fells' work in this period, then, there is a kind of universal inward spirituality that cuts across outward differences of rank, religion or gender. Indeed, in 1656, Fox wrote a defence of women's speech, *The Woman Learning in Silence*, which argued that 'Christ in the male, and in the female is one, which makes them free from the law', thus allowing women the right to preach and prophesy.[50] In *For Menasseh ben Israel*, then, Fell makes it clear that there is no difference between Jews and non-Jews, or between women and men in terms of their salvation through future Quakerism as she urges 'yee men of Judah' 'to take away the foreskin of your hearts' and predicts that 'the Lord shall have washed away the filth of the daughter of Sion'.[51] Neither women nor Jews are prevented from becoming 'inward' Jews through circumcision of the heart.

There were, however, some obvious reasons for Fox and Fell's temperance. In 1656 and 1657, though many radicals and theologians were disappointed that the Whitehall Conference had failed formally to allow Jews back into England to be proselytised, Fell and Fox were still hopeful that mass Jewish conversion to Quakerism would soon occur.[52] The conclusion of *For Menasseth ben Israel*, for example, 'charges' the rabbi 'as thou wilt answer it before the living God, that thou let this be read and published among thy Brethren'.[53] Similarly we can also see from the publishing history of Fell's 1656 and 1657 pamphlets how timely and urgent she believed her interventions to be. Both Fox and Fell were concerned to have their pamphlets distributed amongst the Jewish community in the Netherlands.[54] To this end Fell, in 1657, wrote to fellow Quaker John Stubbs,

---

48   Fox, *To All that would Know the Way to the Kingdom*, *Works*, IV, 15, 18.

49   Ibid., 19.

50   George Fox, 'The Woman Learning in Silence', in *Gospel Truth Demonstrated in a Collection of Doctrinal Books* (London: T. Sowle, 1706), p.78.

51   Fell, *For Menasseth ben Israel*, 15–16.

52   See David Katz, *The Jews in the History of England*, pp.107–44; see also Kaplan, Méchoulan and Popkin, eds, *Menasseh ben Israel and His World*.

53   Margaret Fell, *For Menasseth ben Israel*, 20.

54   Indeed Fell's sense of urgency in 1657 may have been aggravated by

prior to his journey to Holland, asking him to prepare her tracts to the Jews for publication. Another Quaker, Samuel Fisher, was asked to translate the texts first in Latin, and then into Hebrew. However, Fisher clearly had problems with this latter task and, in order to disseminate Fell's ideas to the Amsterdam Jewish community who were, according to William Caton, 'hungering for' her texts, another translator was engaged in 1658.[55] According to Caton, demand for Fell's texts amongst Dutch Jews was considerable. He describes the way in which, in May 1658, he collected Fell's *A Loving Salutation* from 'the presse and the same day that I came from thence I gott about 170 of them dispersed Among the Jewes who willingly and greedyly received them, (they being in the Hebrew tongue) I proposed to have brought halfe a hundred of them with mee to England but I disposed of them in Zealand their being severall Jewes'.[56] Fox's attempts to get his pamphlets circulated amongst Jews were somewhat less successful. Though he made considerable efforts to have his pamphlets translated into Yiddish (seeing this language, rather than Hebrew, as a medium more likely to secure a wide Jewish audience) Fox's texts were never actually published in any language other than English.[57]

The reaction of the Amsterdam Jewish community to Fell's proselytising is difficult to gauge. Certainly no Jews are recorded as having converted to Quakerism, though Caton, rather optimistically, asserted that this was caused not by an aversion to Quakerism but by a fear of 'intolerable persecution … specially from their brethren' if they were to become Christians'.[58] Indeed William Ames, in a letter to Fell written from Utrecht on 17 February 1657, describes 'a Jew at amsterdam

---

opposition to her publishing plans from her husband, Judge Fell. In a letter to George Roberts in London, referring to another text, she appears anxious that the book be sent abroad to be published in the Netherlands as soon as possible. She instructed Roberts: 'Let it come forth speedily and be sent abroad, before my husband come up to London, lest he [get] light of it and prevent the service of it.' Though this text was, in fact, never published, it seems that such opposition only strengthened Fell's desire that Jews be allowed access to her preaching. See Kunze, *Margaret Fell and the Rise of Quakerism*, 35.

55   This translator, 'A Jew … expert in several languages', is believed to be Baruch de Spinoza, who had been excommunicated from the Amsterdam synagogue on 27 July 1656. See Richard Popkin, 'Spinoza's Relations with the Quakers in Amsterdam', *Quaker History*, 73 (1984), 14–29.

56   Quotation taken from David Katz, 'The Marginalization of Early Modern Anglo-Jewish History', in Tony Kushner (ed.), *The Jewish Heritage in British History: Englishness and Jewishness* (London: Frank Cass, 1992), pp.60–77.

57   For further details concerning Fox's efforts, see Lesley Hall Higgins, 'Radical Puritans and Jews in England 1648–1672' (unpublished Yale University PhD thesis, 1979), pp.143–5.

58   Cited by Isobel Ross, *Margaret Fell: Mother of Quakerism*, p.91. For a discussion of the likely reaction of the Jewish community to these pamphlets, see ibid., pp.90–91; Kunze, *Margaret Fell and the Rise of Quakerism*, p.223; see also Popkin, 'Spinoza's Relations with the Quakers in Amsterdam', pp.19–21.

that by the Jewes is cast out' who 'sayde toe read of moses and the prophets without was nothing toe him except he Came toe know it within' and 'he sent me word he would Come toe oure meeting but in the mean-time I was imprisoned'.[59] We can assume, then, that Fell's pamphlets did not provoke hostility amongst European Jewish readers. Though Caton asserted that the Amsterdam Jews he spoke to 'could scarce endure to have Christ mentioned', as we have seen, Fell had been careful to use an Old Testament frame of reference for her pamphlets. After talking 'at their Synagogue' to various 'Rabbyes, and some to the Doctors', Caton believed that they did not 'have anything against it, but only they apprehend that the Author doth judge that the Mesias is come already and they look for him yet'.[60]

II: Fell's Later Pamphlets: Reactions to a Jewish Messiah

Caton's statement exposes a key difference between Fell's Quakerism and the Jewish religion: Fell believed that Jesus was the messiah, and the Amsterdam Jews 'look for him yet'. This fundamental religious distinction underpins Fell's change in tone between her 1650s pamphlets and the ones published in the mid-to-late 1660s. Fell's August 1664 pamphlet, *A Call to the Universal Seed of God*, written at the beginning of her incarceration in Lancaster Castle, is intermediary in tone between her 1650s work and the harsher line she took against the Jews by 1668.[61] The 1664 pamphlet is primarily concerned to establish Jesus Christ as the Son of God and the messiah. Gone from this pamphlet is the rhetorical diplomacy of her earlier work as, using New Testament quotations, she emphasises the divinity of Jesus and the depravity of biblical Jews who failed to listen to Jesus' words. When describing Jesus' actions at the Jews 'polluted and corrupted' Temple in Jerusalem, Fell makes clear that the Jews failed to understand Christ's message. According to Fell, Jesus said:

> Take these things hence, and make not my Fathers house a house of
> merchandize, when the Jewes saw this, they asked a sign ... Jesus
> answered, and said unto them, destroy this Temple, and in three days I
> will raise it up; but he spake of the temple of his body, which is the
> some and substance of that which their Temple was a figure of, which
> they looking upon it to be their Temple, made those words the matter.[62]

---

59   William Ames to Fell, 17 February 1657, from Utrecht. Friends' House Library, London; Swarthmore Manuscripts, iv, 28. For further details see Lesley Hall Higgins, 'Radical Puritans and Jews in England 1648–1672', pp.99–100. See also William I. Hull, *The Rise of Quakerism in Amsterdam 1655–1665* (Swarthmore, PA: Swarthmore College, 1938), pp.204–6.

60   Popkin, 'Spinoza's Relations with the Quakers in Amsterdam', p.20.

61   Margaret Fell, *A Call to the Universal Seed of God, Throughout the whole World*, (London?, 1665).

62   Fell, *A Call to the Universal Seed of God*, p.7.

Fell uses this misunderstanding between Jesus and the biblical Jews as a way of explaining her distinction between inward and outward worship. Fell believed that the death of Jesus 'hath slain … all dead worships, all dead Ministers and ministrations, all dead offerings and sacrifices'.[63] Instead Jesus left 'an everlasting Covenant [which is] written in the heart, and purges the Conscience'. Jesus has, according to Fell's Quaker beliefs, become internalised and resides within each believer as the 'Light within'.[64] The Jews, who persist in practising what she calls 'vain oblations which were corrupted, defiled and polluted', need to recognise the depravity of their outward 'fleshly' worship and turn to the Light within, the legacy of Jesus Christ.[65] However, though this pamphlet is certainly more caustic in tone than her previous work, it is clear that Fell still imminently expected the conversion of the Jews:

> And the Lord hath set his hand again the second time to recover the remnant of his people, for he hath set him up as an Ensigne to the Nations, and shall assemble the out-casts of Israel, and gather together the dispersed of Juda from the four corners of the Earth … so that the day of … Judgement is come.[66]

By 1668, when Fell published her final pamphlet to the Jews, *A Call Unto the Seed of Israel*, she placed it with two other Quaker tracts which were, similar to her 1664 pamphlet, concerned to establish Jesus as the Messiah. This placement is significant; it seems that Fell no longer had any real expectation of Jewish conversion. Furthermore, no attempt was made to translate these 1664 and 1668 pamphlets into Hebrew or Yiddish.[67] It seems safe to assume, therefore, that the intended readership for these tracts was Christian.

The primary reason for Fell's change in attitude was the passing – without mass Jewish conversion – of the important date of 1666 in the apocalyptic calendar. Christopher Hill has argued that the expected mid-century millennium, which never occurred, had a profound effect on many radicals.[68] Fighting for what they thought of as God's cause, groups such as the Diggers, the Levellers and the Fifth Monarchists, amongst others, hoped that the Second Coming would achieve the social and political goals the Revolution had failed to deliver. The failure of the English Republic gradually led to the defeat of these political and

---

63   Ibid., p.8.
64   Ibid., p.7.
65   Ibid., p.8.
66   Ibid., p.6.
67   William Ames, the Amsterdam Quaker instrumental in attempting to get both Fox's and Fell's 1650s pamphlets translated into Hebrew or Yiddish, was by the 1660s no longer interested in the mission to the Dutch Jews and concentrated on working with the general Quaker community in Amsterdam. See Kunze, *Margaret Fell and the Rise of Quakerism*, pp.215–16.
68   Christopher Hill, *The Century of Revolution, 1603–1714* (New York: Norton, 1982).

religious hopes. Hill writes, 'the radical sects in their desperation first became wilder and more millenarian and then gradually concluded that Christ's kingdom is not of this world'.[69] Fell's 1668 pamphlet, *A Call Unto the Seed of Israel*, conforms to this movement since God's cause is shown to be an internal moral one, rather than an external political or religious one.[70] In her 1664 pamphlet there had been an emphasis on the internal workings of Christ in the form of the spirit on the believer. In 1668, this message is even clearer as Fell retreats from the idea of an imminent apocalypse to the position that 'the prophet is risen, in the consciences of men, and he is teaching his people by his light'.[71] Persecuted for her beliefs under the Corporation Act (1661), the Act of Uniformity (1662) and the First Conventicle Act (1664), Fell became increasingly scathing about the religious situation in England. Indeed, in *A Call Unto the Seed of Israel*, she calls the 'Priests and Teachers of this Nation of England ... blind Pharisees', and states that they, like Jews, 'deny the Law of God and cast it behind [their] backs'.[72] In another pamphlet written in 1668, 'M.ff. Answer to A. Smallwood Dr. priest of Grastock in Cumberland', Fell also equates non-Quaker Christian practices with Jewish ones. For example, when describing the way the Anglican Church supported the imprisonment of Quakers for refusing to participate in public oathtaking and swearing, Fell disparagingly wrote: 'Doe you not doe as the high priests did when they delivered X^t upp to Pilate and cryed, "crucify him, crucify him".'[73]

Additionally, Fell's lack of sympathy for Jews in this later pamphlet can be further explained by her reaction to the messianic pretensions of Sabbatai Sevi.[74] This movement engulfed the whole of Jewry, from England to Persia, from Greece to Morocco, from Poland to the Yemen, in 1665 and 1666. It was aroused by a young kabbalist rabbi from Smyrna, the 'messiah' Sabbatai Sevi, and his prophet Nathan of Gaza. After convincing Jews in Smyrna that he was the messiah, Sevi travelled to Constantinople in order to persuade the Turkish sultan

---

69   Hill, *The Century of Revolution*, p.187.

70   Margaret Fell, *A Call Unto the Seed of Israel, that they may come out of Egypt's Darkness* (London: Robert Wilson, 1668).

71   Fell, *A Call Unto the Seed of Israel*, p.9.

72   Ibid., p.5.

73   Margaret Fell, 'M.ff. Answer to A. Smallwood Dr. priest of Grastock in Cumberland. 1668', in Bonnelyn Young Kunze, 'An Unpublished Work by Margaret Fell', *Proceedings of the American Philosophical Society*, 130 (1986), 424–52.

74   For further details, see Gershom Scholem, *Sabbatai Sevi: The Mystical Messiah* (Princeton: University of Princeton Press, 1973); Jacob Bernai, 'Christian Messianism and the Portuguese Marranos: The Emergence of Sabbateanism in Smyrna', *Jewish History*, 7 (1993), 119–26; Richard H. Popkin, 'Jewish Messianism and Christian Millenarianism', in Perez Zagorin (ed.), *Culture and Politics from Puritanism to the Enlightenment* (Berkeley: University of California Press, 1980), pp.67–90; Richard H. Popkin, 'Three English Tellings of the Sabbatai Zevi Story', *Jewish History*, 8 (1994), 43–54.

to establish a Jewish state in Palestine, and throughout Europe Jewish peoples prepared to travel to Palestine to join him. In England there was also great interest in this news. Henry Oldenburg, Secretary to the Royal Society, wrote to Baruch de Spinoza on 8 December 1655, asking his opinion of Sevi's activities.[75] On 19 February 1666, Samuel Pepys reported in his *Diary* that a London Jew was accepting wagers of large sums in the confidence that Sevi would shortly be recognised by the Grand Turk. The Jewish community in London received the news of Sabbatai Sevi with considerable enthusiasm. Benjamin Levi the Elder, the scribe and slaughterer for the Synagogue in Creechurch Lane, was an important conduit for the dissemination of information about Sevi's activities. He received letters from several correspondents that were published in pamphlet form and sold throughout London. The Quakers also received the news of the messiah with intense curiosity. Indeed the news of the messianic movement among the Jews gave rise to a rumour that a boat had sailed from Bristol (a focus of Quakerism) 'from a people called Quakers ... without any merchandise, [merely] in order to know the truth of the matter'.[76]

However, later in 1666, Sevi, when faced with a choice between death or conversion to the Islam faith, became an apostate.[77] News of the apostasy only spread slowly through Europe. The first accounts reached Amsterdam, and then London, early in November 1666. Initially even some Christians disbelieved the report. Oldenburg, writing on 10 November 1666, reported that, according to news received from Amsterdam, 'the King of the Jews was turned Turk' but that confirmation of the report was needed.[78] Reactions among Jews in Europe to this information were divided: some followers of the movement interpreted Sevi's apostasy in the light of their faith; thus Sevi was still king of Israel, and his merit and apparent apostasy had saved Israel from disaster: other Jewish peoples explained the messianic failure in terms of the Devil's work and excommunicated Sevi and Nathan: still other disappointed believers evolved the theory that the whole messianic theory had been founded on deception and intrigue.[79]

In Fell's 1668 pamphlet, we can detect references to Sabbatai Sevi's

---

75   For further details see Cecil Roth (ed.), *Anglo-Jewish Letters (1158–1917)* (London: Soncino Press, 1938), p.69. For information concerning English reactions to Sevi's movement, see Michael McKeon, 'Sabbatai Sevi in England', *Association of Jewish Studies Review*, 3 (1977), 131–69.

76   Cited by Scholem, *Sabbatai Sevi*, p.548. The MS of the anonymous 'A Notebook from Italy', from which this quotation is taken, is in the library of the Jewish Theological Seminary, New York.

77   The exact events of Sevi's apostasy are hard to ascertain, and vary according to whether they are described in Jewish, Christian or Turkish sources. See Scholem, *Sabbatai Sevi*, pp.687–92.

78   Quoted by Scholem, *Sabbatai Sevi*, pp.753–4.

79   See Scholem, *Sabbatai Sevi*, pp.687–814.

messianic movement as she chastises 'changeable' religious leaders who 'sit deckt with Christ's words, and Apostles words, and saints words, and with these they go deceiving poor people, and making merchandise of their souls'.[80] Moreover this pamphlet seems concerned to distance itself from the notion of the imminent arrival of an earthly messiah. Following James Nayler's impersonation in 1656 of Christ's triumphal entry into Jerusalem by entering Bristol on a horse led by women, and the subsequent persecution of the sect, Quakers became particularly sensitive to the charge of Christ-like behaviour. As late as 1669, the Nayler incident was still being used to marshal opposition against enthusiasts. For example, in the first English book on Sabbatai Sevi, John Evelyn's *History of the Three Late Famous Imposters* (1669), the biography of James Nayler appears next to that of the Jewish messiah.[81] As a result, in the late 1660s and during the 1670s, as historians of the early Quakers have demonstrated, enthusiasts were keen to represent the Quaker movement as moderate and respectable. For instance, Fox's *Journal*, only posthumously published in 1694, but thought to have been largely composed between 1675 and 1677, was anxious to play down the movement's radical past as well as minimise the role of challengers, like Nayler, to Fox's authority.[82] Margaret Fell's 1668 text functions, it seems, as a precursor of the revisionary process undertaken by the Quaker movement in the late seventeenth century. But there appears to be another impulse at work in Fell's late 1660s texts as her radical ideas are more focused on issues of gender than of race.[83] For the last section of this chapter I want to return to the quotation with which I began ('There is neither Jew nor Greek, there is neither bond nor free, there is neither male nor female ... for ye are all one in Christ Jesus') in order to examine the ways questions of race, religion and gender intersect in Fell's work.

III: 'Circumcision of the Heart': Women's Speaking Justified

In 1667, Margaret Fell published her tract *Womens Speaking Justified, Proved and Allowed by the Scriptures* which, as its title indicates, sought to defend women's speaking and prove that they, as well as men, could be mouthpieces for

---

80   Fell, *A Call Unto the Seed of Israel*, p.14.

81   John Evelyn, *The History of the Three Late Famous Imposters* (London?, 1669).

82   See Thomas N. Corns, 'No Man's Copy: The Critical Problem of Fox's Journal', *Prose Studies*, 17 (1994), 99–111.

83   For a fuller discussion of women's writing and women's influence within the radical sects, see Phyllis Mack, *Visionary Women: Ecstatic Prophecy in Seventeenth-Century England* (Berkeley and Oxford: University of California Press, 1992); see also Hilary Hinds, *God's Englishwomen: Seventeenth-Century Radical Sectarian Writing and Feminist Criticism* (Manchester: Manchester University Press, 1996).

God. In order to silence 'men of this generation' who are 'blinded ... and pervert the Apostles words' as they 'endeavour to stop the Message and Word of the Lord God in Women', Fell details both Old and New Testament godly women who function as precedents for preaching by contemporary women.[84] For example, Fell describes how the Apostles refused to listen to Mary Magdalene and the other women's prophecy concerning Jesus' imminent resurrection. These women's 'hearts [were] ... so united and knit unto him [Jesus] in love, that they could not depart as the men did'.[85] Consequently because their 'hearts' were so attuned to Jesus, or 'the light within', they were able, unlike their menfolk, to foretell the resurrection. However, except in this example, Fell is careful in *Womens Speaking Justified* to argue for equality between sexes, rather than the superiority of women's rights to speak in Church. For example, in both *Womens Speaking Justified* and *A Call Unto the Seed of Israel*, Fell uses the Old Testament story of Hagar and Sarah, bondservant and wife, respectively, to the patriarch Abraham, to highlight the importance of women's positive and negative relationships with God.[86] What is striking, though, is the different implications the same story possesses in her two pamphlets.

In *Womens Speaking Justified*, Sarah, because her son Isaac was born through God's initiative and supernatural grace, represented, according to Fell, true Christian faith and was 'a mother in Israel'.[87] In this text, Fell uses Sarah as an example of the efficacy of women's prophecy: 'In all that Sarah hath said to thee, harken to her voice (Mark here) the Husband must learn of the Woman and Abraham did so.'[88] Fell compares Sarah to Hagar and describes the latter as the mother of all false churches. Hagar represents all servile, 'false' Christians who are 'tatlers and busie-bodies' and cling to the practices of God's Old Covenant.[89] Hagar and her progeny are now to be cast out, since Sarah's 'Seed', 'the Jerusalem which is Free' is about to descend triumphantly from Heaven.[90] In this pamphlet there is an identification between the priests Fell is attempting to silence and the corrupt woman Hagar. The tone of this pamphlet is militant and aggressive, as the persecutions carried out by Hagar's progeny on the faithful are shown as about to be avenged.

By contrast, in *A Call Unto the Seed of Israel*, the Sarah/Hagar dichotomy is used to emphasise the differences between Quakers and non-Quakers. Unlike Sarah, who faithfully trusted in God's providence, with the result that she was miraculously made fertile, Hagar's son Ishmael was born through earthly effort

---

84 Margaret Fell, *Womens Speaking Justified, Proved and Allowed by the Scriptures*, (London, 1667) Bv.

85 Fell, *Womens Speaking Justified*, A3r.

86 Ibid., B2r; Fell, *A Call Unto the Seed of Israel*, Ii4r.

87 Fell, *Womens Speaking Justified*, B2r.

88 Ibid., C1r.

89 Ibid., B4v.

90 Ibid., B2r.

rather than divine potency. Consequently, in this text, Hagar and her descendants represent the old laws – 'Egypt's Darkness' as Fell calls it in the subtitle of the pamphlet – which remained literal rather than spiritual. It seems here that Sarah's position is analogous to Fell's own as a Quaker, a true believer, surrounded by non-believers. The example of Sarah, who was 'Barren that barest not' but became 'the Mother of us all', is used to comfort Quakers who are disheartened by the scale of the task of mass-conversion before them. If Sarah, through faith, was able to give birth to a son, then Quakers, through faith, will be able, eventually, to convert all non-believers. Hagar and her descendants' banishment and continued 'bondage' to the old outward, fleshly practices mark this lineage out as a suitable one to represent non-Quaker Christians and Jews. What is seen as important is that Sarah conceived a child through faith in God, a miraculous event that acts as a harbinger to the birth of Jesus Christ. In this representation, then, it seems that the description of Hagar is less hostile. Fell's mode of address is much more intimate as she repeatedly asks all 'dear hearts' to remain patient. According to Fell in this pamphlet, Hagar and her tribe will all eventually convert to the 'light within' which will be a spiritual, internal change, not an earthly literal one. But what is noticeable is that Fell has appropriated the term 'Seed of Israel' to refer to Quakers; Jews, like all other non-Quakers, are imprisoned in 'Egypt's darkness'.

There are two conclusions from this analysis that I would like to draw. First, it seems that, in these pamphlets, Fell continues the tradition by which male Christian commentators, including George Fox, had appropriated Paul's distinction between 'inward' and 'outward' Jewishness but, significantly, she applies it to women's positions. In *Womens Speaking Justified*, in the example of Mary and the other women who waited outside Jesus' tomb, it emerges that women are especially appropriate voices for God since their 'hearts' are more susceptible to the words of Jesus Christ than were those of their menfolk. Thus in this example it seems that, according to Fell, it is easier for women to be 'inward' Jews; in other words women, because they possess no penis or 'flesh', can more easily be circumcised of the heart.[91] Consequently Renaissance theologians' complex debate over the merits of male 'fleshly' as opposed to 'spiritual' circumcision, which James Shapiro describes, is modified when women are discussed.[92] Fell's implicit argument, then, is that women's bodies are better expressions of God's covenant since literal circumcision cannot be performed on them. Unlike the bodies of male Jews who convert to Christianity,

---

91   According to James Shapiro, 'In the late sixteenth century the word flesh was consistently used, especially in the Bible, in place of penis.' See Shapiro, *Shakespeare and the Jews*, p.122; see also Howard Eilberg-Schwartz, *The Savage in Judaism: An Anthropology of Israelite Religion and Ancient Judaism* (Bloomington: Indiana University Press, 1990), pp.170–71.

92   Shapiro, *Shakespeare and the Jews*, pp.113–30.

which remain circumcised despite their membership of the Christian Church, the female body does not demonstrate such ambiguous signs.[93] Since, as we have seen, 'inward' Jewishness is the state which all Quakers were seeking, the logic of Fell's argument is that, because women's bodies are clearer expressions of God's true Law of faith, their voices should be heeded as well.

Indeed, such a reading is taken further in a later text written by the Lancashire Women's Quarterly Meeting and sent out to 'women's meetings everywhere'.[94] This text is believed, according to Fell's biographer Isabel Ross, to have been written between 1675 and 1680 by Fell's daughter Sarah, who was then clerk of the Meeting, in conjunction with the women of the Swarthmoor Women's Monthly Meeting.[95] We can presume that Fell's influence on this text was considerable since she had set up this forum in 1671 and continued to preside over it until her death, for, as Kunze describes, 'Fell's name always appeared first in larger, bolder letters on the list of signatures of women in attendance.'[96] This text argues, as Fell did in *Womens Speaking Justified*, for the salvational equality of both men and women before God. Using as a precedent the importance of godly women in 'primitive times', the epistle goes on to urge that 'we may be encouraged in the Lords name, power and spirit, to follow their examples and practises: And having the same rule, which is in Christ Jesus, where neither circumcision, nor uncircumcision availeth; but a new creature; and as many as walk according too, and in this rule, peace be unto them, and mercy upon the Israel of God'.[97] Here it seems that the Fell women are representing the salvational equality of all those converted to Quakerism (those that are 'all one in Christ Jesus') as beyond bodily distinctions. A person's status (male or female) as circumcised or uncircumcised is no longer important since what this text imagines is a 'new creature' where such bodily distinctions are wholly subordinate to spiritual equality. What this development between *Womens Speaking Justified* and this later text reveals, then, is a move to a rhetoric of gender equality which replaces the confusion of bodily demarcations of

---

93   Shapiro writes, 'the religious difference of Jewish women is not usually imagined as physically inscribed in their flesh, and the possibility of identifying women as Jews through some kind of incision never took hold in England, though for a brief time in the fifteenth century in northern Italy the requirement that Jewish women have their ears pierced and wear earrings served precisely this function.' See Shapiro, *Shakespeare and the Jews*, p.120; and on the concept of 'uncircumcision', see 128–30.

94   'From our Country Women's meetings in Lancashire to be Dispersed abroad, among the Women's meetings everywhere'; the Philadelphia copy of this letter has been transcribed. See Milton D. Speizman and Jane C. Kronick, 'A Seventeenth-Century Quaker Woman's Declaration', *Signs*, 1 (1975), 231–45. All references will be to this transcription. For a discussion of this letter, see Kunze, *Margaret Fell and the Rise of Quakerism*, pp.159–66.

95   Isabel Ross, *Margaret Fell: Mother of Quakerism*, pp.290, 298–9.

96   Kunze, *Margaret Fell and the Rise of Quakerism*, p.165.

97   'From our Country Women's meetings in Lancashire', p.241.

circumcision or uncircumcision with respect to maleness and femaleness. In this pamphlet, the 'new creature' of spiritual equality is beyond such bodily concerns.

Second, what this analysis suggests is that in the late 1660s and beyond, Fell was appropriating signs of Jewishness as motifs to discuss other religious concerns. Rather than directing her pamphlets solely at practising Jews, as she had done in the 1650s, when she believed the conversion of the Jews and the subsequent return of the messiah to be imminent, in her 1668 pamphlet she also addressed another group. The 'Seed of Israel' referred to the non-Quaker English who lived in 'bondage' in 'Egypt's Darkness'. The crucial date of 1666 in the apocalyptic calendar had passed without Jews expressing any interest in converting to Quakerism. Indeed Jews had found their own messiah, who had turned apostate. Fell's caustic tone in this pamphlet and her lack of sympathy with the Jews who chase after 'changeable priests' can be explained as a response to Sevi's conversion and, more importantly, by the fact that the Jews still looked for a Messiah on earth rather than recognising that it was the 'light within' which they should be seeking.[98] Under a restored monarchy which was committed to religious uniformity, and prepared to punish non-conformists strenuously, Fell sought to move away from the explicit millennial messages of her 1650s tracts. Thus Fell's change in attitude to the Jews from breathless proselytising to rebuke was a response to continental Jewish messianism, English politics and changes within the Quaker movement. In 1656 and 1657, Fell expected the imminent apocalypse and urged the Jews to convert in order to fulfil this divinely ordained timetable. By 1668, her attitude to the Jews was shaped by a very different situation. It was clear that by 1668 Fell saw God's cause solely in terms of an internal moral victory of the 'light within'. She no longer hoped for external religious or political success. Under the Commonwealth and the Protectorate, at least until the impersonation of Christ by Nayler in 1656, the Quakers had not been harshly persecuted. Writing after four years of incarceration, Fell, in 1668, was understandably anxious to present a less radical theology to a draconian regime. Consequently neither messianism nor Jewish tolerance were her priorities as she sought to rally faithful Quakers and offer them spiritual comfort. The conversion of practising Jews was, for Fell, no longer a central concern. Rather, by appropriating metaphors of Jewishness (particularly the label 'inward' and 'outward' Jew), Fell sought, by arguing for women's rights to speak in Church, to organise and modify the Quaker movement. At a time when the Quaker Church was attempting to rewrite its past in order to shape the movement's future it should not perhaps be regarded as surprising to find Fell's emphasis shifting from the concerns of race and religion with which she theoretically sympathised to considering her own and other women's positions within the Quaker movement itself. By 1675, issues of ethnic difference, which

---

98   Fell, *A Call Unto the Seed of Israel*, p.14.

were necessarily represented by using the metaphor of circumcision, were discarded in favour of the utopian rhetoric of a 'new creature' of non-gendered Quaker equality.

Acknowlegments

I would like to thank Chris Woolgar of the Hartley Institute and Tony Kushner of the Parkes Institute, both at the University of Southampton, who encouraged and supported this work. For helpful critical readings of earlier drafts of this essay, I would like to thank the following: Andrew Hadfield, Sarah Prescott, Carola Scott-Luckens, Kevin Sharpe, Greg Walker and Diane Watt. This article first appeared in *Reformation*, 4 (1999), 139–67. It is reprinted here with permission.

Chapter 10

Enlightenment and Exclusion: Judaism and Toleration in Spinoza, Locke and Bayle

Adam Sutcliffe

Of all the philosophical building-bricks of the post-Enlightenment edifice of modern liberal democracy, the foundation stone of toleration is perhaps particularly vulnerable to cracking under strain. While toleration is today almost universally celebrated as a key moral good, Western political culture is simultaneously haunted by a fear of descent into an ethically anchorless world of permissiveness and cultural relativism. Intolerance of diversity, we affirm, is barbarous; but so is any violation of the universal imperative to respect the rule of law and decent standards of public morality. There is an inevitable tension between these two core values: any legally enforced standard of behaviour potentially encroaches on the tolerance of those who wish to live according to other standards. The political realisation of tolerance requires a negotiated delineation of the subjective, shifting boundary between the legally or ethically absolute and the culturally variable.

In the intellectual climate of liberal–rationalist triumphalism that has suffused so much of post-Enlightenment political discourse, the inescapable difficulties inherent in defining the practical meaning and the appropriate parameters of tolerance are easily occluded. An unhesitatingly confident commitment to toleration as a transparent and self-evidently necessary moral good first emerged amongst the *philosophes* of the mid-eighteenth century, for whom trenchant opposition to intolerance was enshrined as one of the central tenets of enlightened thought. In the eighth volume of the *Encyclopédie*, published in 1765, Diderot very briskly dealt with the issue in his article headed 'Intolérance'. He opens his essay by swiftly drawing a sharp distinction between the thoroughly laudable ecclesiastical intolerance – 'regarding as false every religion apart from one's own' – and barbaric civil intolerance: the violent treatment of people of different religious faiths.[1] He regarded the case against civil intolerance as so obvious that it scarcely merited exposition:

> A few lines drawn from Holy Scripture, from the Fathers and Councils,
> will suffice to show that the intolerant person taken in this last sense is

---

1 Denis Diderot, *Encyclopédie* article 'Intolérance', in *Diderot: Political Writings*, trans. and ed. J.H. Mason and R. Wokler (Cambridge: Cambridge University Press, 1992), p.29.

a wicked man, a bad Christian, a dangerous subject, a poor politician and a bad citizen.[2]

However, in the intellectually formative period of the Early Enlightenment, approximately from 1675 to 1715, the tone in which the issue of toleration was discussed was very different. The validity or otherwise of the notion of tolerance was one of the most keenly contested and intensely debated issues within the self-consciously international scholarly community of the late seventeenth-century Republic of Letters. Particularly during the 1680s, arguments both for and against the principle were widely aired, and the newly-established literary periodicals, which were the most important channel of communication between *savants*, published numerous essays on the subject. Indeed there are signs that some felt the issue was in danger of being debated to death. The review in the *Histoire des Ouvrages des Savans* of April 1688 of a supplement to Pierre Bayle's *Commentaire Philosophique* – the most astute essay on toleration of the period, to which this essay will return shortly – begins almost apologetically:

> Even though this subject, which has been debated to-and-fro so much over the last few years, has lost the attraction of novelty, we won't let that stop us, because the author of the *Philosophical Commentary* has a particularly vigorous, original style that makes everything appear new in his hands.[3]

Whereas the *philosophes* of the mid-eighteenth century generally considered the arguments in favour of toleration to be manifestly obvious to any individual capable of basic rational thought, there was no such assured confidence among the pioneering proponents of toleration of the final quarter of the seventeenth century. The three key theorists of toleration in this period – Baruch Spinoza, John Locke and Pierre Bayle – each developed careful arguments to counter the deeply-felt political and theological objections of their opponents, who were deeply hostile to what they saw as a newfangled and highly dubious principle. For many Protestant and most Catholic thinkers, the idea of tolerance was a dangerous absurdity, implying an abandonment of any commitment to the absolute and unitary authority of the true revealed religion. The dismissive impatience of the Catholic scholar Pellison, in dispute with Leibniz on this subject, is representative of the widely-held orthodox view in the 1690s: 'From this the dogma of Tolerance, so-called, is born; and another, even newer word, "Intolerance", of which people accuse the Roman Church as if it were some terrible crime.'[4]

A recognition of the necessity of some form of confessional coexistence among Christians was not in this period an entirely new idea. In Germany, a

---

2   Ibid.
3   *Histoire des Ouvrages des Savans*, Rotterdam, April 1688, p.529.
4   M. Pellison, in G.W. Leibniz, *De la Tolérance des Religions* (Paris: 1692), p.46.

widespread acceptance of religious diversity had emerged in response to the devastation wrought by religious zeal during the Thirty Years' War. In England, religious toleration had been widely debated during the Interregnum period, with some, such as Richard Overton, in his pamphlet, *The Arraignment of Mr. Persecution* (1645), arguing for the full toleration of all faiths, including, notably, the Jews, 'the apple of God's eye'.[5] However, Louis xiv's revocation of the Edict of Nantes in 1685, and the resulting creation of a large, articulate and embittered Huguenot diaspora, was the key causal factor behind the emergence of the extensive and tightly argued toleration debate in the closing decades of the seventeenth century. Many leading Huguenot exiles, notably Henri Basnage, Jean Le Clerc, Isaac Papin, Gédéon Huet and Jacques Bernard as well as Pierre Bayle, sought to underpin their passionate opposition to the Revocation, and to the persecution of those Huguenots remaining in France, by appealing to the abstract principles of toleration and liberty of conscience.

However, their arguments were vehemently opposed by other Huguenots aligned with the 'zealot' party, led by the theologian Pierre Jurieu. Rather than countering absolutism with abstract theories of political justice, Jurieu directed his polemical fury against the evils of Popery, in the name of which Louis was oppressing the true faith. For Jurieu, acceptance of the idea of toleration implied indifference towards religious truth. The opposing 'moderate' party of Huguenot refugees in the Netherlands, led by Pierre Bayle, argued strenuously against this assertion. In doing so, they were forced to grapple with the extremely difficult philosophical issue of how to allow for dissent and diversity without losing all possible foundations for a notion of absolute truth.

This question, so starkly faced by the refugee Huguenot community, resonated more generally throughout the entire Early Enlightenment toleration debate. In the terms of our own age we recognise their dilemma as the familiar perennial of how simultaneously to defend toleration and reject relativism. In the language of the late seventeenth century, the great fear was not relativism, but the anathema of atheism. Unbelief, it was almost universally assumed, led inevitably to private amorality and public anarchy; and concessions to toleration, in undermining absolute standards of knowledge, belief or behaviour, appeared to many to lead towards this peril. Once we account for this difference of conceptual terminology, we can clearly recognise in these early attempts to theorise toleration the negotiation and the occlusion of this fundamental and inescapable conundrum.

The remainder of this essay will focus on the question of the status of Judaism within the most significant Early Enlightenment texts in support of toleration. This specific issue will be used as an analytical tool with which to attempt to probe and prise open the occlusions and tensions that nestle in the roots of this

---

5   Henry Kamen, *The Rise of Toleration* (London: Weidenfeld and Nicolson, 1967), pp.173–4.

crucial political notion. To claim that the Jewish case offers a particularly penetrating insight into Early Enlightenment thinking on this subject might seem surprising, or even absurd. The Jews were numerically an extremely small group in Western Europe, and were a marginal issue within the toleration debates of the period, the practical concern of which was the acceptability or otherwise of diversity in Christian worship. However references to and invocations of the Jews occur frequently and in many different guises in these essays and treatises. The unique, foundational relationship of Judaism to Christianity also drew the Jews into the heart of the struggle between traditional theology and Enlightenment rationalism, which lay embedded at the core of the debate over toleration.

Since the beginning of the Diaspora the Jews had lived dispersed amongst Christians. For this reason they could be invoked by advocates of toleration as the prime example of a religious minority that had always, in certain places and under certain conditions, been tolerated by their hosts. It was argued by some that the fact that the toleration of Judaism had historically been so widely accepted clinched the case in favour of the civil toleration of all religious groups. If *even* the Jews were tolerated, the argument ran, what possible grounds could there be for denying toleration to any other group? This case is powerfully put in an anonymous essay on civil tolerance in the Dutch Republic, published in the *Histoire des Ouvrages des Savans* of January 1692:

> Let us take the example of the Jews. There is no doubt that they are tolerated for no other reason than the advantages they bring for commerce ... One could even argue that they are not simply tolerated. Buildings that in use and design could not be taken as anything other than Temples, devoted to the cult of Religion, imply a bit more than tolerance. However, taking the Jewish religion into consideration, there is nothing that is more odious to Christianity. The attack wherever Jews are present on the victorious Messiah is a blasphemy against Jesus Christ, who they reject; and their ancestors have had the audacity to boast that their sacrilegious hands crucified the Christian God. If it is argued that we must tolerate them, because they are destined to be recalled, and miraculously converted, and that there is besides no reason to fear that their impiety might spread, I answer that we must therefore tolerate all idolaters ... One cannot push tolerance any further than in the case of the Jews; and so the implications of their case are unanswerable.[6]

This argument highlights several ambiguities clustering around the meaning of toleration for the early theorists of the concept. Does toleration entail nothing more than allowing the physical presence of members of a minority, or must this be accompanied by certain rights and guarantees? Can pragmatic considerations, such as the particular theological and economic justifications for the toleration of

---

6   *Histoire des Ouvrages des Savans*, Rotterdam, January 1692, pp.240–41.

the Jews, be incorporated into general, abstract arguments for toleration? Can cogent arguments for universal toleration be derived from an avowedly Christian theological perspective? And how compatible can toleration of a minority, such as the Jews, be with a deep-seated contempt for that minority, on religious or other grounds? These and similar difficulties resonate through much of the corpus of Early Enlightenment writings on toleration. Despite the aspiration of many Protestant thinkers to develop a justification for toleration that was free from confessional bias, and grounded instead in the scholarly language of the avowedly non-denominational, meritocratic Republic of Letters, their frequent reversion to exceptionalist and theological modes of thought when considering the case of the Jews reveals how incomplete and troubled this project was.

Any discussion of the late seventeenth century debate on toleration and the rights of conscience must start with the contribution of a Jew: Baruch (later Benedict) Spinoza. His *Tractatus Theologico-Politicus* culminates with the claim that he has conclusively demonstrated 'that in a free commonwealth every man may think as he pleases, and say what he thinks'.[7] Fundamental to Spinoza's argument is the careful distinction he draws between faith and philosophy which, he states in the fourteenth chapter, is 'the main object of this entire treatise'.[8] Whereas faith offers a pathway to salvation for all, through simple obedience to God's revealed commands, philosophy enables those few people who have sufficient mental capacities to find wisdom and happiness guided by the natural light of reason alone. Whereas authority over matters of religion has always rightly been subject to the authority of the sovereign, philosophical thinking is impossible to control, and so must inevitably be free.[9]

Spinoza's argument, though, is crucially not one in support of *religious* toleration. Having distinguished so sharply between faith and philosophy, it is exclusively with the freedom of the latter that he concerns himself. It is largely because of the sharp distinction that he draws between authoritarian faith and truth-seeking philosophy that he was almost universally derided by his contemporaries as an atheist, despite his own assertions to the contrary. Spinoza's attitude towards the Christian faith is in fact somewhat ambivalent. Although institutionally and traditionally shackled within unphilosophical structures of religious authority, he regarded Christianity as grounded in the teaching of Jesus that '[God's] covenant is no longer written in ink or engraved on tablets of stone, but is inscribed by God's spirit in men's hearts.'[10] This interpretation of the essence of Christianity casts it as in accordance with Spinoza's own philosophy, which bears many traces of the possible influence of

---

7 Baruch Spinoza, *Tractatus Theologico-Politicus* [1670], trans. Samuel Shirley (Leiden: E.J. Brill, 1991), p.291.

8 Ibid., p.221.

9 Ibid., pp.280–90.

10 Ibid., p.272.

contacts he may have had with the groups of English conversionist Quakers active within the Dutch Jewish communities in the 1650s, spearheaded by the Hebrew-speaking Samuel Fisher.[11]

In contrast with Christianity, Judaism, for Spinoza, represents the unambiguous and total subjection of a people to God's authority. The ancient Jewish state, he writes, was a theocracy, under the direct command of God. He discusses at length both the strengths and the weaknesses of this polity, which 'might have lasted indefinitely',[12] but argues that it is no longer a model to be imitated.[13] Although there are many features of the Mosaic Hebrew Republic that Spinoza admires – most notably its close union of religious and secular authority – he nonetheless characterises it as fundamentally unphilosophical. The fact that the ancient Jews needed such an explicit covenant bears witness to their intellectual underdevelopment: 'To the early Jews,' he writes, 'religion was transmitted in the form of written law because at that time they were just like children.'[14] Rather than aspiring to rational argument, the Scriptural writings were 'adapted to the intellectual level ... of the unstable and fickle Jewish multitude'.[15] Although these vivid prophetical imaginings and rigid laws were appropriate to the predicament and the capabilities of the ancient Jews, they now constitute, as law, an obsolete remnant of an extinct covenant and, as narrative, a text the interpretation of which can reveal nothing about truth itself, but which merely offers a primitive account of the early history of the Jewish tribe. Philosophical thought, for Spinoza, is utterly antithetical to revealed dogma. As they are presented in the *Tractatus*, the Jews represent the inverse case of a people dependent on dogma, to the total exclusion of independent thought.

It is hardly surprising that Spinoza should regard Judaism as dismally blinkered and unthinking. 'By the decree of the Angels and the word of the Saints we ban, cut off, curse and anathemize Baruch de Espinoza ... with all the curses written in the Torah': thus the communal record book of the Portuguese Jewish community of Amsterdam for 27 July 1656.[16] Spinoza was only twenty-four years old when this punishment for his 'horrible heresies' was pronounced, forbidding all members of the community to have any contact with him whatsoever. It is eminently understandable that, as Yirmiyahu Yovel puts it, 'When it comes to his fellow Jews, Spinoza loses his philosophical cool'.[17] However biographical reasons why Spinoza may have been disposed to portray

---

11   Richard. H. Popkin, 'Spinoza and Samuel Fisher', *Philosophia*, 15 (1985), 219–36.

12   Spinoza, *Tractatus* (see note 7), p.272.

13   Ibid., p.272.

14   Ibid., p.205.

15   Ibid., p.220.

16   Quoted in Yirmiyahu Yovel, *Spinoza and Other Heretics – The Marrano of Reason* (Princeton: Princeton University Press, 1989), p.3.

17   Ibid., p.178.

Judaism negatively do not alter or displace the fact that reverence of the Old Testament is deeply structured into his writings as a defining polar opposite of his own positive philosophy.

Again unsurprisingly, Spinoza says nothing that directly brings into question the right of the Jews to be tolerated politically. However, if we accept that a toleration of any depth must incorporate some measure of respect, Spinoza's philosophical attitude to Judaism remains problematic. If this religion is seen as so relentlessly authoritarian, and so deeply inimical to the values of individual intellectual freedom, how can it nonetheless fall within the bounds of a toleration that is based on those very values? As Efraim Shmueli has argued, Spinoza was not in favour of an indiscriminate toleration: most basically, the discipline of his geometrical method set a standard of rigorous logic to which all ideas that merited any respect had to conform.[18] The fact that Judaism represents in Spinoza's thought the starkest case of a world-view that utterly fails to conform to these standards and values throws into relief an edge of judgmental inflexibility that problematises the intellectual foundations on which his argument for tolerance is based.

Although not as argumentatively subtle or original as the work of Spinoza or Bayle, the most influential English text on toleration in the late seventeenth century was undoubtedly John Locke's *Letter Concerning Toleration*, first published, anonymously and in Latin, in 1689. In contrast to Spinoza, Locke emphatically does not argue in favour of a general freedom of thought. He firmly excludes the rights of atheists, asserting that 'all men know and acknowledge that God ought to be publicly worshipped'.[19] Locke interprets toleration primarily as the right to freedom of worship. He advocates this from a distinctively Calvinist perspective, emphasising the importance of the individual's obedience to their own personal conscience. However, although he arrives at his commitment to the underlying autonomy of individual religious practice from a very different perspective to that of Spinoza, he nonetheless enunciates a very similarly particularist and exclusionary attitude towards the Jews.

A number of ambiguities are apparent in Locke's *Letter*. Most immediately apparent among these is the problem of the parameters of his consideration of the question of toleration, which are far from clear. At times, he seems to be aspiring to the formulation of a general theory, applicable to all. Indeed, at one point he specifically asserts this: 'Nay, if we may openly speak the truth, and as becomes one man to another, neither pagan, nor Mahometan, nor Jew, ought to be

---

    18   Efraim Shmueli, 'The Geometrical Method, Personal Caution, and the Idea of Tolerance', in R.W. Shahan and J. I. Biro, eds., *Spinoza: New Perspectives* (Norman: University of Oklahoma Press, 1978), pp.197-234 (pp.213-4).

    19   John Locke, *A Letter Concerning Toleration* [1689], ed. John Horton and Susan Mendus (London: Routledge, 1991), p.32.

excluded from the commonwealth because of his religion. The gospel commands no such thing.'[20]

With regard to the Jews, he goes out of his way to endorse their right to open synagogues (a right which they did not yet have in Britain, where the first synagogue was built in London only in 1701):[21]

> If we allow the Jews to have private houses and dwellings amongst us,
> why should we not allow them to have synagogues? Is their doctrine
> more false, their worship more abominable, or is the civil peace more
> endangered, by their meeting in public, than in their private houses?[22]

However, in the first few lines of the *Letter*, Locke defines his subject matter as 'my thoughts about the mutual toleration of Christians in the different professions of religion', and states that his argument in favour of toleration is fundamentally a Christian one: 'I esteem that toleration to be the chief characteristical mark of the true church.' Locke's religious commitment is often neglected by readers who are eager to interpret him as the supreme prophet of modern liberalism. Cautioning against this, John Dunn has stressed the fundamental importance in Locke's political thought of the traditional Calvinist concept of the calling, which exposes the wide gulf between his own thinking and that of our own, secular age.[23] It is striking, however, that Locke's more theological politics leads him to a denigration of Judaism that is almost identical to that of Spinoza.

Like Spinoza, Locke constructs the Judaism of the Old Testament as antithetical to his own positive values. Against the traditional Christian distinction between the moral, judicial and ceremonial elements of the Mosaic law, which held that, although the latter two categories were no longer binding for Christians, the first retained a general validity, he insists that the entire Mosaic law is now defunct. The ancient Jews were bound by such rigid laws because of their unique situation:

> The commonwealth of the Jews, different in that from all others, was an
> absolute theocracy: nor was there, nor could there be, any difference
> between that commonwealth and the church. The laws established there
> concerning the worship of one invisible Deity, were the civil laws of
> that people, and a part of their political government, in which God
> himself was the legislator.[24]

The Jewish Commonwealth, then, is a world in which the necessary space for the

---

20   Ibid., p.51.

21   N.I. Matar, 'The Controversy over the Restoration of the Jews in English Protestant Thought', *Durham University Journal*, 49 (1987–8), 241–56.

22   Locke, *Letter Concerning Toleration*, p.51.

23   John Dunn, *The Political Thought of John Locke* (Cambridge: Cambridge University Press, 1969), pp.245–261.

24   Locke, *Letter Concerning Toleration*, p. 39.

kind of individual moral calling that stands at the crux of Locke's politics and ethics is uniquely obliterated. Judaism is thus implicitly represented as the inverse of Locke's own values of personal religious, ethical and political responsibility.

As with Spinoza, this philosophically extremely negative view of the Jews stands in Locke only as an implied consequence of his arguments. Nowhere does Locke directly attack the Jews in venomous or derisory tones. He did, however, later modify the explicit argument in favour of the toleration of Jews that he makes in his first *Letter*. Locke wrote two subsequent letters on toleration, in response to the sustained critiques of Jonas Proast. The principal objection of Proast was to Locke's extension of toleration to non-Christians, which, he wrote, 'can do no service to the True Religion'.[25] In response, Locke defended the toleration of Jews on a different basis, in stridently conversionist terms:

> we pray every day for their Conversion, and I think it our duty so to do;
> But it will, I fear, hardly be believed that we pray in earnest, if we
> exclude them from the other ordinary and probable means of
> Conversion; either by driving them from, or persecuting them when
> they are amongst us.[26]

In his correspondence with the Dutch Remonstrant Phillip van Limborch, Locke appears, like van Limborch, as an ardent conversionist, extremely eager to hasten the expected mass Jewish conversion that will herald the Day of Judgment.[27] The ease with which Locke slides from an apparently unconditional advocacy of the toleration of Jews to a more conventional conversionist position demonstrates the superficiality of his consideration of the Jewish case. More profoundly, though, and taken together with Locke's moral hostility towards Judaism, a tension is apparent between a willingness to accept Jews as citizens and a marked ambivalence over whether they can truly be accepted as Jews. The tangled jumble of attitudes towards Judaism displayed by Locke exposes an unthought strand of arrogance that lies deeply woven into his notion of enlightened toleration.

The most comprehensive and intricate defence of toleration in the late seventeenth century was that of Pierre Bayle, the great Huguenot refugee scholar of Rotterdam. Although Henri Basnage de Beauval's slightly earlier *Tolérance des Religions* (1684) was the first extended Huguenot defence of the principle of toleration, Basnage's text is polemic rather than reflective in tone. He devotes most of this essay to a vehement attack on the violent intolerance of the French

---

25   Jonas Proast, *Argument of the Letter Concerning Toleration, Briefly Consider'd and Answer'd* (London: 1690), pp.2–3.

26   John Locke ['Philanthropus'], *A Second Letter Concerning Toleration* (London: 1690), p.2.

27   N. Matar, 'John Locke and the Jews', *Journal of Ecclesiastical History*, 44 (1993), 45–62.

Catholic Church since the beginning of the Wars of Religion, comparing their zeal to the ferocity of 'a tiger intoxicated by blood',[28] in contrast to the stoic and honourable peacefulness of the Huguenots, 'who know how to bear misfortune bravely'.[29] Bayle's theorisation of toleration was far broader in scope and more sophisticated in argumentation.[30] Published in 1686, his *Commentaire Philosophique* is structured around a refutation of the literal interpretation of Jesus Christ's words in Luke's gospel: 'Go out into the highways and hedges, and compel them to come in, that my house may be filled',[31] which since the original exegesis of St Augustine had been used by theologians as a traditional justification for the use of coercive methods to drive heretics back to the true faith.

In a broadly similar but much more outspoken manner than Locke, the linchpin of Bayle's argument in the *Commentaire Philosophique* is his insistence on the paramountcy of conscience. The starting-point of the text is a defence of the self-evident necessity of basing all understanding on the insights of the individual 'natural light'. For Bayle, the inner voice of conscience is the voice of God. Even if the dictates of this voice are in fact mistaken, the individual nonetheless should not act against what he believes to be the true divine voice. Bayle emphasises at the outset of the *Commentary* that he is writing as a philosopher, not as a theologian. His argument against the literal reading of his biblical text is, he states, based purely on a single principle of natural light, which he asserts as self-evident: 'that any literal interpretation which carries an obligation to commit iniquity is false'.[32] Such is Bayle's conviction of the self-evidence of this notion that he equates it with sanity itself:

> As long as a man is not mildly mad, he will never consent to anyone
> being able to command him to hate his God and to scorn his laws clearly
> and distinctly dictated to conscience and intimately engraven in the heart.[33]

In rebuttal of the argument that a distinction must be made between the toleration of truth and of falsehood, Bayle insists that 'an erroneous conscience has the same rights as an enlightened conscience'.[34] Bayle's guiding principle here is what John Kilcullen has called 'the moral irrelevance of being right':[35] the

---

28   Henri Basnage, *Tolérance des Religions* (Rotterdam: 1684; repr. New York and London: Johnson Reprint Company, 1970), p.31.

29   Ibid, p.103.

30   Kamen, *Rise of Toleration*, pp.235–6.

31   Luke 14:23.

32   Pierre Bayle, *Commentaire Philosophique sur ces paroles de Jésus-Christ, Contrains-les d'entrer* (Rotterdam: 1686), trans. and ed. by Amie Godman Tannenbaum (New York: Peter Lang, 1987), p.28.

33   Ibid., p.66.

34   Ibid., p.151.

35   John Kilcullen, *Sincerity and Truth: Essays on Arnauld, Bayle and Toleration* (Oxford: Clarendon Press, 1988), p.80.

individual is always morally bound to follow the dictates of conscience, regardless of what those dictates might be, and of what religious conviction they are based on.

This argument, though, leads to an immediate problem. What of those who believe that precisely the dictates of their conscience require them to persecute others? Such a claim was effectively the argument made by the French Catholic persecutors of the Huguenots, against whom, in deferring to the rights of erring consciences, Bayle stood in danger of depriving himself of any possible grounds for objection. Immediately aware of this, he poses the problem squarely and baldly:

> The second difficulty proposed is that my doctrine, in its consequences, destroys what I would like to establish. My design is to show that persecution is an abominable thing, and yet everyone who believes himself obliged by conscience to persecute would, by my doctrine, be obliged to persecute and would be sinning if he did not.[36]

In his response to this difficulty, Bayle redefines the purpose of his argument as being 'to convince persecutors that Jesus Christ has not commanded violence'.[37] Rather than claiming to have found a universal, philosophical argument for the rightness of tolerance, Bayle implicitly acknowledges that he must ultimately have recourse to faith, and to the teachings of the Christian faith, in order to convince persecutors of 'those errors of conscience which they may harbour in regard to persecution'.[38] He acknowledges nonetheless that, in accordance with his argument, those who remain convinced in conscience of the necessity to persecute those whom they consider heretics must follow their consciences and do so. In order to find firm ground from which to condemn such action, he silently shifts from the terrain of philosophy to that of theology:

> I do not deny that those who are actually persuaded that it is necessary to extirpate sects in order to obey God, are obliged to follow the motions of this false conscience and that, in not doing so, they are guilty of disobedience to God since they do a thing they believe to be in disobedience to God.
> But, (1) It does not follow that they do without sin what they do by conscience. (2) This does not hinder our crying out loudly against their false maxims and endeavouring to enlighten their understandings.[39]

This shift brings into sharp relief the outer limit of Bayle's pyrrhonistic argument in favour of tolerance. Sceptical reasoning here arrives at the point of its own inevitable self-undermining, an inevitability that Bayle himself acknowledges, noting elsewhere, in his *Dictionnaire historique et critique*, that scepticism,

---

36   Bayle, *Commentaire*, p.166.
37   Ibid., p.167.
38   Ibid.
39   Ibid.

despite being an analytical tool of great power, can nonetheless never lead to any form of conclusiveness. The true, self-reflexive sceptic must 'doubt if it is necessary to doubt'.[40] Ultimate recourse to belief is therefore inescapable and Bayle thus, at this point falls back on the convictions of his own moral sense. It is as a moral judgment, impervious to sceptical attack, that he asserts that persecution is sinful; just as elsewhere he expresses his (more contentious) conviction that nobody would ever preach various other things in good faith, such as 'sodomy, adultery and murder'.[41]

A key question that Bayle attempts to address in the *Commentaire* is how to account for and justify the regime of the Old Testament Jews, which, like Spinoza and Locke, he presents in marked contrast to the tolerant polity that he advocates. In the first chapter of his essay, he insists that the Old Testament is included in his critical system:

> God must have marked whatever came from Him with some imprint
> bearing a conformity with that inner light which communicates itself
> immediately to all spirits, or which, at least, should not appear contrary
> to it, and once done, all the particular laws of a Moses or any other
> prophet, were received agreeably and as coming from God, although
> they might have ordained things indifferent in their own nature.[42]

The Mosaic Law, he argues, became for the Jews from Moses' time onward a supplement to the natural light, dependent on it and as valid as it, 'in the same manner as a proposition in geometry once demonstrated from incontestable principles becomes itself a principle with regard to other propositions'.[43] As an elucidation of this, Bayle goes on to discuss a case culled from Guilelmus Arvernus' *De fide et legibus*,[44] concerning a number of medieval Jews who had allegedly renounced Judaism, 'claiming they had found in the ceremonial law of Moses an infinity of useless or absurd precepts which they perceived not to be founded on any solid reason of institution or prohibition, and concluding that such a law did not come from God'.[45] Bayle argues that these Jews were wrong to do so. He judges them guilty of disregarding both 'the incontestable proofs of divinity which God himself had given the mission of Moses' and the 'solid grounds' on which the ceremonial laws were based, given 'the character of the Jewish nation and their penchant to idolatry'.[46]

A paradox is immediately apparent here. Bayle's general argument concerning

40   Pierre Bayle, *Dictionnaire historique et critique* (1697), ed. and trans. R.H. Popkin (Indianapolis: Hackett, 1991) p.206 (article 'Pyrrho', rem. C).

41   Bayle, *Commentaire*, p.168.

42   Ibid., p.31.

43   Ibid., pp.31–2.

44   Guilelmus Arvernus, bishop of Paris, died in 1249. This text was not printed until 1475–6.

45   Bayle, *Commentaire*, p.32.

46   Ibid.

the paramountcy of conscience must logically apply to Jews as well as to all others; but nonetheless he unreservedly condemns these Jews, who followed their consciences in choosing to abandon Judaism. In this case, the rights of conscience are overridden by the authority of the Mosaic revelation, and its binding, legislative hold on the Jewish people. Whereas for Christians, knowledge of God and of virtue is above all discovered through the individual's personal relationship with their 'inner light', for Jews personal conscience is displaced by the binding authority of the Mosaic law.[47] In imposing direct theocratic government on the Jews, God exceptionally 'limited the immunities of conscience'.[48]

Bayle does not flinch from the difficulties that this presents for his argument in support of toleration. Once again, he poses directly the possible objection: since the law of Moses allowed absolutely no toleration for idolators and false prophets, and that the prophet Elias mercilessly put to death the priests of Baal, could not God in the Gospels also have commanded similar intolerance towards heresy?[49] His response is measured and enigmatic: 'I avow in good faith that this objection is strong and seems to be a mark that God wishes us to know hardly anything with certainty, by the exceptions He put in His words for almost all the common notions of reason.'[50]

The mysteriousness of revelation, and the incommensurability of faith and reason, is fundamental to Bayle's philosophy. His greatest work, the immense *Dictionnaire historique et critique* (1697), largely consists of a meticulous exploration of this insoluble tension. Although passionately committed to rational inquiry, Bayle was fascinated by the helplessness of reason when confronted with the fundamental questions of epistemology and ethics. At these points, he argues, we have no option but to turn for guidance to the inner authority of faith. In the *Dictionnaire*, Bayle largely ignores the New Testament – devoting to it only one, relatively brief article on John the Baptist – but he examines the Old Testament at length, repeatedly highlighting the discrepancies between conventional standards of morality and good conduct and the conduct of heroic figures such as David. Whereas he does not doubt that the message of the gospels, when interpreted sincerely and correctly, stands fully in accordance with reason, the Old Testament stands for Bayle largely as a repository of mystery. The Jews thus emerge in Bayle's thought as implicitly bearing witness not simply, as in traditional Christian theology, to the historical truth of the gospels, but to a much more abstracted confirmation of the mystery of revelation. The apparent absurdities and breaches of moral standards in the early Jewish past and in the Mosaic Law serve as a reminder of the limits of reason, and of the inscrutability of God's word to the limited capacities of the human mind.

---

47   Ibid., p.119.
48   Ibid., p.120.
49   Ibid., p.117.
50   Ibid., p.118.

This special significance accorded to the Jews effectively ejects them from Bayle's moral world. This applies equally to the Jews of his own time as to those of the biblical period: he explicitly states that the Mosaic law is 'a general law with regard to the Jews, enunciated absolutely and without restriction to time or place'.[51] He thus imposes a unique theologically and legally endorsed rigidity on the Jew. The divine legislation for the Jews does not command tolerance, and therefore the principle does not apply in their case. (Bayle does, however, note that the Jews are not commanded to proselytise, and so their intolerant law 'applied only to those of their own nation' who abandoned the Jewish faith.[52]) In Bayle's philosophy, Judaism is primarily defined by a crucial absence: its negation of any form of individual conscience.

Bayle's construction of Judaism as fundamentally alien to the notion of personal conscience is of great importance within his general philosophy. As we have seen, it is on his commitment to the paramountcy of the individual conscience that Bayle's own ethics are absolutely dependent. The Jews occupy the outside of the conceptual sphere within which his philosophy applies – and it is in opposition to that outside that he is able to define the parameters of his fideistic philosophy. In contrast to the theocracy of the ancient Jews, Bayle's Christian God is purely spiritual, leaving each individual free to choose their form of worship, following the inner wisdom of their personal natural light. Unlike Judaism, in which moral judgment is effaced by the laws of the Covenant, in Bayle's interpretation of Christianity it is the interior natural light of moral sense that forms the basis for universal ethical unity, beyond which, in minor matters, consciences may differ. Most fundamentally, it is in the Christian world only that the two intellectual forces of reason and faith strain so powerfully in opposing directions. It is this tension, and the ultimate paramountcy of faith in the contest between the two, that is at the heart of Bayle's philosophical investigations. Judaism, as a legally ordained religion impervious both to personal faith and to reason, thus emerges as not only excluded by the assumptions of Bayle's philosophy, but also starkly alien to his concept of philosophy itself.

If, then, Judaism represents for Bayle the very antithesis of his own values of personal moral and religious sincerity, is it really possible for Jews to be incorporated into a toleration that is predicated on those values? As with Locke, we find that Bayle's explicit commitment to the toleration of Judaism is problematised by his presentation of the Jewish religion as itself irredeemably and shamelessly intolerant. As he extends toleration to Jews with one hand, with the other Bayle excludes them from his progressive community of the tolerant. This fundamental antinomy is lodged inextricably within the theory of toleration as formulated by Bayle, and in the Early Enlightenment in

---

51   Ibid., p.121.
52   Ibid., p.121.

general. Underlying it stands a philosophical inevitability. The idea of tolerance could not and cannot be proclaimed as a political cause without the simultaneous condemnation of those who do not share the assumptions on which this ideal is based. Enlightenment can only advance dialectically, defining itself against the myths and orthodoxies that it strives to displace. Although there is certainly no perennial reason why Judaism should necessarily be the primary antagonistic partner of Reason, in the late seventeenth century powerful theological and historical factors singled it out as the obvious candidate.

Today we are probably more likely to see much the same conceptual role being attached to Islam. Angry crowds of anonymous Moslems, frequently labelled as 'fanatical', 'extremist' or 'fundamentalist' when they appear on television or are described in the press, are implicitly thereby represented as incapable of understanding the self-evidently true and simple principles of liberty, democracy and freedom of speech. Conceptually placed beyond the outer limits of the community of the tolerable, they offer the liberal, moderate consumer of the mass media a fleeting sense of security and superiority, safe within the perimeter walls of the world of the reasonable – until, perhaps, we remember that, if toleration is defined in terms of what it excludes, then it is based in its very emergence on a particularly problematic instance of precisely the intolerance that it is intended to supersede.

The meaning of the concept of toleration remains blurred by a fundamental linguistic ambiguity. In its narrow sense, tolerance implies the acceptance of opinions or forms of behaviour that the tolerator would nonetheless rather not have to put up with. As Maurice Cranston has put it, 'only the undesirable – or at any rate, the undesired – is a candidate for toleration'.[53] The grudging spirit of such toleration stands at odds with the equally widespread understanding of the notion as a moral imperative, and as a positive good in itself. The English Toleration Act of May 1689, in accepting religious dissent but imposing significant economic and social impediments on dissenters, was clearly tolerant only in the narrow sense. For this reason, it has been widely criticised by historians as representing a hasty, unsatisfactory compromise; an 'incomplete' achievement.[54] It was not for another 200 years that what might be described as 'completion' was attained in Britain. The repeal of the Test Laws in 1828 and the passing of the Catholic Emancipation Act in 1829 enabled non-Anglican

---

53   Maurice Cranston, 'John Locke and the Case for Toleration', in Susan Mendus and David Edwards (eds), *On Toleration* (Oxford: Oxford University Press, 1987), pp.101–21.

54   See, for example, Hugh Trevor-Roper, 'Toleration and Religion after 1688', in Ole Peter Grell, Jonathan Israel and Nicholas Tyacke (eds), *From Persecution to Toleration: The Glorious Revolution and Religion in England* (Oxford: Oxford University Press, 1991), pp.389–408.

Christians to participate fully in public life, but it was not until 1858 that a Jew was able to sit in the House of Commons, and not until 1890 that Parliament comprehensively abandoned religious restrictions on the holding of almost all official positions and honours.

Without in any sense belittling the great importance of this historical process, it is salutary to remember both that the extension of equal civil rights to minority groups does not necessarily create a society that is tolerant in the broad sense, and that the constitutive requirements of such a broad, positive toleration are themselves far from simple. The Early Enlightenment advocates of toleration regarded the individual's freedom of thought and conscience as a fundamental positive imperative. However, their commitment to toleration was set within the context of an optimistic assumption that the extension of this freedom would not lead to chaotic diversity and disagreement. They were confident that the sincere examination of conscience, or, for Spinoza, the precise use of philosophical reasoning, would on the contrary facilitate the emergence of an enlightened ethical consensus, which would underpin the toleration of relatively insignificant differences in outward forms of worship. Locke, Bayle and Spinoza all share a broadly common view of the ethical subject as autonomous, lucid, analytical and committed to some form of relatively minimal and sharply circumscribed faith. For all three philosophers, the possibility of discovering ethics within culture or tradition is foreclosed, and ways of engagement with culture other than the analytical and critical – such as through symbolic and metaphoric thought – are similarly derided.

It is in these exclusions that the potential severity of the Enlightenment is hidden; and it is in the response of these thinkers to Judaism that such exclusionary patterns come closest to the surface. The casting of Judaism as fundamentally intolerant (and thus inevitably also in some sense intolerable) that we have discovered in slightly different forms in each of these thinkers, does not negate the sincerity or the significance of their arguments in favour of the right of Jews to worship freely. However it does bring into relief the problematic implications of their dogged refusal to accept any form of philosophical and ethical thought that differs on a profound level from their own. They offer no consideration of the possibility that Judaism might evolve, or that it might occupy a space between the two poles of absolute legalism and full dependence on individual conscience. Their rejection of Judaism is thus representative of a wider tendency of the early thinkers of the Enlightenment sweepingly to dismiss all forms of traditional, mythic or metaphorical thought that were alien to their own philosophical project.

It is not until relatively late in the eighteenth century, among the first shoots of the Romantic critique of the Enlightenment, that we find the earliest signs of a recognition of this troubling arrogance that lies entangled within the Enlightenment idea of toleration. Amongst the maxims of Goethe is the following acute observation:

Toleration should really only be a transitory attitude. It must lead to recognition. To tolerate is to insult.[55]

---

55   Johann Wolfgang von Goethe, *Nachlaß*, trans. cited in Joachim Whaley, *Religious Toleration and Social Change in Hamburg, 1529–1819* (Cambridge: Cambridge University Press, 1985) p.209.

Chapter 11

The Limits of Toleration in Enlightenment Germany: Lessing, Goethe and the Jews

Ritchie Robertson

Gentile attitudes to Jews in Enlightenment Germany serve to illustrate two basic positions on toleration which have reappeared in present-day debates on multiculturalism. I shall call them a toleration based on indifference and a toleration based on recognition. A toleration based on indifference corresponds to the widespread liberal view that the state should show its respect for individual citizens by letting them pursue their various goals within the law, without making any assumption about the value of these goals. It is not the business of the polity to teach virtue, only to ensure observance of the laws. A toleration based on recognition, on the other hand, would show a positive appreciation of cultural diversity, assuming that respect of other people implies a recognition of their individual characters and of the cultures which have helped to shape them as individuals, and would promote dialogue among diverse groups.[1]

Both conceptions are problematic. What happens, for example, when the limits of toleration are challenged, as in the case of Salman Rushdie's *Satanic Verses*? Is it acceptable for the law to allow publication of a book deeply offensive to a substantial minority? But is it acceptable for members of that minority to claim religious justification for resorting to the generally abhorred practice of book burning? Can liberalism enter into dialogue with people who reject its premises? Equally serious problems surrounded the limits of toleration in eighteenth-century Germany. In particular, should it extend beyond the Christian denominations to include Jews? Should Jews be required to convert to Christianity, and/or to adopt the manners and appearance of the Gentiles around them, to qualify for admission to civil society? Could unconverted Jews be recognized as different but equal? Or did they mark the limit of any possible politics of toleration?

To many spokesmen of the Enlightenment, a toleration based ultimately on indifference seemed the best escape from the religious conflict that had ravaged sixteenth- and seventeenth-century Europe.[2] The Treaty of Westphalia which

---

1   See Charles Taylor, 'The politics of recognition', in Amy Gutmann (ed.), *Multiculturalism* (Princeton: Princeton University Press, 1994), pp.25–73.

2   See Walter Grossmann, 'Religious toleration in Germany, 1684–1750', *Studies on Voltaire and the Eighteenth Century*, 201 (1982), 115–41; Joachim Whaley,

concluded the Thirty Years' War in 1648 guaranteed the rights of Catholics, Lutherans and Calvinists within the Holy Roman Empire, leaving some states unitary in religion, and others mixed with two religions being granted parity. Enlightenment philosophers based their arguments for toleration above all on the freedom of the individual conscience. Thus Locke's *Letter on Toleration* (1689) assumes that the Church must be quite separate from civil society. Religion becomes a purely private, individual matter: 'the care of each man's salvation belongs only to himself'.[3] The ruler must not interfere with his subjects' religious belief and practice, unless they endanger the peace of society. Rulers themselves, however, granted toleration more on pragmatic grounds. Following the principles of mercantilism, they sought to maximise the productive capacity of the state, including the state's human resources, and could not accept that large sections of the population should be excluded from citizenship and service simply because of religious beliefs. This motive underlay the toleration practised by Frederick the Great, who in 1751 declared his indifference to the private beliefs of the many sects tolerated in Prussia:

> All these sects live here in peace, and contribute equally to the welfare of the state; no religion differs much from others on the subject of morality; so the government can regard them all indifferently, and allow each person the freedom to go to heaven by whatever path he likes; all that is asked of him is that he should be a good citizen.[4]

Frederick's pragmatism went further than most philosophers recommended. Besides Huguenots, Jews and sectarians were allowed to settle, and Frederick showed his tolerance by accepting a Roman Catholic as citizen in the second week of his reign (June 1740), with the note: 'All religions are equal and good, as long as the persons who profess them are decent; and even if Turks and Heathens were to come and populate the country, we will be ready to build mosques and churches for them' (quoted in Grossmann, 1982, p.127). Similar reasoning justified the much further-reaching toleration introduced by the reforming Habsburg Emperor Joseph II, whose Toleration Patents of 1781 and 1782 granted freedom of worship and access to education not only to Protestants but also to Jews. His resolution on Jewish emancipation begins by announcing its purpose: 'in order to make the members of the Jewish nation who are so numerous in my hereditary lands more useful to the state than they could be when their range of occupations was so restricted and the means of

---

'Pouvoir sauver les apparences: the theory and practice of tolerance in eighteenth-century Germany', *British Journal of Eighteenth-Century Studies*, 13 (1990), 1–16.

3   John Locke, *Epistola de Tolerantia / An Essay on Toleration*, ed. Raymond Klibansky, trans. J.W. Gough (Oxford: Clarendon Press, 1968), p.125.

4   [Frederick the Great], *Mémoires pour servir à l'histoire de la Maison de Brandenbourg* (Berlin: Au Donjon du Chateau, 1751), p.396.

enlightenment were not adequately available and thus seemed to them superfluous'.[5]

In eighteenth-century Germany, as in Austria, the most obvious candidates for religious and social toleration were the Jews. Around the mid-century they lost the communal self-government that had previously helped to keep them separate. But while there were pressing practical reasons for governments to promote their economic integration, they were hampered by restrictions on their economic activity, their mobility, their residence and even the age at which they could marry. Better-off Jews increasingly sought and acquired a European-style education and adopted the clothes and manners of the Germans among whom they lived. By the late eighteenth century, Jewish men in Berlin, where acculturation was most advanced, dressed indistinguishably from non-Jews, with wigs or three-cornered hats instead of the traditional flat hat; many were beardless, as was normal for Gentiles, and even the philosopher Moses Mendelssohn retained only a small narrow beard. By his writings, which gained the respect of Gentile contemporaries including Kant, Mendelssohn provided less superficial evidence that Jews could master the rational and polished discourse of the Enlightenment, and demonstrated in his person the injustice of the restrictions that debarred him from membership of Berlin's learned societies.[6]

If Jews were becoming less visibly different, then social prejudice might follow theological prejudice into obsolescence. Jews might be integrated into German society as useful and productive citizens. That was the argument put forward by the Prussian civil servant Christian Wilhelm von Dohm in his treatise *Über die bürgerliche Verbesserung der Juden* (On the Civic Improvement of the Jews, 1781). Combating the common view of Jews as morally inferior, he argued that they were made so only by centuries of Christian oppression, but that freedom from social and economic restrictions would allow their humanity to flourish: 'The Jew is a human being still more than he is a Jew, and how is it possible that he should not love a state in which he could acquire property and enjoy it freely, where his taxes were no higher than those paid by other citizens, and where he too could gain honour and respect?'[7] Dohm's treatise was both beneficial and fateful, for it helped to ensure that Jewish emancipation in Germany was understood as a

---

5   'Resolution Josephs II an den böhmischen Obersten und österreichischen Kanzler Graf Blümegen. Toleranz gegen die Juden', 13 May 1781, in Harm Klueting (ed.), *Der Josephinismus. Ausgewählte Quellen zur Geschichte der theresianisch–josephinischen Reformen* (Darmstadt: Wissenschaftliche Buchgesellschaft, 1995), pp.241–2. All translations are mine unless otherwise stated.

6   The fullest account of Mendelssohn's activity remains Alexander Altmann, *Moses Mendelssohn: a Biographical Study* (London: Routledge & Kegan Paul, 1973), now supplemented by David Sorkin, *Moses Mendelssohn and the Religious Enlightenment* (London: Halban, 1996).

7   Christian Wilhelm von Dohm, *Über die bürgerliche Verbesserung der Juden* (Berlin and Stettin: Nicolai, 1781), p.28.

contract, 'a quid pro quo in which the Jews were to be regenerated in exchange for rights'.[8] In contrast to France, where restrictions on Jewish citizenship were abolished at a stroke, German Jews, even after full civil rights were granted in 1871, continued to be suspected of a residual, increasingly indefinable 'Jewishness' which made their 'regeneration' impossible to complete.[9]

Among the writers of the German Enlightenment, the strongest advocate – though, as I have argued elsewhere and shall briefly argue here, not a wholly unequivocal one – was Gotthold Ephraim Lessing (1729–86).[10] Lessing supported Jewish emancipation long before it seemed a practical possibility. He describes his own early play *Die Juden* (The Jews; written 1749, published 1754) as 'the result of a very serious reflection on the disgraceful oppression in which a nation must groan whom a Christian, I should think, cannot regard without veneration'.[11] Lessing's reputation as a militant supporter of toleration is beyond question. It is based not only on prose writings but also on *Die Juden* and his late dramatic masterpiece *Nathan der Weise* (Nathan the Wise, 1779). But these plays, as imaginative creations, do not simply translate Lessing's principles into dramatic form, but introduce complexities and ambiguities which, without undermining his principles, nevertheless qualify them.[12]

---

8   David Sorkin, *The Transformation of German Jewry, 1780–1840* (New York: Oxford University Press, 1987), p.20.

9   See Ritchie Robertson, *The 'Jewish Question' in German Literature, 1749–1939: Emancipation and its Discontents* (Oxford: Oxford University Press, 1999).

10   See Harald Schultze, *Lessings Toleranzbegriff: Eine theologische Studie* (Göttingen: Vandenhoeck & Ruprecht, 1969); Karl S. Guthke, 'Lessing und das Judentum. Rezeption. Dramatik und Kritik. Krypto-Spinozismus', *Wolfenbütteler Studien zur Aufklärung*, 4 (1977), 229–71; Peter Freimark, Franklin Kopitzsch and Helga Slessarev (eds), *Lessing und die Toleranz* (Detroit: Wayne State University Press and Munich: text + kritik, 1986); more generally, Klara Carmely, 'Wie "aufgeklärt" waren die Aufklärer in Bezug auf die Juden?', in Ehrhard Bahr, Edward P. Harris and Laurence G. Lyon (eds), *Humanität und Dialog: Lessing und Mendelssohn in neuer Sicht* (Detroit: Wayne State University Press; Munich: text + kritik, 1982), pp.177–88; Peter R. Erspamer, *The Elusiveness of Tolerance: The 'Jewish Question' from Lessing to the Napoleonic Wars* (Chapel Hill, NC: University of North Carolina Press, 1997); Klaus L. Berghahn, *Grenzen der Toleranz: Juden und Christen im Zeitalter der Aufklärung* (Cologne, Weimar and Vienna: Böhlau, 2001).

11   Lessing, 'Vorrede' to *Schrifften. Dritter und vierter Theil* (1754), in his *Werke*, ed. Herbert G. Göpfert *et al.*, 8 vols (Munich: Hanser, 1970–79), ii. 645. Future references to this edition are made in the text by L with volume and page number.

12   I have argued this more fully in '"Dies hohe Lied der Duldung?" The ambiguities of toleration in Lessing's *Die Juden* and *Nathan der Weise*', *Modern Language Review*, 93 (1998), 105–20; some material is reproduced here by permission of the Modern Humanities Research Association. For a reply, see H.B. Nisbet, 'Lessing, *Nathan der Weise*: a landmark in the history of tolerance', in Peter Hutchinson (ed.), *Landmarks in German Drama* (Oxford, Berne and Frankfurt a.M.: Peter Lang, 2002), pp.11–29, which I think fails to acknowledge that the imaginative expression of a belief is bound to be more complex and qualified than its formulation in discursive prose.

The play *Die Juden* exhibits a philosemitism that is ultimately restricted. A traveller saves a Baron from two highway robbers who are in fact the Baron's own servants, disguised as Jews. To protect themselves, the servants hold forth about godless, thieving Jews, while the Baron remarks that the Jews' deceitful character is apparent from their faces. He does not yet know that the traveller he is addressing is himself a Jew. The Baron offers the traveller, out of gratitude, his daughter and hence his fortune. The traveller replies that he cannot marry his daughter because he is a Jew. Thus the standard happy ending of comedy is frustrated, for the traveller's religion excludes him from the real integration represented by intermarriage, and his acceptance in Gentile society is confined to social and intellectual intercourse. In other ways, too, limitations are set to the philosemitism expressed by the Baron's words: 'Oh, how admirable the Jews would be if they were all like you!' (L i. 414).[13] The traveller replies smartly: 'And how charming the Christians would be, if they all had your qualities!' But his response does not diminish the impression given by the play that this Jew is admirable because untypical, both in his goodness and in having no readily perceptible Jewish qualities (though we learn that he avoids eating pork, and evidently follows Jewish law). Lessing is adumbrating a utopia in which people, whether Jews or Christians, are judged by the standard of universal morality: the traveller says it was 'universal benevolence ('die allgemeine Menschenliebe', L i. 378) that obliged him to save the Baron. But this is not a utopia in which difference is acknowledged, rather one to which people are admitted in so far as they erase their difference and conform to a common model, that of the universal, rational, enlightened human being. The traveller's comically stupid Christian servant exclaims: 'There are some Jews who aren't Jews. You're a fine man' (L i. 414; *The German–Jewish Dialogue*, p.35). Unwittingly he has blurted out the truth: Jews can only be admitted to the society of the Enlightenment if they are not Jews. At the beginning of the twentieth century, the same conclusion was drawn about the play by the Jewish critic Moritz Goldstein, as part of his contention that Jews could not hope to be fully accepted within German culture: 'To be a Jew without anyone noticing it, and yet to be a good Jew: that was the dream that enraptured Jews and Christians.'[14]

Lessing returned to the theme of Jewish–Christian relations in his last play, *Nathan der Weise*, after a controversy with the orthodox Lutheran cleric, Hauptpastor Goeze of Hamburg, over some investigations into the historical authenticity of the Gospels and the story of Moses written by the theologian

---

13   Quoted from the translation in *The German–Jewish Dialogue: An Anthology of Literary Texts, 1749–1993*, ed. Ritchie Robertson (Oxford: Oxford University Press, 1999), p.35.

14   Goldstein, 'Die geistige Organisation des Judentums', *Ost und West*, 6 (1906), p.515, quoted in Elisabeth Albanis, *German-Jewish Cultural Identity from 1900 to the Aftermath of the First World War* (Tübingen: Niemeyer, 2002), p. 64.

Hermann Samuel Reimarus and published after his death by Lessing.[15] Lessing's employer, the Duke of Brunswick, ordered him to end his pamphlet war with Goeze, so Lessing resorted to the theatre to explore the relations among dogma, free inquiry and morality. The resulting play is one of three dramatic masterpieces of the German Enlightenment, all written in the same decade, and all setting the individual conscience against political and ecclesiastical authority. The others are Goethe's *Iphigenie auf Tauris* (Iphigenie in Tauris, 1787), which will be discussed below, and Friedrich Schiller's *Don Carlos* (1786), in which the demand for freedom of conscience is addressed to King Philip IV of Spain and finally crushed by the sinister figure of the Grand Inquisitor.[16] Lessing, like Schiller, shows a political potentate as more approachable than an ecclesiastical potentate: Saladin, the Muslim ruler, helps arrange the happy ending in *Nathan*, whereas the Patriarch of Jerusalem represents the play's anti-comic force. Lessing's play won him admiration among subsequent generations of Jewish readers who celebrated him as the advocate of Jewish emancipation.[17] Others, however, recognized that the play's message about toleration is not as straightforward as one would like to think.

Nathan is set in Jerusalem at the time of the Third Crusade, during a truce between the Muslim ruler Saladin and the Christian population represented by the Patriarch. The action turns on the fact that Nathan, a rich Jewish merchant, has brought up as his daughter a girl who is in fact of Christian parentage. If this became known, he would be in danger of being burnt alive by the intolerant Patriarch. The image of fire runs through the play. At the beginning, Recha has been saved from a fire by a Christian, the Knight Templar, whose life has earlier been inexplicably spared by his captor Saladin. Having fallen in love with Recha, the Templar learns of her parentage from her pious Christian nurse, Daja; thinking that Nathan will refuse to let him marry Recha, he is tempted to betray Nathan to the Patriarch, but, for all his outward antisemitism, he is at bottom a decent and humane person and keeps Nathan's secret. At the end, it turns out that the Templar and Recha are brother and sister. Both are the children of Saladin's brother who married a German woman, so that the Templar was brought up in Germany. Lessing uses this standard comic ending to show how illusory are the

---

15   On Goeze, see Joachim Whaley, *Religious Toleration and Social Change in Hamburg 1529–1819* (Cambridge: Cambridge University Press, 1985); on the theological issues, see H.E. Allison, *Lessing and the Enlightenment* (Ann Arbor: University of Michigan Press, 1966).

16   On the resemblances among these plays, see F.J. Lamport, *German Classical Drama* (Cambridge: Cambridge University Press, 1990), ch.5, and, in a more historical context, see T.J. Reed, 'Talking to tyrants: dialogues with power in eighteenth-century Germany', *Historical Journal*, 33 (1990), 63–79.

17   For tributes paid at the Lessing bicentennial of 1929, see Barbara Fischer, 'Lösungsansatz "Raum" versus "Zeit": Jüdische Reaktionen auf Lessings *Nathan der Weise* im Vor-Shoah-Deutschland', *Lessing Yearbook*, 32 (2000), 325–39.

religious differences among people who are linked by blood and friendship. But since the Templar and Recha cannot marry, the ending is sexless. As in *Die Juden*, the expected happy ending represented by marriage is frustrated.

To recount the plot, however, says little about this play, which consists largely of tense and exciting argument. The characters embody various standpoints. Religious belief is set in opposition to natural human affection and honesty. This natural morality made the Templar save Recha's life and makes him, despite the contempt for Jews that he owes to his upbringing, warm to Nathan's palpable sincerity; it makes him unwilling to obey the Patriarch, who wants him to assassinate his benefactor Saladin, and restrains him from revealing to the Patriarch the identity of the Jew who has brought up a Christian child. This natural solidarity among people, based ultimately on family ties, is symbolized in the general embraces with which the final curtain falls. By contrast, Christian dogma encourages inhumanity. Daja, shown as a superstitious believer in miracles, thinks it wrong for Recha to be brought up in a non-Christian faith. The Patriarch, the only evil figure in the play, denies that there are any moral obligations towards non-Christians, or any moral commands that cannot be overridden by the (supposed) divine imperative. As his reluctant emissary, the Lay-Brother, puts it when transmitting to the Templar the Patriarch's proposal that he should murder Saladin,

> The Patriarch says what counts as villainy
> For men, may not be villainy to God. (L ii. 230)

The Patriarch corresponds to Schiller's Grand Inquisitor and to King Thoas in Goethe's *Iphigenie*, in that all represent a 'theological politics' in which ecclesiastical power takes precedence over natural bonds of affection and gratitude.[18] The Grand Inquisitor orders Philip to have his own son killed, and Thoas contemplates compelling Iphigenie to sacrifice her own brother to the gods. In all cases, natural emotion is set against the unnatural, corrupting and calculating demands of ruthless power-politics strengthened by religious conviction.

The Patriarch's dogmatic intolerance is in turn based on the illusion that one's own religious belief is the one true faith and that one is therefore entitled to criticize members of other faiths. As the Templar points out, this exclusivism originates from the Jews, who first called themselves the chosen people, but has been bequeathed both to Christians and to Muslims, and is at present showing its pernicious character in the Crusades:

---

18   See Hans Reiss, '"Theological" politics in Goethe's *Iphigenie auf Tauris*', in Dorothy James and Silvia Ranawake (eds), *Patterns of Change: German Drama and the European Tradition. Essays in Honour of Ronald Peacock* (New York, Berne and Frankfurt a.M.: Peter Lang, 1990), pp.59–71.

> You are surprised that I,
> A Christian and a Templar, speak like this?
> The pious frenzy whereby men believe
> They have the better God, and are entitled
> To force him on the whole world as the best,
> Has never shown itself in darker hue
> Than here, than now! (L ii. 253)

The representation of Christianity is hardly unbiased. With the few decent Christian characters – the Templar and the Lay-Brother – their decency is shown as conflicting with the obligations of their religion; Daja illustrates naive superstition, the Patriarch intolerant bigotry. Daja encourages Recha to suppose that the Templar who rescued her from the fire was an angel. Nathan not only dismisses this belief as showing too little trust in humanity but analyses its origins in medical terms: disappointed at finding her expressions of thanks rebuffed by the Templar, Recha defends herself against the feeling of rejection by resorting to 'Schwärmerei', superstitious emotionalism. By reminding her that the Templar, as a human being, may be ill and in need of help, Nathan provides a cure ('Arznei', L ii. 218) for her emotionalism. Thus religious behaviour of which Lessing disapproves is explained away in medical terms. No other outlook is allowed seriously to challenge the practical benevolence upheld by Nathan. Nathan's benevolence is in turn based on the cognitive theories of ethics, as based on rational knowledge of the good and the translation of knowledge into action, which were put forward in the early Enlightenment by Leibniz and Wolff; Lessing preferred these theories to the affective theory of morality proposed by Shaftesbury and developed in Francis Hutcheson's theory of moral sentiments.[19]

Neither Judaism nor Islam is represented in any detail. Nathan is never shown as engaging in any specifically Jewish religious practices. He stands for a universal, humane benevolence. As for Islam, Lessing brings in a dervish, or pious mendicant, who intends to join the Ghebers (members of a Zoroastrian sect in Persia) and do penance with them on the banks of the Ganges. It seems that, for Lessing, Islam was not distinct from Zoroastrianism or Hinduism. But then Judaism and Islam are present in the play only as sticks with which to beat Christianity.

It is doubtful whether Nathan is meant to typify the Jewish people.[20] The other characters remark more than once how different he is from most Jews. His friend the Dervish says of him:

---

19   See H.B. Nisbet, 'Lessing's ethics', *Lessing Yearbook*, 25 (1993), 1–40.

20   See Gunnar Och, *Imago judaica: Juden und Judentum im Spiegel der deutschen Literatur 1750–1812* (Würzburg: Königshausen & Neumann, 1995), pp.151, 157.

> He is,
> What's more, a Jew the like of whom there are
> Not many. He has sense; knows how to live;
> Is good at chess. (L ii. 245)

Besides having these civilized accomplishments, Nathan is also unusual in not lending money. He is a merchant, not a usurer. Nathan himself refuses to identify himself with his people. He tells the Templar, in a famous passage:

> Despise
> My nation as you please. We did not choose
> Our nations, either you or I. Are *we*
> Our nations? What does 'nation' mean? Are Jews
> And Christians first and foremost Jews and Christians,
> And human only second? Would that I
> Had found in you another person who
> Is happy to be human [*ein Mensch*]! (L ii. 253)

Nathan and the Templar have evidently transcended the restrictions of religion and nationality and joined a freemasonry of pure humanity. A 'Mensch' (a human being, independent of nationality, religion, or indeed gender) is presented as the ideal norm, just as it is in that other Enlightenment masterpiece, *The Magic Flute*.

There is another side to Nathan, though, which does not wholly harmonise with his morality of practical benevolence. Nathan's own goodness fully emerges when we learn that, long before, his wife and seven sons were burnt in a pogrom by Christians, and that he accepted this as God's will. One may feel that there is a gulf between Nathan's Enlightenment maxims of practical benevolence and the saintly submission to the divine will that he exhibits here. He lay in dust and ashes for three days and nights; he wept, protested against God, cursed the Christians; but gradually, he tells the Lay-Brother, he yielded to the voice of reason, which told him that the death of his wife and sons resulted from God's decree. This submission to the divine will recalls the Book of Job and Job's assertion, 'Though he slay me, yet will I trust in him' (Job 13:15). Such submission may seem almost superhuman. Certainly the power to accept grief and bereavement as part of the divine will comes from quite different sources than the rational benevolence exhibited by Nathan. There seems to be a discrepancy in Lessing's presentation of his character. Nathan's profound goodness presupposes a life devoted to God; yet such devotion is not expressed in the rational maxims he utters. But this discrepancy is hardly a fault: Lessing's imagination has enabled him to create a compelling portrait of a truly good person which far exceeds his rather meagre theory of rational benevolence.

The centre of the play is generally taken to be the parable of the three rings. Thanks to his reputation for wisdom, Nathan is summoned before the Sultan Saladin and asked which of the three religions is the true one. Nathan sidesteps this embarrassing conundrum by telling how a ring that made its possessor pleasing to God and man was handed down through the generations till it came to a father with three sons. He engaged an artist to make two externally similar rings, so that each son received one. Wondering which was the true ring, they took their problem to a judge, who told them that the authenticity of the ring could only be demonstrated by the upright conduct of its owner, and advised each to assist the ring's power by his benevolence, peacefulness and devotion. Thus moral action becomes the test of a religion's truth. This answer reflects Lessing's private scepticism about all religions: 'all positive and revealed religions are equally true and equally false'.[21]

It is important to note that the parable is not saying that the other two rings are as good as the true one. Rather, as the German–Jewish novelist Berthold Auerbach noted in 1879, all three rings must be false.[22] The beneficent power of the original ring lay in its iridescent opal, and since, as contemporary reference works affirmed, the opal is the only precious stone that cannot be imitated, all three rings must be forgeries.[23] Similarly, all three sons, we are told, behaved equally badly in their dispute (L ii. 277), though the owner of the true ring ought to have behaved more magnanimously than the other two. The inner truth of each religion is not its divine or magical origin, but its incitement to moral action. Indeed the judge speculates that the true ring may have got lost and that each facsimile will serve provided its possessor lives up to it. Tradition (the historical content of religion) cannot establish any absolute religious truth, because everyone believes the traditions in which he was brought up; rather, the historical element of religion is a fiction, and the only proof of any religious pudding is in the eating. Is this really toleration? The other religions are not accepted as being other, but as being secretly identical, as Nicholas Boyle has argued: 'The representatives of the three major religions, Judaism, Christianity, and Islam, are not here shown to tolerate one another's differences, for it is only temporary misunderstanding that prevents them from recognizing that they all think alike: they are shown rather to be agreed in a fourth, secret, religion of agnostic humanism.'[24] The bearers of this humanism are human beings independent of nationality or religion. Lessing has done little to represent his main characters as

---

21   'On the Origin of Revealed Religion', in *Lessing's Theological Writings*, ed. Henry Chadwick (London: A. & C. Black, 1956), p.105.

22   Berthold Auerbach, 'Gedanken über Lessing's "Nathan"', in *Lessing-Mendelssohn-Gedenkbuch. Zur hundertfünfzigjährige Geburtsfeier von Gotthold Ephraim Lessing und Moses Mendelsohn, sowie zur Säcularfeier von Lessing's 'Nathan'*, herausgegeben vom Deutsch-Israelitischen Gemeindebunde (Leipzig: Baumgartner, 1879), pp.321–8.

23   Rüdiger Zymner, '"Der Stein war ein Opal ...": Eine versteckte Kunst-Apotheose in Lessings morgenländischer "Ringparabel"?', *Lessing Yearbook*, 24 (1992), 77–96.

24   Nicholas Boyle, *Goethe: The Poet and the Age*, vol.1: *The Poetry of Desire* (Oxford: Clarendon Press, 1991), p.33; cf. p.273.

representatives of different cultures, different thought-worlds. As a commentator complained as long ago as 1909:

> Lessing was too remote from positive religion to be able to portray a particular faith sympathetically. His Nathan is no longer a Jew, nor his Saladin a Muslim, nor his Lay-Brother a Christian – if they ever were; for apart from their name and station, nothing about them recalls their confession. [...] Their tolerance cannot make a deep impression; what they have to tolerate in one another amounts to nothing at all.[25]

Without diminishing Lessing's achievement as a pioneer of toleration, one can still draw attention to the weaknesses within the type of toleration based on indifference that he espouses. By translating religious belief into moral action, he risks trivializing its specifically religious content as false consciousness and reducing the remainder to a set of ethical maxims on which all can agree. In so far as this type of toleration interprets other people's beliefs as being only superficially different but fundamentally the same as our own, it becomes a pseudo-tolerance which tolerates different beliefs only on the assumption that they are not really different. Masquerading as toleration of others, it actually makes the implicit claim that its own intellectual or ethical values are universal and unchallengeable. Its own values are taken to constitute an Archimedean point outside religious belief, from which religious disagreements can be dismissed as trivial. Hence such toleration excludes dialogue: for either the other people hold beliefs different from and incommensurable with our own, to which we can only listen uncomprehendingly, or else they really hold the same beliefs as we do, and there is nothing to hold a dialogue about.[26] One can tolerate opinions because one assumes that none of them is true anyway, as in Gibbon's well-known account of the religious toleration practised under the Roman Empire: 'The various modes of worship, which prevailed in the Roman world, were all considered by the people, as equally true; by the philosopher, as equally false; and by the magistrate, as equally useful.'[27]

A different approach to toleration can be found in the writings of Goethe, and has recently been the subject of an important book by Paul Kerry.[28] Goethe sums it up in his aphorism: 'Tolerance should really be only a transitory attitude; it should lead to recognition. Putting up with anything means insulting it.'[29] Taken

---

25   Christoph Schrempf, *Lessing als Philosoph* [1909] (Stuttgart: Frommann, 1921), p.165.

26   This argument is pursued by Ian C. Markham, *Plurality and Christian Belief* (Cambridge: Cambridge University Press, 1994).

27   Edward Gibbon, *The Decline and Fall of the Roman Empire*, 6 vols (London: Dent, 1910), i. 29.

28   Paul E. Kerry, *Enlightenment Thought in the Writings of Goethe: A Contribution to the History of Ideas* (Rochester, NY: Camden House, 2001).

29   'Toleranz sollte eigentlich nur eine vorübergehende Gesinnung seyn; sie muß zur Anerkennung führen. Dulden heißt beleidigen', in Johann Wolfgang Goethe,

out of context, this aphorism, especially its last few words, can easily be misunderstood. Ole Peter Grell and Roy Porter assimilate it to the view, gaining ground in the late Enlightenment, that freedom of conscience is not a privilege to be granted by a tolerant prince but a natural right which could neither be granted nor withheld. Thomas Paine said so trenchantly in *The Rights of Man*: 'Toleration is not the *opposite* of Intolerance, but is the *counterfeit* of it. Both are despotisms. The one assumes to itself the right of withholding Liberty of Conscience and the other of granting it.'[30] Kant wrote in his essay, 'An Answer to the Question: What is Enlightenment?' (1783), with which Goethe was familiar, that a truly enlightened prince would not even claim to be tolerant:

> A prince who does not regard it as beneath him to say that he considers
> it his duty, in religious matters, not to prescribe anything to his people,
> but to allow them complete freedom, a prince who even declines to
> accept the presumptuous title of *tolerant*, is himself enlightened.[31]

Goethe, however, is not making a political but rather a moral point. Tolerance should not be conceived as simply putting up with something that we dislike but cannot change, as in the Stoic conception of *tolerantia* or passive endurance. Merely to put up with something is to deny it any value and thus insult it. Instead Goethe recommends the active and positive recognition ('Anerkennung') of traditions different from our own. And this acknowledgment of different traditions means acknowledging also that I inhabit my own life-world of tradition. Far from being poised on an Archimedean point or floating free above the battle among beliefs, I am myself a participant. Goethe thus separates himself from the mainstream Enlightenment tradition of toleration. As Sylvana Tomaselli has pointed out, Enlightenment thinkers rarely presented toleration as a virtue, in the way that the concept is widely understood nowadays. They presented it rather as a pragmatic means to an end.[32] Goethe, however, treats toleration in individual rather than political terms, and regards it as a positive human quality associated with other virtues.

Goethe's understanding of toleration shows the lasting influence of the radical Pietist Gottfried Arnold (1666–1714). In his monumental work, *Unpartheyische Kirchen- und Ketzer-Historie* (1699–1700), Arnold interprets the history of the Church as a steady decline from the purity of early Christianity. He laments the

---

Sämtliche Werke. Briefe, Tagebücher und Gespräche, 40 vols (Frankfurt a.M.: Deutscher Klassiker Verlag, 1986–99), I, xiii, 249. Future references to this edition are given in the text by G with division, volume and page numbers.

30 Quoted in Ole Peter Grell and Roy Porter (eds), *Toleration in Enlightenment Europe* (Cambridge: Cambridge University Press, 2000), p.46, and associated with Goethe on p.16.

31 *Kant: Political Writings*, 2nd edn, ed. Hans Reiss, trans. H.B. Nisbet, (Cambridge: Cambridge University Press, 1991), p.58.

32 Sylvana Tomaselli, 'Intolerance, the virtue of princes and radicals', in Grell and Porter (eds), *Toleration in Enlightenment Europe*, pp.86–101.

disputes, conflicts and devastation caused by religious zeal. He thinks that true Christianity is to be found among those obscure people whom the Church of their day punished as heretics. Yet it was through such people, not through the official Church, that the Holy Spirit worked:

> And herein lies the reason why at all times and among all parties, nations and languages the true Church of Christ must be invisible, hidden, oppressed and in the wilderness. For the Kingdom of God has always been inward and thus imperceptible to bodily sight, and has consisted in a few despised outcasts who have recognized one another only by their inner connection and relationship in the Spirit, not by external forms, ceremonies, principles, kinds, times or other circumstances.[33]

For Arnold, the standard of true Christianity is not rational; but neither is it simply emotional. The true Christian is one who lives his faith with the aid of an inward illumination. Contemporaries accused Arnold of setting up inward illumination as more important than the Scriptures, but he replied that the inspired person would not negate or reject the Scriptures, but would enter into their life in a new and original way. Arnold did not think himself obliged to agree intellectually with all the heretics whose lives and ideas he recounted. Hence we find a sympathetic account of Muhammad, maintaining that he was justified in criticising Christianity since it had fallen away from its own teachings, and ascribing his popularity in part to his allowing freedom of conscience and prohibiting theological disputation. True religion is to be found wherever the Holy Spirit circulates.

Goethe read Arnold enthusiastically in his youth. He recounts in his autobiography, *Dichtung und Wahrheit* (Poetry and Truth, 1811–33), how pleased he was to find people whom he had heard of as heretics presented in a favourable light (G I xiv 382). It encouraged him to believe that one should work out religious views of one's own. One result was the curious cosmology drawn from Neoplatonic sources that Goethe sketches in the following paragraphs of *Dichtung und Wahrheit*, and that has often been adduced to elucidate *Faust*. Another was an attractive little text published in 1773, 'Brief des Pastors zu *** an den neuen Pastor zu ***' (Letter from the vicar at *** to the new vicar at ***), in which a French Protestant clergyman of very liberal views welcomes a new colleague, urges him to avoid both the dogmatism of the orthodox, with their warnings about damnation, and the intolerance of enlightened philosophers who constantly talk about tolerance without displaying it: 'They care about nothing so much as tolerance, and their mockery of all who do not share their opinion shows how little peace one can expect from them' (G I xviii 122). He thinks theological

---

33   *Gottfrid Arnolds Unparteyische Kirchen- und Ketzer-Historie / von Anfang des Neuen Testaments biß auff das Jahr Christi 1688*, 2 vols (Frankfurt: Thomas Fritsch, 1699 and 1700), ii. 846.

disputes are pointless, because we lack the knowledge to resolve them, and in any case, 'if you look at the matter by daylight, everyone has his own religion' (G I xviii 125). But he insists that his tolerance is very far from indifference. What counts is not intellectual belief, which easily degenerates into dogmatism, nor works, but faith, which the Vicar interprets as a warm assurance of God's love. As for non-Christians, the Vicar privately suspects that they may get a second chance through reincarnation (an answer often proposed in the Enlightenment to explain the elusiveness of Divine justice in this life),[34] and expects, even if they despise him as a Christian, to be eventually united with them: 'What joy it is to think that the Turk who considers me a dog, and the Jew who considers me a pig, will one day be glad to be my brothers' (G I xviii 123). Thus even the most obdurate will ultimately, in some future state, be brought into communion with God and the rest of humankind. The activity of the Holy Spirit, evoked by Arnold, is transmuted into a circulation of emotion which must eventually draw in all humanity.

Goethe's metaphor of light, implicitly opposed to the obscurantism of the ultra-orthodox, makes one ask how far he can justifiably be associated with the Enlightenment. Isaiah Berlin has drawn a famous distinction between the Enlightenment proper, which upheld a universal ideal of civilization based on natural law and reason, and the Counter-Enlightenment, represented centrally by Johann Gottfried Herder (1744–1803), which transfers the emphasis from the universal to the particular, from universal civilization to specific cultures, from rational contemplation to empathetic understanding, from materialism to vitalism, and from thought to feeling and action.[35] In his autobiography, Goethe is at pains to dissociate himself and his German contemporaries from the French Enlightenment, giving a distinctly cool appreciation of Voltaire, admitting that he found Rousseau congenial, and expressing admiration for Diderot. The *Encyclopédie* is compared to a great factory, and D'Holbach's *Système de la nature* is condemned for giving a dreary materialist analysis instead of a living portrayal of nature (G I xiv 530–36). Instead, Goethe tells how his acquaintance with Herder, though often tense and prickly, led him to understand poetry, including that of the Old Testament, as a product not of a cultivated elite but of the creativity of the people, and how Herder further directed him towards the writings of Justus Möser, whose essays on the town of Osnabrück recounted in vivid detail and with detached humour both its legal and commercial history and the changes in its citizens' domestic lives (G I xiv 699–700). Goethe's early poetry expresses vigorously the presence of the whole person, with feelings,

---

34   See Lieselotte E. Kurth-Voigt, *Continued Existence, Reincarnation, and the Power of Sympathy in Classical Weimar* (Rochester, NY: Camden House, 1999).

35   Isaiah Berlin, 'The Counter-Enlightenment', in his *Against the Current: Essays in the History of Ideas*, ed. Henry Hardy (Oxford: Clarendon Press, 1979), pp.1–24.

moods, physical movements; the early scenes in *Faust*, dating from the 1770s, famously evoke Nature as a force transcending the power of humankind to grasp it intellectually; and his historical drama *Götz von Berlichingen* (1773) celebrates locality and personality against the centralising forces of early modern Germany.

On the other hand, even the young Goethe cannot simply be set in opposition to the Enlightenment without caricaturing both, and the complexities of Goethe's position can be illustrated from a strongly worded letter he wrote to Herder in May 1775, thanking him for the gift of some writings on the New Testament in which Herder opposed the overintellectual, analytic approach of rationalist theologians.

> I got your books and enjoyed them. God knows, that's a deeply-felt
> world! A heap of rubbish brought to life! And so thank you! thank you!
> – I'd need to fill all the pages with markings to show the transition and
> yet – If only the whole doctrine of Christ were not such shit [*so ein
> Scheisding*], that infuriates me as a human being, as a limited needy
> thing, then I would like the object as well. Even if it's God or the Devil
> who is *treated* in that way, I like him, for he's my brother. – And so in
> your whole character I feel, not the shell and husk from which your
> Castors or harlequins emerge, but the brother who is always the same,
> man, God, worm and fool. – Your manner of sweeping things away –
> and not sieving gold from the rubbish, but turning the rubbish through
> palingenesis into a living plant, always puts me on the knees of my
> heart. (G II i 451)

Goethe's powerful feelings render his syntax incoherent (so that my translation can only be tentative). He seems to mean that, though the theologians Herder is attacking are a pile of rubbish, Herder has brought them to life through the vigour of his attack. But though Goethe likes the books, that does not make him like their subject-matter; on the contrary, he hates and despises the Christian doctrine that man is a limited being, in need of divine grace. Goethe, however, is prepared to feel brotherly affection towards anyone, whether God or the Devil, who is treated sympathetically (but the letter is particularly obscure here), and he senses such sympathy in Herder's writing. Superficially Herder mocks his antagonists, making them into harlequins. (The word 'Castors', recalling the mythical brothers Castor and Pollux, refers to the New Testament epistles by James and Jude, supposedly the brothers of Jesus, about which Herder had written.) But behind his mockery Goethe senses a warm brotherly feeling not only towards every fellow-human but towards every being, however high (God) or low (worm), and no matter how foolish. For this activity of Herder's Goethe borrows the concept of palingenesis or rebirth, implying a faint parallel between Herder's creative power and that of God in making the universe out of chaos.

In its headlong emotional style, its hostility to rationalist theology, and its warm appreciation for Herder's empathetic approach, this letter could be taken as a document of the Counter-Enlightenment. But, in rejecting the orthodox Christian view of man as dependent on divine grace, Goethe is affirming not only man's natural goodness, but also man's autonomy, and this stance aligns him rather with the Enlightenment.

Humankind's attainment of autonomy, our liberation from dependence on God or gods, is also the theme of Goethe's drama *Iphigenie auf Tauris* (1787), which of all his major literary works is closest to Enlightenment ideals of universal humanity. Here prejudice is represented initially by the barbarian king Thoas, civilized humanity by the Greek priestess Iphigenie who has found refuge in his kingdom. Learning that other Greeks have arrived to take her home, the jealous Thoas threatens to restore the human sacrifices which he abolished under her humane influence, and ignores his promise to let her leave for Greece as soon as an opportunity should arise. However the play soon transcends the opposition between civilised Greeks and barbarous Taurians. For when Iphigenie recounts her family history, it appears that the original impiety of her ancestor Tantalus has been punished by a curse which has led the family into repeated acts of gruesome murder; and when Iphigenie and her fellow-Greeks are planning their departure, Pylades' opportunistic readiness to deceive Thoas and transfer responsibility to the Fates illustrates a 'theological politics' as immoral as that of Thoas himself.

Refusing to deceive Thoas, Iphigenie has to confront him, and she wins him round by a number of strategies. One is her appeal to the universal claims of natural law: she obliges him to keep his earlier promise to let her go, and ends the play by arranging a treaty of friendship between Mycenae and Tauris.[36] Another, produced in response to Thoas' ethnocentric argument that barbarians can hardly be expected to behave better than Greeks, is the claim that humane values are not the possession of any one nation, but truly universal:

> THOAS   You think the rude
> And barbarous Scythian will hear the voice
> Of truth and of humanity, unheard
> By Atreus the Greek?
> IPHIGENIE   It's heard by all,
> Born under every sky, provided only
> The spring of life flows through the bosom, pure
> And unimpeded. (G I v 612)

Humane values are available to everyone, as salvation was in the opinion of Goethe's Vicar. But while the Vicar relied on God to draw obdurate Turks and Jews into the fold, the initiative in *Iphigenie* has passed from the gods to humanity. Much in the play suggests that, though the gods may have been effective in the semi-mythic past, they are now projections of human emotions. Thoas' claim that the gods require human sacrifices is countered by Iphigenie's argument that anyone who thinks the gods bloodthirsty is simply imputing to

---

36   See Alois Wierlacher, 'Ent-fremdete Fremde. Goethes *Iphigenie auf Tauris* als Drama des Völkerrechts', *Zeitschrift für deutsche Philologie*, 102 (1983), 161–80.

them his own unacknowledged cruelty (or, in Thoas' case, his anger at Iphigenie's refusal to marry him). As Wolfdietrich Rasch has shown, this argument reflects eighteenth-century controversies about whether cruel and immoral actions could be required by God.[37] Was it really possible to claim divine sanction for the countless cruelties perpetrated by the Christian Churches? Surely such actions could only be excused by the relative childishness of earlier humanity, a state too often exploited by power-hungry priests like the savage priests of 'Pluton' in Voltaire's tragedy *Les Guèbres, ou la Tolérance* (1769). The progress of humanity must lead to a more exalted morality, exemplified by Iphigenie, in the light of which diverse conceptions of the divine could be judged. Iphigenie, far from submitting to the gods' will, issues an almost Promethean challenge, demanding that they should live up to the sublime image of them she carries in her soul (G I v 605).[38] The aura of divinity seems to pass from the gods to the noblest representatives of humanity.

Orest, coming to Tauris to recover, as he supposed, the statue of Apollo's sister Diana, finds that the real object of his quest is the person of his own sister; and the magical power by which Diana, before the play began, transported Iphigenie to Tauris has now been transmuted into the overwhelming personal presence which enables Iphigenie to soften the harshness of Thoas, to assist in Orest's cure from the depression induced by guilt at his matricide, and finally to reconcile the conflicting parties without resorting to treachery or violence. Even more than in *Nathan der Weise*, it is personal presence, as well as argument, that defeats prejudice. Almost a century earlier, Christian Thomasius (1655–1728) argued that prejudices resulted partly from intellectual impatience, partly from misdirected love which caused people to imitate models before they were intellectually mature enough to choose models worthy of imitation.[39] Goethe's play, like Lessing's, shows how far enlightenment is brought about by individuals who inspire love.

In the crucial scene where Iphigenie confronts and convinces Thoas, she resorts, as Martin Swales has noted, to the imagery of 'free flow' which occurs at other key moments.[40] Like the activity of the Holy Spirit described by Gottfried Arnold, the circulation of emotion creates a secularized equivalent of

---

37 Wolfdietrich Rasch, *Goethes 'Iphigenie auf Tauris' als Drama der Autonomie* (Munich: Beck, 1979).

38 On the status of the gods here, see Wolfgang Wittkowski, '"Bei Ehren bleiben die Orakel und gerettet sind die Götter"? Goethes *Iphigenie* – autonome Humanität und Autorität der Religion im aufgeklärten Absolutismus', *Goethe-Jahrbuch*, 101 (1984), 250–68, esp. p.261: Iphigenie acts 'im prometheischen Widerspruch gegen die Götter'.

39 Christian Thomasius, '*De Praejudiciis* oder Von den Vorurteilen', in *Aus der Frühzeit der Aufklärung*, ed. F. Brüggemann (Leipzig: Reclam, 1928), pp.29–59.

40 Martin Swales, '"Die neue Sitte" and metaphors of secular existence: reflections on Goethe's *Iphigenie*', *Modern Language Review*, 89 (1994), 902–15.

the invisible church, consisting now of the enlightened and of those capable of enlightenment. Salvation into the international community of the enlightened is now to be brought about not by divine providence but by human agency. The resulting version of toleration is in some ways more confident and more generous than Lessing's. To Nathan, the servant's superstitious belief in miraculous rescue by an angel is fair game for mockery, and the Patriarch, with his mechanical repetition that the Jew must be burnt, is represented as so inflexibly dogmatic that there could be no point in appealing to him. In *Iphigenie*, however, the despot (admittedly a secular figure, not a priest) does soften in response to Iphigenie's appeal, though he is clearly an alarming character who is quite capable of forcing anyone to do his will.

Nevertheless, Goethe's toleration does have limits, both in principle and in practice. For recognition is a mutual process and, in Goethe's imagery, it depends on the circulation of emotion. Anyone through whose bosom the stream of life runs pure is able to hear the voice of reason and humanity. Toleration is thus a dialogical process. In appealing to Thoas, Iphigenie gives him recognition as a person capable of enlightenment, and he responds, not just with formal agreement, but with the warmth of feeling expressed in the handshake and the cordial farewell that end the play. But suppose there are people who are cut off from such feelings, who do not share in the circulation of emotion, and who will not engage in dialogue? If so, their claim to receive toleration must be limited by their inability to give toleration in return. And many representatives of the late Enlightenment were inclined to think the Jews were such people.

Modern Judaism, as opposed to that of Old Testament times, was widely seen by Enlighteners as a narrow, ungenerous religion, in which futile reasoning took the place of emotion. This picture derived, not from empirical information, but ironically in large part from the critical presentation of orthodox Jewry by its opponents Spinoza (in the *Tractatus theologico-politicus*) and Mendelssohn (in *Jerusalem*, 1783). The long-established Christian doctrine that the Jews, by their blind rejection of Christ, had confined themselves to a sterile religion of works without faith was transmuted into the claim that a religion based on external ritual had become fossilised by the tyrannical authority of rabbis and the practice of Talmud exegesis. Even in New Testament times, according to Lessing, rabbis had imparted 'a petty, crooked, hairsplitting understanding' by the overingenious allegorisation of their sacred texts (*Theological Writings*, p.91). Schiller maintained that Moses had imparted to the ancient Hebrews a sublime monotheism which they accepted blindly without being unable to understand it.[41] Kant argues that Judaism is merely external, a church without religion, and needs to pass through an at least partial acceptance of Christianity in order to die peacefully and be reborn as the religion of pure morality in which ultimately all

---

41 'Die Sendung Moses', in J.C.F. v. Schiller, *Sämtliche Werke*, ed. Gerhard Fricke and Herbert G. Göpfert, 5 vols (Munich: Hanser, 1958), iv. 783–804.

faiths will converge.[42] The young Hegel sharply contrasts Jesus' gospel of love with the legalism of Moses, which kept the Jews in loveless isolation from nature and the rest of humankind; their servile relation to God was enforced by the Law in which 'the holiest of things, namely the service of God and virtue, was ordered and compressed in dead formulas'.[43] Although some Jews, like the Essenes and John the Baptist, had loftier conceptions of virtue, the multitude were unable to recognise the divinity of Jesus: 'The lion has no room in a nutshell, the infinite spirit none in the prison of a Jewish soul, the whole of life none in a withering leaf.'[44] And the Romantic theologian Schleiermacher, for whom the essence of religion is the feeling of absolute dependence on God, disqualifies Judaism as a religion on the grounds that its original childlike core has long since been corrupted by its refusal to accept Jesus as the Messiah:

> It has long persevered, as a single fruit, after all the life force has vanished from the branch, often remains hanging until the bleakest season on a withered stem and dries up on it. Its limited vantage point afforded this religion, as religion, a short duration. It died when its holy books were closed; then the conversation of Jehovah with his people was viewed as ended; the political association that was linked to it dragged on in an ailing existence, and its external parts were preserved even longer still, the unpleasant appearance of a mechanical movement after the life and spirit had long since departed.[45]

Goethe's own attitude to Jews and Judaism is complex. He was friendly with many individual Jews, such as the salon hostess Rahel Levin and the composer Felix Mendelssohn-Bartholdy (both converts), the Kantian philosopher and physician Marcus Herz, the playwright Michael Beer (brother of the composer Meyerbeer), the composer Ferdinand Hiller and the painter Moritz Oppenheim, not to mention the cultivated Jewish ladies from Vienna whom he got to know on his holidays in Carlsbad and with whom he afterwards corresponded.[46] Yet though there are no grounds for calling him an antisemite, his writings do contain numerous casual and clichéd disparagements of Jews, which were gleefully quoted, often out of context, in the antisemitic compendia of the nineteenth and twentieth centuries.[47] He also

---

42   *Der Streit der Fakultäten*, in G. Kant, *Werke*, ed. Wilhelm Weischedel, 6 vols (Frankfurt a.M.: Insel, 1964), vi. 320–21.

43   G.W.F. Hegel, *Early Theological Writings*, trans. T.M. Knox and Richard Kroner (Chicago: University of Chicago Press, 1948), p.68.

44   Ibid., p.265. Translation amended: Hegel wrote 'in einer Nuß', which Knox mistranslates as 'in a nest'.

45   Friedrich Schleiermacher, *On Religion: Speeches to its Cultured Despisers*, trans. Richard Crouter (Cambridge: Cambridge University Press, 1988), p.213.

46   See Florian Krobb, '"Überdies waren die Mädchen hübsch …": Goethes Jüdinnen', *Oxford German Studies*, 20–21 (1991–2), 33–45.

47   See, for example, Theodor Fritsch, *Handbuch der Judenfrage* (Leipzig: Hammer-Verlag, 1942; first published in 1887 as *Antisemiten-Catechismus*), pp.446–9; Adolf Hitler, *Mein Kampf* (Munich: Eher, 1943), p.341.

upheld conventional prejudices against the admission of Jews to civil life. He thought that proposals for their emancipation would endanger social order (G I xv 615). When Duke Carl August of Weimar in 1823 granted Jews freedom to practise their religion, marry non-Jews, attend grammar schools and universities, and practise trades, Goethe deplored this ordinance as a 'scandalous law' which would 'undermine all moral feelings in families, which rested entirely on religious feelings', and even wondered if it had been engineered by bribes from 'the almighty Rothschild' (G II x 112). One commentator concludes that, in some ways, 'he failed to soar beyond the prejudices of a courtier in a small eighteenth-century German princedom'.[48]

To see how Goethe shares in the philosophical critique of Judaism as a religion without feeling, we need to look at a notorious passage from Goethe's late novel *Wilhelm Meisters Wanderjahre* (Wilhelm Meister's Journeyman Years, 1821 and 1829). The passage occurs only in the second and longer version of the novel (1829). Its context is the recurrent theme of founding a new community in order to promote enlightenment and the brotherhood of man, inspired especially by the Quaker settlement in Pennyslvania; William Penn is mentioned admiringly (G I x 342). A body called the 'Weltbund' (World League), including the protagonist Wilhelm Meister, intends to found such a community in America. Its principles include freedom of religion, explained as follows:

> All religions insist that man must accept the inevitable; each tries to cope with this task in its own way.
> The Christian religion helps delightfully through faith, love, hope; thence arises patience, a sweet feeling that existence remains a valuable gift even if, instead of the desired enjoyment, it burdens one with hideous suffering. We adhere to this religion, but in a particular way; we teach our children from their infancy onwards about the great benefits it has brought us; but the last thing we tell them about is its origin and development. That makes its founder truly dear and precious to us, and all the information relating to him becomes sacred. In this sense, which may be called pedantic, we do not tolerate any Jew among us; for how should we grant him a share in the highest civilization, when he denies its origin and history? (G I x 686-7)

Their teaching begins by inculcating an emotional outlook on the world, a positive appreciation of life and a willingness to endure adversity through the Christian cardinal virtues. Only when these virtues have been established, however, are people told about the person of Christ and the Bible. Instead of religious knowledge being used to excite religious feeling, religious feeling is

---

48   William Rose, 'Goethe and the Jews', in his *Men, Myths and Movements in German Literature* (London: Allen & Unwin, 1931), pp.157–80. Of many studies on this topic, the most recent, with a review of earlier ones, is Klaus L. Berghahn, 'Ein klassischer Chiasmus: Goethe und die Juden, die Juden und Goethe', *Goethe Yearbook*, 10 (2001), 203–21.

implanted first and generates a desire for religious knowledge. Such knowledge is wasted on Jews, because they disbelieve in the religious authority of Jesus and the New Testament. But why should the same educational process not bring Jews to respect, even revere, the person of Jesus? After all, one could consider him 'heilig' without actually accepting the doctrine of the Incarnation. The passage implies that this educational method cannot be tried on Jews, because they are not susceptible to the Christian virtues of hope, faith and charity.

Many attempts have been made to explain away this passage as harmless or even ironic (reviewed in Kerry, 2001, pp.181–8). However there seems no reason to doubt the obvious interpretation: Goethe, in putting forward a post-Christian type of religiosity, assumes that to attain it you have to pass through Christianity; and Jews, who have not made this passage but are stuck at an earlier stage in religious history, are thereby excluded from it. We can recognize here another, secularized version of the thesis that their failure to recognize Christ has paralysed the development of Judaism and stunted their capacity for religious feeling. Even in the religious freedom envisaged by Goethe's post-Christian utopia, therefore, the Jews continue to mark the outer limit of toleration.

Chapter 12

The Slave, the Noble and the Jews: Reflections on Section 7 of Nietzsche's *On the Genealogy of Morals*

David M. Seymour

Introduction

The ambit of this chapter is clearly circumscribed; it is a reappraisal and re-evaluation of the allegations of anti-Judaism or antisemitism in section 7 of the first essay of *On the Genealogy of Morals*,[1] 'Good and Bad', 'Good and Evil'. It is in this section that the Jews, there characterised as 'that priestly people', are given the role of overcoming the noble in the name of the slave and replacing the former's mode of evaluation of 'good and bad' with that of 'good and evil'.

The reasons for this seemingly narrow focus are twofold. First, as have many others, I have always been puzzled not just by the anti-Judaic and antisemitic sentiments Nietzsche expresses in that section, but also by the venom with which they are expressed. My sense of puzzlement only increases when section 7 is set beside Nietzsche's oft-expressed and evidently sincere opposition to contemporaneous antisemitism.[2] The enigmatic nature of this seeming contradiction is brought into even greater relief when set against the fact that Nietzsche was amongst the first commentators to identify, chronicle and offer a diagnosis of this phenomenon.

The second reason for my choice of focus stems from my dissatisfaction with the manner in which the proliferating commentaries on Nietzsche's work treat this issue. On the one hand, many of them simply choose to bypass the very real problems that section 7 raises.[3] More often than not, they are dealt with

---

1   Ed. Keith Ansell-Pearson (Cambridge: Cambridge University Press, 1994).
2   For examples and illustrations see Yirmiyahu Yovel, *Dark Riddle: Hegel, Nietzsche, and the Jews* (University Park, PA, Pennsylvania State University Press, 1998); 'Nietzsche, the Jews, and *Ressentiment*', in R. Schat (ed.), *Nietzsche, Genealogy, Morality: Essays on Nietzsche's On the Genealogy of Morals* (London: University of California Press, 1994). For an extended debate on this question and related issues, see also J. Golomb (ed.), *Nietzsche and Jewish Culture* (London: Routledge, 1997) and Jacob Golomb and Robert Wistrich (eds), *Nietzsche: Godfather of Fascism: On the Uses and Abuses of a Philosophy* (Princeton, NJ: Princeton University Press, 2000).
3   See Daniel W. Conway, *Nietzsche and the Political* (Oxford: Routledge,

perfunctorily though noting Nietzsche's philosemitic or anti-antisemitic credentials.[4] On the other hand, there are those accounts that address the issue directly but in isolation from other aspects of his thought. The general consensus of this strand of thinking is to emphasise Nietzsche's 'ambivalent' attitude toward the Jews.[5] This conclusion is premised upon the idea that Nietzsche distinguishes and evaluates three different periods within the internal history of 'the Jews': the biblical, the priestly and the modern. Sympathetic and complimentary to the first and last, section 7 represents his distaste of the middle period. Even if this were the case, and one of the aims of this chapter is to open this account to question, it still does not fully account for the hostility manifested by Nietzsche.

In contradistinction to both these approaches, this chapter argues that section 7 has *nothing whatsoever to say about the Jews*. However it does contain a great deal of insight about the antisemite. This argument is premised upon reading this work in the spirit in which it was written, that is, *genealogically* and *polemically*. Treating genealogy[6] as the ability to umask[7] the diverse types whose will to power constitutes the meaning of words, concepts and ideas, a link is established between the fate of the concept 'good' and the fate of the figure of the 'noble'. In both instances, Nietzsche's genealogy illustrates that these concepts are expressions of the same type, the slave or man of *ressentiment*.

Nietzsche's self-styled description of the *Genealogy* as a polemic draws on two of the word's common meanings. The first, a controversial and disputatious contribution to a current theological debate is evidenced by his insistence on the

---

1997); Brian Leiter, *Nietzsche on Morality* (London: Routledge, 2002).

4   See, inter alia, R. Safranski, *Nietzsche: A Philosophical Biography* (London: Granta Books, 2002); Robert Wicks, *Nietzsche* (Oxford: One World, 2002); Keith Ansell-Pearson, *An Introduction to Nietzsche as Political Thinker* (Cambridge: Cambridge University Press, 1994).

5   Yirmiyahu Yovel, *Dark Riddle*; M.F. Duffy and W. Mittleman, 'Nietzsche's Attitude Toward the Jews', *Journal of the History of Ideas*, 49(2) (1988), 301–17. It is interesting to note that this evaluative typology is also found in Gilles Deleuze's *Nietzsche and Philosophy*, trans. Hugh Tomlinson (London: Athlone Press, 1983) which, in almost all other ways, offers an iconoclastic view of such historical accounts. For criticisms of this tripartite approach, see Menahem Brinker, 'Nietzsche and the Jews', in Golomb and Wistrich, *Nietzche: Godfather*; Gillian Rose, 'Nietzsche's *Judaica*', in *Judaism and Modernity: Philosphical Essays* (Oxford: Blackwell, 1993).

6   Whilst discussions and interpretations of the meaning of Nietzsche's genealogy appear in almost all commentaries of his work, useful collections of essays include Richard Schact, *Nietzsche, Genealogy, Morality* and John Richardon (ed.), *Nietzsche* (Oxford: Oxford University Press 2001) (a collection that includes Michel Foucault's 'Nietzsche, Genealogy, History').

7   For a discussion of the importance of masks to understanding Nietzsche, see W.D. Williams, 'Nietzsche's Masks', in Malcolm Pasley (ed.), *Nietzsche* (London: Methuen, 1978). See also Alisdair MacIntyre, 'Genealogies and Subversion', in Richard Schact, *Nietzsche, Genealogy, Morality*.

non-divine origins of morality. The second meaning of 'polemic' which applies to the *Genealogy* (and to Nietzsche's writings as a whole) is its style of almost warlike confrontation with the objects of critique: the Church, Richard Wagner, Ernst Duhring, moralists, cultural philistines and so on. One of the weapons utilised to great effect by Nietzsche in these wars was that of irony,[8] as the case of the noble indicates. Gillian Rose's description of Adorno's *Minima Moralia* is an example of how irony is useful as polemic,

> [it] is ironic in the two standard senses of the word: 'expression of
> meaning by use of words normally conveying the opposite meaning',
> and 'apparent perversity of fate or circumstance' … Sometimes he uses
> the original phrase and conveys the ironic inversion in the discussion.
> Sometimes he just states the inversion and does not discuss it.[9]

Reading section 7 ironically, the tactic of ironic inversion becomes increasingly visible: what appears as the voice of the noble is unmasked as that of the slave, as the man of *ressentiment*. This irony of misrecognition is doubled when the reader realises that, as a man of *ressentiment*, the noble is unable to see himself as such. On this realisation, a further irony presents itself. Far from the noble's self-representation offering a challenge to the decadence of contemporary culture, Nietzsche shows how this noble is, rather, an expression of its exhaustion.

This genealogy of the noble is constituted through a comparison of two of Nietzsche's most sustained commentaries on this figure, both of which are centred around the person and persona of Richard Wagner, *The Birth of Tragedy Out of the Spirit of Music* and the first essay of *On the Genealogy of Morals*. The next section of the present chapter offers a depiction of the noble in the earlier study. The third section compares and contrasts this descriptive and normative account with that provided in the *Genealogy*. The chapter concludes with a discussion of the impact this genealogy has for recognising Nietzsche as one of the earliest analysts and critics of the modern phenomenon of antisemitism.

The Genealogy of the Noble: *The Birth of Tragedy Out of the Spirit of Music*

Nietzsche's earliest sustained treatment of the noble is found in his study *The Birth of Tragedy Out of the Spirit of Music*. It may be noted, however, that it could be better titled 'the *Re*-birth of Tragedy'. Having traced its birth and demise in the context of ancient Greece, Nietzsche sees the possibility of the

---

8   For a fuller discussion of Nietzsche's use of irony, see Gillian Rose, *The Melancholy Science: An Introduction to the Thought of Theodore W. Adorno* (London: Macmillan Press, 1978).

9   Ibid, p.26.

potential revival of tragedy in the Germany of the time under the auspices of whom he believed to be the new tragic noble, Richard Wagner.

Nietzsche located the expression of the glories of pre-Socratic Greece in the mythologies articulated through the art of its great tragedies. These mythologies reflected the strength of the Ancient Greeks and their culture built upon the edifice of a terrible and potentially overawing power of a raw and directionless nature. The greatness of the tragedies lay in drawing all involved, actors and spectators, into the immediacy of these creative–destructive forces. Expressing this phenomenon through the gods Dionysus and Apollo, Nietzsche argued,

> The Dionysiac is the basic ground of the world and the foundation of all existence. In the final analysis, it must be thought of as the eternal and original artistic power that calls into being the entire world of phenomena. The Apolline is secondary, the source of those illusions with which the Dionysiac world must, for our own sakes, be transfigured. As far as human awareness is concerned, the two impulses manifest themselves in a strict relation: only so much Dionysiac experience is permitted to the individual consciousness as can be controlled by the Apolline and translated into self-sustaining terms. The present emergence of the Dionysiac thus implies the co-presence of the Apolline and, in turn, an efflorescence of Apolline art in the years ahead. The scale and perfection of the Apolline manifestations among the Greeks, conversely, attests the powerful hold that the Dionysiac must have among them. Let us bear in mind how much they must have suffered to achieve such beauty. Above all, let us acknowledge the two principles, Dionysiac and Apolline, as the basis of tragedy, their highest achievement.[10]

This 'golden age' was brought low through the historical intervention of the figure of Socrates. The effect of Socratic reason and rationality was to block life from the danger and spontaneity of Dionysian nature. Nature, human and otherwise, now became an object of enquiry through which its apparent purpose could be divined and chance substituted by order. The death of the old tragedy of pathos was replaced by the new tragedy of logos,[11] the Dionysian laid low by the Apolline, and myth replaced by history (section 23).

The world-historical significance of this defeat of spontaneity was the almost uninterrupted victory of a life divorced from its creative spark. In place of the life-affirming noble, this shift brought with it a humanity characterised by 'abstract man ... abstract education, abstract morality; abstract law; the abstract state'. The ripples of this epochal transformation continue to be felt centuries later; 'the present age', is, for Nietzsche, 'the result of that Socratism which is bent on the destruction of myth' (section 23).

---

10   M.S. Silk and J.P. Stern, *Nietzsche on Tragedy* (Cambridge: Cambridge University Press, 1981), p.88.

11   Safranski, *Nietzsche: Biography*, p.63.

Central to Nietzsche's thesis is that the demise of myth and of its expression in tragedy go far beyond the confines of purely 'aesthetic' interest. It reaches into the very essence, heart and nature of 'national life' and 'national character':

> It had to appear to us that the demise of Greek tragedy was brought
> about through a remarkable and forcible dissociation of these two
> primordial artistic drives [Dionysus and Apollo]. To this process there
> corresponded a degeneration and transformation of the character of the
> Greek people, which calls for serious reflection on how necessary and
> close the fundamental connections are between art and the people, myth
> and custom, tragedy and the state. (Ibid.)

From this perspective, the death of the old tragedy brought about the death of the Greek national character: nobility. Its defeat by Socrates, although himself a member of the noble caste, was symptomatic of the victory of its nemesis, the slave caste. In recognisable terms, Nietzsche has this to say about their intervention onto the world stage: 'There is nothing more terrible than a class of barbaric slaves who have learned to regard their existence as an injustice, and now prepare to avenge, not only themselves, but all generations.'[12]

One avenue, or, rather, one person, pointed the way to a potential overcoming of this lifeless existence: Richard Wagner. Wagner's tragedies, Nietzsche predicted, would rip asunder the art and opera that had developed under Socratic influence – abstract, soulless, flippant entertainment – through the unbinding of life from nature, and the renewal of the Dionysian and the Apolline. In what reads as a plot from one of Wagner's own music-dramas, Nietzsche presents the figure of Wagner as the Redeemer of the German spirit:

> nevertheless in some inaccessible abyss the German spirit still rests and
> remains undestroyed, in glorious health and profundity, and Dionysian
> strength, like a knight sunk in slumber; and from this abyss the
> Dionysian song rises to our ears to let us know that this German knight
> is still dreaming his primordial Dionysian myth in blissfully serious
> visions. Let no one believe that the German spirit has forever lost its
> mythical home where it can still understand so plainly the voices of the
> birds that tell of that home. Someday it will find itself awake in all the
> morning freshness following a tremendous sleep: then it will slay
> dragons, destroy vicious dwarfs, wake Brunnhilde – and even Wotan's
> spear will not be able to stop its course. (Section 24)

Subsumed within this belief in the potential of the rebirth of tragedy is, of course, the rebirth of the noble. The myths and their manner of articulation that defined Wagner's work were intended as an expression of the reincarnation of the pre-Socratic Greek noble. It was only this noble who had the strength and power to stare into the abyss of the terror of human existence, to confront and subsume

---

12   Section 18, *Birth of Tragedy Out of the Spirit of Music*, trans. Walter Kaufman, (London: Random House, 1967).

within himself the god, Dionysus, and not only survive in the face of that knowledge, but render it visible to others through his own Apolline structures.

The Genealogy of the Noble: *On the Genealogy of Morals*

In certain important respects, many of the themes present in *The Birth of Tragedy Out of the Spirit of Music* remain in *On the Genealogy of Morals*. These include, inter alia, the cultural decadence of contemporary Germany, the absence of life-affirming creativity and the coldness of triumph of reason and rationality. Yet it is also the case that these matters are approached from different perspectives. In the present context, however, it is the comparison between the two works and their discussion and evaluation of the noble that is of importance.

In the preface to *On the Genealogy of Morals*, Nietzsche announces the object of his enquiry: the origins and roots of the moral evaluation inherent within the concept 'good'. Approaching this subject-matter genealogically, Nietzsche immediately identifies it as the expression of a given type's will to power:

> It is of no little interest to discover that, in these words and roots which
> denote 'good', we can often detect the main nuance which made the
> nobles feel they were men of higher rank … But the names [they adopt
> for themselves] also show a *typical character trait*: and this is what
> concerns us here. (Section 5)

It is this connection between 'noble' and 'good' that is relevant within the context of Nietzsche's overarching thesis. The two modes of moral evaluation that contain the concept 'good' – good and bad and good and evil – are the products of two distinct character traits or types, the noble and the slave, respectively. As Nietzsche develops his ideas it becomes clear that the concept of the noble is intimately tied to the fate of the concept 'good'; that, just as 'good' becomes the product of slave morality, so too the slave becomes the content of the concept 'noble'. Implicit within Nietzsche's argument is the recognition that, just as the slave wilfully inverts his own moral evaluation from evil to good, so the concept of the noble masks its shift of content to the slave.

In the earlier *Birth of Tragedy Out of the Spirit of Music* it is more the 'objective' product of the noble that is discussed, that is the nature of myth and tragedy. In the later work, it is the subjective element that Nietzsche depicts. For example, the idea of the cruel beauty and suffering that had infused Nietzsche's earlier account of pre-Socratic Greek culture appears now from the point of view of the noble's subjectivity:

> It was the noble races which left the concept of 'barbarian' in their
> traces wherever they went; even their highest culture betrays the fact
> that they were conscious of this and indeed proud of it (for example,
> when Pericles, in that famous funeral oration, tells his Athenians, 'Our
> daring has forced a path to every land and sea, erecting timeless

memorials to itself everywhere for good *and ill*). This 'daring' of the
noble races, mad, absurd and sudden in a way it manifests itself, the
unpredictability of their undertakings – Pericles singles out the
rhyathymia of the Athenians for praise – their unconcern and scorn for
safety, body, life, comfort, their shocking cheerfulness, and delight in
all destruction, in the debauches of victory and cruelty – all this, for
those who suffered under it, was summed up in the image of the
'barbarian', the 'evil individual', perhaps the 'Goth' or 'Vandal'.
(L. 245, section 11)

A similar pattern emerges when Nietzsche discusses the causes of the noble's
demise. In both books its demise is brought about by figures who emerge from
the noble caste itself. In each instance, the figures are presented as the expression
of the slave caste and the mode of their evaluation. Yet it is in the discussion of
this overcoming of the noble by the slave that the two studies diverge. In the
earlier work, it is the figure of Socrates that is central, whilst in the *Genealogy* it
is, at least in the majority of the work, the figure of the Priests that predominates.
It is only in section 7 that it is the Jews who are attributed this role.

Whilst commentators have reflected on the move from Socrates to Priests,
little comment has been made concerning the shift from Priests to the Jews. More
often than not, the reduction of the Priests to 'the Jews' tends to be assumed
without further comment. To appreciate more fully this latter transition, it is
necessary first to return to Nietzsche's relationship with and changing evaluation
of Wagner and his works; that is, to present this relationship genealogically,
noting the changes and transformations that occur within the name 'Wagner';[13] a
genealogy that is matched by Nietzsche's own attitude toward antisemitism.

From their first meeting, Nietzsche's notebooks and writings contain frequent
and increasingly hostile references to Richard Wagner.[14] Prominent amongst
these sketches are *Wagner at Bayreuth*, *The Case Against Wagner*, the collection
of notes published under the title, *Nietzsche contra Wagner*, as well as sections 2
to 5 of the third essay of the *Genealogy*, 'what do ascetic ideals mean.' Yet
perhaps the most seething commentary on Wagner that Nietzsche offered is

---

13   It must be noted in passing, of course, that the venom of Nietzsche's pen is
directed not only at Wagner himself, but also the acolytes of the 'Bayreuth idealism' who
centred around the *Bayreuth Blatter*. A further target of Nietzsche's polemic were also
those 'nobles' of an Aryan 'new world' associated with his sister Elisabeth and his brother
in law, Berhard Foster. As is well documented, Nietzsche's attitudes to this latter group is
one of exasperated irritation and annoyance at the attempts to seek his stamp of approval
for their madcap schemes and for their wilful misquotations of his works. See also
Yirmiyahu Yovel, 'Nietzsche *Contra* Wagner on the Jews', in Golomb and Wistrich,
Nietzsche: Godfather.

14   See Joachim Koehler, *Nietzsche and Wagner: A Lesson in Subjugation*,
trans. Ronald Taylor (New Haven: Yale University Press, 1998); M.S. Silk and J.P. Stern,
Nietzsche on Tragedy (Cambridge: Cambridge University Press, 1981); Barry Millington,
Wagner (Oxford: Oxford University Press, 2000).

contained in the first essay of the *Genealogy*, 'Good and Bad', 'Good and Evil'. Although no mention is made of Wagner by name, close parallels exist,[15] between the genealogy of his type, and Nietzsche's depiction of the slave, the man of *ressentiment*.

Despite reservations that remained secreted in Nietzsche's notebooks, *The Birth of Tragedy Out of the Spirit of Music* looked to Wagner's work as inaugurating a new epoch in which German culture would be reawakened and revitalised, a view that Nietzsche later retracted. As is well documented, Nietzsche broke with 'the Master' shortly after the publication of this first book. Accounts of this split have varied over the years, but there is now general consensus that the parting was hastened by the spectacle of the first Bayreuth festival. Far from reviving the *praxis* of ancient tragedy that Nietzsche had hoped, and Wagner had professed, the nature of that event confirmed the troubling thoughts he had been nursing for some time. In both his personality and his creative works, Nietzsche recognised that Wagner had become 'a representative of the bourgeois culture [Nietzsche] so loathed'.[16] Safranski describes the scene that greeted Nietzsche confirming his suspicions:

> [Nietzsche] was horrified, and even nauseated to witness the
> ostentatious arrival of Kaiser Wilhelm I, [Wagner's] fawning
> demeanour on the festival hill at Wahnfried, the Wagners' villa in
> Bayreuth), the unintended comicality of the staging, the racket about
> the mythical enterprise, and the high-spirited, prosperous spectators to
> this artistic event who were in search not of redemption,[17] but of a good
> meal.[18]

Over the ensuing years and culminating in his critique of *Parsifal*,[19] Nietzsche came to realise that the Wagnerian myths (in which he included Wagner's meticulous cultivation of his self-image) were far from representing the potential for an overcoming of what he saw as the decadence of Bismarckian culture. Rather, Nietzsche viewed them as an expression of that culture; a culture Nietzsche defined precisely as one that lacked the noble spirit of its pre-Socratic antecedent. In this process, Nietzsche unmasks Wagner the noble to reveal Wagner the slave, his masquerade a mere, but nonetheless dangerous, pose. This

---

15   The views expressed by the slave in this essay mirror many of Wagner's writings, old and new, especially those since labelled 'regeneration', as well as those of his circle; see Millington, *Wagner*.

16   Millington, *Wagner*; Koehler, *Nietzsche and Wagner*. See also the introductory essay by Siegried Mandle in Lou Salome, *Nietzsche* (Chicago: University of Illinois Press, 2001), for a discussion of Nietzsche's attendance at Bayreuth.

17   Safranski also makes the interesting point that, where Wagner believed in *redemption* through art, Nietzsche believed in art's power of *transcendence*.

18   Safranski, *Nietzsche: Biography*, pp.106–7.

19   Although the centrality of Nietzsche's critique of *Parsifal* has been overstated in recent years. See Millington, *Wagner*.

point emerges clearly when section 7 is read through the prism of section 10, Nietzsche's discussion of the nature of *ressentiment*. Before so doing, it is necessary first to place section 7 into the context of the preceding discussion, notably sections 5 and 6.

It is in sections 5 and 6 that Nietzsche develops his genealogical thesis concerning the concept 'good'. He argues that the conflict between the moral evaluations of 'good and bad' and 'good and evil' arose originally as the expression of a conflict within the noble caste itself: that between warrior and priest. As in the *Birth of Tragedy Out of the Spirit of Music*, Nietzsche is at pains to stress that the outcome of the conflict was the slave's overcoming of the noble. So complete was this victory that the noble, once so powerful, was brought down to the level of the slave.

It is this thesis that in section 7 becomes subject to Nietzsche's striking irony. The tone and content of section 7, both within itself and in relation to the previous sections, imply that the history of the ignoble and irretrievable defeat of the noble has been written by the noble himself. The irony here is that the voice of the ancient noble, defeated centuries earlier, can no longer be heard, at least in the first person. Instead it can only be the voice of the man of *ressentiment*, the slave, the one who masquerades as the noble. In other words, section 7 offers an account of the practical outcomes of the developments of sections 5 and 6, the way in which the concepts of 'good' and 'noble' have suffered a shared fate of inverted meaning.

The rather academic explanatory style of sections 5 and 6 is replaced by the boorishness of section 7 through which a bowdlerised and vulgarised version of the same events is repeated. In place of reflection and a certain open-endedness, the reader is suddenly confronted with the crudity and siren of simple assertion. This transition is evidenced by reference to the following two quotations. Despite Nietzsche's aversion to the priestly intervention in history, the section concludes with a sensitive and ambivalent reflection on the place and role of the priest in the trajectory of moral and cultural development:

> Priests make *everything* more dangerous, not just medicaments and healing arts but pride, revenge, acumen, debauchery, love, lust for power, virtue, sickness; – in any case, with some justification one could add that man first became an *interesting animal* on the foundation of this *essentially dangerous* form of human existence, the priest and the human soul became *deep* in the higher sense and turned *evil* for the first time – and of course, these are the two basic forms of man's superiority, hitherto, over other animals!

This nuanced and 'objective' account can be compared to the expression of the same point in section 7:

> The history of mankind would be far too stupid a thing if it has not the intellect [*Geist*] of the powerless injected into it: – let us take the best example straight away. Nothing which has been done on earth against

'the noble', 'the mighty', 'the masters' and 'the rulers', is worth
mentioning compared with what *the Jews* have done against them.

In the transition from section 6 to section 7, Nietzsche's undoubtedly severe
anticlericalism and anti-asceticism,[20] which includes a vast span of historical
references including that of Brahminism and Buddhism, and *not*, it is to be noted,
Brahmins and Buddhists, is now reduced to one single group, 'the Jews'. In place
of evidence of depth and breadth of learning along with nuance of argument and
presentation, section 7 speaks of 'the Jews' as if they are the personification of
the unrelenting and unending misfortune that has befallen the noble from time
immemorial to the present.

This vulgar conception of 'the Jews' can be compared with that of Nietzsche's
comments elsewhere in the *Genealogy* as well as his other published works.
These other discussions of the Jews either emphasise their 'positive' intercession
in world history or, in more measured and less effusive terms, present the role of
such intervention more in keeping with the tone and content of sections 5 and 6.
Again, therefore, the subtlety of thought associated with Nietzsche is replaced by
the thuggery of thought identified with the man of *ressentiment*.

Perhaps the most significant clue to the identity of the narrator of section 7
surfaces in the characterisation of the priests, now reduced to that of 'the Jews,
that priestly people', as 'the most *evil* enemies'. This 'slip of the tongue'
prefigures the concluding comments of Nietzsche's portrait of the man of
ressentiment in section 10:

> How much respect a noble man has for his enemies! – and a respect of
> that sort is a bridge to love … For he insists on having his enemy to
> himself, as a mark of distinction, indeed, he will tolerate as enemies
> none other than such as have nothing to be despised and a *great deal* to
> be honoured! Against this, imagine 'the enemy' as conceived by the
> man of *ressentiment* – and here we have his deed, his creation: he has
> conceived of this 'evil enemy', '*the evil one*' as a basic idea to which
> he now thinks up a copy and counterpart, the 'good one' – himself.

As the quotation makes clear, this perception of the Jews as 'the most *evil
enemies*' – and the emphasis is Nietzsche's – unequivocally points to its origins
within the mind of the slave and not that of the noble. This interpretation is in
keeping with the force of Nietzsche's essay: to trace the trajectory of the
overcoming of the noble's moral evaluation of 'good and bad' by that of the
slave's 'good and evil'.

This *trompe l'oeil* continues when the narrator offers an answer to his own
rhetorical question as to why these enemies, their enemies, are evil. The reason
proffered is 'because they are the most powerless'. Unable to fight physically,
that is, in a noble manner, the Jews are said to undermine their counter-caste

---

20   Whilst this point should not be overstated, Wagner's proclaimed respect for
Schopenhauer should not be forgotten.

through subtle subterfuge. Their very passivity becomes the measure of their strength. Yet, in this outpouring of righteous indignation, the modern noble overlooks his own impotence, his own unwillingness to confront his enemy in a noble way that is open and honourable. Not only does this point illustrate the passivity of this modern noble, but it is projected onto their enemies through the prism of moral inversion, in which 'lies are turning weakness into an *accomplishment* … and impotence which doesn't retaliate is being turned into goodness' (section 13).

Echoing a point made by the 'noble' himself, that, 'out of this powerlessness, their hate swells into something huge and uncanny to a most intellectual and poisonous level' Nietzsche notes, in section 10,

> When *ressentiment* does occur in the noble man himself, it is consumed
> and exhausted in an immediate reaction, and therefore it does not
> *poison*; on the other hand, it does not occur at all in countless cases
> where it is unavoidable for all who are weak and powerless.

The effects of this poison are clearly evidenced in the venomous tone of section 7 and the almost absurd claims made by the narrator. These include the figure of the Jew as evil, their bringing down all nobility, their destruction of culture for millennia. This image of 'the Jews' as the destroyer of all noble things, especially its expression in culture,[21] is a prevalent theme in the antisemitic canon and is on all fours with the description of the man of *ressentiment*'s art of portraiture. It is this crude representation that replaces the nuanced role of the diverse instances of Priestly castes that have existed from Ancient Greece to the present day and which Nietzsche discusses in the previous sections.

This pervasive and obsessive paranoia that is present in this list of accusations, brought about by this poisoning, is traced by Nietzsche to a further symptom of a *ressentiment* unable to discharge itself. This symptom expresses itself as a paranoia in which the enemy appears in gigantean and uncanny forms. Paradoxically this belief in one's own conspiratorial fantasy grants to the slave's adversaries far more power that they in fact possess:

> While the noble man is confident and frank with himself … the man of
> *ressentiment* is neither upright nor naïve, nor honest and straight with
> himself. His soul *squints*; his mind loves dark corners, secret paths and
> back-doors, everything secretive appeals to him as being *his* world, *his*
> security, *his comfort*; he knows all about keeping quiet, not forgetting,
> waiting, temporarily humbling and abasing himself … To be unable to
> take his enemies, his misfortunes and even his *misdeeds* seriously for
> long – that is the sign of strong, rounded natures with a superabundance
> of a power which is flexible, formative, healing and can make one
> forget … A man like this shakes from him, with one shrug, many
> worms which would have burrowed into another man.

---

21   It is to be noted that this was one of Wagner's enduring complaints: that the Jews had destroyed German culture (see Millington, *Wagner*).

It is at this point that the gap between the ancient and modern noble is most apparent. As noted in the previous section, a prime characteristic of the ancient noble was his ability to live in the knowledge of the terrors of raw nature. The power of the Ancient Greek tragedy, Nietzsche argues, was to articulate that fear without denying its force. Conversely the modern noble's mythologies act in the opposite way. The mythology of the Jews, a parody of ancient mythology, is created through a spiralling relationship between the modern noble and his own warped and poisoned imagination. The Jews and their imagined power become the *idée fixe*[22] of the modern noble, an idea whose power accumulates with the memory of each and every fictitious slight and injury to their noble sensitivities. The entire world comes to be seen in terms of a hermetic, self-replicating system of conspiracies and secret cabals,[23] all of which ensnare him in their grasp.[24] Thus this paranoid relationship acts as a boundary to the intrusion or recognition of nature's power in the act of creation. Wrapped in a world of its own delusion, the noble's detachment from nature, from what Nietzsche saw as the spark of life-creativity, is almost complete.[25]

Nietzsche recognises the nature of this disease of the mind in which self-perpetuating delusions and dark fantasies stand in for the nature of the real world. Again its cause is the presence of a destructive and dangerous *ressentiment*:

> When the noble method of evaluation makes a mistake and sins against
> reality, this happens in relation to the sphere with which it is *not*
> sufficiently familiar, a true knowledge of which it has indeed rigidly
> resisted: in some circumstances, it misjudges the sphere it despises, that
> of the common man, the rabble; on the other hand, we should bear in
> mind that the distortion which results from the feeling of contempt,
> disdain and superciliousness, always assuming that the image of the
> despised person is *distorted*, remains far behind the distortion with
> which the entrenched hatred and revenge of the powerless man attacks
> his opponent – in effigy of course. Indeed, contempt has too much
> negligence, nonchalance, complacency and impatience, even too much
> personal cheerfulness mixed into it, for it to be in a position to
> transform its object into a real caricature and monster.

The implication of this insight is quite startling. 'The Jews' that appear in section 7 of the first essay of *On the Genealogy of Morals* are 'caricatures' and 'distortions'. They are but 'effigies', their form and substance a product of what Nietzsche saw as deranged and pathological minds. It was only later that the fate

---

22   Note the musical origins of this term utilised by Nietzsche.

23   See section 14 for an account of this phenomenon, but this time from the perspective of the 'free-spirit'.

24   It is this point, and the paranoia to which it is connected (see below) that explains the paranoid fantasy that Christianity is a Jewish plot for world domination. See Rose, *Judaism and Modernity*, on the historical relationship between Judaism and Christianity and Nietzsche's knowledge of their connections.

25   In painting an image of this type, Nietzsche offers what must rank as one of the finest portraits of the antisemite and his traits.

that awaits effigies at the hands of their opponents was transferred onto millions of unique and particular individuals.

Conclusion

Whilst it is clear that section 7 of the first essay of the *Genealogy* has nothing to say of Nietzsche's 'attitude' to the Jews, and offers no sensible account of the development of Judaism over the centuries, it does offer an early insight into the psyche of the antisemite, as well as re-establishing Nietzsche's anti-antisemitic credentials.

In many ways, the portrait that Nietzsche paints of the modern 'noble' is as a parody of his venerable predecessor. Both types, for example, stand in a negative relationship to 'logos', but in a different position. The ancient noble was left behind at reason's dawn, whilst the modern noble confronts the latter at reason's dusk. Correspondingly, whilst the ancients lived in and for the present, their erstwhile successors looked only to the future through a retreat into the past. Put another way, the myths of the ancient Greeks for Nietzsche offered a 'yes' to life, the myth of the antisemite screams out a conformist 'no'; Apollo has secured dominance over a defeated Dionysus.

The nature of the myths each constructed was equally of a different kind. The myth of the pre-Socratic Greeks accepted the contingency of life and the arbitrariness of nature; the antisemitic myth, on the other hand, refused all chance by making the universe amenable to some negative grand design driven by the conscious action of one particular entity, 'the Jews'. Unlike the ancient noble, the modern noble's action is always reaction, and one that brings with it the verbiage of moral outrage.

In offering this portrait of the antisemite, Nietzsche can claim the status of one of the first commentators to recognise and criticise the appearance of a social and cultural phenomenon that had only appeared on the scene recently. This figure of the slave–noble is distinguished from the man of reason and the man of science as well as the old anti-Judaic religious bigot. Yet, despite his perception, it would be wrong to characterise Nietzsche as a prophet heralding the events of the following century. At the time of writing, antisemitism was not the only symptom of cultural exhaustion, nor had it achieved its victory over all other competing 'isms'.[26] Nonetheless, it is equally the case that Nietzsche's genealogy of the noble offers a pessimistic view of the world in which the 'inversions of well-known ideas imply that society has undergone an extremely perverse fate, and has turned into the obverse of its ideals'.[27]

---

26 See Hannah Arendt, *Origins of Totalitarianism* (London: Harcourt and Brace, 1975), p.9

27 Rose, *Judaism and Modernity*, p.26; see also T.W. Adorno and M. Horkheimer, *Dialectic of Enlightenment* (London: Verso, 1997).

Chapter 13

Antisemitism in Canada: The Legal Dimension in Context

Thomas S. Kuttner

The deeply personal has driven my commitment to combat anti-Semitism as it did James Parkes, the man whose life and memory we here celebrate.[1] He once

---

1   By way of introduction to this paper at the Southampton Conference held in September 1996, I gave the following eulogy to my father, to whose memory it is dedicated.

   Sixty three years ago almost to the day, a young scholar left Berlin with his new bride for Rome, there to embark upon a lifetime of study in Medieval Canon Law. Raised a Lutheran by his own father, also a scholar, who at the turn of the century had abandoned his orthodox Jewish faith, he himself, like so many others of his generation, had converted to Catholicism. Yet, as a Jew, he was unable to take the oath of racial purity imposed upon all who aspired to embark upon a career in the academy, and so was disqualified from making his *Habilitation*, stripped of the academic appointment which had been earlier awarded to him. I have in my office the form letter from the Reichs Minister of Justice, so advising.

   It was Pius XI who had invited him to the Vatican, as he did so many other scholars spurned because of their 'racial impurity' by a world gone horribly mad, Pius XI who several years later would proclaim to the world, 'Spiritually we are all Semites.' Seven years later it was Pius XII who secured for him and his young family a place of refuge in America as the evil forces let loose throughout Europe overwhelmed even the Eternal City.

   That young scholar was my father, Stephan Kuttner, a man for whom the Church was a living community of faith which transcends the bounds of nation, land and people, and those of time as well. A man for whom the words of the Apostle Paul in 1 Corinthians 12 were a lived experience: 'For by one Spirit are we all baptized into one body, whether we be Jews or Gentiles, whether we be bond or free: and have been all made to drink into one Spirit.'

   He raised me a Catholic, but long ago I, as a young scholar too, returned to the traditions of my People. I confess to a bitterness at that time, one directed at both my father and his father before him for the choices each had made. That bitterness has long since dissipated for 'When I was a child, I spake as a child, I understood as a child, I thought as a child: but when I became a man, I put away childish things' (I Cor. 13.11). As you can see, he raised me well in his adopted tradition and its cadences still resonate in my consciousness. It is just short of one month now that my father in his ninetieth year 'breathed his last, dying at a good ripe age, old and contented; and he was gathered to his kin' (Gen. 25:8). So too do the cadences of his and my original tradition continue to resonate.

   The bitterness, now past, has been replaced by a deep sorrow. A sorrow that my father, his father and so many scores of thousands like them were impelled to make that choice by a complex of interacting forces, stretching over many hundreds, even thousands

wrote that 'Anti-Semitism is the oldest and most comprehensive of modern political neuroses',[2] a neurosis which he analysed in terms of its linkage to other expressions of prejudice; its particularity rooted in the dismal history of the relations between Jews and Christians; and its use as a political weapon aimed at the destruction of democracy. In his numerous writings, Parkes established that the foundations of antisemitism are to be found in a deeply rooted and malevolent falsification of Jewish history in the Christian tradition. As a believer, he found the continued persistence of that falsification within a segment of popular Christian tradition to be deeply offensive, and as a social critic to be exceedingly dangerous. One need not be a believer to feel a particular affront when antisemitism is pleaded as a Christian virtue, and none should shrink from attacking it for the perversion of Christianity which it is. Indeed the battle against modern antisemitism is futile unless its foundations in Christian tradition, once recognized, are irrevocably refuted.

In 1946, Parkes wrote a Penguin Special entitled *An Enemy of the People: Anti-Semitism*, a work of widespread impact and immense importance.[3] Although recognizing the phenomenon as a threat to the democratic polity, he hesitated to rely upon the legal apparatus of the state to defend society from its encroachments. For him education was the weapon of choice. It is instructive to read this early work of Parkes, revealing as it does his familiarity with the use elsewhere of law as an instrument to combat antisemitism during the period between the two World Wars. 'Many people say that the first thing to do is to make the propagation of anti-Semitism illegal,' he wrote;

> that is pass a law against community libel. Legal proceedings have been taken in many countries; and, unfortunately, the evidence from those countries is not very encouraging. In Republican Germany many Nazi leaders were brought into court, tried and convicted for blasphemy on various occasions before 1933! They found the court proceedings a rather valuable platform for making anti-Semitic utterances, and that any fines they paid were well spent. If the punishments are not very severe they will not stop the offense; if they are savage, they will turn the convicted offender into a martyr. Those are the disadvantages. In the Soviet Union such a law also existed, and had no such disadvantages; but that is because it was part of a whole campaign, and

---

of years, – forces which they knew consciously only in part and saw 'as through a glass darkly' (1 Cor. 13.12) as do I yet. But there is joy too, that by those choices I, my children and my children's children are part of the Remnant saved, who can join with the Psalmist and rejoice: 'Behold how good and pleasant it is for brethren to dwell together in unity!' (Ps. 133.1).

2   James Parkes, 'Introduction' *Anti-Semitism* (London: Vallentine, Mitchell, 1963) p.ix.

3   James Parkes, *An Enemy of the People: Anti-Semitism* (New York: Penguin Books, 1946); this was a revised edition of a work, originally published by Penguin Books Limited, Harmondsworth, 1945).

not the most important part. For the attack on anti-Semitism took place on a basis of increasing security and employment; in other words, the general situation was favorable. Moreover the center of the campaign was education in racial tolerance within the proletarian society, and anti-Semitism was pilloried as 'bourgeois' and 'reactionary', which was much more serious than just making it 'illegal'. Legislation might be a useful adjunct in a general campaign; it cannot take the place of other methods of dealing with the disease, or even occupy the central position among other methods. It certainly could not be of the slightest value if we are not at the same time tackling the removal of insecurity and frustration from the lives of ordinary men, and from the Jewish community.

It is more valuable to make fascist propaganda unattractive than to make it illegal. Openly fascist bodies will, doubtless, be proscribed in many countries; but crypto-fascism can be just as dangerous. From the purely legal point of view the prohibition of uniforms, of para-military parades and organizations, and of secrecy in finance, would be legitimate measures, and possibly do more than direct prohibition of community libel. They cut a little nearer the source of the evil. But the main emphasis must be on education.[4]

Twenty years later his views had undergone a significant transformation. In the final chapter to his 1963 study, *Anti-Semitism*,[5] significantly entitled 'The Sterilization of Prejudice', Parkes acknowledged a change in perspective. He still remained convinced that '[l]egal action by itself will never be enough',[6] and that it had to be coupled with a programme of civic and communal education in which the Churches have a critical role to play. But he had come to recognise as well four fields in which legislative controls would be advantageous, even essential. These were (i) the prohibition of racial discrimination in employment and services available to the public; (ii) the expansion of the protective embrace of the law to counter group libel and defamation; (iii) the exclusion, from freedom of expression, of speech designed to destroy that freedom; (iv) the prohibition of marching and the wearing of uniforms for political purposes.[7] In the same work he refuted a *Times* editorial opposed to any legislation prohibiting incitement to racial hatred, and in doing so refuted too the arguments brought forward by himself twenty years earlier.

> Such legislation might have two prongs which, to mix the metaphor, might usefully interact upon each other. To protect democracy it would make use of the prong which forbade the group libel, and to improve relations between the majority and the minority it would discourage various forms of discrimination against minority groups. This is an indirect way of achieving the objective but it well may be wisest.

---

4   Ibid., p.142.
5   See note 2.
6   Ibid., p.174.
7   Ibid., p.168.

> Legislation about libel (written) and defamation (oral) of a living individual already exists in all civilized communities. There is also legislation making it an offense to speak or write obscenities and blasphemies. There is therefore already a recognized limitation upon freedom of speech. It seems difficult to claim that there is so erroneous a difference between the attacking of an individual and the attacking of a group, or between sexual obscenity and racial calumny, that laws about the one are possible and about the other are impossible.[8]

It is interesting to note that Parkes' fourfold recommendation reflected developing public policy initiatives undertaken in many liberal democracies in the 1960s and 1970s, including Canada. This was the era of adoption of human rights legislation crafted to prohibit discrimination in accommodation, employment and public services on the basis of race, creed, national origin, colour and sex. To these were later added age, disability and, most recently (but not without controversy), sexual orientation. So too was prohibited the displaying of signs and symbols emblematic of discrimination or an intent to discriminate on these forbidden grounds – a variation of Parkes' aversion to the political marches of the brownshirts and blackshirts.[9] Parkes had written his prescription for a legal assault on antisemitism when its latest manifestation was yet in its incubation. The bacillus now thrives and displays that same virulence which has always characterised Jew-hatred in the past.

Holocaust denial is often termed 'the new antisemitism', but it takes only cursory analysis to grasp that it reeks of the old. The same tiresome litany – the Jew as fiend, the Jew as conspirator, the Jew as a canker, exploitative, amoral, depraved and always foreign – in short all that led Hannah Arendt to identify antisemitism as 'an outrage to common sense' is to be found there.[10] The society in whose name this outrage is perpetrated must respond forcefully, at least to hold it in check, if not to blot it out. But how? Parkes advocated expansion of the common law torts of libel and defamation, a project judges have not embraced, nor legislatures on the civil side. Rather the instrument to which the state has traditionally turned in the common law world to curb asocial behaviour that threatens public order is the criminal law. This is the case in Canada, whose *Criminal Code*[11] contains three offences that deal directly or indirectly with what is compendiously termed 'hate propaganda': advocating genocide;[12] public incitement of hatred likely to lead to a breach of

---

8   Ibid., p.171. The *Times* editorial is reproduced at Appendix I, pp.180–82.

9   The New Brunswick Human Rights Act, R.S.N.B., 1973 c.H-11, discussed *infra*, is representative of such legislation in Canada.

10   Hannah Arendt, *The Origins of Totalitarianism* (New York: Harcourt, Brace and World, 1966). This is the title to chapter I, pp.3–10.

11   *Criminal Code*, R.S.C. 1985, c.C-46.

12   Section 318 (1) Everyone who advocates or promotes genocide is guilty of an indictable offense and liable to imprisonment for a term not exceeding five years.

the peace;[13] wilful promotion of hatred other than in private conversation;[14] and, until recently, a fourth, spreading false news.[15]

As Parkes was acutely aware, each of these offences raises profound issues of the reach of freedom of speech and freedom of belief as fundamental liberties on which modern democratic societies are grounded. In Canada, both freedoms are a legacy of our British heritage, for ours is 'a Constitution similar in Principal to that of the United Kingdom'.[16] More recently these fundamental liberties have found expression in the Canadian Charter of Rights and Freedoms,[17] where they are entrenched as informing values against which the validity of state action must be measured: a profound restraint upon the British principle of the sovereignty of Parliament. However, even apart from the Charter, the tension between these freedoms and the state interest in public order is evident. In addition, there are procedural safeguards to prosecution in the case of hate propaganda offences (although not in that of the false news offence), the consent of the Attorney General being required in order to institute proceedings. Within the Charter the balance between fundamental freedoms and the democratic principle is found in its provisions, saving harmless limitations on the freedoms it guarantees which are 'demonstratively justified in a free and democratic society'.[18]

There is a great tension here, and nowhere is it as evident as in the major Holocaust denial criminal cases, *R. v. Keegstra*,[19] and *R. v. Zundel*.[20] Zundel is a neo-Nazi propagandist who was convicted of spreading false news: the publication of a pamphlet of the revisionist genre entitled 'Did Six Million

---

13   Section 319 (1) Everyone who by communicating statements in any public place, incites hatred against any identifiable group where such incitement is likely to lead to a breach of the peace is guilty of (a) an indictable offense and is liable to imprisonment for a term not exceeding two years; or (b) an offense punishable on summary conviction.

14   Section 319 (2) Everyone who, by communicating statements, other than in private conversation, wilfully promotes hatred against any identifiable group is guilty of (a) an indictable offense and is liable to imprisonment for a term not exceeding two years; or (b) an offense punishable on summary conviction.

15   Section 181 Everyone who wilfully publishes a statement, tale or news that he knows is false and that causes or is likely to cause injury or mischief to a public interest is guilty of an indictable offense and is liable to imprisonment for two years.

16   The Constitution Act, 1867 originally enacted as the British North America Act, 1867 (U.K.), 30 & 31 Vict., c. 3, Preamble.

17   The Canadian Charter of Rights and Freedoms, being part I, Constitution Act, 1982, schedule B to Canada Act, 1982 (U.K.), 1982, c. 11. The Charter stipulates at section 2: 'Everyone has the following fundamental freedoms: (a) Freedom of conscience and religion; (b) Freedom of thought, belief, opinion, and expression, including freedom of the press and other media of communication.'

18   The Charter stipulates at section 1: 'The Canadian Charter of Rights and Freedoms guarantees the rights and freedoms set out in it subject only to such reasonable limits prescribed by law as can be demonstrably justified in a free and democratic society.'

19   *R. v. Keegstra* [1990] 3 S.C.R. 697.

20   *R. v. Zundel* [1992] 2 S.C.R. 731.

Really Die?', the work of a British neo-Nazi, Richard Verral. Keegstra was an Alberta high school teacher convicted of wilful promotion of hatred against an identifiable group in the course of his teaching. His was a more classic antisemitism coupled with Holocaust denial. In both cases, the convictions were challenged on the basis that the provisions of the *Code* under which they were obtained are an unconstitutional interference with freedom of speech guaranteed by the Charter. In December 1990, the Supreme Court of Canada, by a narrow majority, upheld the conviction in *Keegstra*. A majority of four justices found the criminalization of wilful promotion of hatred in the *Code* to be a reasonable limit of freedom of expression 'demonstrably justified in a free and democratic society' under section 1 of the Charter. Three justices filed a strongly worded dissent, finding the same provisions of the *Code* violative of the Charter freedom.

It is noteworthy that the two groups of justices were in agreement that hate propaganda, despite its failure to further the ends of the free speech guarantee (said to be threefold: seeking and attaining truth; participation in societal and political decision making; and individual self-fulfilment and human flourishing) nevertheless falls within its embrace as communication which conveys or attempts to convey meaning.[21] Where they parted company was in their measuring of that expression against the section 1 Charter limitation. Chief Justice Dickson, speaking for a bare majority, concluded that the detrimental effects of hate propaganda justify its suppression when juxtaposed against the informing values of a free and democratic society which underlie the freedom of expression guarantee. The effects of hate propaganda he identified as twofold: the threat to the dignity of the target group members and the possibility that prejudicial messages might gain some credence in society at large, and so threaten social discord. Hate propaganda repudiates and undermines democratic values, and in particular the value of equal respect and dignity to which each citizen is entitled.[22] The minority was not prepared to accede to the criminalization of hate propaganda, arguing that alternative, less punitive, mechanisms were available to Parliament to blunt its pernicious effects.[23]

Less than two years later, a panel of the Court, differently comprised, struck down the conviction in *Zundel*, an equally narrow majority holding the criminalization of spreading false news to be violative of freedom of speech and not saved by the section 1 Charter exculpatory clause.[24] The decision of the

---

21   Ibid., p.728.

22   For Chief Justice Dickson's reasons for judgment, see note 19, pp.713–96.

23   The dissenting reasons of Justice McLachlin for the minority are found in ibid., pp.796–868.

24   In the interim the composition of the court had changed. Of the majority in *Keegstra*, Chief Justice Dickson and Justice Wilson had retired, replaced by Justices Cory and Iacobucci. In *Zundel*, Justice L'Heureux Dubé crossed over to join Justices McLachlin, Sobinka and La Forest (who had comprised the minority in *Keegstra*) to form

majority was penned by Justice McLachlin, the leading justice in dissent in *Keegstra*. She considered the false news provisions of the Code to be too broadly framed to withstand Charter scrutiny, rooted as they were in thirteenth-century legislation intended to preserve political harmony in the state. In contrast to the hate propaganda provisions of the Code so narrowly upheld in Keegstra, the false news provisions were said to be overextended in contextual reach, to be particularly invasive in their reliance upon criminal sanction, and to threaten a chilling effect on legitimate social and political comment, which in some circumstances might actually include knowingly false statements.[25] Again three Justices filed a strongly worded dissent, which would have found the false news provisions of the *Code* saved harmless as a reasonable limit under section 1 of the Charter, on the same basis as the majority had determined in the *Keegstra* case.[26] Needless to say, all of the justices engaged in this appeal, as in that of Keegstra, were in agreement that the evil of hate propaganda is beyond doubt. Nevertheless it was inevitable that, in the case of Zundel, his acquittal would be proclaimed by some as endorsement of his conduct as legitimate, and so it was.

At the crux of the general debate as well as of the clash between the two groups of justices is the disturbing use of the state's criminal law-making power to control the conduct of the citizen. Traditionally the courts, when faced with criminal law strictures, strive to enhance individual liberty against state interference. The complex structure of the criminal law of evidence is a legacy of that tradition. The trial process is a poor crucible in which to test historical events of overwhelming significance. The Holocaust demands the art of the muse Clio for explication, if explication there can ever be. It cannot be weighed upon the scales of justice. It requires the craft of the historian, not that of the lawyer, for to submit Auschwitz to cross-examination is to commit the ultimate blasphemy. In *Zundel*, it was only with shame that we witnessed the historian Raul Hilberg subjected to the barbs, the vacuous badgering, the gratuitous insults and vapid philosophising of defence counsel, and with even greater shame that we were forced to accept as 'expert witnesses' equal in the eyes of the law to one of Hilberg's stature, the revisionist propagandists Faurrison and Felderer. That was during the first *Zundel* trial, and to his credit Hilberg refused to testify at the second.[27] It was at the second that the presiding judge took judicial notice

the new majority. This left of the original majority in *Keegstra* only Justice Gonthier who, together with Justices Cory and Iacobucci, filed the dissent in *Zundel*.

25   The origins of the false news provisions of the Code were traced to the offence of *De Scandalis Magnatum* enacted in the Statute of Westminster, 1275, 3 Edw. I, c. 34. For Justice McLachlin's reasons for the majority, see note 20, pp.731–78.

26   For the dissenting judgment, see ibid, pp.778–843.

27   Zundel's conviction after his first trial was overturned by the Ontario Court of Appeal because of errors in the admission of evidence and the charge to the jury. It was Zundel's conviction at the second trial that was the subject of the Appeal to the Supreme Court of Canada here being considered.

of 'the mass murder and extermination of Jews in Europe by the Nazi regime during the Second World War' as a fact and so directed the jury.[28] Yet he refused to take judicial notice of the facts challenged in Zundel's pamphlet: that six million were murdered, that the gas chambers existed, that there was a premeditated state policy to annihilate the Jewish people. These disputed facts the Crown had to prove to the satisfaction of the jury in a Toronto courtroom in 1987.

The differing outcomes in the *Keegstra* and *Zundel* cases confirm that rarely is the criminal law an appropriate vehicle to vindicate a collectivity grievously harmed. Collective values (group dignity, sensitivity and sensibility) all fare poorly against the liberty of the subject when the latter is threatened, regardless of the nature of the act which has given rise to public obloquy. Group defamation, such as that epitomised by classic antisemitism, presents a particularly intractable problem as it often reflects deep-seated and entrenched animosities in the dominant civilization, the expression of which has only relatively recently become, within that civilization itself, unacceptable. Orthodoxy in the dominant civilisation now condemns not merely as heterodox but even as heresy that which was once doctrine or creed worthy of its *imprimatur*. This is certainly the case with antisemitism which is deeply embedded as a social practice in Christian culture to a degree with which that culture has only in the last century come to terms. The tensions then are doubly drawn, for the modern dissenter sees himself as a true believer, returning to the true faith by articulating one of its earlier, openly expressed, even fundamental tenets.

A Zundel or a Keegstra who trumpets his beliefs with almost messianic fervour presents then a particular difficulty for the dominant culture, even if the dominant culture is determined to distance itself from him. He does so by skilfully playing on another of the fundamental values of the dominant culture, this one shared with the minority culture or group, namely freedom of speech or freedom of religion. He calls these in aid in order to force the dominant culture to allow him to articulate that which the culture itself has now rejected. This is the cunning of the hatemonger. Zundel, for instance, cynically styles his publishing house *Samisdat Publishers*. This arrogation of the values of free speech and freedom of belief to shield antisemitic expression horrifies us as Jews for whom the expression of such ideas was always anathema, whether espoused by the majority or not. Indeed, in both *Keegstra* and *Zundel*, the Canadian Jewish Congress, which was a party to the proceedings, strenuously argued that neither embraced antisemitic speech, but to no avail.[29] The majority culture has still not

---

28   See note 20, p.782.

29   Both the trial judge in *Keegstra* and the Court of Appeal in *Zundel* were prepared to find antisemitism to fall outside the scope of free speech, but the Supreme Court's subsequent decisions to the contrary, giving an expansive reading to the freedom such as to embrace all expression short of violence, are determinative.

fully so internalized its rejection of the discredited social practice to the extent that it is willing to sacrifice the principles of freedom of speech and freedom of belief where the latter are used – or should I say abused – as a vehicle to articulate the once orthodox, but now heretical, doctrine of antisemitism.

Ironically it is only in a dominant culture which has itself been so traumatized by the offending doctrine, to the point of collapse because of its virulence, that one witnesses a forthright and absolute rejection of its free expression. Thus, in the case of present-day Germany, notwithstanding the constitutional entrenchment of freedom of speech, any public espousal of Nazi ideology, in particular antisemitism, whether orally, pictorially or otherwise has been criminalized. The democracy of the Federal Republic, with the example and image of Weimar before it, is not prepared to chance an internal assault by the virus of Nazism, particularly under the guise of freedom of speech. It was there that Zundel was convicted for purveying hate propaganda. To the contrary, it is the Western democracies that have not experienced first-hand the oppressive and destructive force of fascist ideology which harbour doubts as to its curbing through mechanisms that challenge the overarching value of freedom of speech and freedom of belief. The classic case was the neo-Nazi march in Skokie, Illinois in the mid-1960s, an incident that fractured the American Civil Liberties Union, some say irreparably. The leadership supported the right to march in that heavily Jewish suburb of Chicago, prompting a sizable segment of the membership to depart in protest from the organisation as a result.

This gives one pause to ponder whether one should turn to the criminal law process at all to address the canker of group defamation in general, and of antisemitism in particular. The Canadian experience seems to indicate that to subject the hatemonger to the criminal law process in an effort to vindicate and champion the maligned collectivity leads only in the best of cases to a painful cauterisation and, in the ordinary case, to something much more painful, a continuing festering of the wound with the possibility of much worse, an outbreak of the secondary tumour; that is, the well-known phenomenon adverted to by Parkes that such trials publicise the views of the diabolic and win to their cause new converts. This was certainly the view of Zundel himself, who gloated that the trial had given him 'a million dollars' worth of publicity'.[30] In the case of Keegstra, repeated reversals of his conviction on technical grounds caused many to question why, ten years later, he continued to be 'hounded' by the state. Indeed, in dissent in *Keegstra*, Justice McLachlin opined on the danger of creating a 'martyr' and sympathy for his cause.[31]

There is another model which is distanced from that of the criminal law process, its traditions and institutions and which holds more hope for realistically

---

30   This was following Zundel's first conviction in 1985 (*Globe and Mail*, 1 March 1985, as cited by Justice McLachlin); see note 19, p.853.
31   Ibid.

and effectively confronting the challenge of antisemitism. That model is the regulatory control of conduct between management and labour in modern collective bargaining legislation. Central to the legislative regime is the regulation of anti-union conduct by employer. The unfair labour practice, its definition, control and eradication are a principal feature of our labour codes. Employer free speech, where expressive of anti-trade union animus, is severely restrained. We are now outside the criminal arena and its pitfalls. The governing principle under the labour codes is not the preservation of the liberty of the subject, but rather the furtherance of collective bargaining and the championing of the rights of the individual worker as part of a collectivity. A collectivist ethos informs the work of our labour boards. This was most memorably expressed by the great American justice, Learned Hand, almost fifty years ago when he wrote the following:

> The privilege of 'free speech', like other privileges, is not absolute; it has its seasons; a democratic society has an acute interest in its protection and cannot indeed be without it; but it is an interest measured by its purpose. That purpose is to enable others to make an informed judgement as to what concerns them, and ends so far as the utterances do not contribute to the result … [w]ords are not pebbles in alien juxtaposition; they have only a communal existence; and not only does the meaning of each interpenetrate the other, but all in their aggregate take their purport from the setting in which they are used, of which the relation between the speaker and the hearer is perhaps the most important. What to an outsider will be no more than the vigorous presentation of a conviction, to an employee may be the manifestation of a determination which it is not safe to thwart. The Board must decide how far the second aspect obliterates the first.[32]

For fifty years labour boards have developed a jurisprudence sensitive to the reality that, in the labour context, employer free speech, masked as simply 'the vigorous presentation of a conviction', must give way to the collective values of labour and be constrained precisely because in practice it reveals itself to be 'the manifestation of a determination which it is not safe to thwart'. Within this context, there is no longer any magic to the rubric 'freedom of speech' which must give way to a competing, even overriding value: the dignity of the individual as expressed in collectivist action.

There is much to be learned here. Group defamation must be regulated through institutions and structures that are sensitive and responsive to collectivist values. Human rights codes, themselves near constitutional instruments, entrench the values of equal dignity and respect which inform any multicultural and pluralistic society. As in the case of the labour boards, human rights tribunals sensitive to those values are much more likely to recognise and unmask false

---

32 *National Labor Relations Board* v. *Federbush Co., Inc.*, 121 F. 2d 954 (1941, U.S.C.A. 2d circuit), p. 957.

invocation of freedom of speech or freedom of belief to justify vicious and destructive assaults on the integrity of our society. In moving from the realm of the criminal law to the regime of the regulatory agency, we shift the focus of our attention from the hatemonger to the victim of hate propaganda. We strive not to mete out punishment to the offender, but to ameliorate the condition of the aggrieved. To this end, remedies can be fashioned to blunt and to restrict the destructive impact of hate propaganda. To be sure attempts will be made to infuse the ethos of the criminal law process into that of the human rights tribunal. Indeed it is precisely this tack which is often employed to undermine the proceedings of human rights tribunals. The pitfalls are many and the temptation to adopt the hostile attitude of the courts towards collective interests great. Nevertheless there is room for cautious optimism that, within the context of such an inquiry, the collective values of group dignity and respect, so viciously assaulted through antisemitic hate propaganda, can be vindicated. An opportunity to test that optimism presented itself in the *Moncton School Board* case, to which I now turn.[33]

Malcolm Ross is a Moncton, New Brunswick school teacher who, over a fifteen-year period commencing in the 1970s, published a series of books, the titles of which alone reveal their dismal content: *Web of Deceit* (1978), *The Real Holocaust* (1983), *Spectre of Power* (1987), *Christianity vs. Judeo-Christianity* (1987).[34] They are all of them a turgid amalgam of Jewish conspiracy theory, drawing directly on the *Protocols of the Elders of Zion* (naturally without attribution, but the parallelisms are unmistakable), Holocaust denial literature and classic Christian anti-Judaism. In addition to his writings, which were widely available throughout New Brunswick, Ross made himself a public figure as well, appearing variously in the media and remonstrating in the press. The flavour of his warped belief system is captured in the following excerpt from a newspaper commentary written in the mid 1980s:

> How then could these capitalists support communism?
> These questions troubled me, and several years after leaving university I began to hear about an 'international conspiracy'. Most disturbing of all, this 'conspiracy' seemed to be headed by those that many Christians held to be God's 'Chosen People', the Jews.
> My work is not 'disguised' as Christian, as Dr. Israeli insists, but is completely faithful to the spirit of the Christian faith from earliest Christian times to at least our 'post-Auschwitz Christian' church when the Jewish infiltration of top offices in the Vatican and elsewhere led to the sorry state of the Christian church and Christian society today.

---

33   I acted as Counsel *pro bono* for the New Brunswick Human Rights Commission in the *Moncton School Board* case before the Courts of New Brunswick and the Supreme Court of Canada between 1988 and 1996. I draw upon that experience in my discussion of the case.

34   All bear the imprint of the Stronghold Publishing Company Ltd., Moncton, N.B., Canada.

It is indeed the 'Judeo-Christian society' our society has fought against for years, a society under the control of a Jewish controlled mass media, Jewish controlled international finance, and now a Jewish-dominated 'Christianity' where every 'evangelist' who appears on our television spews out the same old line, 'The Jews are God's Chosen People so we must support them no matter what they do.' I believe many of the evils in our land stem from the fact that we have denied the kingship of Christ in our society and have allowed those 'who hate the Lord' to rule over us.

My whole purpose in writing and publishing is to exult Jesus Christ and to inform Christians about the great Satanic movement which is trying to destroy our Christian faith and civilization.[35]

Several attempts were made to commence criminal charges against Ross under the hate propaganda provisions of the *Criminal Code*, particularly once they had been laid against *Keegstra* in Alberta, but these foundered on the requirement for the consent of the Provincial Attorney-General to do so. Two different Attorneys-General under two different governments declined to grant their consent. Perhaps their refusal lay in the fact that, in contrast to the *Keegstra* case, there was no evidence that Ross had openly advocated antisemitism in his teaching or mentioned his pathological world view to pupils. Perhaps it lay in the disturbing fact that Ross claimed it was his Christian faith which fuelled his antisemitism.[36] Be that as it may, Ross's penchant for the soap box increased his notoriety and the local School Board became the scene of a protracted struggle between those (a minority) who sought to restrain his off-duty conduct, and a majority unwilling to pursue the matter vigorously. At one point it appeared that civic virtue would triumph, and the School Board actually instructed Ross to cease the public articulation of his views under threat of greater sanction, but on his breach of that order no further action was taken against him. Indeed a joint School Board–Teacher's Federation investigative committee, on finding no evidence of in-classroom misconduct on the part of Ross, came to the conclusion that the Board could do nothing to interfere with his conduct. The Teacher's Federation perceived the case solely as one in which what was at stake was the right of a teacher to be free of employer dominance while off-duty and away from the workplace. Both the Board and the Federation refused to acknowledge any responsibility for that conduct, and in the case of the Board this was in the face of legal advice to the contrary.

This was the situation when, in 1988, a courageous Moncton parent, David Attis, a Jew, filed a complaint before the New Brunswick Human Rights

---

35 *Board of Inquiry Report* (1991), pp.52–3. An edited version of the *Report* can be found at (1992) 41 *UNBLJ*, 238–68. The cited excerpt is on p.259.

36 Good faith opinion on a religious subject is a defence to the wilful promotion of hatred offence under the *Criminal Code*, s.319 (3). The requirement to obtain the consent of the Attorney General in order to institute criminal proceedings for the offence is found at section 319 (6).

Commission alleging that, in failing to act against Ross, the School Board was in breach of its statutory obligation to provide educational services to the public free of bias, prejudice and intolerance contrary to the Provincial Human Rights Act.[37] After a great deal of legal wrangling, a one-person Board of Inquiry was established to inquire into the complaint, and following five weeks of hearing in late 1990 and early 1991, at which hundreds of exhibits were filed and thousands of pages of testimony heard, it issued its decision.[38] The decision was a complete vindication of Attis and all those convinced that our democracy is sufficiently robust to defend its weakest from the depravity of the hatemonger without threat to the integrity of our polity.

After an extensive review of the voluminous evidence, the Board determined that the antisemitic activities of Ross had contributed to the creation of a 'poisoned environment' within the school district. Moreover the failure of the School Board to restrain Ross implicated it in his misconduct such that the Board had failed to provide educational services in the district free of discrimination against the complainant, contrary to the Human Rights Act. By way of remedy, the Board issued a two-pronged order: immediate removal of Ross from the classroom, with the opportunity to be given to him to take up a non-teaching position, and the continued restraint of Ross from further publication or public articulation of his antisemitic views so long as he remained in the employ of the School Board in any capacity. The action of the School Board was swift.[39] Within a week it found for Ross a non-classroom teaching position as a modified resource teacher.

In its decision, the Board of Inquiry had eschewed consideration of the free speech and religious belief arguments tendered by Ross in support of his activities. Ross applied immediately to the Court of Queen's Bench to have the order of the Board of Inquiry quashed as an unjustifiable interference with these Charter rights. At the Queen's Bench he was partially successful. The restraint order was quashed, but the removal order was upheld as a reasonable limit justified in a free and democratic society.[40] On appeal, the removal order too was struck down by a majority of the New Brunswick Court of Appeal.[41] At neither

---

37   See above, note 9. Section 5(1) of the Act stipulates:

No person directly, or indirectly, alone or with another, by himself or by the interposition of another, shall
a) ...
b) discriminate against any person or class of persons with respect to any accommodation, services or facilities available to the public because of race, color, religion, national origin, ancestry, place of origin, age, physical disability, mental disability, marital status, sexual orientation or sex.

38   See above, note 35.
39   See above, note 35, pp.69–71; (1992) *UNBLJ*, p.269.
40   (1991) 121 N.B.R. (2d) 361.
41   (1993) 142 N.B.R. (2d) 1.

level were the Charter issues probed deeply. That task was left to the Supreme Court of Canada to which the matter came up on further appeal in September 1995. In April 1996, a full bench of the Court, comprising nine justices, unanimously upheld the order of the Board of Inquiry removing Ross from the classroom, but struck down the restraining order as to future antisemitic conduct for lack of an evidentiary basis sufficient to warrant its imposition in the circumstances.[42]

Mine was the singular honour to appear before the Court on behalf of the New Brunswick Human Rights Commission in order to defend the decision and order of the Board of Inquiry. My argument before the Supreme Court was driven more by didactics than by tactics. By this I mean that I envisaged the case as a vehicle of instruction, even of self-discovery, which would enable the judiciary to confront and formally acknowledge the particularity of antisemitism, and the complex problem it presents for our society. In both *Keegstra* and *Zundel* that complexity was masked behind the term 'hate propaganda' , in short, Jew-hatred was submerged into the universalised 'racial hatred' , its deep imbrication into our culture ignored. The thrust of the argument was to peel off those layers of universalisation and put into relief the distinctiveness of antisemitism, for my sense is that to isolate intolerance from its context risks debasement of its profound destructive impact. My endeavour was only partially successful, for although the Court for the first time tentatively acknowledged the particularity of antisemitism as an evil and a threat to social stability, it drew back from grappling with the conundrum of its roots in Christian Jew-hatred, despite a clear invitation to do so. Let me set out the structure of the Commission's argument and that of the Court's decision.

Canadian constitutional jurisprudence calls for contextualisation of the values underlying the rights and freedoms guaranteed by the Charter when these are pleaded against state action. The Court accepted the Commission's invitation to consider the *Moncton School Board* case within three contextual circumstances: within the context of the public education system, within the context of an employment relationship in the public sector and within the context of antisemitism as a pathological belief system. For our purposes here, the first two contexts need be addressed only briefly. The first, that of a public education

---

42   (1996) 1 S.C.R. 825. This was the first time that the Court had been unanimous in a freedom of speech case. The three justices who would have struck down the conviction in *Keegstra*, and who together with one other struck down that in *Zundel* (Justices La Forest, McLachlin and Sopinka) joined their colleagues in the *Moncton School Board* case. Indeed, it was one of their number, Justice La Forest, who wrote the judgment for the full Court. In *Ross* v. *Canada* (2001), 10 B.H.R.C. 219, the U.N. Human Rights Committee dismissed a complaint filed by Ross alleging that the decision of the Supreme Court of Canada was violative of his rights to freedom of speech and freedom of religion under articles 18 and 19 of the International Covenant on Civil and Political Rights 1966 (UN HRC Communication 736/1997).

system, explored the tension between two values deeply entrenched in our political culture, a tension of which already the Greeks were aware. Although the state has no role in deciding for the citizen the content and contours of the good life, paradoxically it is its role to inculcate in its youth civic virtue, for the shaping of character and of culture is a function of the community. Speaking for the Court, Justice LaForest agreed that the state, in a manner unparalleled by any of its other functions, when providing public education services is engaged in nurturing and sustaining those underlying values and principles of a free and democratic society which are the genesis of the rights and freedoms guaranteed by the Charter. Citing first an earlier judgment of the Court, penned by himself, he wrote, 'Whether one views it from an economic, social, cultural, or civic point of view, the education of the young is critically important in our society', and he continued:

> There can be no doubt that the attempt to foster equality, respect, and
> tolerance in the Canadian educational system is a laudable goal. ...
> Education awakens children to the values a society hopes to foster and
> to nurture. [...] The importance of insuring an equal and discrimination
> free educational environment, and the perception of fairness and
> tolerance in the classroom, are paramount in the education of young
> children. This helps foster self-respect and acceptance by others.[43]

Within the context of employment in the public sector as a teacher, the Court agreed with the argument that the standard of behaviour which a teacher must meet is greater than the minimum standard of conduct otherwise tolerated, given the public responsibilities which a teacher must fulfil and the expectations which the community holds for the educational system. Again the words of Justice LaForest are apposite:

> It is on the basis of the position of trust and influence that we hold the
> teacher to high standards both on and off duty, and it is an erosion of
> these standards that may lead to a loss in the community of confidence
> in the public school system. [...] Where a 'poisoned' environment
> within the school system is traceable to the off duty conduct of a
> teacher that is likely to produce a corresponding loss of confidence in
> the teacher and the system as a whole, then the off duty conduct of the
> teacher is relevant.[44]

The third contextual prism the Court had been invited to consider was that of antisemitism. As the starting point of its own analysis the Court cited the principal submission put forward in the Commission's factum, as follows:

> After Auschwitz it is simply not feasible to consider the Constitutional
> values of freedom of expression and freedom of religion where these
> are proclaimed to shield anti-Semitic conduct, without contemplating

---

43   (1996) 1 S.C.R. 825, p.873.
44   Ibid., p.858.

the centrality of that ideology to the scourge of death and destruction
which swept across Europe during the era of the Third Reich.[45]

As noted earlier, in its analysis the Court gave tentative recognition to the
particularity of antisemitism and for the first time acknowledged, in a way it had
scrupulously avoided in both *Keegstra* and *Zundel*, the specific and focused harm
it occasions. The references are short, but significant.

In an earlier judgment, Chief Justice Dickson had warned that the courts must
be cautious to ensure that the Charter not become an instrument in the hand of
better situated individuals used to roll back legislation crafted to improve the
condition of the disadvantaged. Picking up that theme, Justice La Forest identified
Jews as disadvantaged, thereby implicitly demolishing the grotesquely drawn
stereotype Ross had put forward. The Jews are 'an historically disadvantaged
group that has endured persecution on the largest scale', the Judge wrote.[46]
Accepting the determination made by the Board of Inquiry that the primary
purpose of Ross's form of expression, despite his assertions to the contrary, was
to attack the truthfulness, integrity, dignity and motives of Jews, Justice La Forest
concluded that this manifestation was incompatible with the very values sought to
be upheld in a Charter inquiry. Consequently only an attenuated justificatory
analysis had to be undertaken under Section 1 of the Charter when measuring
Ross' activities against the informing values of freedom of expression and
freedom of religion. In his analysis, Justice La Forest concluded that, rather than
further the search for truth, Ross' writing 'muzzles the voice of truth'; rather than
further individual autonomy and self-development, incitement to contempt of
Jews 'hinders the ability of Jewish people to develop a sense of self identity and
belonging'; rather than further participation in civic culture, antisemitism
'undermines democratic values' and, by impeding Jews from meaningful
participation in social and political decision making accomplishes an end 'wholly
antithetical to the democratic process'. As to freedom of religion, inasmuch as
Ross' belief system denigrates and defames the religious beliefs of others, it
'erodes the very basis of the guarantee' of freedom of religion in the Charter.[47]

The Court accepted that the object of the impugned Order of the Board of
Inquiry was to remedy the discrimination which had been found to have
poisoned the educational environment in Moncton. It found that objective
compatible with its own jurisprudence, with Canada's international obligation to
eradicate discrimination in general and with the values entrenched in the Charter.
Indeed it accepted that 'the pernicious effects associated with hate propaganda,
and more specifically anti-Semitic messages, undermine basic democratic values
and are antithetical to the "core" values of the Charter'.[48] Finally, in his

---

45 Ibid., p.875.
46 Ibid.
47 Ibid., pp.878–9.
48 Ibid., p.880.

concluding disposition of the Appeal, Justice La Forest identified Ross as 'a notorious anti-Semite', a characterization adopted by the full Court, although interestingly a descriptive never articulated as a finding by the Board of Inquiry.[49]

So the judgment acknowledged, for the first time in Canada in a sustained manner, the particularity of antisemitism as a form of race hatred. What it did not do was to unmask the illegitimacy of Ross's argument that Jew hatred was central to his Christian belief system. This is regrettable. One can understand that the Court would shy away from inquiring into the *validity* of any belief system, but that does not require that it refrain from commenting upon the legitimacy of its self-characterisation. This is the way the argument was put to the Court:

> 35. The invidiousness of anti-Semitism is compounded by its deep roots, historically ingrained as social practice in Western Christian culture. The literature is vast and was recently surveyed by the Canadian theologian, Alan Davies. That it has found expression in Canada throughout its history is chronicled in his edited study *Anti-Semitism in Canada*. In his writings, the Respondent Ross taps into a particularly virulent form of anti-Semitism – the myth of a Jewish conspiracy to dominate the world in all its facets – social, political and economic – so as to destroy Christian civilization. That these views parallel and replicate those propagated in the notorious forgery *Protocols of the Elders of Zion* is evident at a glance.
>
> 36. The Respondent Ross professes anti-Semitism to be 'completely faithful to the Christian faith' which he professes. Below, the Court of Appeal characterized such belief as 'religious' and 'sincerely' held. In *R. v. Jones* this Court declined to question the validity of a religious belief assuming sincerity of conviction by an adherent. Nevertheless, it should not hesitate to challenge the characterization of a dogmatic belief as 'Christian' in the face of overwhelming evidence to the contrary. This is particularly important given the Christian heritage of the majority in our society, a sociological factor recognized in *R. v. Edwards Books and Art Ltd*. Given the constitutional imperative to preserve and enhance the multicultural heritage of Canadians, the Court must be mindful of the threat to social cohesion and mutual respect between Canadians which could arise were grossly distorted characterizations of the dogmatic belief system of the Christian majority to go unchallenged. Curial deference need not be paid to the assertion by the Respondent Ross that his is a 'Christian' belief. To the contrary this Court should affirm that anti-Semitism is inimical to the dogmatic belief system of the overwhelming majority of Christian faith communities in Canada.
>
> 37. Throughout its history the relationship between the Christian Church and the Jewish people has been a complex one, at times painful and marked with anti-Jewish beliefs, practices and measures. The Respondent Ross has his proof-texts.[50] That they represent Christian

---

49   Ibid., p.886.
50   In his writings and before the courts, Ross pleaded in support certain

dogma and practice at certain times in the past when tolerance was not an informing value for the Church, is sadly too true. That they represent Christian dogma and practice today is emphatically not. The Respondent Ross espouses an atavistic Christianity, a petrified theology and fossilized dogma of a distant era now repudiated and categorically rejected by each branch of the Christian Church – the Roman Catholic, the Protestant and the Eastern Orthodox. That the living Christian Churches categorically reject anti-Semitism as any part of Christian belief cannot be over-emphasized, and to this they bear witness.[51]

Rather than take up the challenge, the Court demurred. It would not enter into such a discussion. To be sure, from its decision it is clear that the Court intuitively grasped the significance for its consideration of the antisemitic conduct of Ross, of the near destruction of the Jewish People in the Holocaust. But it failed to go further by excavating, in a sense, the antecedents of mid twentieth-century antisemitism perversely tapped into by Ross under the claim of fidelity to a faith tradition which has now consciously purged itself of its earlier social practice of Jew hatred. The Court had before it sufficient materials to have stated unequivocally that the Christian Churches now resolutely reject antisemitism and Jew-hatred in whatever guise as inimical to Christian belief and tradition. Such a statement, issuing from what is arguably the 'high priesthood' of our civic culture, would have vindicated the enlightened Christian belief tradition of the great bulk of Canadians which was besmirched by Ross's grotesqueries. However, all of this was consciously avoided by the Court. Here was an opportunity missed. It rests with forums such as this, continuing in the spirit of James Parkes, to fill the gap.

---

scriptural passages and the classic attacks against Jews and Judaism by several of the Church Fathers, Luther and other Christian polemicists.

51   *Factum of the Appellant Human Rights Commission*, Supreme Court file no. 24002 (March 1995), citations omitted. The Court's attention was drawn to the Vatican II document *Nostra Aetate* and other well-known condemnations of antisemitism by the World Council of Churches, the Lutheran World Federation and the Eastern Orthodox Churches, as well as by several denominations in Canada including the Anglican, United and Presbyterian Churches.

Chapter 14

Offending the Memory?
The Holocaust and Pressure
Group Politics

Tony Kushner

James Young has written with regard to the work of Sylvia Plath:

> To remove the Holocaust from the realm of imagination ... to sanctify
> and place it off-limits, is to risk excluding it altogether from public
> consciousness. And this seems to be too high a price to pay for saving it
> from those who would abuse its memory in inequitable metaphor.
> Better abused memory in this case, which might then be critically
> qualified, than no memory at all.[1]

This chapter will explore the issues raised by Young through several case studies,
which have evolved a quarter of a century after the end of the Second World War,
involving what can be generally described as pressure group politics. The subject
matter of these debates can all be linked to 'progressive' causes: anti-racism and
campaigns on behalf of immigrants and refugees. Space will only permit passing
reference to other issues such as the welfare of animals and the need for
Holocaust education/museums. The memory of the Holocaust has, of course,
been central to the last-mentioned, but it has also surfaced in a critical manner in
the others. What follows then is an analysis of the legitimacy of using the history
and memory of the Holocaust in the political sphere in the postwar world. Is it
automatically illegitimate to use references to the murder of the Jews even if it is
to achieve a worthy moral goal? Or can or even must there be lessons from the
Shoah that speak to problems faced by modern society?

The destruction of the Jews was a central core of Nazi ideology and then
practice, even if historians legitimately debate about the place of antisemitism in
Hitler's electoral success. The Second World War also witnessed the
intensification of antisemitic tendencies present since the late nineteenth century
and before in the state policies of many countries within the Nazi area of
influence.[2] It is, however, one of the most troubling features of internal and

---

1 James Young, *Writing and Rewriting the Holocaust: Narrative and the
Consequences of Interpretation* (Bloomington, IN: Indiana University Press, 1988), p.133.

2 Although now dated, Michael Marrus, *The Holocaust in History* (London:
Weidenfeld & Nicolson, 1988) remains the best overview of the historiographical debate.
See also Donald Bloxham and Tony Kushner, *The Holocaust* (Manchester: Manchester
University Press, 2004).

external politics of the Western Allies (and, of course, even more so, the Soviet Union) that the fate of the Jews was so underdeveloped. The issue surfaced once and briefly on an international level with the Allied Declaration on behalf of persecuted Jewry in December 1942 (the result of Jewish, Christian and Polish lobbying), but the resultant Bermuda Conference was largely hidden from the public gaze. Its results were meagre and all official references to it deliberately refrained from highlighting Jewish suffering.[3] Moreover, on a domestic political level, only at one time and in one country in the Allied world did the murder of European Jewry threaten to become a national political issue. Faced with the prospect of embarrassing revelations about State Department inaction on circulating and responding to the news of the 'Final Solution', President Roosevelt was pressurised into creating the War Refugee Board, whose particular function was to explore by all means the rescue and relief of persecuted Jews.[4]

Even at the end of the war the tragedy of European Jewry remained outside the political arena. It is true that in Britain, the left–liberal world utilised the revealed horrors of the liberated Western concentration camps to condemn what they saw as the moral failure of Conservative appeasement during the 1930s. In this case, however, the emphasis was placed on the *continuities* in Nazi policy: it was stressed that the nature of camps such as Buchenwald and Dachau had been known about, through publicity by progressive forces, before the war, yet this had not stopped 'the men of Munich', or 'the guilty men' as they became known, from doing business with Herr Hitler. The early Nazi camps were particularly connected, not inaccurately, with victims on the left. This, plus the failure to recognise that a new development of concentration camps during the war, whose function was mass murder, led to a failure to recognise the specific extermination of European Jewry.[5] With more puerility and no success, Winston Churchill 'in a sudden descent to the bottom of the electoral barrel' warned in his first election broadcast in 1945 that the Labour Party programme would impose a Gestapo state on Britain.[6]

At an international level this lacuna continued with the war trials immediately

---

3   Bernard Wasserstein, *Britain and the Jews of Europe 1939–1945* (Oxford, Oxford University Press, 1979), pp.169–221; Tony Kushner, *The Holocaust and the Liberal Imagination: A Social and Cultural History* (Oxford: Blackwell, 1984), part 2; Louise London, *Whitehall and the Jews 1933–1948: British Immigration Policy and the Holocaust* (Cambridge: Cambridge University Press, 2000); David Engel, *In the Shadow of Auschwitz: The Polish Government-in-Exile and the Jews, 1939–1942* (Chapel Hill, NC: University of North Carolina Press, 1987).

4   Richard Breitman and Alan Kraut, *American Refugee Policy and European Jewry, 1933–1945* (Bloomington, IN: Indiana University Press, 1987), chs 9 and 10.

5   Kushner, *The Holocaust and the Liberal Imagination*, p.217.

6   Paul Addison, *The Road to 1945* (London, Jonathan Cape, 1975), p.265, who comments through Mass-Observation reports on how the speech caused 'disappointment and genuine distress'.

after the conflict had ended. At best, the destruction of the Jews was a marginal theme at the Nuremberg and other trials, even if the evidence collected there would form the basis of early histories of the Holocaust.[7] In short, the Holocaust would have been difficult to politicise for any purpose, even if nations, groups or individuals had wanted to do so, because the very concept of a discrete Jewish tragedy remained to be fully crystallised in the immediate postwar period.

This was true even of much Zionist politics with perhaps the major exception of the progressive World Jewish Congress, which had been so influential in passing on the news of the extermination plan in the war.[8] The emphasis throughout the conflict in 'free world' Zionism, including in Palestine, had been first and foremost on the need to establish a postwar Jewish state. There was of course stress on Jewish immigration to Palestine and thereby the growing conflict with Britain.[9] After the war, as Jewish–British tensions grew, a Holocaust rhetoric developed within Zionist rhetoric to attack Britain, which included comparisons between the British Foreign Secretary, Ernest Bevin, and Hitler.[10] They did not end in 1948. Eight years later, in the middle of the Suez Crisis, David Ben-Gurion responded to the pleas of Labour left-wingers for Israeli restraint by a blatant invocation of Holocaust memory:

> We still recall that there were leaders of the Labour Party who did not take seriously Hitler's threats physically to exterminate the Jewish race until it was too late. Six million Jews perished in the gas chambers of the Nazi dictator. I am sorry that you do not see the dangers of the Fascist dictator of Egypt.[11]

In the late 1950s and particularly after the Eichmann trial in Jerusalem and then the Auschwitz trials in Germany during the 1960s, and also thanks to the persistence of survivors such as Elie Wiesel, a better understanding of the unique enormity of the destruction inflicted on the Jews entered general consciousness and the term 'Holocaust' came into popular usage. Nevertheless this awareness had immense regional and national variations. In Britain, for example, as a result of the tiny size

---

7   Donald Bloxham, *Genocide on Trial: War Crimes Trials and the Formation of Holocaust History and Memory* (Oxford: Oxford University Press, 2001). For a different perspective, see Michael Marrus, 'The Holocaust at Nuremberg', *Yad Vashem Studies*, vol.26 (1998), 5–41.

8   See, for example, World Jewish Congress (British Section), *Bermuda – and after* (London: World Jewish Congress, 1943).

9   Dina Porat, *The Blue and the Yellow Stars of David: The Zionist Leadership in Palestine and the Holocaust* (Cambridge, MA: Harvard University Press, 1990).

10   Alan Bullock, *Ernest Bevin: Foreign Secretary* (London, Heinemann, 1984), p.164.

11   Ben Gurion to Tony Benn, Sydney Silverman, Ian Mikardo and two other Labour MPs, 3 November 1956, quoted in Jad Adams, *Tony Benn* (London, Macmillan, 1992), p.122. See David Ben-Gurion, *Reply to Bevin* (no publisher, 1946) based on a speech given on 28 November 1945.

and marginalisation of survivors, the avoidance of the subject by other Jews as a result of their insecurity in a liberal society intolerant of difference (what Bill Williams has dubbed the 'the antisemitism of toleration') and the preciousness of the specific British war memory, consideration of the Holocaust was particularly underdeveloped.[12] There were outlets for the study of the Holocaust and the publication of research, autobiography and literature on it such as the Wiener Library and its *Bulletin*, *The Jewish Quarterly* and Vallentine, Mitchell (the last of which were to publish *The Diary of Anne Frank* for the first time in English in 1952).[13] Yet it remains that those interested were largely outside the mainstream of British culture. The situation was not much different in the USA, except that the memory of the war was less significant in the formation of contemporary national identities and the survivor community was larger.[14] The centrality of war memory in the British case was made clear in 1970 when, for the first time since 1945, an explicit link was made between internal British politics and Nazi atrocities in the concentration camps.

The 1960s had witnessed the failure of both major political parties in Britain to deal with problems of racism and immigration. There was, by 1963, a consensus on the need for controls specifically aimed particularly at black migrants, although this was always publicly denied. The Labour Party was more committed to anti-discrimination legislation but the legislation it produced in the form of the Race Relations Acts of 1965 and 1968 tended in practice to deal only with blatant and extreme cases rather than the ordinary day to day problems faced by racial minorities in Britain.[15] There was, in fact, a legacy from earlier debates dating from the 1930s when sections of the Jewish community and its supporters demanded legislation to protect Jews from libel and physical attack from fascist and antisemitic organisations. Dealing with racism that could somehow be seen as Nazi-inspired and therefore unBritish was less threatening to the national esteem, although liberal considerations of freedom of speech and the reluctance to single out minorities for particular protection for fear of making matters worse meant that no legislation was ever agreed.[16]

---

12   Kushner, *The Holocaust and the Liberal Imagination*, ch. 7; Bill Williams, 'The Anti-Semitism of Tolerance: Middle-Class Manchester and the Jews, 1870–1900', in A.J.Kidd and K.W.Roberts (eds), *City, Class and Culture* (Manchester: Manchester University Press, 1985), pp.75–102.

13   See, for example, Natasha Lehrer (ed.), *The Golden Chain: Fifty Years of the Jewish Quarterly* (London: Vallentine Mitchell, 2003) on its engagement with the history and representation of the Holocaust.

14   For the construction of memory in Britain and the USA, respectively, see the contributions of David Cesarani and David Wyman in David Wyman (ed.), *The World Reacts to the Holocaust* (Baltimore, MD: Johns Hopkins University Press, 1996), pp.599–641 and 693–748.

15   See John Solomos, *Race and Racism in Contemporary Britain*, 2nd edn, (London: Macmillan, 1993).

16   See PRO HO 45/25398 and Board of Deputies of British Jews archive, C4/1 and 2; C6/7/3/2.

A problem emerged in 1967 and 1968, when several prominent Conservative politicians, and especially Enoch Powell, began their concerted attempt to make what they called 'race' the central issue of British politics. Powell, after his notorious 'Rivers of Blood' speech in Birmingham in April 1968, was sacked from the Conservative shadow cabinet by Tory leader Edward Heath. Powell was attacked for the extremity of his language, particularly by *The Times*.[17] He was not, however, prosecuted in 1968 or beyond under the clauses of the Race Relations Acts relating to using language likely to provoke racial tension. Furthermore Powell can take little responsibility for the ease of conscience with which the Labour Party passed the second Commonwealth Immigration Act in February 1968, aimed explicitly at stopping the feared flood of Kenyan Asians with British passports from entering the UK. Indeed both parties were committed to extending immigration controls, which remained their key response to dealing with the 'race' problem in Britain.[18]

Underlying Powell's speeches in 1968 and responses to them was the memory of the Second World War. Powell's use of a mythical woman old age pensioner in Wolverhampton who was now the only white person in her street was at the heart of his Birmingham speech. This, according to Powell, was her story:

> She lost her husband and both her sons in the war. So she turned her
> seven-roomed house, her only asset, into a boarding-house. She worked
> hard and did well, paid off her mortgage and began to put something by
> for her old age. Then the immigrants moved in. With growing fear, she
> saw one house after another taken over. The quiet street became a place
> of noise and confusion. Regretfully, her white tenants moved out ...
> She is becoming afraid to go out ... She finds excreta pushed through
> her letter-box. When she goes to the shops, she is followed by children,
> charming, wide-grinning piccaninnies. They cannot speak English, but
> one word they know. 'Racialist,' they chant. When the new Race
> Relations Bill is passed, this woman is convinced she will go to prison.
> And is she so wrong? I begin to wonder.[19]

The social anthropology of this story is important. Variations of it were told across the country. It was what would now be seen as a classic urban myth with the key features of the honest hard-working war widow whose neighbourhood is invaded and overtaken by black aliens remaining central throughout.[20]

Heath's response to Powell – sacking him as shadow secretary of state for

---

17   *The Times*, 27 April 1968 editorial, 'Appeal for Tolerance'. The Birmingham speech is reproduced in Bill Smithies and Peter Fiddick, *Enoch Powell on Immigration* (London: Sphere Books, 1969).

18   Ann Dummett and Andrew Nichol, *Subjects, Citizens, Aliens and Others: Nationality and Immigration Law* (London, Weidenfeld & Nicolson, 1990), ch. 11. See also Shamit Saggar, *Race and Politics in Britain* (London and New York: Harvester Wheatsheaf, 1992), pp.113–16.

19   Reproduced in Smithies and Fiddick, *Enoch Powell on Immigration*, p.41.

20   Ibid, pp.59–60; *The Times*, 24 April and 8 May 1968.

defence – has been seen as opportunistic, as the latter was seen as a rival for the former: 'the events did provide an opportunity for him to sideline the man who had slowly become the main threat to his authority in the [Conservative] party'.[21] It did not stop Heath sponsoring the 1971 Immigration Act, which included many softened Powellite tendencies including support for voluntary repatriation and patrial preference.[22] And yet Heath was also genuinely appalled at the ferocity of Powell's language and his blatant singling out of a racial minority: 'That way lies tyranny, and it must be fought wherever it raises its ugly presence. It had to be fought in Germany in the 1930s, in America in the 1950s, and wherever it happens today it must be fought.'[23] Here Heath was offering a different memory and interpretation of the Nazi era and beyond. Rather than seeing the legacy of the war, as articulated by Powell, as decline from imperial greatness to multiracial degeneracy, Heath, if only obliquely, was suggesting a different tradition of resistance to the excesses of racism if left untamed.

Beyond 1968, Powell remained an outsider in terms of British power politics although his influence continued on a popular level and also in setting a framework of exclusive, new right Englishness for later politicians to follow, most significantly Margaret Thatcher.[24] Powell persevered obsessively with the race theme and it was no surprise in the 1970 general election that he produced his own manifesto, the major theme of which, apart from his opposition to Britain joining what was the EEC, was a call for a complete halt to Commonwealth immigration (including the spouses and children of those already here), a new citizenship law to distinguish between people who 'belonged' to the UK and the rest of the world, and voluntary repatriation. Such measures were designed to avoid 'a threat of division, violence and bloodshed of American dimensions'.[25] Powell received relatively little media attention and the hope of both Labour and Conservative party leaders that 'race' could be kept out of the election appeared to be succeeding. Four days later, however, the Minister for Technology, Tony Benn, set the election campaign alight in an unrestrained and massively publicised speech.

Benn's presentation to a student audience only dealt in passing with Powell,

21 Simon Heffer, *Like the Roman: The Life of Enoch Powell* (London, Weidenfeld & Nicolson, 1998), p.459.

22 Dummett and Nichol, *Subjects, Citizens, Aliens and Others*, pp.216–27.

23 *The Times*, 18 November 1968, in response to Powell's speech in Eastbourne.

24 See especially Paul Gilroy, *There Ain't No Black in the Union Jack: the Cultural Politics of Race and Nation* (London, Hutchinson, 1987), ch. 2; Tom Nairn, *The Break-up of Britain*, 2nd edn (London: Verso, 1981), ch. 6; Patrick Wright, *On Living in an Old Country: The National Past in Contemporary Britain* (London, Verso, 1985), p.179.

25 Douglas Schoen, *Enoch Powell and the Powellites* (London, Macmillan, 1977), ch. 3; John Wood (ed.), *Powell and the 1970 General Election* (Kingswood, Surrey: Paperfront, 1970).

but it was the two or three minutes of concerted attack on the maverick Tory that received all the attention:

> The flag of racialism which has been hoisted in Wolverhampton
> [Powell's constituency] is beginning to look like the one that fluttered
> 25 years ago over Dachau and Belsen. If we do not speak up now
> against the filthy and obscene racialist propaganda, still being issued
> under the imprint of Conservative Central Office, the focus of hatred
> will mark up their first success and mobilize for the next offensive ...
> Already Powell has spoken against the Irish. Anti-semitism is waiting
> to be exploited as Mosley exploited it before.[26]

On the surface, the critique, drawing heavily on the Second World War, echoed that of Edward Heath made less than two years earlier. Yet, whilst the latter had been commended by both sides of the political spectrum, Benn faced an avalanche of criticism, including some from within his own party. Benn, although not yet the full-blown Labour radical of the 1980s, was accused of opportunism and, much worse, was seen to have committed an unpardonable sin: abusing the memory of the Second World War.

To understand the emotions unleashed by Tony Benn, it is essential to take account of the critical importance of Belsen in the formation of British postwar national identity. Belsen, as the only major concentration camp liberated by the British, represented both what Britain had been fighting against *and* the moral integrity of the British war effort. Although the war was to continue for nearly a month, the liberation of Belsen by the British army marked a symbolic ending of the Second World War.[27] Quite simply, by connecting the horrors of the Nazi camps with mainstream British politics on race, Benn was in essence accused of tarnishing not only the Conservative Party but also Britain's special relationship with the Second World War. Benn's comments need to placed alongside those of Colonel Bird when burning down the last of the huts at Belsen, alongside an Iron Cross flag and portrait of Hitler, in May 1945:

> I cannot help feeling ... that in the razing to the ground by fire of this
> pestilence-ridden camp there is a great symbol. It is, I feel, a symbol of
> the final destruction for all time of the bestial, inhuman creed of Nazi
> Germany; the creed by which criminals tried to debase the peoples of
> Europe to serve their own devilish ends.

Simultaneously, the British troops hoisted a Union Jack which, as Bird continued,

---

26   Denis Taylor, 'Onslaught on Powell by Wedgwood Benn', *The Times*, 4 June 1970. The speech was reported in detail in most of the British national press – Benn had put out a press release beforehand. See Tony Benn, *Office Without Power: Diaries 1968–72* (London: Hutchinson, 1988), p.287, entry for 3 June 1970.

27   See Tony Kushner, 'The Memory of Belsen', in Jo Reilly, David Cesarani, Tony Kushner and Colin Richmond (eds), *Belsen in History and Memory* (London: Frank Cass, 1997), pp.181–205.

had never stood for cruelty and bestiality. That is why it has never yet
flown over Belsen Camp. It will fly in a few moments. There too is a
symbol; the symbol of the completion of the great task of liberation for
which the Allied Nations have striven for six long years, the completion
of the task begun by the British Liberation Army when it landed on the
beaches of Normandy on June 6th [1944], and the completion, in
particular, of the grim but inspiring task with which units of the 2nd
Army were confronted here a short while ago.[28]

Not surprisingly, therefore, Tony Benn received what he described as very
unpleasant letters 'stressing the theme of patriotism, how Powell was a Christian
gentleman and how the last war against Hitler had been a patriotic war'.[29] It is no
accident that, whilst Benn referred to Dachau first and Belsen later, and then on
the radio two days later emphasised the former camp, references were made only
to his 'Belsen speech'.[30] And although most but not all national newspapers
distanced themselves from Powell's stance on immigration and race, the
Conservative MP's response to Benn's attack was widely and supportively
published: 'In 1939 I voluntarily returned from Australia to this country to serve
as a private in the war against Germany and nazism. I am the same man today.'[31]
Powell, too, could instrumentalise the memory of the Second World War for his
own ends – far more successfully in this case than Tony Benn.[32]

What then was the impact of Benn's attack on Powell's racism? Was it an
abuse of Holocaust memory or a legitimate if somewhat crude and simplistic
evocation and utilisation of the past to confront the intolerance of the present?
One basic measure is the effect it had on the General Election of 1970. Given the
expected easy Labour victory and subsequent Conservative success, it is not
surprising that Benn was widely blamed within and outside his party for the
unexpected defeat. The race card, it was argued, had lost Labour the support of
some working-class voters in key marginal constituencies who feared that
Labour were going to be 'soft' on immigration. Four years later, in the run-up to
the next general election, Labour leader Harold Wilson warned senior members
of his party to 'Ignore Enoch Powell, because last time the attack on him [by
Tony Benn] lost [us] five seats.'[33] There were certainly some Conservatives who

---

28   Derrick Sington, *Belsen Uncovered* (London: Duckworth, 1946), p.149.

29   Benn, *Office Without Power*, p.289, entry for 8 June 1970.

30   BBC radio, *Any Questions?*, 5 June 1970; Benn, *Office Without Power*,
p.288 diary entry of 4 June 1970; John Whale, 'What the Papers Say', *Sunday Times*, 7
June 1970 outlines how six daily papers led with the 'Belsen flag' attack on Powell.

31   See, for example, *Daily Mirror*, 4 June 1970.

32   Heffer, *Like the Roman*, ch. 3 and pp.556–7.

33   On the impact of immigration on the 1970 election, see Zig Layton-Henry,
*The Politics of Immigration: Immigration, 'Race' and 'Race' Relations in Post-War
Britain* (Oxford: Blackwell, 1992), pp.83–7; David Butler and Michael Pinto-Duschinsky,
The British General Election of 1970 (London, Macmillan, 1971), pp.160–61, 208–9,
252–5; Schoen, *Enoch Powell and the Powellites*, ch. 3.; Wilson, quoted in Tony Benn,

were anxious to give that impression. It is surely no accident that the only two national newspapers not to lead or give prominence to the Benn onslaught on Powell were at the heart of the campaign to intensify immigration controls: the *Daily Mail* and the *Daily Express*. Indeed the *Express* added an utterly unsupported line to the Benn speech that 'The question raised is whether Labour is contemplating a greatly relaxed immigration policy after the General Election.'[34] Benn, in fact, had supported the Labour party line that good race relations depended in part on immigration controls alongside anti-discrimination legislation. As a *Times* leader reminded its readers, when it had come to the Bill to exclude Kenyan Asians in 1968, Mr Benn 'happily remained a member of the Government which passed that Act'.[35] There were certainly those who wrote to Powell claiming that they were so

> roused by Wedgwood Benn's immoderate attack on you, I placed my cross not for the Conservative candidate, not for the party of Ted Heath, but, in sympathy with you, for the party of Enoch Powell. I suspect there are many more like me in constituencies where it did count who did the same. Hence the victory.[36]

In reality, the impact of Benn's speech was more complex. There were less than a handful of marginal seats with candidates of a Powellite persuasion. These were more than matched by the twenty-five marginal constituencies in which Afro-Caribbean, Asian and white ethnic minorities played a key role.[37] There is no doubt that Benn's interest in highlighting the dangers of racism was appreciated by many non-whites in Britain and confirmed their support for the Labour Party. Tony Benn wrote in his diary that although two-thirds of the many people writing to him after the speech were against him, there were 'some very sympathetic ones saying that my speech was overdue, the first speech that indicated the deep feeling of black people about racism'.[38] It is possible that aside from the question of marginal seats in which the evidence works against a negative Benn factor, the prominence he gave to Powell helped to alienate further previous Labour supporters, but there were far too many other factors at work during the election, even if this was its most prominent media moment, to

---

Against the Tide: diaries 1973–76 (London: Arrow Books, 1990), p.91, entry for 16 January 1974.

34   *Daily Mail*, 4 June 1970; *Daily Express*, 5 June 1970.

35   Editorial, 'Mr Benn Makes an issue of race', *The Times*, 5 June 1970.

36   Letter from Brigg, Lincolnshire in Wood (ed.), *Powell and the 1970 General Election*, p.31.

37   Schoen, *Enoch Powell and the Powellites*, pp.55–67, argues that Powell's role 'was quite possibly decisive in the Tories' election triumph'; for an alternative analysis, see Nicholas Deakin and Jenny Bourne, 'The Minorities and the General Election, 1970', *Race Today*, 2.7 (July 1970) and Lewis Chester, 'The Black Backlash', *Sunday Times*, 7 June 1970.

38   Benn, *Office Without Power*, p.289, entry for 8 June 1970.

evaluate in electoral terms the impact of Benn's 'Dachau and Belsen' intervention. As the political commentator Peter Jennings put it: 'The effect could not be measured; it felt important.[39]' Was it, however, a useful contribution beyond the impact it did, or did not, make at a political level?

Tony Benn was clear in his own mind of his intentions in what was very much a premeditated speech:

> The truth is that Harold [Wilson, the Labour Prime Minister] had hoped to keep race out of the Election. But an issue as important as this can't be left out, because an election is a period when the public engages in a great debate about its future and as race is one of the most important questions in the future, it is quite wrong to try to keep it quiet.[40]

Benn was not mistaken about the desire of the Labour Party to avoid the race question – it was an open secret[41] – but did he succeed in opening up the debate constructively by his use of Nazi analogies?

To analyse this further, it is necessary to examine first why Tony Benn chose the words that he did. The public explanation given by the Labour politician was that the thing that moved him more deeply than anything that had happened to him was the event of Dachau and Belsen. He remembered Mosley and the Blackshirts and what was said about Hitler in the 1930s.[42] In his diary, Benn, clearly worried that he had gone too far, was encouraged that Doug Constable, a curate in Bristol and a good friend of his in the local Labour Party, 'was in favour of the words I used on the grounds that if you were going to fight evil, you had to use fairly strong weapons'.[43] But what did 'the event of Dachau and Belsen' mean to Benn? Did he, for example, have in mind particularly the attempted genocide against the Jews (in which Dachau, the first Nazi camp which was set up in 1933 against *political* opponents of the regime, was of relatively limited significance) or something more general, reflecting the contemporary importance of Dachau in left wing circles as a symbol of the reactionary and anti-leftwing nature of the Third Reich?[44]

Tony Benn, especially through his mother Lady Stansgate, a prominent member of the Council of Christians and Jews and also a trustee of the Parkes Library in the 1960s, was familiar from an early age with Jewish issues,

---

39   Jennings, in *Encounter*, 35.2 (August 1970), 15.

40   Benn, *Office Without Power*, p.288, entry for 5 June 1970.

41   See Deakin and Bourne, 'The Minorities and the General Election'; Richard Crossman, *The Diaries of a Cabinet Minister*, vol.3, *Secretary of State for Social Services 1968–70* (London: Hamish Hamilton and Jonathan Cape, 1977), p.939, entry for 7 June 1970, which quotes Wilson as stating, 'the Campaign Committee had decided they wouldn't play up Enoch Powell and now Benn has gone completely against the directive'.

42   Benn, on *Any Questions?*, 5 June 1970.

43   Benn, *Office Without Power*, p.288, entry for 5 June 1970.

44   World Committee for the Victims of German Fascism, *The Brown Book of the Hitler Terror* (London: Gollancz, 1933), ch. 11.

including the 1930s refugee crisis.[45] He had, however, no direct connections to the camp liberations in 1945, being on active service in the Middle East. In fact, it must be argued, his use of Holocaust-related imagery owed as much to a left-wing romantic anti-fascist reconstruction of the British war effort as it did to honouring the memory of the murdered Jews. He thus resented the idea that the conflict had been merely a nationalistic one, which would lose sight of its also 'having been a moral war against the racialism of the Nazis'.[46] There is no doubting Benn's genuine horror at the persecution of the Jews, but he remained hazy about the specific history of the Holocaust. Twelve years later, at a time of labour strife in Britain, he attacked journalists who refused to write independently of those who employed them: 'Their role could be likened to the Jews in Dachau who herded other Jews into the gas chambers.'[47] Aside from the inappropriateness of this comparison, it is also notable for revealing a common misconception in British culture – that the western as opposed to eastern Nazi camps contained mass extermination facilities. Benn, though emotionally engaged in learning 'the lessons' of the Holocaust, attempted to appropriate its memory through progressive patriotism. It was an instrumentalisation that was almost inevitably problematic because of his simplistic and often factually incorrect understanding of the subject matter.

From the perspective of the dawning of a new century, when Holocaust remembrance and awareness has developed spectacularly, even in Britain, compared to three decades earlier, it is remarkable that, in all the criticisms aimed at Tony Benn, not once in 1970 was he accused of besmirching the memory of Holocaust victims. No Jewish publication mentioned his speech even though it was covered exhaustively in the media as a whole. It was only the British war memory that had been affronted. In April 1970, five thousand people gathered at Bergen-Belsen concentration camp for a memorial ceremony, one in a series of small-scale events that had occurred since the end of the war. The West German President Gustav Heinemann stated that 'the names of Bergen-Belsen and the other concentration camps have not lost their terrible meaning' and accepted that 'Germany bears the responsibility for what happened here'.[48] In Britain, however, as the *Jewish Quarterly* pointed out:

> The 25th anniversary of the liberation by the Allies of the Nazi camps
> has passed almost unnoticed. Yet it is a date which must not be
> forgotten. The survivors who emerged from the camps, often crippled
> in spirit and body, looked at their own shattered world, hardly
> comprehending what had happened to them, and even less

---

45   See Adams, passim; *Guardian* obituary of Lady Stansgate, 23 October 1991, and correspondence in Parkes papers, University of Southampton archive.

46   Benn, *Office Without Power*, p.289, entry for 8 June 1970.

47   Reported in *The Times*, 26 January 1982. I am grateful to Jad Adams for supplying me with relevant material on this incident.

48   Reported in Association of Jewish Refugees, *Information*, June 1970.

comprehending the world at large which appeared eager to forget, and refused to be reminded of, this darkest chapter in recent history.

It thus dedicated its issue of summer 1970, consisting of Holocaust testimony, poetry, songs and stories, 'to the memory of the murdered millions, and to the courage of the survivors to start a new life'.[49] The special issue coincided with the General Election, but the milieu of the *Jewish Quarterly* and the cultural environment of British politics were worlds apart. There was little specific or detailed knowledge of the Holocaust in British society and culture, certainly not enough, say, to differentiate between the function and history of camps such as Dachau, Belsen and Auschwitz. In Britain, Belsen had by far the most resonance, the images from the newsreels, radio and newspaper reports having left a deep impact on the British psyche, presumably as was the case with Tony Benn. But who were these victims? The poet and writer Mervyn Peake, who witnessed the early scenes of liberation, was one of the few to reflect on this question and to have the self-honesty to realise that he could not see them as human beings deserving compassion.[50] Thus, when the comment was made on Benn that his analogy was 'irresponsible and untrue', the concern was not over the memory of the piles of corpses and skeleton survivors at Dachau and Belsen but the 'guttersnipe abuse' which had left Powell, Heath and the Conservatives 'vilely slandered'.[51]

In his public defence of his speech, Benn had hoped to show that 'once you embark on racialism, where is it going to end?' He added, ' I have always asked the question: if this were to start here when should we try to stop it?'[52] Only one contemporary commentator, Tom Baistow in the left-wing *New Statesman*, supported Benn's reasoning and the exception was to be explained by the life history of the individual concerned:

> Mr Wedgwood Benn used the lurid Nazi analogy to shock people into awareness of what race-consciousness can lead to. Perhaps I have an unfair advantage … in that I visited Germany in the Thirties and saw the first baiting of the Jews ('unassimilable aliens who can never be true Germans') and 10 years later entered Belsen at its liberation to find the logical conclusion to that kind of *untermenschen* philosophy.[53]

A problem remains, however, with Benn's analysis and Baistow's support of it. In both, the danger of racism in Britain remains in the future. On one level Benn was trying to explode the myth of British decency and fairness by saying

---

49   *Jewish Quarterly*, 18.2 (Summer 1970), 23.

50   See Joanne Reilly, *Belsen: The Liberation of a Concentration Camp* (London: Routledge, 1998), p.30.

51   Editorials in *The Times*, 5 June 1970 and *Daily Telegraph*, 5 June 1970.

52   Benn on *Any Questions?* and in a speech at Weston-super-Mare reported in *The Times*, 5 June 1970.

53   *New Statesman*, 12 June 1970.

it could happen here. On another, he was marginalising that threat by evoking the memory of racism/fanaticism in its most extreme form in the modern era. The issue would arise later in the 1970s when the neo-nazi National Front briefly threatened to become the fourth force in British politics. From the perspective of the time, as the novelist Hanif Kureishi has written in *The Buddha of Suburbia* (1990), the prospect of white people in Britain turning

> on the blacks and Asians and … forc[ing] us into gas chambers or
> push[ing] us into leaking boats … wasn't as ludicrous as it sounded…
> At night [the neo-fascist groups] roamed the streets, beating Asians and
> shoving shit and burning rags through their letter-boxes … There was
> no evidence that these people would go away – no evidence that their
> power would diminish rather than increase.[54]

This perhaps explains why all energy was concentrated by its opponents in declaring that the 'National Front was a Nazi Front'. Nevertheless, once the electoral threat of the Front had passed, the wider problem of non-extremist (including state) racism and discrimination remained. In particular, as Paul Gilroy and others have argued, the Anti-Nazi League, by concentrating on a form of racism that could be readily identified with Britain's former enemy, reinforced a patriotic xenophobia generated by war memories which actually worked against the security of New Commonwealth immigrants. This hostility, in which culture rather than biology was seen as the key to difference, had as its main spokesman and populariser Enoch Powell.[55]

In fact, the Gilroy critique was anticipated by the liberal *Guardian* after Benn's speech in an editorial entitled 'Belated sledgehammer':

> It is easy to brand Mr Powell as a way-out extremist who is not
> integrated into the mainstream of British life, a kind of political alien.
> The sad thing is that Mr Powell does strike a chord for many people.
> Not only that, but he has managed to swing the whole immigration
> issue his way, and that includes the Labour Party …
>
> Britain has a long tradition of what might be called 'lace curtain
> racialism', or how to keep inferior breeds down without hurting their
> feelings by saying 'no' to them outright … Mr Powell's sin was to strip
> the curtain off. Racialism is a deeper, more unpleasant and more
> pervasive phenemenon than Mr Benn implies. It is not so alien to parts
> of the Labour Party.[56]

It is at this point that the context of the Powell/Benn conflict in terms of British 'race relations' in 1970 should be made clear. Although these were the early days of the National Front, some of whose skinhead supporters acted as

---

54   Hanif Kureishi, *The Buddha of Suburbia* (London: Faber & Faber, 1990), p.4.

55   Gilroy, *There Ain't No Black*, chs 2 and 4.

56   *The Guardian*, 5 June 1970.

unofficial bodyguards to Enoch Powell in the election campaign, it was the heyday of what was known as 'Paki-bashing'. As one Liberal candidate put it at the election: 'The main difference between Mr Enoch Powell and the skinheads is that he does his Paki-bashing verbally and they do theirs physically. Clearly they are going to derive encouragement from his ... views on immigration.'[57] To put this on an individual level, the film maker John Akomfrah relates the impact Powellism had on him as a youngster at a street level in West London at this time: 'Neighbours told me I couldn't possibly be black and British ... I grew up listening to Powell being quoted by every street corner race expert as the last word on Englishness.'[58]

More drastically, racial violence increased markedly after every major Powell speech on the alleged dangers represented by New Commonwealth immigrants. Racial violence, although not monitored as it is today, was part of everyday life for British black people in 1970.[59] This, plus endemic discrimination and the general sense of unwelcome was leading to more West Indians leaving Britain by the end of the 1960s than coming in.[60] And as *The Guardian* pointed out, both Labour and Conservatives in power had legislated to keep black people out of the country. The problem with Benn's Holocaust analogy was not that it was *necessarily* inappropriate in pointing out what uncontrolled hatred could lead to, but that it failed to do justice to the very real problems faced by minorities in Britain when he gave his speech.[61] It also, however, exposed the deep ignorance within British society about the Holocaust. Nowhere was this exposed more crudely than in the monthly journal of the Institute of Race Relations, *Race Today*:

> Nothing could ever justify what happened at Dachau and Belsen, but death would be more merciful than the proposed financial inducement to encouragement 'repatriation' to countries of origin where chronic mass unemployment and under-employment deny the majority of people ... an opportunity to provide for their basic human needs as outlined in the United Nations Declaration of Human Rights.[62]

Twenty-four years later, some of the same issues, with a different emphasis, re-emerged in a heated debate about Britain's immigration, asylum and nationality policies. The Churches Commission for Racial Justice published a

---

57   Ernest Palfrey, letter to *Daily Telegraph*, 5 June 1970.

58   John Akomfrah, 'A Touch of the Tar Brush', Black Audio Film Collective for BBC, 1991.

59   Layton-Henry, *The Politics of Immigration*, pp.125–6; Benjamin Bowling, 'The emergence of violent racism as a public issue in Britain, 1945–81', in Panikos Panayi (ed.), *Racial Violence in Britain in the Nineteenth and Twentieth Centuries*, 2nd edn (London: Leicester University Press, 1996), pp.193–6.

60   Phil Sealy, 'Repatriation and the Numbers Game', *Race Today*, July 1970.

61   *The Guardian*, 5 June 1970.

62   Sealy, 'Repatriation and the Numbers Game'.

booklet, *Breaking Up the Family*, highlighting twenty families some of whose members were threatened with deportation.[63] According to one of its authors, Revd Theo Samuel, Moderator of the Churches Commission for Racial Justice, the 'booklet illustrate[d] just a little of the misery people face in the present immigration system. It is a modern form of the terror Jewish families faced under the Third Reich'. The Revd Dr Leslie Griffiths, President of the Methodist Conference, added, in relation to the story of a young Nigerian girl who faced an early death if deported, that the administrators of the law were stressing that 'Rules are the Rules, and go she must'. Griffiths commented that 'These are the thought patterns of the Gestapo.'[64]

These remarks led to a media storm but, unlike that nearly a quarter of a century earlier, some of the comments, such as that by columnist Bernard Levin, were that the comparisons 'cheapened, soiled, diminished and tainted the deaths of six million Jews'.[65] Nevertheless the majority of comments made were to defend Britain's record against the 'profoundly offensive', 'distorted' 'obscene rubbish' offered by Samuel and Griffiths. On the BBC Radio's flagship, *Moral Maze*, all the resident experts, including the Holocaust survivor Hugo Gryn, stated not only that the analogy was false but also that Britain's immigration policies, whilst firm, were also fair.[66]

Should we conclude then that utilising the memory of the Holocaust has no place in politics, no matter how just the cause (including fighting racism)? Are we better, as Elie Wiesel suggests, with silence rather than any risk of abusing the memory of the victims?[67] We are back with James Young's conundrum with which we started. It is clear even with the progress made in Holocaust education in recent years and films such as *Schindler's List* that there is massive ignorance of the hows and whens of the Holocaust and its devastating impact on the Jewish world. Thus whilst *Breaking Up the Family* made an explicit comparison to the Holocaust, it nevertheless exposed the same crudity of understanding illustrated by *Race Today* with the Benn–Powell debate a quarter of a century earlier.

Even from a self-interested point of view, campaigners should be wary of drawing upon the Holocaust when their claims can be so easily dismissed. In 1970, Auberon Waugh poked fun at Harold Wilson after the Benn speech, asking when he thought the Conservatives would establish concentration camps in Britain.[68] In 1994, another right-wing commentator more seriously pointed out

---

63   Churches Commission for Racial Justice, *Breaking Up the Family* (London: CCRJ, 1994).

64   Quoted in *The Runnymede Bulletin*, no.279 (October 1994), 6.

65   In *The Times*, 16 September 1994. See *Jewish Chronicle*, 30 September 1994 for Christian apologies to the Jewish community.

66   *Moral Maze*, BBC Radio 4, 8 September 1994.

67   See, for example, his 'Art and the Holocaust: Trivializing Memory', *New York Times*, 11 June 1989.

68   Waugh, quoted in Benn, *Office Without Power*, p.291, diary entry for 11 June 1970.

that, 'however rotten and cruel are the procedures of Britain's immigration laws, they do not include putting the would-be immigrants into gas chambers by the millions and there murdering them'.[69] In the confusion, hurt and anger of the Churches Commission report, the chance to compare meaningfully British refugee policy, including its moments of generosity and timidity, in the Nazi era with that in the 1990s was lost. And yet crass comparisons do not always fail to gain support, as those campaigning on behalf of exported animals from Britain going to the continent for slaughter revealed. Holocaust imagery and comparisons were made freely by animal rights activists who gained massive public support and some practical success.

One of the major prices to be paid for increased Holocaust awareness is such possible abuse as the writer and animal rights campaigner Carla Lane shouting, 'Murderers, the Nazis did this to the Jews'.[70] Better abused memory than none? Were Benn, Samuel and Griffiths wrong to draw the parallel? It is very easy with the Holocaust to stand on the moral high ground. Surely it was right for a prominent politician to be able to say that Powell's contributions to discussions over race were pernicious and for two prominent church figures to say that Britain's immigration and asylum policies were mean-spirited and in the worst tradition of British xenophobia and racism. Importantly black people who were bearing the brunt of governmental, state and popular racism whether in 1970 or 1994 gained heart from the parallels made with the Holocaust – a racism that could not be defended. Wiesel has stated that writing about the Holocaust acts as an 'invisible tombstone, erected to the memory of the dead unburied'.[71] The approach of Wiesel can come close to mystification in which the Holocaust becomes utterly beyond human comprehension: its subject matter, in his words, 'is made up of death and mystery, it slips away between our fingers, it runs faster than our perceptions'.[72] And yet Wiesel is surely right to demand a memorial process and engagement.

In 2000, the Imperial War Museum opened its permanent Holocaust exhibition. Its painstakingly detailed approach to the chronology and implementation of the 'Final Solution' will help the process of removing the all too easy assumption that 'we' know what happened during the Holocaust and, from there, to appropriating its memory for contemporary usage.[73] Nevertheless those responsible for the exhibition, in contrast to the Holocaust museum in

---

69   Bernard Levin in *The Times*, 16 September 1994.

70   Carla Lane, 'The song of Shoreham', *The Guardian*, 8 February 1995.

71   Quoted in Alvin Rosenfeld, *A Double Dying: Reflections on Holocaust Literature* (Bloomington, In: Indiana University Press, 1980), p.27.

72   Yehuda Bauer, 'Against Mystification', *The Holocaust in Historical Perspective* (London: Sheldon Press, 1978), pp.30–49; Wiesel, quoted by Rosenfeld, *A Double Dying*, p.6.

73   Steve Paulsson, *The Holocaust: The Holocaust Exhibition at the Imperial War Museum* (London: Imperial War Museum, 2000).

Washington, DC, largely eschew a memorial function. History without memorialisation of the victims is hard to justify, just as utilisation of the memory of the Holocaust without knowledge is equally inappropriate. Any reference to the Holocaust should first and foremost do justice to its victims, which is why it is unacceptable to compare Jews to animals awaiting slaughter. The Nazis referred to Jews as rats, lice, dogs. What is the difference? The six million were humans, not helpless animals or those carrying diseases. But surely part of honouring that memory is to ensure that no form of racism or intolerance continues in the world.

The Guardian in 1970 stated that 'What Mr Benn said needed saying, but sooner, more subtly, and more often.'[74] The problem remains that the obscenity of Auschwitz and the vileness of racism today cannot be said quietly. We still need to find ways of making connections between history and memory, then and now, that go beyond mere platitudes, and recognise, as Yehuda Bauer puts it, that 'The Holocaust has no end. We still live in a world in which the Holocaust took place. We do not deal with a past, but a present.'[75] Auschwitz is not, as one major British educational venture which tried to make connections between the Nazi era and Thatcherite Britain, claimed: 'Yesterday's racism'.[76] Finally, I would suggest, it is through the serious contemplation of the life work and writings of those rare individuals such as James Parkes, who worked before, during and after the Holocaust to combat all forms of prejudice, that we can start to make the very real and necessary connections in a manner that is both sensitive and challenging to the 'then' as well as the 'now'.

---

74   *The Guardian*, 5 June 1970.
75   Yehuda Bauer, 'The significance of the Final Solution', in David Cesarani (ed.), *The Final Solution* (London: Routledge, 1994), p.308.
76   On the educational pack, see Kushner, *The Holocaust and the Liberal Imagination*, pp.261–2.

Bibliography

The essays in this collection cover a great variety of specific topics although they all address the generic issues raised by the study of Jewish/non-Jewish relations across the ages. The following bibliography is not intended in any way as exhaustive but it highlights key works that address general issues raised by many of the contributors.

H.E. Allison, *Lessing and the Enlightenment* (Ann Arbor: University of Michigan Press, 1966).

Roger Arnaldez, *Three Messengers for One God*, trans. Gerald W. Schlabach (Notre Dame: University of Notre Dame Press, 1994).

Elazar Barkan, *The Retreat of Scientific Racism: Changing Concepts of Race in Britain and the United States Between the World Wars* (Cambridge: Cambridge University Press, 1992).

Yehuda Bauer, *The Holocaust in Historical Perspective* (London: Sheldon Press, 1978).

David Berger (ed.), *History and Hate: The Dimensions of Anti-Semitism* (Philadelphia: Jewish Publication Society, 1986).

Jan Blommaert and Jef Verschuren, *Debating Diversity: Analysing the Discourse of Tolerance* (London: Routledge, 1998).

Donald Bloxham, *Genocide on Trial: War Crimes Trials and the Formation of Holocaust History and Memory* (Oxford: Oxford University Press, 2001).

Eugene B. Borowitz, *Exploring Jewish Ethics: Papers on Covenantal Responsibility* (Detroit: Wayne State University Press, 1990).

Daniel Boyarin, *Intertextuality and the Reading of Midrash* (Bloomington and Indianapolis: Indiana University Press, 1990).

——, *A Radical Jew; Paul and the Politics of Identity* (Berkeley: University of California Press, 1994).

Benjamin Braude and Bernard Lewis (eds), *Christians and Jews in the Ottoman Empire: The Functioning of a Plural Society*, vol. 1 (New York and London, 1982).

Richard Breitman and Alan Kraut, *American Refugee Policy and European Jewry, 1933–1945* (Bloomington, IN: Indiana University Press, 1987).

Israel W. Charny (ed.), *Toward the Understanding and Prevention of Genocide: Proceedings of the International Conference on the Holocaust and Genocide* (Boulder and London: Westview Press, 1984).

Robert Chazan, *Daggers of Faith: Thirteenth-Century Missionizing and Jewish Response* (Berkeley, Los Angeles and London: University of California Press, 1989).

Bryan Cheyette, *Constructions of 'the Jew' in English Literature and Society: Racial Representations 1875–1945* (Cambridge: Cambridge University Press, 1993).

Bryan Cheyette and Laura Marcus (eds), *Modernity, Culture and 'the Jew'* (Cambridge: Polity Press, 1998).

Jeremy Cohen, *The Friars and the Jews* (Ithaca: Cornell University Press, 1982).

—— (ed.), *Essential Papers on Judaism and Christianity in Conflict: From Late Antiquity to the Reformation* (New York: New York University Press, 1991).

——, *Living Letters of the Law: Ideas of the Jew in Medieval Christianity* (Berkeley, Los Angeles and London: University of California Press, 1999).

Mark Cohen, *Under Crescent and Cross: The Jews in the Middle Ages* (Princeton, NJ: Princeton University Press, 1994).

Dan Cohn-Sherbok (ed.), *Many Mansions: Interfaith and Religious Intolerance*, (Canterbury Papers Series) (London: Bellew Publishers, 1992).

Gavin D'Costa, *Theology and Religious Pluralism* (Oxford: Blackwell, 1986).

Ann Dummett and Andrew Nichol, *Subjects, Citizens, Aliens and Others: Nationality and Immigration Law* (London, Weidenfeld & Nicolson, 1990).

S. Eidelberg (trans. and ed.), *The Jews and the Crusaders: The Hebrew Chronicles of the First and Second Crusades* (Madison: University of Wisconsin Press, 1977).

Peter R. Erspamer, *The Elusiveness of Tolerance: The 'Jewish Question' from Lessing to the Napoleonic Wars* (Chapel Hill, NC: University of North Carolina Press, 1997).

Paul Foot, *Immigration and Race in British Politics* (Penguin: Harmondsworth, 1965).

Marvin Fox (ed.), *Modern Jewish Ethics: Theory and Practice* (Columbus: Ohio State University Press, 1975).

——, *Interpreting Maimonides* (Chicago and London: University of Chicago Press, 1990).

John G. Gager, *The Origins of Anti-Semitism* (New York: Oxford University Press, 1985).

Sander Gilman and Steven Katz (eds), *Anti-Semitism in Times of Crisis* (New York: NYU Press, 1991).

Paul Gilroy, *There Ain't No Black in the Union Jack: the Cultural Politics of Race and Nation* (London, Hutchinson, 1987).

——, *Between Camps: Nations, Cultures and the Allure of Race* (London: Allen Lane, 2000).

David Theo Goldberg, *Racial Subjects: Writing on Race in America* (New York: Routledge, 1997).

——, *The Racial State* (Malden, MA: Blackwell, 2001).

—— and John Solomos (eds), *A Companion to Racial and Ethnic Studies* (Malden, MA: Blackwell, 2002).

J. Golomb (ed.), *Nietzsche and Jewish Culture* (London: Routledge, 1997).

Martin Goodman, *Mission and Conversion: Proselytizing in the Religious History of the Roman Empire* (Oxford: Clarendon Press, 1994).

S. Grayzel, *The Church and the Jews in the Thirteenth Century*, rev. edn (New York: Hermon Press, 1966).

Ole Peter Grell and Roy Porter (eds), *Toleration in Enlightenment Europe* (Cambridge: Cambridge University Press, 2000).

——, Jonathan Israel and Nicholas Tyacke (eds), *From Persecution to Toleration: The Glorious Revolution and Religion in England* (Oxford: Oxford University Press, 1991).

A.C. Hepburn (ed.), *Minorities in History* (London: Edward Arnold, 1978).

David Heyd (ed.), *Toleration: An Elusive Virtue* (Princeton, NJ: Princeton University Press, 1996).

Michael Hilton, *The Christian Effect on Jewish Life* (London: SPCK, 1994).

Margaret T. Hogden, *Early Anthropology in the Sixteenth and Seventeenth Centuries* (Philadelphia: University of Pennsylvania Press, 1971).

John Y.B. Hood, *Aquinas and the Jews* (Philadelphia: University of Pennsylvania Press, 1995).

John Horton (ed.), *Liberalism, Multiculturalism and Toleration* (London: Macmillan, 1993).

John Horton and Susan Mendus (eds), *Aspects of Toleration: Philosophical Studies* (London: Methuen, 1985).

Richard G. Hovannisian, *The Armenian Holocaust. A Bibliography relating to the Deportations, Massacres and Dispersion of the Armenian People 1915–1923* (Cambridge, MA: American Heritage Press, 1980).

Michael Ignatieff, *Blood and Belonging: Journeys into the New Nationalism* (London: Vintage, 1994).

Jonathan Israel, *European Jewry in the Age of Mercantilism, 1550–1750* (Oxford: Clarendon Press, 1985).

Sian Jones, Tony Kushner and Sarah Pearce (eds), *Cultures of Ambivalence and Contempt: Studies in Jewish/non-Jewish Relations* (London: Vallentine Mitchell, 1998).

Henry Kamen, *The Rise of Toleration* (London: Weidenfeld and Nicolson, 1967).

Yosef Kaplan, Henry Méchoulan and Richard H. Popkin (eds), *Menasseh ben Israel and his World* (Leiden: E.J. Brill, 1989).

David Katz, *The Jews in the History of England 1485–1850* (Oxford: Clarendon, 1994).

Jacob Katz, *Exclusiveness and Tolerance: Jewish–Gentile Relations in Medieval and Modern Times* (Oxford: Oxford University Press, 1961).

——, *From Prejudice to Destruction: Anti-Semitism, 1700–1933* (Cambridge, MA: Harvard University Press, 1980).

Menachem Kellner, *Maimonides on Judaism and the Jewish People* (Albany: SUNY Press, 1991).

Paul E. Kerry, *Enlightenment Thought in the Writings of Goethe: A Contribution to the History of Ideas* (Rochester, NY: Camden House, 2001).

Hans Köchler (ed.), *The Concept of Monotheism in Islam and Christianity* (Vienna: Wilhelm Braumüller, 1982)

Hans Küng, *Does God Exist?* (New York: Vintage Books, 1981)

Leo Kuper, *Genocide: Its Political Use in the 20th Century* (New Haven: Yale University Press, 1981).

Tony Kushner, *The Holocaust and the Liberal Imagination: A Social and Cultural History* (Oxford: Blackwell, 1994).

Gavin Langmuir, *History, Religion and Antisemitism* (London: I.B. Tauris, 1990).

——, *Toward a Definition of Antisemitism* (Berkeley: University of California Press, 1990).

Zig Layton-Henry, *The Politics of Immigration: Immigration, 'Race' and 'Race' Relations in Post-War Britain* (Oxford: Blackwell, 1992).

Mark Levene, *War, Jews and the New Europe: The Diplomacy of Lucien Wolf 1914–1919* (Oxford: Littman Library, 1992).

Louise London, *Whitehall and the Jews 1933–1948: British Immigration Policy and the Holocaust* (Cambridge: Cambridge University Press, 2000).

Hyam Maccoby, *Judaism on Trial: Jewish–Christian Disputations in the Middle Ages* (Rutherford, NJ: Fairleigh Dickinson University Press, 1982).

E. Manuel, *The Broken Staff: Judaism Through Christian Eyes* (Cambridge, MA: Harvard University Press, 1992).

Michael Marrus, *The Holocaust in History* (London: Weidenfeld & Nicolson, 1988).

Nur Masalha, *Expulsion of the Palestinians: The concept of 'transfer' in Zionist political thought 1882–1948* (Washington, DC: Institute for Palestine Studies, 1992).

Susan Mendus (ed.), *Justifying Toleration* (Cambridge: Cambridge University Press, 1988).

—— and David Edwards (eds), *On Toleration* (Oxford: Clarendon Press, 1987).

Robert Miles, *Racism and Migrant Labour* (London: Routledge & Kegan Paul, 1982).

——, *Racism after 'Race Relations'* (London: Routledge, 1993).

R.I. Moore, *The Formation of a Persecuting Society: Power and Deviance in Western Europe, 950–1250* (Oxford: Blackwell, 1987).

Benny Morris, *The Birth of the Palestinian Refugee Problem 1947–1949* (Cambridge: Cambridge University Press, 1989).

L. Nochlin and T. Garb (eds), *The Jew in the Text: Modernity and the Construction of Identity* (London: Thames and Hudson, 1995).

H. Oberman, *The Roots of Antisemitism in the Age of Renaissance and Reformation* (Philadelphia: Fortmore Press, 1984).

Panikos Panayi (ed.), *Racial Violence in Britain in the Nineteenth and Twentieth Centuries*, 2nd edn (London: Leicester University Press, 1996).

James Parkes, *The Jew and His Neighbour: A Study of the Causes of Anti-Semitism* (London: Student Christian Movement Press, 1930).

——, *The Conflict of the Church and the Synagogue: A Study in the Origins of Anti-Semitism* (London: Soncino Press, 1934).

——, *The Jew in the Medieval Community: a Study of his Political and Economic Situation* (London: Soncino Press, 1938).

——, *An Enemy of the People: Anti-Semitism* (New York: Penguin, 1946).

——, *Emergence of the Jewish Problem 1878–1939* (London: Oxford University Press, 1946).

——, *The Foundations of Judaism and Christianity* (London: Vallentine Mitchell, 1960).

——, *Anti-Semitism* (London: Vallentine, Mitchell, 1963).

——, *Prelude to Dialogue: Jewish–Christian Relations* (London: Vallentine Mitchell, 1969).

——, *Voyage of Discoveries* (London: Gollancz, 1969).

Richard Popkin and Gordon Weiner (eds), *Jewish Christians and Christian Jews from the Renaissance to the Enlightenment* (Dordrecht: Kluwer Academic Publishers, 1993).

Uri Ra'anan, Maria Mesner, Keith Ames and Kate Martin (eds), *State and Nation in Multi-Ethnic Societies, The Breakup of Multinational States* (Manchester: Manchester University Press, 1991).

Alan Race, *Christians and Religious Particularism* (London: SCM Press, 1983).

Ritchie Robertson, *The 'Jewish Question' in German Literature, 1749–1939: Emancipation and its Discontents* (Oxford: Oxford University Press, 1999).

Gillian Rose, *Judaism and Modernity: Philosophical Essays* (Oxford: Blackwell, 1993).

Shamit Saggar, *Race and Politics in Britain* (London and New York: Harvester Wheatsheaf, 1992).

E.P. Sanders (ed.), *Jewish and Christian Self-Definition* (London: SCM Press, 1980).

Milton Shain, *Antisemitism* (London: Bowerdean, 1998).

James Shapiro, *Shakespeare and the Jews* (New York: Columbia University Press, 1996).

W. J. Sheils (ed.), *Persecution and Toleration* (Studies in Church History, vol. 21) (Oxford: Blackwell, 1984).

Yvonne Sherwood, *A Biblical Text and Its Afterlives: The Survival of Jonah in Western Culture* (Cambridge: Cambridge University Press, 2000).

Shlomo Simonsohn, *The Apostolic See and the Jews* (8 vols) (Toronto: Pontifical Institute of Mediaeval Studies, 1991).

John Solomos, *Race and Racism in Britain*, 3rd edn (Basingstoke: Palgrave Macmillan, 2003).

David Sorkin, *The Transformation of German Jewry, 1780–1840* (New York: Oxford University Press, 1987).

——, *Moses Mendelssohn and the Religious Enlightenment* (London: Halban, 1996).

Kenneth Stow, *Alienated Minority: The Jews of Medieval Latin Europe* (Cambridge, MA: Harvard University Press, 1992).

Adam Sutcliffe, *Judaism and Enlightenment* (Cambridge: Cambridge University Press, 2003).

Charles Taylor, *Multiculturalism and the Politics of Recognition* (Princeton, NJ: Princeton University Press, 1993).

Hanne Trautner-Kromann, *Shield and Sword: Jewish Polemics Against Christianity and the Christians in France and Spain from 1100–1500* (Tübingen: J.C.B. Mohr, 1993).

Bernard Wasserstein, *Britain and the Jews of Europe 1939–1945* (Oxford: Oxford University Press, 1979).

Laurence Weinbaum, *A Marriage of Convenience, The New Zionist Organisation and the Polish Government 1936–1939* (Boulder: Westview Press, 1993).

Joachim Whaley, *Religious Toleration and Social Change in Hamburg 1529–1819* (Cambridge: Cambridge University Press, 1985).

Diana Wood (ed.), *Christianity and Judaism* (Oxford: Blackwell, 1992).

David Wyman (ed.), *The World Reacts to the Holocaust* (Baltimore, MD: Johns Hopkins University Press, 1996).

James Young, *Writing and Rewriting the Holocaust: Narrative and the Consequences of Interpretation* (Bloomington: Indiana University Press, 1988).

Yirmiyahu Yovel, *Dark Riddle: Hegel, Nietzsche, and the Jews* (University Park, PA: Pennsylvania State University Press, 1998).

Index